MY MEMORIES OF BERLIN

MY MEMORIES OF BERLIN
A YOUNG BOY'S AMAZING SURVIVAL STORY

To: Ghia Leonardo-Kuhn

Best wishes,

[signature]

Herbert R. Vogt Ph.D

Copyright © 2008 by Herbert R. Vogt Ph.D.

Library of Congress Control Number:		2007906248
ISBN:	Hardcover	978-1-4691-8361-9
	Softcover	978-1-4691-8360-2
	Ebook	978-1-4691-8362-6

All rights reserved. No part of this book may be reproduced or transmitted in any form or by any means, electronic or mechanical, including photocopying, recording, or by any information storage and retrieval system, without permission in writing from the copyright owner.

This book was printed in the United States of America.

To order additional copies of this book, contact:
Xlibris Corporation
1-888-795-4274
www.Xlibris.com
Orders@Xlibris.com

Contents

PREFACE		9
CHAPTER I:	LIFE AROUND KIELER STRASSE	15
	Background and Early Upbringing	17
	My First Political Experience	24
	A Visit to the Red Baron	31
	The Gang at Kieler Strasse	36
CHAPTER II:	YEARS OF PREPARATION IN TEGEL	55
	From Kieler Strasse to Tegel	57
	A Girl Named Gisela	65
	The Beginning of German and British Air Raids	78
CHAPTER III:	INDOCTRINATION AND HIGHER EDUCATION	83
	Moving Away from My Parents	85
	My Return to LBA-Neisse	101
	Operation Barbarossa	105
	My First Major Air Raid	109
	The Balance of the War in Russia	113
CHAPTER IV:	BERLIN: BOMBS AND BODIES	125
	Back to Brandenburg and Berlin	127
	Tragedy in the Family	135
CHAPTER V:	MORE DEATH AND STARVATION	147
	To a New School and More Hardships	149
	From the School Bench Into the Fire	155
	Premilitary Combat Camp	166

CHAPTER VI:	TO HELL OR SIBERIA	171
	Getting Ready for the Inferno	173
	Escape from an Air-raid Shelter	189
	Capitulation Is No Option	199
CHAPTER VII:	MORE HAPPENINGS OF 1944	207
	A Strange Funeral at Midnight	209
	Acquaintance with a Fighter Ace	220
	A Visit at the Eckard Mansion	227
	My Last Days with Gisela	236
	Christmas of 1944	240
CHAPTER VIII:	THE BATTLE OF ARMAGEDDON	247
	1945 Summary of Disasters	249
	Death in Cold Blood	254
	Destruction of a Flak Battery	260
	Inside a Werewolf Training Camp	265
CHAPTER IX:	BERLIN: THE EYE OF THE HURRICANE	271
	The End of War at Humboldthain Bunker	273
	Cease-fire and Back on the Road	282
	My First Encounter with the Opposite Sex	287
CHAPTER X:	LIFE AFTER THE WAR	299
	Drifting With the Wind	301
	The Call of the Werewolf	310
	Accident at the Last Mission	321
CHAPTER XI:	THE AMERICAN CONNECTION	331
	My Struggle as a Student	333
	Getting a Job at the American Club	339
	A Conflict in Political Ideology	349
CHAPTER XII:	FINAL ESCAPE TO FREEDOM	353
	Last Year in Berlin	355
	Isolation and Civil Insurrection	366
	My First Steps to Freedom	380
	Storm Over the Atlantic	386

The supreme purpose of history is a better world. Yesterday's records can keep us from repeating yesterday's mistakes.
—Herbert Hoover

If you don't know the past you can't cope with the future.
—Golo Mann

Preface

Two reasons made me write this book at a later part of my life. For some time, because of being educated in an Adolf Hitler school, I was too biased to the events of the Hitler time and WW II. After living in America, I became more objective of the past. Secondly, for many years, the information published by the media did not always correspond with the truth. History eventually will report the past in a more realistic light. Since I have personally experienced and lived through the misery of WW II, I hope that my story will make a small contribution to what it really was like in those days. Even so that by now my mind has formed an opinion of its own, I must accept certain facts and figures; after all, statistics don't lie. However, when I wrote this book, it was not my intention to rewrite history, but rather, to give the reader a background of events in politics, on the home front and at the battlefield parallel to my own story. Too many books have already been written about Hitler and WW II, but not enough individual stories came out from ordinary people giving testimony as to what it was like and how they survived.

After WW I, millions of Germans embraced, in order to escape starvation, a new worker's party called Nazi Party (National Socialist German worker's Party). Not only was it a new party, but it promised to deliver a better life and future for the lower class. No other party or form of government was able to reverse the injustice of the Versailles Treaty. The nation had no other option, and in good faith, the people voted for the Nazi Party. The unemployed men on the street had no intention to conquer the world, all they wanted was a job and food on the table. Without bread and butter, any nation will undergo the risk of revolution. We have learned that from history, but politicians have not learned their lesson. Among the Allies, only one topic was under discussion. How can we cut up Germany and collect more on reparation? An outrageous amount went to France alone. Germany rejected democracy because the Western nations were no longer interested in a free and prosperous Germany. The Weimar Republic could not survive without foreign assistance and turned into a republic without republicans. Whatever material things the German people still possessed were taken from them by the great depression and inflation of 1929, that year I was born into a world of little hope for a better life and greater future. Adolf Hitler was the man of the hour and came to power. Trusting a single man with all the decisions to be made that concerned the welfare of a nation with eighty million people required the utmost and greatest faith in that person by all citizens. Many nations in the past had experienced that any order coming from the mind of one man was far from infallible. In reality a critical opposition is needed to check the validity of rules and laws handed down by a one-man government. Then why would a civilized nation that is governed by the Weimar Republic revert to a dictatorship? The reasons are numerous, but above all, it was an act of desperation. Germany was a place of total chaos. Hitler's speeches were promising and spiritually uplifting. Since the end of WW I, the German people had been demoralized and in fear of being shot crossing the street. Hitler seemed to have the only power to restore law and order; to most Germans, it was worth risking one's life over. Their beloved president, Hindenburg, had no choice but to select Hitler in order to keep communism out of Germany. Not knowing what they were doing, they went directly from the frying pan into the fire. After Hitler's Blitzkrieg victories faded away, so the people's trust in him eroded, but by then it was too late. Even with all the failed assassination attempts against Hitler; Germany could not surrender. Its population, either soldiers or civilians, were condemned to be killed either by the Allies or by Hitler's henchmen.

As the average German at one time or another would lose the trust to follow Hitler, there remained one population among them that would fanatically believe Hitler, fight and die for him to the last day of the war and beyond. If any other citizen joined the Nazi Party for personal gain or advancement, the Hitler Youth was purely motivated to fight for Führer and *Vaterland*. The Nazi hierarchy was aware of it. They took them away from their parents at the tender age of ten, put the children into camps to be indoctrinated, and trained the young boys to be overzealous fighters. Near the end of the war when all the manpower resources were depleted and all the hopes to win the war was gone, it was the Hitler Youth that defended Berlin. These boys, ten to eighteen years old, were slaughtered by the Russians from the Seelow Heights to downtown Berlin by the thousands, just to give Hitler an extra few days before he ended his miserable life in his underground bunker on April 30, 1945. Few survivors were left to testify to the needless sacrifice of the Hitler Youth.

Throughout the ages, the many events of history are told and written based on memories of survivors. For instance, nobody would ever know anything about the multitude of human tragedies if the sinking of the *Titanic* had no survivors. Every life has a story. Some are eventful, others are not too important, and a few of us have been challenged to live through situations where life and death hang in the balance. Not always do we have the choice to live our lives the way we want to. Time, place, and circumstances dictate our destinies. The environment we are born into is not voluntary but strictly by random. After we are born, we become a member of a certain culture or society that raises us; teaches us; and, according to our upbringing, expects us to believe in a certain way.

After we are old enough and have developed a mind of our own, we may or may not approve of what surrounds us. If we have the freedom to adapt our behavior to our own conviction, we may change to a different style of life and create our own philosophy.

However, if you are born into a system where the state is ruled by a dictator, you may not know anything else, and it becomes very difficult to differentiate between good and bad. Even if you have arrived at the conclusion that you live in an evil empire, you still don't have the luxury to walk away from it. The regime owns you, and you must shut up and perform, or else become a statistical number in a concentration camp.

It is easy for an outsider to criticize the willingness of a misguided nation to follow their leader. We will never know how the individual reacts in his own mind to doing his duty. I want to believe that the majority of people, if they have the freedom of choice, would immediately turn around and live a life in peace and harmony. Instead, as prisoners in their own country, they must fight and die to the bitter end. It makes no difference if the dictator is a fascist, communist, or a ruler of a Chinese or Muslim state; the moment human rights are violated, brutality applied, and political opponents imprisoned, then such a dictator must be removed from the government. If not possible by the people of his own country, then it becomes the responsibility of the free world to act as a liberator. This must be viewed as a police action sanctioned by the United Nations before it escalates into a major war. One of the best examples in recent history is the outbreak of World War II. We can only guess how many millions of people would have not been killed, and endless tragedy would have been avoided among civilians if the leaders of the free world had made the right decision. The first time Hitler violated the Versailles Treaty, which had been freely signed by Germany, was reason enough for the Allies to march into Germany and remove the dictator from office. There was no risk involved as the German military, other than a few SS (Schutzstaffel) regiments, would not have resisted. Early in 1935, Hitler openly denounced the military restrictions of the peace treaty. In public he announced that Germany would have a peacetime conscript army of thirty-six divisions. England and France were also aware of the speedy buildup of a German air force and navy. A second violation of the peace treaty occurred a year later on March 7, 1936, when units of the new army were sent into the demilitarized zone of the Rhineland facing France on the western border of Germany. At this time, France could have easily stopped the invasion as they still had the strongest military force in Europe. Hitler admitted to his generals that, had the French marched, it would have been the end of him and of National Socialism. The military resources at Hitler's disposal were wholly inadequate for even the slightest resistance. The fact that the great Western democracies did not call Hitler's bluff and refused to go to war, they missed the last chance to keep the peace in Europe for a small cost to themselves. Instead they gave Hitler the green light to plunge the world into the bloodiest war in history. The handwriting was on the wall when Germany engaged in a feverish rearmament. For a false hope of peace, the Allies have gambled away the lives of millions of innocent people on both sides. May this be a lesson to future leaders of the free world not to make the same mistake and stop an evil maniac before he has a chance to destroy them. Unfortunately, history repeats itself, and people seem to forget or are blinded by an illusion that bad things could not happen to them. Not so with survivors of a disaster; they never forget, and they relive their sufferings over and over again. That is especially the case when your traumatic experiences occur in your childhood or the formative years of your youth. Memories don't go away; they become your vade mecum, your shadow, and subsequently, they affect your consciousness and your behavior toward other people.

Eventually every survivor has to ventilate his feelings, that's why I am writing this book at the end of my life, dedicating it in particular to my grandchildren and their generation. Since the end of World War II, so many changes have come along, giving the earth a completely different environment. Time is an ongoing process. It will not stop for anything and will not leave anything permanent behind it. Sooner or later the last eyewitness of a past event will not be alive anymore to describe what really happened in those days. At this point in time, history will rely on the written reports of survivors; anything else in history is more or less just speculation. One person's life is only a small piece of history, but it comes closer to the truth of long-past events than any other interpretation of history. The story left behind, based on the memory of a survivor, must be seen as a building block of history. Many history books are written without any passion or feelings for the subject matter. They are just a summary report in the form of a textbook, stating previous events in chronological order. The information contained in these books are often obtained from other writings. In contrast, reading the story of a survivor is like bringing back a piece of the past to the present.

The reader is actually witnessing and reliving the joy, pain, and suffering of the survivor as every event of the past is described in detail. A good reported human story becomes a small window for future generations to look back and learn more about the past. We can learn from the disaster and misery of other people in order not to make the same mistakes by taking action or avoiding certain steps that can lead to catastrophe. Even if a story does not relate to the problems of present times, it is at least educational for someone who is interested to explore past events in history. The author hopes that this book, if nothing else, stays in the family as a meaningful inheritance.

CHAPTER I

LIFE AROUND KIELER STRASSE

Background and Early Upbringing

My Parents and I

The story of my life started insignificantly when I was born on a rainy day in Berlin on the nineteenth of July 1929. I was the only child, my mother was nineteen and my father twenty-five years old when I was born. Max and Margarete Vogt came from bourgeois families who had to struggle to make ends meet. Both of my grandfathers were killed in WW I, and the oldest boy in each family had to become the breadwinner and the head of the household at an early age. There was no time or money for them to get an education or learn a profession. Luckily my father got a job with the government, but in the beginning, he got paid less than an ordinary laborer. Fortunately my mother was very thrifty and knew how to handle the money. Every morning she would run up and down the market to find the cheapest soup bones or whatever food was on sale. Thanks to her, nobody went to bed hungry; and we managed to get us through the depression, hoping for better times to come. We lived in a very small apartment in a tenement on a third building in the rear with the toilet located one floor below where the sun never shined. Our domicile was located right in the heart of Kreuzberg in the old downtown Berlin. After World War II, all Turk immigrants chose that particular part of Berlin to settle down, and it later became known as Little Istanbul as it turned into a sanctuary for all Muslims living in Berlin. In the old days, the streets in Kreuzberg were clean, and there were beautiful parks and churches that no longer exist now. When I was a child, my mother many times would take me to play in the biggest and highest park in Kreuzberg that displayed a huge cross on top.

On Sundays my parents would take me out to a lake or forest, which Berlin has so many, for "kaffee und kuchen" coffee and cake in a restaurant or beer garden. As I got older, I became aware that my parents and I did not go to church regularly on Sundays like other folks did with their children. Of course, they had a reason, and my mother told me about it later when I attended school. My father was raised as a Catholic, and my mother came from a Lutheran family. The trouble started when my parents wanted to get married and my grandmother on my father's side insisted that they get married in the Catholic Church. My mother had no objection but refused to change her faith and become a Catholic. The church in turn closed the door and told them to get married someplace else, but the old Lady Martha Vogt, my grandmother, did not want to hear about a marriage in the Lutheran Church, so the wedding was off. Time went by, and in the meanwhile, my mother was six months pregnant. My parents did not want me to be born illegitimate. My father got mad as hell and went to see the bishop. Finally, the church agreed to marry them under two conditions. The marriage could not be performed at the main altar in front of the tabernacle containing the Eucharist. My mother had to sign papers where she swore to raise all children as Catholics. My mother agreed, and they were married on a Monday evening in April 1929 in the empty church of St. Norbert, by a small altar next to the exit on the left side of the church. As only guests and mandatory witnesses appeared my father's two brothers Rudolf and Herbert. The whole thing was an in-and-out affair. Thereafter everything went smoothly; my mother kept her promise, prayed with me, and took me to a Catholic church on Sundays. After my father's mother died in 1937, my father became a nonpracticing Catholic, and the only time I remember seeing him in church was on my first Holy Communion. As I grew up, I also developed my father's attitude, attending church became secondary for me. Even though, when I was a young cadet at the LBA Neisse and it was forbidden for us to go next door to church at the monastery, at the risk of being caught, I would climb a ten-foot wall to go to mass on Sundays.

My parents

Working for the government was a long stony road. It guaranteed a lifelong job security and a pension at the end. The servants of the state didn't get paid for overtime and didn't get rich, but promotions were given out periodically. Such an advancement occurred to my father at the end of 1932. Finally Dad was making more money, and he was moving his family to a bigger apartment in a new neighborhood. Mama was thrilled with her new kitchen, and there was even some money left to buy some extra furniture. We didn't have to tighten our belts anymore, but the weekly ritual of counting out the money went on. In the old days, employees did not get a payroll check to take to the bank to cash it; everybody received a little sealed brown paper bag with their name on it. On Friday nights when my father came home from work, we would sit at the kitchen table and have supper. After my mother cleaned the table, my father would take out the little brown paper bag, tear it open, and dump the contents in the middle of the table. "There you have it," he said, smiling and starting to count the money—a few big bills, some small bills, and a bunch of coins. The first thing they did was separate from the pile a portion for the monthly payment for the rent and utilities. Then my mother held her hand open to receive a weekly allowance to buy her groceries. She kept her hand stretched out and looked at him till he topped it with another shiny coin. Ultimately she folded the money very neatly and stashed it away in her apron pocket. Whatever was left, they put it in a cookie jar to pay miscellaneous bills or as reserves for a rainy day.

My mother

To supplement her income, my mother was pretty handy in knitting all kinds of tablecloths in her spare time that people ordered to buy. The new apartment was really the first place in my life that I remembered vividly. It was the home of my first Christmas that I remembered and the real candles that would burn brightly on that festive, decorated *tannenbaum* (Christmas tree). My fascination of my new world I was now living in was endless. Every day I discovered something new, and slowly I began to explore my new environment. I felt the protection of my parents, giving me a sense of security. I proceeded to play and learn very innocently. I made new friends in my neighborhood. The house we lived in was on Kieler Strasse 2, still being an apartment in a tenement, but we had our own bathroom and one bedroom. The living room had large windows inviting the sun to shine in and warming up the place. As in most European cities, people did live in apartment houses. Usually, four-house buildings, several stories high, make a square complex with a rectangular courtyard in the center. These complexes were lined up side by side to fill up a whole city block with streets going all the way around. This arrangement provided more security, and each complex had access to a street. A huge ornamental door or iron gate would allow service or emergency vehicles to drive into the courtyard. Apartments facing the street had balconies; all others in the center of the complex had only a view from their windows to the courtyard. Some courtyards were landscaped; most of them had only a big square area of concrete, but all of them served as a playground for children. Adults did come out to relax, and women were gossiping when they had time, watching their children play. The end of the block was next door at Kieler Strasse 1. It was also the end of the west side of the street. On the same side of the street on the dead-end corner was a bakery and pastry shop, then suddenly you were facing the Nord Hafen Kanal flowing from the Humboldt Hafen north to the Nord Hafen Kanal terminating in the much bigger Hohenzollern Kanal.

Incidentally, Berlin has more lakes, rivers, and waterways than any other city in Europe. Going back east on Kieler Strasse, on our side of the street, we found a grocery store and the noisy neighborhood beer bar. Now we were already on the corner of Kieler Strasse and Scharnhorst Strasse. Making a right turn, we were going toward Invaliden Strasse. This street was a very big interesting street with large government buildings, beautiful parks with old gothic and Romanesque churches. There was the Invaliden Krankenhaus (veterans hospital) and the Invaliden Friedhof (veterans cemetery). As busy as this main street was, it was always attractive to me going there for a walk since our home was within walking distance. I am describing the surroundings of the place we were living in as our neighborhood became eventful to me in many ways.

The year 1932 was coming to an end. The streets were covered with snow and ice. Even though it was cold and windy, it did not dampen the spirit of the people to prepare for the holidays. It was the last Christmas we were celebrating in freedom and peace, and nobody really had an idea, that beginning the following year, life would change for us forever. It was a good thing that nobody knew; the great depression was almost over, and everyone was optimistic about the future. The stores were busy, and people were running around doing their last-days Christmas shopping. The biggest surprise for me on Christmas Eve was a train set going around in a circle under a beautiful decorated Christmas tree. My father was playing with it, and I was watching him make it go. Later on he got tired and let me play with the train. I was very excited, not been able to go to sleep that night. That was how I remembered my first Christmas.

The day after, my mother was taking me to Hertie, a big department store not far from where we lived. We were walking through knee-high piles of snow, I was cold and my hands were frozen. Finally we made it to the store, it was warm inside, my mother was taking me to a heater. I put my little hands on it, and pretty soon I was able to move my fingers again. On the second floor was a cafeteria where we found a cozy corner to sit down and rest for a while. My mother ordered a cup of coffee for her and a glass of hot chocolate with whipped cream on top for me. After we finished our drinks, I could hardly wait to go to the fifth floor. The entire fifth floor was the toys department, and the biggest attraction was the annual Christmas show. People from all over Berlin came with their children to see and admire the colorful and beautifully decorated exhibition. Lights were changing, and puppets were moving, making sounds that gave you the impression that they were alive. All together, the show was mechanically a well-coordinated play holding young and old in a firm grip of amazement. It was hard to believe that such an exhibition was possible to put together at a time long before the advent of computers. A last look at the rest of the toys, and then we must go home.

Hanging on to each other, stepping through ice and snow again, we took the shortest way back. Approaching the corner of Scharnhorst Strasse and Kieler Strasse, we noticed a bunch of people standing around. As we got closer, we found a horse lying at the intersection in front of an overloaded wagon, stopping the traffic in both directions. Next to the horse was a mad driver hitting the animal with a whip, demanding it to stand up again. The horse was trying desperately to get on its feet but was unable to do so. The accident occurred when the horse pulled the heavy wagon and slipped on the icy road. Falling down, the horse broke one of its legs and was lying helpless on the road. Somebody must have called the police to take care of the situation because shortly, a policeman arrived at the scene. The policeman was having an argument with the driver, but soon they reached an agreement. With the permission of the driver, the policeman stepped closer to the animal, who was screeching in pain. He pulled his revolver and fired a shot into the head of the horse to put it out of its misery. I got sick to my stomach witnessing the horrible death of the horse. My mother pulled me away from the dreadful event. I was not able to control myself. Uncomposed, I cried all the way home.

A few days later, I began to get the horrible episode out of my mind. It was still cold, but the sun was shining. Children were playing in the courtyard and in front of the house, showing each other the new toys they received for Christmas. There were shiny bicycles and all kinds of wagons and wooden sleds the kids were trying out in the snow. The little girls were pushing around tiny baby carriages, showing off their new dolls. For the bigger boys, it was firecrackers and ice skates. If you didn't have any skates, you amused yourself on the *schlitterbahn*, which was a narrow frozen runway where you slid on it in full speed on top of the ice only with your shoes. The ice was so smooth and slippery that one must keep perfect balance. It took some coordination, and till you got the hang of it, you might as well be in the beginning sliding several times on your butt. Sylvester, that was New Year's Eve, was just around the corner. The noise in the streets was getting louder, firecrackers starting to pop more often, and people everywhere were beginning to ring in the New Year. People were happy, celebrating the arrival of 1933, but very few of them knew what the future would bring.

My First Political Experience

At the termination of WW I in 1918, the German emperor (Kaiser) abdicated and fled to Holland. In 1919 the German assembly met in Weimar and adopted a constitution to form a government with Frederich Ebert as its first president. Upon his death, Field Marshal Paul von Hindenburg succeeded him. The Weimar Republic, as it was known, governed from 1919 to 1933. It was to be a socialistic and democratic government with the objective of establishing in Germany more equitable ownership of the land and the tools of production—a land where plenty should be the lot of all. The German people for the first time in their history, after they lived for centuries under the rule of a monarchy, tried to establish their own democracy. In the beginning it was successful under Ebert and Stresemann, but it did not last very long. Leaders of the free world had hoped that World War I would be the war to end all wars. But their hopes were in vain. In 1929 the world became involved in a great economic depression, especially Germany, the only country that had to pay for the damages of the war and suffered more than any other nation.

The Weimar Republic was a feeble attempt to achieve a government in which every man would be free and could earn a living. Democratic reforms were difficult, and the people were hungry, hoping that the burden of the Versailles Treaty would be lifted. Since the fourteen-point peace treaty proposal by the U.S. president Wilson was defeated and the economic chaos became unbearable, the majority of the Germans refused to live under a democratic system. The republic was destroyed, "not in anger nor in battle," but by the results of starvation in Germany. The last chancellor at that time was Brüning, a man known for corruption and also responsible for Germany's economic and financial chaos. Consequently, the people were seeking a strong leader who would restore law and order. The Nazi Party from 1924 to 1929 was rejected by most Germans. The Communist Party was also considered extreme and not suitable for an industrialized nation not willing to give up free enterprise.

As the democrats were no longer in favor of either the Nazi Party or the Communist Party, they were left fighting each other in the streets of Berlin in an attempt to come to power. Paul von Hindenburg, the hero of World War I, was the last president in 1932, and his decision to make Hitler the chancellor was respected by all Germans. He did not give up on the reestablishment of a new democratic government. Hitler, on the other hand, was pleased to see high unemployment, economic chaos, and civil insurrection, hoping that the government would collapse. He took advantage of the opportunity to come to power, it was now or never. In all his speeches, he promised the public exactly what they wanted to hear—from new jobs, social security, abolishment of the Versailles Treaty, and reunification of German territory to total prosperity of Germany. Out of frustration and desperation, the German people were beginning to see Hitler as their new leader for the salvation of Germany. The attitude in general was, "We had so many governments, let's give him a chance." Very few people, mostly the upper class, would fear a bigger disaster and rejected Hitler as their new chancellor. The president also refused as long as he could to make Hitler a part of the new government. He really had only two options, either the Communist Party or the Nazi Party. In the end, he chose what he believed to be the lesser evil. As the pressure on him increased, he compromised at the last last minute and made Hitler chancellor but insisted Franz von Papen, a democrat, to be the vice president. His reasoning was that the democrats by far had more seats in the cabinet and in the Reichstag (the headquarters of the legislature) and would be able to control Hitler and make all political decisions. By persuading the aging Hindenburg to give the chancellery to Hitler, the destruction of the republic was done. Thereafter, the entire propaganda of Adolf Hitler was built on a foundation of lies.

He advocated hate, murder, treachery, brutality, and revolution. Never in the history of government had propaganda been so vile, vulgar, and disgusting as it was during the reign of the Third Reich. The first attempt made by Hitler to obtain leadership of the German people by force in München in 1923 ended in the death of sixteen men and a five-year prison sentence for himself, a term of which he served six months. This defeat convinced him that there was a better way—that of propaganda and flattery, thereby gaining enough votes to get elected to the desired position. After his election, Hitler had his own dark plan to make himself a dictator and the absolute ruler of Germany.

On February 27, 1933, he committed another criminal act by burning down the Reichstag and blaming it on the communists. As soon as Hitler was made chancellor, the Reichstag passed an enabling act on March 5, 1933, giving Hitler absolute power and control over all activities in the country—political, economic, industrial, commercial, and cultural. The Nazi regime immediately passed emergency laws allowing them to arrest people suspected of being enemies of the Third Reich (without evidence) and to ban all other political parties. By eliminating the parliament of the German people, Hitler was one step closer to becoming a dictator. The next year, on August 2, 1934, President von Hindenburg suddenly died. He was buried with full military honors, organized by the new regime, in Neudeck, East Prussia. Under Hindenburg's military leadership, the Russians were defeated in the battle at Tannenberg in WW I, so Hitler erected the biggest war memorial in his honor. The same day that Hindenburg died, Hitler merged the offices of the president and the chancellor, appointing himself as the sole leader of Germany and assuming all political power as the new Führer und Reichs Kanzler (leader and prime minister). From that day on, the Führer was now a dictator with no opposition. All German military had to swear an unconditional oath of obedience and loyalty to Hitler personally as the new and only leader of Germany.

It was then in August 1934 that Hitler finally controlled every aspect of the German societies. He had become a dictator. That same month, Hitler started his long line of territory annexations.

On August 26, Hitler, in an emotional address to a throng officially estimated at three hundred thousand people, asked the world, and especially France, to be prepared for the return of the Saar to Germany, when that rich region voted on the question next January. "The Saar is the greatest problem now separating France from us," Hitler said. "We shall not give up the conviction that the other side eventually will view this problem as it really is, and that France will not deny her assistance in solving it. There is no reason whatsoever why two great nations should remain forever hostile on this issue." The chancellor was greeted with frenzied "Heils" when he arrived from Cologne, where he had attended the inauguration of the huge Saar exposition. The throng, apparently almost to a man, seemed intensely Nazi in its sympathies. Hitler spoke from the topmost bastion of the historic Rhine fortress from which the Stars and Stripes flew in the period of the postwar occupation. The address was a strong appeal for understanding abroad, especially on the part of France, that the return of the Saar to the Reich on January 13, 1935, was inevitable. "Ties of blood and race bind the Saar population indissolubly to the fatherland," he said.

However, the actual beginning of the Nazi cult and the twelve years of unbelievable terror and destruction started in Berlin when Hitler came to power on January 30, 1933, and ended with the capitulation of Germany in the ruins of Berlin on May 8, 1945.

Here was what I remembered and what I had seen with the eyes of a four-year-old boy on January 30, 1933. My uncle Rudolf, the oldest brother of my father, came to visit us many times. He was honest, hardworking, and a patriot who would do anything to serve his country. He did not drink or smoke, had a good job, and took good care of his family. As a young man, he attended one of Hitler's meetings that put a spell on him. Being an idealist, he sincerely believed in the cause of the Hitler party. He became an early member, joined the SA (Sturmabteilung) as a storm trooper and was convinced to do the right thing to help Germany to recover. His men liked him, and he would bring many of the unemployed to his home for a meal. His idealism and leadership soon gained him the rank of *Obersturmbannführer* (the equivalent of an army colonel; a *Sturmban* was the size of a regiment). He talked to my father many times, trying to convince him that it was his duty to join the Nazi Party in order to get Germany going again. My father, a nonbeliever in politics, had mixed feelings and decided to stay clear of any party affiliation whatsoever.

At about noon on January 30, 1933, my uncle Rudolf came to us very happy and excited to bring us the good news. "This morning Adolf Hitler was appointed by President Hindenburg as the new chancellor of Germany, a day that will live on in history and will change Germany forever," he exclaimed. My parents were not too thrilled about his good news but tried to share his enthusiasm. "Get ready and come to join the victory celebration," he said. My father agreed to come and got his instruction how to get there. "Be early and wait in front of the chancellery, the Führer will come and talk to us. In the evening will be a torchlight parade by the SA marching through the Brandenburg Gate."

It all sounded very good, and my parents promised to be there on time for the big event. He left to go home, and we were sitting down to have *mittag essen* (the meal of the day). After that we would rest for a short time, then my mother took out all our winter clothes, and we started dressing for the night. On the way out, my mother went back to the kitchen to grab in a hurry some cookies and candies, leftover from the holidays, for the long night to come.

Following my uncle Rudolf's direction, we walked up Seller Street to get to the U-Bahnhof Reinickendorfer Strasse, catching the metro that goes to Stadtmitte. Here we switched trains and went one more station to Bahnhof Kaiserhof. When we arrived, practically everybody disembarked from the train, rushing up the stairs to get out of the metro. My parents and I were right in the middle of a tight stream of people going up the Wilhelm Strasse to the final destination, the chancellery. Slowly the flow of people came to a halt, and nothing was moving anymore. A big crowd was now gathered in front of the chancellery, looking up the big windows on the first floor of the building, waiting impatiently for the Führer to come and greet them. We managed to find a spot in the center of the street facing the main window. It was like a huge balcony bathed in a bright light coming from the inside. On the outside were also many lights firmly attached on the building or freestanding in the street, illuminating the whole plaza of the Kaiserhof. It was getting dark now, but all the bright lights were replacing daylight, not letting you become aware of the onset of the night. I could not tell what time it was, but it really does not matter. Constantly a wave of excitement and euphoria was inflaming the masses. Nobody was tired or bored; everybody was singing, and voices were getting louder, calling the Führer to come.

The happiness of the people reflected a visible relief that fourteen years of afterwar chaos was over and an area of national unity was on the way. Maybe not everybody standing here tonight was convinced about Hitler's sincerity, but certainly the hope for a better future was on everybody's mind. Suddenly, after hours of waiting, people were jumping and screaming, trying desperately to get a good look at their Führer appearing above them in the window. I could not see anything, being a small person as I was, but my father lifted me up and put me on his shoulders. Instantly I was taller than everybody else, having a front-row seat. I could see Hitler perfectly; he was holding his right arm up, moving from left to right over and over again, leaning as far as he could over the windowsill to give everybody a chance to see him. To talk to the people was impossible for him as they constantly shouted, "Sieg Heil, sieg Heil, sieg Heil!" Hail to the chief! Before my father put me down again, he said to me, "Son, take a good look at our Führer. With God's help, he will save Germany."

After a couple of minutes had passed, Hitler left his well-wishers and returned to the inside of the building. Other dignitaries came to the window, but the main event at the chancellery was over. During the two-day celebration starting on the night of January 30 to January 31, perhaps the biggest spectacle was the torch parade of the SA, which lasted five hours. My parents took me by the hand, and my father made sure to work his way through the multitude of people heading to the Brandenburg Gate. However, a lot of others had the same idea. The lines in front of the Reichs-Kanzlei were almost as long as those in the Wilhelm Strasse. A slow pilgrimage toward downtown was on the way. It was not possible to get lost as everybody was pushing in the same direction. The human avalanche was slowing down the moment we were getting closer to the Pariser Platz. Everybody was trying to get a standing place by the Brandenburg Gate to watch the torchlight parade. The only chance to get out of this congested area would be an attempt to break away to the left and head for the Tiergarten, a huge park nearby.

Once we reached the Tiergarten, the traffic of people walking around without crowding each other was almost normal. We followed a small road leading to the Charlottenburger Chaussee. Finding a place on the sidewalk was difficult, so we kept walking in a westerly direction a little longer till we found a spot. We were able to look up and down the Charlottenburger Chaussee. Looking back east, we could see the Brandenburg Gate. The whole parade was going in a circle; it started coming down the Charlottenburger Chaussee through the Brandenburg Gate, turning right into the Wilhelm Strasse. At the end of the Wilhelm Strasse, the parade turned right again at the Bellevue Allee back to the Charlottenburger Chaussee. We just arrived as already the first regiment of brownshirts came in sight. They marched in rows of twelves, holding their flaming torches in front of them. The first unit of the SA was a marching band playing military music. Behind them was a column of officers bearing swastika flags. Each regiment had their own banner, emblem, and insignia. It was almost as bright as daylight and getting brighter every minute the storm troopers came closer to our place. The air was warm from the thousands of torchlights, and the air was filled with songs and music. The jubilation of the spectators was like a wave that moved along with the approaching of the endless column of brownshirts. The steady sound of their marching boots was getting louder by the minute. The smell of the burning torchlights became stronger, and the flaming lights appeared brighter as the parade was slowly rolling down the street, looking like a long stream of burning lava in the darkness of the night.

Once the head of the parade had passed us, there was no end of the ongoing column. Only every ten minutes or so came another group of flag bearers followed by a marching band. We were already standing on the same spot for two hours, and it was getting close to midnight. My mother was ready to go home, but my father wanted to see his brother marching in front of his battalion. The parade was scheduled to go on for five hours through the night till early in the morning of January 31, 1933. Shortly after midnight, my father spotted Uncle Rudolf coming close to us. As he passed us, we waved our arms and called his name, but he did not see us. Neither could he hear our voices among all the screaming people.

Now my mother insisted that we go home, arguing that it was way past my bedtime. She let us have the rest of the cookies and rubbed my hands to warm them up. Lots of the people had the same idea; where there was a tide wall of spectators for many hours, it was now beginning to break up, and slowly everybody was starting to disburse in a different direction. The main destination seemed to be the closest metro station or the local railroad station. A bygoing policeman told us that buses and streetcars were no longer in operation till early in the morning. The nearest subway still open and going all night long was at the Postdamer Platz. It would not be so bad if everybody would go in one direction; instead, people were bumping into each other as they were coming and going, trying to get out of what seemed to be a human blockade. In all that commotion, two Red Cross workers in uniform carrying a woman on a stretcher were unable to find an opening to evacuate the victim of an apparent heart attack. Their destination was toward Stadtmitte; they had to reach the nearest first aid station. We were trying to break through on a side street, holding our course, aiming for the subway at the Postdamer Platz. I was scared looking at all these people pushing and running to get ahead. I was holding on to my parents with both hands, afraid to get lost. It seemed like a long time to get to the metro. Finally we got to within the entrance to the subway. A unit of policemen was regulating the traffic and orderly directing the flow of people down the stairs. Coming out of the cold air, it was a relief to get inside the heated terminal. Special trains were arriving every ten minutes, minimizing the waiting time of all the desperate people anxious to get home. After we entered the train, someone offered my mother a seat, and she held me in her arms. I must have fallen asleep; all I remembered was when we left the train and the cold air hitting my face, waking me up.

    The short familiar walk back to the house presented no problem. At this time of the night, most people were in bed. Only a few partygoers coming home or some men going early to work were visible. Even though the streets were empty, I noticed something I had never seen before. All of a sudden, practically every window displayed the new flag—red and white with a black swastika. A few days after the historical event in Berlin, Uncle Rudolf came to visit us. Every week on Wednesday, come rain or shine, he would go to the huge indoor public swimming pool to train for the Olympics. Since our place was not too far from it, he would make it a habit to stop by on the way home to see us. He also liked my mother's cooking, and usually, he would have dinner with us. The latest news became the topic of conversation. This particular day, he told my parents all about the parade and how it was organized. I did not understand or remember the political significance of it. All I really cared for and what was important for me was the gift I received from him that day. He gave me a big paper bag and told me that I could keep it as a souvenir courtesy of our Führer Adolf Hitler. I was very excited and full of curiosity to find out what the package contained. Not wasting any time, I removed the wrappers in a hurry, and here was a real torchlight, the kind that the SA would ignite and march with during the victory parade. I kept the torch for many years till one day, in an air raid, it ignited and burned down along with my grandmother's house.

A Visit to the Red Baron

The winter of 1933 was relatively mild and followed by an early onset of springtime. Young and old enjoyed the outdoor activities, children of my age and older were occupying the streets and playgrounds in the neighborhood. It was at this time that I began to meet other children and make my first friendships with them. The boy next door, Egon, and I developed a very close relationship. His father was the owner of the bakery on the corner of Kieler Strasse. Almost every morning we would sit on the sidewalk in front of the bakery and eat *Kuchenkrümel,* cake or cookie crumbs. Egon was a couple of years older than I was and had more street experience, which gave him the right to teach me everything I should know about what was going on in our block. I didn't have any brothers or sisters, and neither did Egon, perhaps that is the reason why we stuck together and looked out for each other.

In the old days, nobody had an entertainment center in the house; only the rich people could afford to buy a gramophone. The only luxury for the poor folks was a squeaky radio, which was not used very often in order to save the radio tubes that could easily overheat and break. An old custom in Berlin gave the people a chance any time of the day to sing and dance and forget for a short time the everyday monotony by listening to real live music. The foremost type of entertainment was provided by unemployed musicians going from one apartment house to the next, singing and playing a musical instrument either solo or in a group. People opened their windows and, after the first song, started throwing small coins wrapped in paper down the courtyard. The band kept on playing till the rain of money stopped. As the musicians went from place to place, they were followed by a tail of children eagerly catching the coins and collecting them for the band. All the nickels, dimes, and quarters went in a big pot. Usually, if there were some pennies, the bandleader would throw them back to the kids. The next popular group were the organ grinders. They too would make a good living, but the children who followed them did not share the profit as the organ grinder normally had his own helper, a trained monkey that collected the money. The moment a boy or a girl tried to help with the money collection, the monkey would not hesitate to bite them. Another favorite was the one-man band that seemed to have become a relic of the past. The operator was hooked up to a contraption where he, with certain movements of the body, played several instruments at the same time. To harmonize the whole thing required that the operator be a good musician and a body artist as well.

The Vogt brothers—Rudolf, Max, and Herbert—were excellent swimmers. They enjoyed the outdoors, and watersport was their favorite activity. Each of them purchased a kayak, and together they belonged to a boat club at Saatwinkel that owned a small private beach at the Lake Tegel. In the summertime my parents would take me out every weekend to the lake, and the two of them would paddle me up and down the Havel River. Saturday night we usually pitched a tent on one of the many islands at the Lake Tegel. At the clubhouse we ate most of our meals and spent the evening together with other members by an open fire. At a very early age, I learned how to swim and dive. We had no life preservers in those days, and in an emergency, everybody had to be prepared to swim long distance back to the beach if necessary.

Our transportation from Kieler Strasse to the clubhouse was by bicycle, taking a shortcut through the Tegeler Forest. My father had a small seat mounted to his bike where I would sit in front of him. All we would take each trip were supplies and provisions to prepare our meals at the clubhouse. Our tent, sleeping bags, and extra clothing stayed in the club's locker room. One Sunday morning at the end of the summer, I had a life-threatening experience. With a group from the club, we stayed overnight at Scharfenberg, an island mainly preserved as a bird sanctuary. Our kayaks were securely tucked away in the reeds by the beach, and everybody was sleeping in their tents. I did wake up early and sneaked out of the tent to go for an early swim. Strolling along the beach, I got away from our camping place and entered the water at a remote section of the island, not knowing that I trespassed a breeding ground of wild swans. Not more than one hundred feet away from the beach, I was suddenly attacked by one of these heavy-bodied aquatic birds. I had seen these big white birds with a black head and neck before, swimming peacefully, remarkable for their grace of movement in the water. The animal that I was confronted with was anything but friendly. Screeching extra loud, the creature shot inches across the surface of the water, aiming at my head, resembling the jump of a serpent expressing disapproval and contempt of my presence in the bird's territory. It happened so fast that there was no time to show fear or to think of what to do about it. Adrenalin rushed to my brain, and my instinct took over.

After I was bitten in the neck and shoulder, I realized that I could not fight the mad swan in the water, and my only chance not to get killed was to escape back to the land. Automatically I took a deep breath and started to swim under the water toward the beach. My eyes wide open, I made sure the beast did not follow me. After about fifty feet, I had to come up for air. Looking around, I found myself out of danger. Another deep breath, and I would make it underwater back to the beach. Totally exhausted, I cringed out of the water and noticed for the first time that I was bleeding from head and shoulder wounds. With my last energy, I pulled myself up and run as fast as I could back to safety. Needless to say that my parents were stricken with panic when I arrived at the camping place. Wrapped in blankets, I was taken to the first aid station, and the only doctor on the island stitched up my wounds. The swimming skills I acquired as a little boy obviously saved my life. In later years it would again help me survive from a death underwater. Somebody else with the same experience might have become phobic and stayed away from water. In my case, I became more ambitious to perfect my swimming and diving endurance.

Unfortunately, most lakes and rivers in Berlin are frozen in the wintertime, and all boating activities are suspended. As I mentioned earlier, not far from Kieler Strasse was the Stadtbad Mitte at Garten Strasse, one of Berlin's biggest and finest indoor swimming pools. The pool was open all year long, heated and had Olympic-size diving boards from three to ten meters. First I would go there with my parents or Uncle Rudolf; later when I went to school, our PE teacher would take the entire class once a week for swimming lessons to prepare for various certificates. From Kieler Strasse, within a few minutes' walking time along the Scharnhorst Strasse, one could reach the Invaliden Friedhof, which was a huge cemetery for veterans that could be compared with Arlington in Virginia. Enclosed within a tall stonewall and the entrance protected by an iron gate high in stature, it had the appearance of a fortress. The interior had the atmosphere of a well-manicured garden with narrow roads surrounded by trees leading to different sections of the cemetery. Graves were well kept with simple tombstones to fancy vaults, and artistic statues and extravagant monuments were erected to the memory of the dead. In the middle of the cemetery was a small plaza with a baroque chapel looking more like a castle than a church. The visitor to the cemetery became overwhelmed with feelings of peace and tranquillity. The first time Egon suggested that we visit the cemetery, both of us were very impressed; I had never seen a cemetery and could not really comprehend what death was all about. I asked my mother on the same day for an explanation, and she told me that the graveyard was a place where people went to sleep and never wake up.

I also told Uncle Rudolf about my visit to the cemetery hoping that he could tell me more about who was buried there. He mentioned a few heroes and told me in particular about Rittmeister Manfred Freiherr von Richthofen, better known as the Red Baron. He was the top gun among all the fighter aces of WW I, credited with the destruction of eighty enemy planes. He was born in 1892 and shot down on the twenty-first of April 1918 in the Vaux-sur-Somme, France. The enemy respected Richthofen and buried him with full military honors in a small cemetery for fallen soldiers of World War I near Amiens in France. The German aviator, decorated with the pour le mérite, was repatriated in 1926 when his remains were removed to the Invaliden Friedhof in Berlin. For the anniversary of his death on April 21, 1934, the new government planned a memorial ceremony at his graveside. It was going to be held under strict security, only for relatives and military, government, and party officials. The public had to wait outside till all the brass was gone. However, some boys and a few girls had climbed the trees and walls around the cemetery to watch the ceremony from above as the birds would view it.

Egon and I were also occupying a spot on the wall close to the graveside. After a short religious ceremony in the chapel, the relatives and their entourage proceeded to Richthofen's grave. Among the highest-ranking military dignitaries were the newly appointed Reichsmarschal Herman Göring and Luftwaffen General Ernst Udet, both were personal friends of Richthofen and leaders of the famous Richthofen Geschwader. Speeches were made, and the military band played the national anthem, the "Horst Wessel Lied," and "Ich hat einen Kameraden." Flags were lowered, and wreaths of flowers were laid by the grave. At the end of the ceremony, a squadron of low-flying fighter planes crossed the cemetery. The new regime became famous for state funerals and military spectacles; obviously, Hitler tried to gain the confidence of German military leaders.

Another spectacular event every year became the May 1 celebration in honor of the German worker. Different types of unions were no longer allowed, and instead the only union allowed was NSDAP (National Socialistic German Workers Party). It was mandatory that every employed German belonged to it and marched. It became an overnight political affair; the first of May was declared a national holiday, and every family or establishment was obligated to display the swastika flag. In Berlin it was not a strange custom since the Communist Party had celebrated May Day long before the Nazi Party came to power. In either case, the Berliners knew how to celebrate; it started early in the morning with a *Frühschoppen*—that was, a drink or two before or after breakfast. By daybreak every public house was open, from the many neighborhood joints to the larger public facilities ready to serve fast food and drinks. Places like Lunapark, Charlottenhof,

Krollgarten with its music pavillon, Lustgarten, and Tiergarten were the favorite get-together establishments for families and larger groups. Many Berliners also took advantage of a holiday by organizing a day's trip to the rural areas of Berlin. They were coming in big numbers by cars, buses, trains, and boats, targeting the resorts and entertainment centers of every river and lake outside of Berlin. Typical for the May celebration was the decoration of everything, from vehicles to restaurants with fresh-cut green branches of the white birch tree.

The Gang at Kieler Strasse

The corner of Kieler Strasse being a dead-end street and virtually cut off by the canal makes it a perfect playground for children. Preschool children are usually playing by the pump or in the courtyard occupying sandboxes and swings. Pumps in Berlin are part of the old street picture and similar playgrounds as the fire hydrants in New York. Those pumps are huge iron columns, round ornamented pillars pressing vertically on its base with a crown on top and a long swinging handle to operate the pump. The spout is often cast in a form of head of a lion or dragon with its mouth wide open to expel the water. Underneath the pump is a shallow basin molded in the concrete of the sidewalk intended for the horses to drink from. Every half kilometer or less, such a pump would be in sight to accommodate horse-driven vehicles.

In the old days, rest places for horses were just as important as filling stations are today for automobiles. I don't believe it is a coincidence that most of the pumps are located in front of a beer bar / restaurant, giving the driver a chance to stop for a quick meal or refreshment. Anytime the pump is not in use for the purpose it was designed for, the children of the street were back there to claim it. For Egon and me and all the rest of the kids, the pump in front of our house was a blessing; it was nice to take a bath under the pump during the hot days of the summer. Pretty soon I outgrew the circle by the pump and started hanging out with the bigger boys behind the bakery or by the canal. Egon already knew the gang, and they all liked him. I liked him too, maybe because he was older than I was, or because he supplied everybody with *Kuchenkrümel*. Anyway, Egon introduced me to Atze, the oldest boy and leader of the gang. His right man was Harry, and his sister Lucy was my age. Both were living in the apartment next to mine, and we were already acquainted. Atze was the kind of guy who was very macho; he surrounded himself only with boys who were tough. If you were tenacious, daring, and able to endure hardships, you stood a good chance to be accepted by the gang at the waterfront. I did not belong to the gang, but I was tolerated coming with Egon since they were using the old storage room behind the bakery as a meeting place.

Atze—Kieler Strasse gang leader. Killed in Russia.

The corner of the block by the bakery to the edge of the canal had a barrier of a six-foot chain-link fence with three tight-connected barbed wires on top. The backyard of the bakery was also blocked by a high stonewall, with large trash cans lined up against the wall, making it easy to climb the wall and gain access to the canal. One time Egon was climbing the wall and was urging me to follow him. I did, and as I was sitting on top of the wall, I was amazed at the beautiful view. Here you could see the canal and all its activities better than from the street. There were tugboats pulling large barges loaded with coal or building material slowly through the canal up north toward the Havel River. Barges are sturdy flat-bottomed boats used mainly to carry bulk cargo. Some barges are pushed or pulled by tugboats; others are powered by their own engines. Barges are used chiefly in sheltered waters such as canals and harbors and are very economic vehicles of transportation.

On the other side of the canal, I could see all kinds of warehouses and industrial storage and parking places. Many dockyard workers were coming over a small wooden bridge after work to go home or head for the nearest beer bar, which was on our side at Kieler Strasse. Many times, especially on Friday nights, they spent a good portion of their paychecks on beer and schnaps. For us kids, it was always fun to hang out by the door waiting for drunks to come out. They were usually singing, having a good time and very generous with their money. The biggest kick for them was to toss coins up in the air and watch the kids struggle on the floor to pick them up. Egon and Lucy got some coins at one time or another, but I never did. There must be an easier way to make money, and Atze and Harry had a bright idea. They decided we should go coin fishing. The best places for that were basement stores and underground dwellings. To connect them to the outside, they had light and air shafts to the floor of the street, usually a square, a few feet wide and deep with a heavy iron grid on top. Such a steel fence could be walked on and had holes from one to two inches between bars. The metro had air ducts every one hundred feet or so for ventilation purposes. Horizontally underneath was a griddle installed to divert rainwater. Now you know where we were going fishing, but I still have to tell you the kind of tool we needed.

We didn't need any bait or a fancy fishing rod; all we needed was a stick with a string and a small magnet instead of a hook at the end of the string. Another helpful contraption was a stick with a big spoon attached at the end. The spoon had to be bent at a ninety-degree angle to scoop up any coins in sight. A flashlight would spot the treasure, and with a lot of patience, you might be able to bring it to the surface. Ready to go, we were starting out in our own neighborhood.

At Kieler Strasse 3 was a grocery store with tables in front of it displaying fruits and vegetables. Most women came here every day just to buy whatever they needed to prepare their daily meals. A custom developed out of necessity as refrigerators were not available, and only the rich people could afford an icebox. Most housewives made their purchases outside the store and paid the greengrocer in front of the fruit stand. It happened quite often that some loose change fell under the table and into the *Kellerloch*, better known as basement grid. At the end of the day, the storekeeper moved everything back in the store, locked the place, and went home. Shortly thereafter, our gang jumped into action. We were lying down on our bellies, manipulating the gear into the hole and trying to get whatever coins we found to the top. Sometimes nothing or a few pennies, and if Lady Luck was on our side, we even retrieved nickels, dimes, and, very seldom, quarters. Making the rounds between Kieler Strasse and Scharnhorst Strasse, we pretty much covered all the retail stores in our neighborhood.

But there was yet bigger fish to fry. Eventually we were working our way up through Seller Strasse to U-Bahnhof Reinickendorfer Strasse, and Wedding. Our fishing results were making good progress, and our skills to get the coins to the top were also improving. A few times we got interrupted and chased away by a street sweeper. At U-Bahnhof Wedding, we had literally found a gold mine. A strategic traffic point where trains were coming and going every five minutes in both directions. All day long people were running up and down the stairs trying to catch a train. There were four ticket counters, and all of us five guys had them covered. Many passengers were so much in a hurry getting away from the window in an attempt to get on the train that was momentarily leaving the station. It happened frequently that they dropped coins and didn't have the time to look for them or pick them up. With a watchful eye, I mastered the situation and put my foot on the coin to protect my loot. Whatever we gathered at the end of a working day would be evenly divided among us. What we collected was not enough to open a bank account, but it sure kept us supplied with candies and ice cream.

One day we were hanging out at the subway Reinickendorfer Strasse, the nearest U-Bahn station to where we lived; with a few copper coins in our pockets, we decided to call it a day. Harry suggested that we first go next block and visit the farmer's market, a busy place where housewives pushed each other around looking for bargains. The smell alone of all the goodies made you hungry. Pooling all our coins, we had just enough money to buy a bag of fresh roasted almonds, sugar coated and delicious to eat. On our way home, we stopped on the corner of Schönwalder and Reinickendorfer Strasse in front of the entrance at the Berliner Kindl Family Restaurant. On both sides of the corner were huge windows covered with painted letters of advertising. Under the windows were long removable iron grills secured with a padlock, designed for street delivery by the brewery to the beer cellar. Looking at each other, we knew we could not pass up the opportunity to check it out.

I was holding the flashlight while Atze tried to get his spoon through one of the holes. There were no coins in sight, but in the far corner of the windowsill, he found something glittering and partially covered with dirt. It was difficult to make out what the small object might be, and Atze kept poking to get a hold of it. Every time he tried to scoop it up, it slipped off the spoon. At a closer glance, it appeared to be a small key chain or something round. Finally Atze was able to manipulate and hook it with the spoon. Slowly he lifted the stick, coming closer to the top, but then suddenly, he loosened his grip, and the claim once more disappeared into the darkness of the cellar. Harry told Atze to bend the spoon more like a hook, that way he might have a better grip to bring the thing to the surface.

Atze agreed, and this time he lifted his bounty to the top. Egon had already one finger in the hole next to the stick and very carefully took the object off the spoon and pulled it through the hole without dropping it. Taking it away to safety, all of us were surprised as Egon opened his hand to show us the treasure. What we were looking at was a little girl's golden bracelet, more valuable than all the coins we ever collected.

Strolling along Seller Street on our way home, we were too excited to make a decision as to what we should do with the bracelet. Harry said we could give it to Lucy. Atze was against it, and he wanted to take the bracelet to a pawnshop. Egon came up with the bright idea to take it back to the restaurant to find the true owner. At the end of the discussion, they were asking me about my opinion, and I told them that I didn't really care one way or the other. We trusted Egon to take it home and hang on to it for a few days. As it turned out, Harry told his mother the whole story, and she agreed to buy it for Lucy, giving each of us one new shiny Reichsmark. Eventually all of our parents found out about it and insisted that we give up our fishing expeditions or else we would be restricted to stay home. That was an ultimatum we could not ignore, but it did not stop us from finding other ways to make money.

Atze and Harry were already going to school for a few years and had connections to other gangs and learned in the schoolyard about their means of getting financial support for their members. One day, as we were sitting in the storage room behind the bakery, Atze told us that he had a plan to send us out to pick up money from the street. That statement made us look stupidly at each other in utter disbelief. "Naturally," he said, "what we are going to pick up has to be turned into money." We still did not know what he was talking about, but he was asking us to follow him for an explanation. He left the room and jumped on top of a trash can and up the wall. Now we were all sitting on the wall, and Atze was pointing to the other side of the canal. Nothing we had not seen before, nothing unusual; but the bigger boys, who swam across the canal all the time, knew more about what was happening on the other side. Many hundreds of shore workers were working there eight hours every day. It was hard work for these dockworkers to keep up with the traffic of the incoming and outgoing merchandise and material. To cool down, they consumed huge amounts of beer by the case every day. In Germany in those days, beer was sold to the consumer in a special beer bottle with a wire-flip top. Those heavy glass bottles were expensive to produce and were not disposable containers. In order to get the bottles back for refilling, the breweries charged twenty cents extra for each bottle as a security deposit. Most of the dockworkers were too busy and too tired after work to collect empty bottles to return them to the store for a refund of deposit. Other gangs in the past from nearby tenements would go over at nights and collect all the bottles they could put their hands on. Sooner or later, they got stopped by a night watchman and turned over to the police, especially when they were caught inside a warehouse.

Atze was a daredevil but did not want to get in trouble with the law. This time Harry came up with a smart idea. "Why don't we buy all the bottles at ten cents apiece and double our money!" he exclaimed. Everyone was patting Harry on the shoulder, showing him our approval. Now it was Egon's plan to solve the problem. How were we going to transport the bottles back to the store? In his grandmother's garden, there was an old rack wagon that would be just dandy for the job.

Each of us was pitching in with one mark that we still kept from the sale of the bracelet. Next morning we were on our way over to the docks. Surprisingly, everything went smoothly; one forklift operator told us that this was no playground and that we were to stay out. Once we told him what we were up to, he became helpful. Anyway, he asked us to stay where we were but was willing to call a supervisor. To make a long story short, the boss appointed one of the apprentices to deal with us.

We gave him the money, and he loaded our wagon with two cases of empty beer bottles. At the store, we doubled our money, but the little greasy grocer told us not to come back; he did not believe us that we legally obtained the bottles.

To avoid any friction, we just went to another store, and this time we had no problems. Our little business went on for quite some time but died down at the end of the summer when we all went back to school. For me, September 1, 1935, was the first time in my life when I started to go to school. Life from now on would never be the same again. The carefree and leisurely days were, after the beginning of school, a thing of the past. Instead, discipline and a regimen of education were the rule and order of the day.

Suddenly going to school one day was not an overnight transition for me. I kept on playing in school and paid very little attention to what the teacher had to say. After I got punished several times, it was clear to me that I had to conform and give in. Once you get used to it, school was not all that bad; certain subjects became interesting, and finally you developed a habit of learning. My favorite subject was sport, and my ambition was to become a member of the swimming team. Atze and Harry already belonged to the school team. Egon and I were not quite ready for the team, not because we were too young or not good enough in distance swimming—no, it was only the missing training from the high diving board that was holding us back from becoming team members. The wall behind Egon's bakery was a solid two-foot wide and twenty-foot high steel-encased concrete edge to the canal. Egon and I were walking on it, looking down, but neither of us had the guts so far to jump down from it. The rest of the gang were constantly jumping from the wall, doing saltos, backward, headfirst, and cannonball.

Atze's inner circle was a special kind of club. Only fearless boys need apply. All the members were tested by Atze in one way or another. They would not last if they were not brave enough to satisfy Atze, and when you met with them, they bragged about this. They didn't hide it. The braver they were, the more credible they were. Egon was seeking a higher level of acceptance, and to reach this point, he must jump from the wall or stay with the status of associated member in the club. One day he said he was ready, and he jumped from the wall headfirst, landing on his belly. He did not come up immediately, and Atze had to jump after him to get him out. Egon was crying with pain and holding his stomach, his skin was red as a lobster from the impact of the water. He was not ready for the Olympics, but his courage to jump earned him the respect of the club. That made me, outsider as I was, the only one who had not demonstrated the willingness to jump. Atze asked me if I was afraid, and I told him I was not but I needed more time to try out from a lower level.

"That is right," everyone said. "But Egon showed no fear without any experience."

"OK," I said, "if you are testing my courage, there are other ways to do it."

"Yes!" someone exclaimed. "I have a pretty good idea how you can show us your courage."

"What do you have in mind?" Atze asked. "Right now is siesta time, and all the stores are closed from one o'clock to three o' clock in the afternoon for *mittag essen* [main meal time]. The greengrocer that called us liars and refused to take our beer bottles should be punished. Suppose somebody would lift the canvas and bring us some of his plums hidden under the cover."

Everybody looked at me, and I said, "That is stealing."

"No," Atze said, "that is courage."

There was no time to think about the consequences, I volunteered as everybody expected me to do the job. There were no people around the store at this time of the day, and it was easy for me to lift the canvas and pull out a small wooden crate of juicy plums. Slowly I walked away, shaking like a leaf, knowing that I did something terribly wrong. I did not relax till I reached the backyard of the bakery. For a moment I was a hero and earned the respect of the gang, but not completely; that would be accomplished when I was able to perform my first swan dive without landing on my belly. Unfortunately, the crime I committed did not go unpunished.

The old lady Hasenfus lived downstairs next to the store in a small apartment. She was a widow suffering from arthritis, sitting in a chair by the window, spending most of her time looking out of the window to see what was going on in the street. I was not aware that she saw me when I was taking off with the box of plums. She told my mother; my mother told my father, and he gave me the beating of my life. Ten lashes with his razor strap on my bare bottom. Bending over the toilet seat, holding my pants down, and facing the bathroom door, I saw my mother stepping close to me. I was hoping that she would come at the last minute to my defense and try to talk my father out of my upcoming ordeal of corporal punishment. Instead she came closer to me, asking me to open my mouth, and then she put a clean washcloth between my teeth and told me to bite on it. That washcloth would keep me from crying or screaming. Now I knew there was no way I could escape. A feeling of fear and total abandonment came over me; at that moment, I closed my eyes and mentally I completely resigned. The physical pain passed, but the psychological pain I suffered had never gone away.

The summer of 1935 went by all too fast and with it the sunny days at the lake. My first year in school had not excited me too much, but I did enjoy my gym classes. The coach in our school was taking a group of students who were interested in swimming lessons once a week to the public swimming pool at Stadtmitte. I signed up in a hurry; it was exactly what I needed to get past the winter month. I knew the place, and I couldn't wait to get in the water. Here was my chance to try out the diving boards. To warm up, I jumped first from the three-meter board; but this was kid's stuff, and I had done it before. The next size was a five-meter board. A few cannonballs gave me the feeling of the impact before I tried a header. The third diving board, also known as Olympic diving board, was the highest diving board of them all. It had a measurement of ten meters, which was equivalent to thirty feet. It was a big step to go from a five-meter board to a ten-meter diving board. Twice the flying time and double the impact. You could hurt yourself badly if you do a belly flap. The style of flying had to be perfect to enter the water correctly; if you would not keep your legs straight and your heels together, you would lose balance and come down with an unbound entry.

I told the coach what my final goal was, but he would not let me go up the ten-meter diving board till I got his green light. Every time we came to the pool, I practiced at the five-meter board, and he was watching me. Hoping to satisfy the coach soon, I did my best to show him clean jumps, and the day had come when he deemed me ready for the big one. The coach gave me a last-minute advice: "Pretend you are diving from a five-meter board, it is the same procedure, it only takes a few seconds longer to come down. Go, you can do it."

Climbing up the ladder to the platform was already scary as I was standing at the edge of the board looking down thirty feet. For a moment, a sudden fright came over me, but then I remembered what the coach told me. I positioned myself, concentrated, and jumped. When I got out of the water, I was really happy, and I felt like an airplane pilot who had delivered his first solo flight.

Next morning in school, I was telling Egon that I had taken the big plunge. "Now you are ready to jump from the wall," he replied.

"Yes, you are right. I am just waiting for warmer days to come."

Never before was my longing as much as it was then to show the gang that I could do anything they were doing. Till summer arrived, we were just sitting on the wall watching the tugboats go by. Some went fast, and others were pulling slower, depending on how heavy of a load they were carrying. One day Atze and Harry were dreaming up a stunt. They were talking about diving underneath a barge and coming out the other side. "It may be possible," said Egon. Some of the barges were fifty feet long and about twelve feet wide. "Let's go to the bridge," Egon said. "We have to find out how long it takes for the barge to travel fifty feet."

We were now going to the bridge waiting for the next slow barge to come. Atze had his watch ready to time the barge from the moment it entered underneath the bridge till the moment the rudder was out of sight. Here came one loaded with gravel, getting very slowly closer to the bridge. The barge was hardly visible with the deck only a couple of feet over the water surface. The pace of the barge was about the speed of a person walking down the street. Barges towed by a tugboat are faster than those without a towboat. Independent barges usually had a smaller engine operating with less speed. The barge we were timing traveled solo and needed twenty seconds to go fifty feet. Even a slow diver would not need more than ten seconds to swim twelve feet underwater. So we figured that there was enough time to get to the other side of the barge. The trick was to start diving at the front of the barge, or else you might get cut to pieces by the screw of the rudder.

In conclusion, we decided that it was safer to target a flat-bottom barge towed by a tugboat, not overloaded, to give us enough clearance between the bottom of the canal and the bottom of the barge. Where exactly the deepest spot of the canal was we didn't know till we did some diving to find out. The canal was approximately fifty feet wide at the most, and I knew that I could dive from our side of the canal to the shore vis-a-vis without coming up for air; I had done it at the pool many times. Talking about it was one thing, but to do it was something else. When the summer came, we would see who had the guts to be the first one to do the stunt.

Baldur von Schirach was appointed by Hitler in June of 1933 to be the leader of the Hitler Youth. In 1936, on Hitler's forty-seventh birthday on April 20, Schirach presented Hitler with a unique birthday present.

Field   exercise

Hitler Youth Tent City

Hitler Youth marching band, author second from right

He created Jungvolk, a subdivision of the Hitler Youth, and to please the Führer, Schirach declared 1936 the year of the newly organized Jungvolk, which encompassed all German boys from the age of ten to fourteen years. After the age of fourteen, everybody became a member of the Hitler Youth till the age of eighteen. To educate young people in the doctrine of the Nazi Party had priority in the new regime.

Mein Kampf was the new bible of the Third Reich, a required reading for all Germans. Its author was Adolf Hitler. Schirach instructed all schools to encourage boys from the ages of six to ten to attend meetings of the Jungvolk to get interested in the activities of the older boys. On Hitler's birthday, all schools were closed. Only a ceremony was taking place in the morning to celebrate the Führer's birthday and the induction of all ten-year-old boys in the Jungvolk. The auditorium in our school was packed with every teacher and their students. The stage was draped with a huge picture of Hitler with swastika flags on both sides. At the beginning of the ceremony, everybody stood up to sing the national anthem and the Horst Wessel hymn. The first speech was given by the principal of our school in his new uniform as a party member to the glory of Adolf Hitler and the Third Reich. Some boys and girls came up the stage to recite a poem fitting the solemn occasion. But the highlight of the celebration was the induction of the new members in the Jungvolk. Leaders of the Hitler Youth were holding a flag in front of them. With their left hand, they touched the flag and, with the right hand held up, they repeated the following oath: "I swear by God this holy oath, that I will render to Adolf Hitler, Führer of the German Reich, unconditional obedience, and that I am ready, to risk my life at any time for this oath."

A passport picture of my Hitler Youth ID

At the end of the induction, each new member of the Jungvolk received an ID card and a metal badge of the Hitler Youth. They were also now allowed to wear uniform and the official Hitler Youth dagger, carrying the Hitler Youth's own slogan—Blood and Honor—engraved in the blade. Part of the ritual was a foregoing initiation test, usually a jump from a three-to-four-story-high building while your comrades on the ground were holding a fireman's net to catch you. From the tender age of ten and up, every boy in Germany was now involved in activities of combative sport and endurance training to make them "as fast as greyhounds and as tough as steel," as Hitler put it. Obviously he had it in mind to turn the Hitler Youth into soldiers, and Schirach was just the man to do it. This year Berlin was also working with great enthusiasm to prepare itself for the Olympic Games to be held from August 1 to 16. Even though Hitler was not interested in the Olympic Games whatsoever, he expected the German team to pick up most of the medals as he was trying to show the world that the Arian race was superior.

As I mentioned earlier, my uncle Rudolf was seriously training for the 1936 Summer Olympic Games in Berlin. He was selected to participate as a swimmer in the German team in the international competition. Unfortunately, he never had a chance to see or be part of the Olympic Games. He suffered a tragic motorcycle accident on March 29, 1936, and died in the night of April 3, 1936. How did it happen? No collision of any kind; he was an excellent motorcyclist and never consumed alcohol. In the capacity of Obersturmführer of the Standarte 5/224, he was in charge of the election on Sunday, March 29, 1936, in Velten. After the conclusion of the election that evening, he left for his hometown, Kremmen, on his motorcycle. Before he arrived in Kremmen, his gasoline tank exploded somewhere in the middle of the road and threw him instantly through the air. His body was found one hundred feet away from the place of the bloody accident; he was still alive and taken to the nearby hospital in Nauen. Doctors were able to stabilize his condition, but he suffered too many wounds and broken bones. As a result, he developed large blood clots, and his heart finally succumbed to a massive thrombosis in the night of the following Sunday. Was it an accident? No, it was not, but let me go back to where it all started.

Rudolf Vogt, leader of Hitler's SA 1934

Two years earlier, in 1934, Hitler faced an inner crisis. He was not the absolute ruler of the Nazi Party and was confronted with an open conflict and opposition that came from General von Schleicher, Gregor Strasser, and the Stabschef of the SA Captain, Ernst Röhm. In order for Hitler to gain complete control over Germany, it was essential that he gained the confidence and support of the German army. Röhm insisted that the Reichswehr should be dissolved and the SA, by now 3.5 million men strong, turned instead into a Volks army. Hitler had no choice and decided to eliminate the SA as a power factor under the leadership of Ernst Röhm, or the Reichswehr would terminate Hitler as the chancellor and create a military government. He promised the armed forces to restore them to the size and grandeur they had known in imperial times before the Treaty of Versailles. Hitler's offer was accepted by the generals, and he received the backing of the army to destroy the SA leadership. Hitler carried out his part of the bargain and launched on June 30, 1934, what became known in history as the Nazi Blood Purge. Under the pretense of stopping Röhm from conspiring against Hitler and his administration, he ordered the summary execution of eighty-five SA leaders, plus the former number two man in the Nazi Party, Gregor Strasser; and the former chancellor General von Schleicher and his wife were shot in their home by the SS.

Rudolf Vogt, shortly before his assassination in 1936

Gustav von Kahr, helper in the suppression of Hitler's 1923 Beer Hall Putsch, was not forgotten by Hitler's thirst for blood and was hacked to pieces with an ax by a gang of SS cronies. His remains were dumped in a swamp near München. Some one thousand persons were massacred on this bloody weekend of June 30, 1934. The executions took place either at the SA leaders' meeting in Bad Wiessee under Hitler's supervision or in Berlin at the Lichterfelder SS Kaserne under the orders of Hermann Göring. As Hitler decided to sacrifice the SA, his loyal brownshirts who believed in him, in favor of his new bodyguard the SS, his old comrades in arms who put him in power felt deeply betrayed and knew at this point that they had followed the wrong leader. In reality, the switch from SA to SS bore more historical importance than the average citizen was aware of. Early membership of the SA came from a handful of party members who gave Hitler protection at meeting places and beer halls when he gave speeches. Anybody who followed Hitler and joined his party must have been convinced of his ideology to help Germany out of its crisis. Among them were former army officers, businessmen, students, and ordinary workers. Those men who advanced to the rank of leaders were educated and dedicated to the cause. Of course, the majority of the storm troopers became engaged in street battles with the communists and other rioters. Contrary to the SS, most members of the party and the SA had jobs, lived with their families, and went to church on Sundays. Members of the SS lived in barracks, had to give up their religion, and were groomed and indoctrinated to kill any human being when ordered to do so without asking any questions. Naturally, characters with criminal tendencies were attracted to such kind of evil organization. After the killing of the upper SA leadership, Hitler considered the rest of the SA unnecessary and troublesome. One way of elimination was to force as many members of the SA as possible to join the ranks of the SS.

The free-thinking spirit of most members of the SA was too dangerous for the new dictator. It was no secret that Rudolf Vogt opposed the idea vigorously and openly advised his men not to join the SS, and for that he had to pay with his life. Only a few people knew about his death, and the truth was only revealed by one survivor after the war. In the eyes of his family, friends, and comrades, he was a hero; and he was buried as such. A state funeral was ordered for him by the new Stabschef of the SA, Lutze, who was a friend of Rudolf Vogt's. The funeral procession started on Sunday, April 5, 1936, at 6:30 PM in Nauen. His coffin was escorted overnight by his SA comrades and arrived the following morning in Warsow, Mecklenburg-Schwerin. The little church was already filled with family members and government dignitaries. After the religious ceremony, the funeral procession proceeded to the nearby cemetery. At the graveside, the funeral oration was given by the Catholic priest and senior officers of the SA. His coffin was decorated with an abundance of flowers and beautiful wreaths from a multitude of people who knew him and paid their last respects.

The graveside of Rudolf Vogt in Mecklenburg

A month before Rudolf Vogt died, Hitler made his first big move. On March 7, 1936, he sent units of his new army into the demilitarized zone of the Rhineland on Germany's western border. This was a breach not only of the Versailles Treaty, which had been forced on Germany, but of the later Locarno Treaty, which Germany had freely signed. Hitler's march into the Rhineland was a daring move. It was pure bluff. The French army, as Hitler well knew, was entitled under the two treaties to throw back the German troops in the Rhineland. And it could easily have done so. It was still the strongest military force in Europe. The new German army was as yet no match for it. Yet the French, restrained by Great Britain, did not move. The two great Western democracies did not want to go to war even though they could easily have won. They wanted peace at almost any price. Hitler's uncanny intuition had convinced him of this. That was why he took the gamble and got away with it.

Summer weather had arrived early in 1936, and the gang at Kieler Strasse was getting ready for their own little game of competition. There would be no medal for the winner who dived the fastest across the canal underneath a floating barge, but it sure would be a prestigious event; best of all, it would build self-esteem and confidence for the winner. Atze broke the ice and jumped from the wall first to dive across the canal underwater, followed by Harry and Egon. Finally it was my turn to pass the test, but somehow I drifted to the right and came up for air under the bridge. Next day I was trying again, compensating my speed to the left, bringing myself in a perfect dive to the other side of the canal. To stay underwater across the canal was no problem; the trick was to dive as close to the bottom as possible. The clearance between the bottom of the barge and the mud of the canal was not more than ten feet. To keep a safe distance from the boat, the diver had to swim within five feet from the bottom of the canal to make a successful passage of the barge. Our first dry run was a simulated barge figured out by Atze. Harry and Egon swam down the canal toward the bridge, hanging on to a fifty-feet string stretched between them, making believe to be a slow barge from bow to stern. I was the observer while Atze, in a calculated jump in front of them, passed, diving close to the bottom underneath the first twenty feet of the line. Theoretically it was a perfect dive. All of us repeated the same maneuver several times till we were confident enough to go for the real thing.

It must be borne in mind that diving underneath a moving barge is a very dangerous project requiring utmost courage, speed, and perfect timing. As our confidence progressed to the highest point of readiness, everybody looked up to Atze to get started. After our training was completed, the long-awaited day came when Atze finally announced that he was ready to make the first dive. A slow-moving barge with a not-too-heavy cargo floating close to the surface was his selection. Atze jumped at the right moment, and all of us stopped breathing till the barge disappeared and Atze came in view at the other side of the canal. As he came back to us, the reception was one of joy and happiness. The successful event called for a special celebration. Egon invited all of us by saying, "I have twenty-five pennies in my pocket, let's go and spend it on ice cream." He was the most endowed kid in the block, making tips by delivering bakery goods after school to the old ladies for their afternoon *kaffee und kuchen.*

The next day Harry and Egon were in line to take the dive, taking last-minute instruction from the champion. Somehow they were less tense knowing that they would make it. Waiting for the right barge to come, Atze told them when to jump. Again it went smoothly, and both of them made it without any problem. That left me as the only one in the group who had not yet proven himself. Even so, being the youngest one in the gang, I didn't want to be left out. To be fully recognized by my peers, I just had to do it; if I could only get rid of the butterflies in my stomach. A few days later, Harry showed me a superlong barge going superslow through the canal. That was my boat, and off I went, reaching the opposite shore with time to spare. Never before in my life did I feel so happy and relieved as the moment when I got out of the water. I was now bursting with self-esteem, and at the same time, I had earned the respect of all gang members.

CHAPTER II

YEARS OF PREPARATION IN TEGEL

From Kieler Strasse to Tegel

As a young boy in the parochial school in Tegel

Moving to a new place was not easy, and saying good-bye to old friends was even tougher. I considered the move to Tegel as the first major interruption in my early life that really left a big impression on me by leaving a home behind that encompassed my comfort and security. The neighborhood, the school, and most of all my friends, the gang on the waterfront, were taken away from me. It all happened very fast and unexpectedly. One day after work, after we had just finished dinner, my dad told us that he had a chance to fill a vacancy in a small post office in a northern district of Berlin called Tegel. My uncle Rudolf was there for some time as assistant postmaster and gave his brother the opportunity for a promotion. Tegel is a small resort surrounded by Lake Tegel, the river

Havel, and a huge forest. It is also the birthplace of the famous brothers Wilhelm and Alexander von Humboldt. The Humboldtschloss (Humboldt Palace) is a twenty-acre estate and beautiful garden near Lake Tegel. Tegel is a historical place; it was favored by King Frederic II.

Tegel is very proud of having four major schools, two elementary schools, and two high schools. The high school for boys is the Humboldtschule, and the girls' own high school is the Lyceum. The two elementary schools are divided by the two major religions, Catholics and Lutherans. According to my denomination, I was now a new pupil at the local Catholic school in Tegel. The schoolhouse was a small two-story stone building erected around the turn of the century. It had a big backyard in a quiet neighborhood adjacent to the Catholic church only two blocks away from Lake Tegel. Most teachers were members of the same parish and were respectable leaders of the congregation.

Contrary to state public schools, parochial schools have a strong religious overtone in the Christian upbringing of their children. A totally new environment from what I was accustomed to when I attended public school before. No more pictures of Adolf Hitler in the classroom, no "Heil Hitler" salute in the morning; instead, there was a crucifix on the wall, a prayer in the morning, and supervised church attendance every Sunday morning. However, all of this gradually changed and disappeared under the influence of the new regime. Nevertheless, I made new friends, and in no time, I felt at home in Tegel. A beautiful sunny apartment with a lovely garden within walking distance to the forest was our new domicile. The new school I was going to was much smaller than the old school in Wedding. I must also say that the curriculum was stricter and the behavior of the children more obedient. The only problem was the distance between the house and the school, more or less two kilometers each way. I didn't mind walking, but it could be miserable on a rainy day or when the road was covered with ice and snow. During the winter months, it happened quite often that we kids arrived at school with wet feet. The teacher encouraged us to take our shoes and socks off and hang them over the steam heater to dry. Each grade had its own classroom and a smaller number of students compared to public schools. Teachers did not belong to the Nazi Party, except the principal. The new minister of education made it mandatory that all principals be members of the party, and parochial schools were not exempted.

Our principal's name was Boese, and his attitude showed no conflict of interest. He was a devoted Catholic and 150 percent Nazi at the same time. He became my mentor in religion and Nazi doctrines, but as it turned out, the latter superseded in my mind. We were now into the year of 1937, and on January 15, Boese announced the opening of the new Adolf

Hitler schools, the Napola and the LBA. The first one stood for National-Politische Erziehungsanstaft, the LBA for Lehrer Bildungs Anstalt. There was not much difference between the two. The Napola was an institution to prepare selected boys for political leadership with military discipline. At the LBA you found a higher academic standard with less emphasis on political indoctrination. The purpose of the LBA was to educate young boys to become teachers. Both schools had special uniforms and lodging, and other arrangements had the character of a military school. Sports activities were on a daily basis. Our principal told us what an honor it would be if someone from our school would meet the criteria of selection. For some of us, his indication became an enticement to learn more and get better grades. In the month of May, a few changes took place in our school. The crucifix hanging in the middle of the wall behind the teacher disappeared overnight, and the next morning, the wall was decorated with a picture of Adolf Hitler. In one corner of all classrooms, swastika flags were posted. The hours of religious teaching were reduced, and new textbooks replaced the old ones. Parochial schools in particular were subject to frequent inspection by an agent of the SS. At his discretion, he could dismiss any principal he deemed not suitable for membership in the Nazi Party. For a long time I could not figure why a man in a black suit would sit in our classroom and listen to the teacher's lecture. I didn't like the guy, he gave me the creeps and reminded me of an undertaker.

Finally the last day of school arrived, and eight weeks of summer vacation were ahead of us. It all worked out perfectly; my father also had his summer vacation scheduled for the same time. Since Uncle Rudolf died last year, we had promised my aunt Erna that we would come and spend next summer with her. She lived now in the big house in Kremmen with her daughter, Ingeborg, and my grandmother, Rudolf's mother. Her place was a new two-story farmhouse on a ten-acre spread near the railroad. She would take care of the garden and the animals while my grandmother did the cooking. On an early morning in July, we took everything we packed the night before to the bus station around the corner. My father had to go back to the house and fetch another big suitcase as we could only carry so much. The bus arrived on time, and the friendly bus driver stacked all our gear in the luggage compartment under the bus. The bus terminal was right in front of the railroad station in Tegel. While my father purchased the tickets to Kremmen, a porter came and placed our luggage on the train. Ten minutes later, the train pulled out, and we were heading for Kremmen. What a lovely ride. The train was pulled by an old steam engine and moving along slowly. My mother let me have the seat by the window, and I was observing everything that we passed by. I must admit it was about the first time that I had a chance to see the open country. Everything was blooming, and the fields were intersected by tiny straight dirt roads, making them look like checkerboard squares.

Ever so often, we passed a small village with a church in the middle or surrounded by a forest. Most of the villages or small towns were connected with the railroad. The train stopped a few minutes; passengers were in a hurry to come or go, and again the train was on its way. Early in the afternoon, the train arrived in Kremmen. We had barely enough time to throw our luggage out of the door and get off the train, as it was now in a hurry to get to its final destination on time—Schwerin, the capital of Mecklenburg. At the end of the Bahnsteig platform, the next-door neighbor's son Fred was waiting with his horse and buggy for us. He went to town to buy some material, and Aunt Erna asked him to pick us up at the train station. As we drove through the gate, we saw Grandmother, Aunt Erna, and my cousin Ingeborg sitting on the front porch, ready to welcome us. After all the greetings were done, we entered the house, and immediately I could smell the bacon. By then I realized how hungry I was and that we had no time to eat breakfast since we left the house early in the morning. Aunt Erna asked us to sit down with them and have a late lunch.

My grandmother was an excellent cook, and what she prepared was the best *Bauernfrühstück* I ever had. A dish of mixed fried potatoes, bacon and scrambled eggs, served with black bread, smoked sausage from Mecklenburg, and a tall glass of cool buttermilk. The bread she baked came fresh out of the oven from the huge wood-burning cast-iron stove in the kitchen. As she placed the hot loaf of bread on a wooden board, she made the sign of a cross with her carving knife over the new bread and started to slice it up. That was the beginning of the *Brotzeit*, and everybody began eating. After the meal, all of us relaxed in the living room, and a lively conversation took place. Sooner or later, the subject of Rudolf's death came up, and Grandma started to cry; she excused herself and went to her room.

Silence filled the room for a few minutes till my father said we should also go upstairs and unpack our things. We had a very comfortable room in the attic, it had fresh linen on the beds and was ready for us. I slept all night till the rooster woke me up in the morning. The women were already up working in the kitchen, and my father planned for the day to do some repairs around the house. Cousin Ingeborg, who was one year younger than me, was eager to show me the place, and we played in the backyard. I told her that my birthday would be the following day, July 19, but it seemed that it was no surprise to her.

I figured that they may have planned a birthday party for me. Sure enough, when I got up the next morning, there was a big bunch of flowers on the table and some birthday greeting cards. Everybody wished me a happy birthday, and my grandma made me my favored breakfast, omelette with *bratkartoffeln* and *sülze*. Aunt Erna told us that her sister Alwine and family would come and visit us in the afternoon. My mother told Ingeborg and me that she would bake a cherry pie if we would go out this morning and pick some cherries. Ingeborg got a basket; and showed me where the tree was, I climbed up the tree and picked enough cherries to fill the basket. Every day I helped my cousin with her chores around the house, and today was no different. First we would bring in firewood for the stove, then we would get drinking water from the pump outside for the house, sweep the sidewalks, and take care of the animals. Feeding the chickens and seeing them produce eggs were most interesting for me. For a kid like me, born and raised in the city, it was very exciting to help gather the eggs from the chicken coop. She took me to the strawberry patch in the backyard, and we picked some fresh strawberries, enough for everybody to have for dessert after dinner. At this time, I was already getting impatient to find out what I would get for my birthday. I knew Ingeborg must have a notion, but according to her, she had no idea. The only information I was getting out of her was the news that Erna's sister Alwine; her husband, Erich; and their son, Dieter, were coming to visit us for coffee and cake this afternoon. Dieter was about our age and a nice fellow to be with. After dinner, the women were getting ready to set the table one more time for coffee and cake, a tradition that is taken very seriously in Germany especially when there is a birthday celebration.

The grown-ups were lounging in the living room, engaged in a vivid conversation, showing no interest to go to the dining room. Finally my grandmother, the respected matrix, took over, inviting everybody to follow her to the dining room. Nobody talked or sat down till Grandmother had taken her place at the head of the table. And what a beautiful table it was, decorated with a white tablecloth, shiny silverware, and fine china porcelain. Placed in the center of the table was a fancy huge three-layer marzipan chocolate vanilla cream cake. On each end of the table were plates with various pastry and diverse confection. The scent of lovely blooming flowers and the aroma of fresh-brewed coffee filled the dining room with a festive atmosphere. Behind me on the wall, on top of the buffet table, I discovered several neatly wrapped packages; obviously, these were my birthday presents. Finally my mother decorated the cake with eight candles and lit them in honor of my birthday. I was very moved, and the moment everybody joined in the "Happy Birthday" song, I was overcome by joy that almost made me cry. This was all new to me; I did not know what to think of when I was asked to make a wish and blow out the candles. Now I was allowed to open my presents, the moment I had long been waiting for. The big package was my first target; it contained exactly what I was hoping for—an erector set with all the nuts and bolts to build a miniature Eiffel Tower. That was what I had been asking my parents for in a long time, but my father kept telling me that it was too expensive; later I found out that my grandma pitched in to make my wish come true. The rest of the gifts were smaller but also nice, like a book, a harmonica, candies, etc. The chocolates and candies I shared with Ingeborg and Dieter. The older folks were now sitting down to enjoy their Kaffeeklatsch; for us kids, it was hot chocolate and cake. Ingeborg could not believe just how much cake Dieter and I were able to swallow. The next day I was not too hungry, and food did not appeal to me. Everybody was busy with cleaning or fixing something. My father was in the barn trying to get the old Opel to start; the car had not been driven since his brother died. There was some gasoline left in the tank, but the ignition did not make a sound. The time the car had been sitting idle in the barn had drained the battery.

The people next door watched my father cranking the motor and offered their help. Together the men pushed the car on the road; then my dad got in the driver's seat, another pushed, and the car went down the road. With plenty of speed and going farther down the hill, he stepped on the clutch, put in the second gear; and to everyone's delight, the engine jumped into action. He drove the car home under its own power, parked it but let the motor running for some time to recharge the battery. The following day, he pushed the starter button, and the motor turned on with no problem. For the remaining days of our vacation we now had a chance to drive around Kremmen, go to the market, and visit all the stores in town. The women in particular appreciated my father for being the chauffeur and taking them places. On the following Sunday, since we had not seen the countryside, Aunt Erna suggested to drive out to the lake for a picnic. A basket with all kinds of goodies was prepared, and we were ready to go, but at the last minute, Grandma decided to stay home. She was not feeling very well as her arthritis gave her some pain, and she had great difficulties walking. Ever since I could remember she always walked with a cane, but today she was mostly sitting in her chair.

My mother suggested that we all stay home, but Grandma insisted for us to get out of the house and have a good time on the shores of the lake. We had mixed feelings about leaving her alone, but she would not have it any other way. It was indeed a beautiful day; the sun was shining and inviting us to come and see nature. At the lake, we find a shady place under the oak trees to stretch out the blanket for relaxation. Ingeborg and I preferred to play at the beach, not wasting much time before we went for a swim. The day went by fast, and then it was time to go home. When we arrived at the house, Grandma was in a good mood. She talked on the phone to her brother Erwin who lived with his wife, Iga, in a new house in Rudow in the south side of Berlin. He called to find out how she was doing. Since they were now living in the big new house without children, he suggested that she come back to Berlin and stay with them. Erwin knew that Martha wanted to go back to Berlin after the death of her son Rudolf, but more important, she needed to be in town for medical treatment. Aunt Erna was kind of surprised, but she agreed to go along with whatever was best for Grandma. In a few days, our vacation was coming to an end, and my father suggested that we take her back to Berlin with us. He called his sister, Lucy, my grandmother's only daughter, the next morning, and she promised to meet us at a certain time at the train station in Tegel to take her mother all the way to Rudow.

The following weekend, we visited Grandma in Rudow to see how she was doing. Sitting in a rocking chair in the veranda, covered with a comfortable blanket, she seemed to be quite content soaking up the last sunrays of the Indian summer. Erwin told us that she never complained, but he noticed that she had great difficulties moving around. It was obvious that the deformity of her bones kept her in constant pain. Two weeks after we visited her, it got so bad that she had to be hospitalized. Iga went to see her every day, but most of the time she was sleeping. The painkiller she was taking kept her pretty much sedated. Also, her immune system was not doing the best job in protecting her. The fact that she was constantly grieving over her son's, Rudolf, death undermined her health severely. One day early in November, she contracted pneumonia, fell in a coma, and died a few days later. It saddened all of us. My grandma lived for her children and was very much concerned not to be a burden to any of them.

Long before she died, she had made arrangements for her funeral. So with elaborate care and religious ceremony, she was buried at the Dorothean Friedhof, a Catholic cemetery in Berlin. All I remembered was the beautiful display she had around her coffin of flowers and burning candles. It was an open-casket ceremony. I went really close to see her face; she looked peaceful. Of all the relatives, Lucy suffered the most; she cried over her mother's body and had to be gently taken away by her two brothers Max and Herbert in order to close the coffin and lower it into the ground. After the funeral, we stayed overnight at Erwin's house, and the next morning Iga wanted to dispose of Grandma's belongings as soon as possible. There was not much to give away. Most of the furniture in her room belonged to Erwin and Iga anyway. Erna made it clear that she did not want any of Grandma's possessions. Lucy took some of her books, and my parents claimed her old Singer sewing machine. All the family photos my grandma kept were equally divided among the surviving children. Since I was about to celebrate my first Holy Communion, Iga gave me a little brown purse containing my grandma's black rosary to keep it in memory of her. I kept it in all the years to come, and it is still in my possession—one of the few things that survived my childhood.

Another year had passed, and we were now entering the year 1938. I was very much involved in schoolwork, and my favorite subjects were literature and history. Not only was I eager to learn about events that happened in the past, but I was also excited by contemporary history as I became a witness of it in the early years of my life. The biggest sensation after Hitler's election that gave him the first triumph of popularity was his successful annexation of Austria to Germany on March 13, 1938. Every German saw the pictures of a peaceful occupation and how the Nazi troops were greeted with flowers by the Austrian people, but it was not known by the average citizen that Hitler jailed Schuschnigg, the Catholic dictator who had succeeded Dollfuss, and started the usual massacres and imprisonments of Jews and anti-Fascists. Hitler's triumphant return to his native land of Austria was a spectacle I shall never forget. Upon his arrival at his hometown of Linz, he gave a speech to his delirious fellow countrymen that he had vowed never to return until he would come as a liberator. Back in Berlin, Hitler also now openly sponsored the aggression against the Jewish population by the members of the Nazi Party. The prejudice against the Jews became with Hitler a terrible fanatical disease which led to the massacre of millions of innocent Jewish people.

The only protest and opposition against Hitler's barbarism, besides quite a few individual mostly unimportant Germans, came from the two big leading churches in Germany. The Roman Catholic Church and the Lutheran Church condemned Hitler's actions under organized leadership by the Vatican and all bishops. Consequently, many church leaders were arrested and taken to concentration camps. At my school, teachers would only say good things about the regime and were given the freedom to teach religion at the same time. Before I joined the Hitler Youth, the Catholic Church was still a domineering factor in my life. My grandmother's wish became reality when on March 31, 1938, I received my first Holy Communion at the St. Josefskirche in Berlin-Tegel.

A Girl Named Gisela

Living in Tegel had also an advantage. I could now walk to the lake, enjoy the beach more often, and watch the boats in the harbor. Across the river Havel, which flowed into the lake, was a huge iron bridge. At one time many years ago, if somebody wanted to cross the bridge, each person had to pay five pfennig (pennies) at the gate. Even though it was no longer the case, people had kept the name Sechser Brücke or, in English, Nickel Bridge. The bridge was an old landmark and was especially popular among the young folks. As tradition has it, if a boy wants to impress his girlfriend, he has to jump from the bridge to gain her acceptance by demonstrating his courage. About half of my classroom were girls. The boys were sitting on the left side and the girls on the right side. My seat was right next to the middle in the back. The desk next to me across the lane belonged to a girl by the name Gisela. She lived just a few blocks from my house, and I would catch up with her in the morning and walked together with her to school. After school, she usually walked with a bunch of other girls; but past the railroad tracks, she walked alone. At this point, I would show up and offer my service to carry her books. I could only describe my desire to be close to her as an attraction to a girl that I had never experienced for any girl before, truly an innocent feeling of nonsexual affinity. It was hard to tell if our feelings were mutual, but when I asked her if she would join me for ice cream next Sunday after church, she agreed to go with me.

As soon as she said yes, she immediately asked me if she could bring her younger cousin along. Of course, I said, being the last of the big spenders, I had no problem with that. Financially, I was in good shape; being the proud owner of a second-hand bicycle put together mostly from junkyard parts, I was finally able to get a paper route with the *Berliner Morgenpost*.

Come Sunday morning, I was the first one out of church. People didn't go home right away; usually they stayed in small groups before they departed. The men would go to the nearest beer bar for some beer, drinks, and breakfast; and the women would congregate in the church hall with coffee and cake. As soon as I spotted Gisela talking to some girls, I motioned to her; and she came toward me with her cousin, and off we went to town. A few blocks away, we entered the Haupt Strasse, or as we call it, main street, which led directly to the lake. On both sides of the street were fancy shops, restaurants, hotels, a one-movie theater, and the only ice cream parlor in town. When we got there, the place was already packed with kids, but we were lucky to find a table under a big chestnut tree in the garden. A few minutes had gone by, Felix and his girlfriend Eva walked into the garden. They had the same problem of not finding a vacant table, so I invited them to come and sit down with us. No introduction was needed as we all were attending the same school and church. Felix was two years older than I was, and I had seen him come to school many times in his Hitler Youth uniform. Eva also was a member of the Hitler Youth Bund for German girls. Here in the garden it was self-service; after asking the girls what they liked, Felix and I went to the counter, took a tray, and ordered all the drinks and ice cream novelties we desired. When we finished our ice cream, Gisela and her cousin talked to Eva, and I got involved, asking Felix all kinds of questions about the Hitler Youth since I was ready pretty soon to join the Jungvolk.

Membership in the Hitler Youth was mandatory for any boy who was planning to attend any of the Adolf Hitler schools. Baldur von Schirach, the leader of the Hitler Youth, tried to draw all schoolboys ages nine to ten years old into the Jungvolk. To create an elite youth, he ordered every school to report the boy with the best grades at the elementary school to the state education office. The brightest boys would then be sent into one of the elite national schools. The director of our school followed his obligation and encouraged me to keep up my grades in order to be nominated for the Nazi institution. I told Felix about my ambition and asked him what was his opinion.

He said, "It must be a great opportunity to get a higher education all paid by the government including uniforms, board and room." "As far as I am concerned," he replied, "I want to become a pilot, and the Air Force Academy is the ticket for me."

The girls got tired of our conversation, and Eva suggested that we go for a walk by the lake. Everyone agreed, and we left the ice cream parlor, heading for the lake. A walk would do us good. On a beautiful day, most people were enjoying the great outdoors. The Nickel Bridge over the Havel was now in sight as Gisela's little cousin was beginning to tease me.

"If you really care for Gisela, why don't you jump from the bridge and show her?"

"Can't you think of something more challenging?" I countered.

"Sounds like you want to back out," said Eva.

"Not at all. If that is all you ask of me, I will get ready for the jump as soon as we reach the bridge."

Gisela objected, not wanting to have any of that nonsense, but I assured her there was nothing to worry about. On top of the bridge, some pedestrian stopped and watched me get undressed. Now I was in my trunks, climbing up the railing, taking a deep breath, and jumping headfirst into the water. So far everything was routine, but after I entered the water, I couldn't remember what happened to me; something hit my head, and the light went out in my brain. Up on the deck, they were waiting for me to come up for air. Felix realized that I was in danger; he wasted no time and jumped in the water where I'd cut the surface. He explained to me later where he found me unconscious and how he got me out of the water. The next thing that came back to me when I woke up was that I was lying in the grass, and Gisela was holding me in her arms and kissing my face. I was exhausted and in severe pain, but soon an ambulance came and took me to the emergency hospital. A deep cut in my forehead and a broken ossa frontalis below were the unfortunate results when my head collided with a big rock under the bridge. Looking at the bright lights on the ceiling of the emergency room, all kinds of thoughts went through my mind as they cleared and stitched up my head. I had to think of the gang at Kieler Strasse and how Atze and Egon would call me an idiot for not checking out the water before jumping. Well, it was all academic now, and I had to pay the piper for being stupid.

Gisela and I celebrating her birthday

One good thing came out from all of this. I was now Gisela's hero, and I knew now that she cared for me. The fact that Felix saved my life made me grateful and dedicated to him, and we became lifelong friends. My parents, however, were not too thrilled for what I did, and my father punished me by taking privileges away from me for a month. Altogether the incident made me a little tougher, providing me with the extra capacity for endurance required to become a member of the Hitler Youth. In the month of July 1938, one week before my ninth birthday, I was inducted into the Jungvolk.

Just as I joined the Hitler Youth, my father very reluctantly became a member of the Nazi Party also in 1938. He was one of many Germans working for the government who were becoming members of the Nazi Party. They seemed regretful of their membership and seldom wore the round badge with the swastika in public. They kept it mostly in the drawer, but they were compelled by the Nazi State Authorities to join the party to keep their jobs. They regarded, rightly or wrongly, their dual membership in the church and the Nazi Party as necessary in order to keep making a living. I recalled that I had no feelings of opposition but rather an honest desire to become a member of the Hitler Youth. We were taught by our leaders that it was an honor to serve our country and become mentally and physically prepared to carry out the orders and duties given to us by our Führer Adolf Hitler. This was what was expected of us, and this was the alliance we had to pledge under oath. Following the induction ceremony, each of us new members were given the Hitler Youth badge to wear on our uniform. Part of the uniform were black pants, a brown shirt, and a dagger with the Hitler Youth emblem. In the blade of each dagger, the slogan Blood and Honor was engraved.

After Hitler annexed Austria, his next victim was Czechoslovakia. He demanded under the threat of war the "return" to Germany of three and a half million Sudeten Germans and the Sudetenland they lived in under the Czechs. The plan was to make it a part of Greater Germany. Chamberlain, the prime minister of Great Britain, wanted to preserve the peace of Europe and gave in to Hitler's demand. On the first day of October 1938, the German army marched into the Sudetenland. Surprisingly, Britain and France did not go to war when Hitler pulled the same stunt again, demanding in his meeting with Chamberlain in München the rest of Czechoslovakia. This democratic republic, which had won its independence from Austria-Hungary Monarchy after it collapsed in 1918, ceased to exist on March 15, 1939, when Germany occupied the rest of the country. For the time being, the threat of war seemed defused. Of course, it was impossible to be absolutely sure about a long-lasting peace. The fact that the two dictators, Hitler and Stalin, negotiated a nonaggression pact between the Soviet Union and Nazi Germany, signed in Moscow on the night of August 23, 1939, left little doubt that Hitler was still out to conquer more territory.

In many ways, the summer of 1939 was a beautiful summer, a time of carefree living. I was enjoying myself tremendously but did not know that there would never be any more summers like it. As a matter of fact, it was the end of my childhood and the beginning of the oncoming war. Marvelously, there were still ahead for me a few happy summer days, a vacation of complete independence. School was over, the apartment was locked up, my parents were on vacation in Bavaria, and they left me for two months with an elderly couple in Heiligensee, a nice little village next to Tegel. These folks were very good friends of my parents and asked if I could stay with them since they were alone and had no children. They were living in a big two-story house with a large backyard filled with all kinds of fruit trees. For the first time in my life, I was sleeping in my own bedroom upstairs overlooking the nearby lake. In the morning, I would get up early, have some hot porridge and a glass of milk, and off I'd go on my bicycle to take care of my paper route. Usually I was back by 10:00 AM.

Mr. and Mrs. Hugo Schultz were retired for some time. They owned at one time a shoe factory with many employees but lost it all during the inflation. Luckily they salvaged enough money to build for their golden years a house in Heiligensee. Hugo was not the kind of man to retire early, so he kept repairing shoes in his new house in a little shop facing the street. He had no employees but had all the business he could handle. Every day when I came back from my paper route I went, after lunch, down to the shop trying to help him. Since I was getting free board and room, I felt like I had to do something to earn my bread and butter. When I asked him to put me to work, he gave me an old pair of shoes and some instructions showing me how to cut the leather and how to swing the hammer. It did not turn out too good, so he gave me an easier job. I was shining shoes now, and I polished them afterward with the electric buffer. That was an easy job and did not take very long with plenty of time to spare. Hugo looked at my bike and said, "I know what you can do. Your newspaper box at the back of the bike has plenty of room for what I have in mind for you to do."

He loaded four pairs of shoes in the back of my bike and prepared a list of names, addresses, and the amount of money to be collected. He asked me if I could do my new job, and I told him that there was no difference between selling newspaper and shoes. I did it every day—delivered the goods and collected the money. My first deliveries were close to the house and easy to find. I found three of the customers at home, delivered the shoes, and collected the money; but one was not at the house, so I returned to the shop with one pair of shoes. This job went on for some time. I enjoyed the outside and being on my bike, and I got to know Heiligensee. Hugo and Paula Schultz were very nice to me. Hugo was my mentor and treated me like a grandson; I saw him as the grandfather I never had. When the time came to say good-bye and I had to return home, Hugo gave me an almost new pair of army boots, unclaimed by a soldier who got his military orders in a hurry. Paula also surprised me with a fresh-baked *Pflaumenkuchen*, plum cake to take home. During the years to come, I visited the old folks many times. They were nice to me, and I helped them out whenever I could.

Bad times were ahead for all of us, and more than ever, we did need each other. It all started on August the 8, 1939, the day when food ration cards were given out to all Germans. No longer was anybody able to buy unrestricted any kind and quantity of food by choice. Nobody could go to a store or restaurant and purchase food items or eat a meal unless you presented a ration card with your name on it. Only if the proprietor clipped out the necessary coupons could you eat a meal or buy some of the food that was available.

All food items—bread, potatoes, sugar, milk, meat, or fat—were measured in increments of one-hundred-, two-hundred-, or five-hundred-gram coupons. All these coupons had to be pasted daily on a sheet of paper and were checked against the inventory by a Nazi officer at the end of the month. Besides food, all other kinds of supplies came under restriction, such as soap, gasoline, and heating material. On November 15, 1939, the people of Berlin received the Reichskleiderkarten, another strict form of rationing for linen, clothing, and all kinds of garments.

All organizations of the NSDAP—from the German Jungvolk, the Hitler Youth, the German Labor Front, to the last German housewife—were instructed to participate in the largest recycling program the world had ever seen. Suddenly there was no more waste. Practically everything from potato peels and table scraps, from animal bones and dirty rags, and from old newspaper to a complete metal fence were either used to feed livestock, to make soap, print books, turn into new clothing, or, what was most important to the Nazis, to turn old iron into new weapons and ammunition.

Every schoolyard in Germany was converted into a collection center for some of those stinking items. Each kid received a small folded index card with the names of all items to be collected, and every item delivered went on a scale and then was separated and dumped on top of a specific pile. Several boys from an upper grade were in charge of receiving, sorting, and making the right entry in the credit card of each student. In the hallway of the school next to the picture of Adolf Hitler hung a small blackboard bearing the name of the top collector for each month. This started a regular collection mania as everybody wanted to be the top banana. Pretty soon, the academic purpose of the school became secondary as every student was involved to compete for free cinema tickets and had no more time to do homework. Adding to the problem was the fact that the schoolyard was running out of space. The truck company hired for the removal was not always on time. Mountains of newspaper were getting wet in the rain or getting blown away by the wind.

Finally the school district came up with a solution. Paper, the biggest item, must be stored inside in a dry building. In our case, we had to give up one side of the gymnasium. Still the truck driver could not handle big volumes of loose material. As a result, our school received a big press to compact paper and rags into heavy square bundles. The compactor operated manually and required muscle power. So again, routinely, every boy had to stay away from the classroom certain hours and report for duty downstairs to make bundles. First, four pieces of wire must be cut twelve feet long and held in place at the bottom and the inside walls of the press. After the box was filled, a heavy plate was put on top; and by cranking the plate from the top downward, the material in the box would be compacted. Before releasing the four removable sides to take out the compressed bundle, all four wires on top must be twisted and tied together with some heavy pliers.

It took four boys to manufacture one bundle. Two smaller boys could evenly fill the box, and the two other bigger and stronger boys were needed to turn the crossbar and twist the wires to secure the bundle. Then it took all four boys to push the bundle away. It was amazing to see all the different items boys and girls were dragging to school every day. Some of these objects were quite new and valuable; it would be a shame to melt them down and make bullets out of them. One day a boy came with a WW I cavalry saber. He would not tell us where it came from, but the saber was in mint condition. Four boys made one team, and they were always working together every time they were scheduled. From 8:00 to 10:00 AM, one team was in charge to receive the collection, separate the items, and make the proper deposit entries according to weight in each student's credit card. After 10:00 AM, the counter was closed, but the same team remained on the job till noon, making bales of paper, rags, or aluminum cans.

The team I worked with were all boys out of my class—Tony Schneider, Klaus Mueller, and Ralph Pfeiffer. The day we received the saber, all four of us agreed not to throw the saber to the heap of scrap metal; instead, we concealed the weapon under the subfloor of the storage building. For the time being, we did not have to worry about it till we decided what to do with it. Our team stuck together for a long time. On days when it was not too busy, we would sit around and read old magazines including those that featured pornographic pictures. To see those kinds of sexual activities for the first time in your life was a hell of a way for a young boy to lose his innocence. First it shocked you, and then it evoked your natural curiosity. Some strange and rare feelings came over you, beginning to impact your mind with an endless inquisitiveness. For the boys already in puberty, their early flow of hormones and sexual arousal may be triggered through the influence of pornography. Pfeiffer could be described as a cool guy, but he was also a daredevil. He managed to sneak one of those X-rated magazines into the girls' powder room.

Not to discard anything and to recycle whatever possible had become a nationwide obsession. The idea of rationing food in peacetime made lots of people suspicious. Pretty soon their suspicion became an ugly reality. The German people also could not understand why Hitler was so much in a hurry to get a nonaggression pact signed between Germany and the Soviet Union. Stalin was eager to accept the deal in Moscow on the night of August 23, 1939. The dictator Josef Stalin, out of unscrupulousness, negotiated at the same time an alliance with the British and French military delegations in Moscow. He publicly agreed to stay out of any war that Hitler might provoke. Secretly the two dictators agreed to divide up Poland, but Stalin wanted more; he made Hitler agree for Russia's right to annex the Baltic states of Latvia and Estonia. Finland was also on Stalin's list as it belonged to Russia until 1919. This cold-blooded bargain with Stalin enabled Hitler to attack Poland in the morning hours of September 1, 1939. Berlin itself was quiet. The German people, though worked up by Nazi propaganda about the seriousness of the Polish situation, did not expect war.

In societies like Germany, which never had a real democracy, the mystique of the dictator's power was enormous. The people believed in the Führer and trusted Hitler when he promised them peace and prosperity. After the war started in Poland, for days people did not believe it. They could not imagine that he had actually broken a promise and started another war just twenty years after Germany survived the six miserable years of World War I. The Sunday of September 3 was a sunny end of the summer day in Berlin when at precisely 9:00 AM, the governments of Britain and France presented Hitler with a two-hour ultimatum to withdraw his armies from Poland or receive a declaration of war against Germany. Hitler ignored the ultimatum, and in the evening before he departed for the front to command his armies, he dispatched a message to Stalin, inviting the Soviet Union to join in the attack on Poland. After the German armies poured across the Polish frontier, the Luftwaffe quickly penetrated the skies over Poland, and a massive formation of bombers attacked the city of Warsaw. The Polish armies were destroyed in less than fifteen days. On the eighteenth, Soviet and German forces met at Brest Litovsk. The Polish government fled into exile, and the Nazi and Soviet conquerors signed a treaty effecting the partition of Poland.

There was now peace in the east, but the war with the enemy in the west was about to start; that was why the German people were not really in the mood for a victory celebration over the outcome of the Polish conflict. The public was very much divided and had mixed feelings about future events. At school and the meetings of the Hitler Youth, all members of the party were praising the Führer and glorifying the German army. No applause was given to the Nazi government when Hitler signed a new law of euthanasia on October 8, 1939. This new law went out as an order to all mental institutions to discretely dispose of all incurable mental patients. The average person did not notice the new law or showed little concern as long as nobody in his family was in danger of being killed. In school we talked about it, and the teacher put it to us as if death, by putting somebody to sleep with an injection if the patient could never be normal again, was an act of mercy. The German people could not stop the barbaric law, no more than they could stop the escalating war.

Many years after the war, my aunt Lucy told me that she had a brother, the second-born son of my grandmother Martha, by the name Alwin. He was named after my grandfather on my father's side. He was fourteen years old when my grandfather got killed in World War I in 1917 in France.

On March 6, 1919, the Berlin civil war began among the Socialist Party, the Communist Party, and the troops of the government. For over a week, the streets of Berlin turned into a battleground. At the end of the revolution, 1,200 people had lost their lives. The victims were mostly civilians, and one of them was a sixteen-year-old boy, Alwin Vogt. He came from school in the afternoon of March 9 and got trapped in a street battle he could not escape. A blow from a rifle bud hit him in the back of the neck and split his head wide open. Some medical workers pulled him out of the street and drove him to the nearest hospital. His wounds healed, and after several days, he came out of the coma, but his speech was not coherent. My grandmother cried when he did not recognize her. No rehabilitation could help him, and young Alwin was permanently brain-damaged. Because it was not possible to care for him at home, he was placed in a mental institution. Early in 1940, the Vogt family received a letter from the administration of the Mental Hospital Wittenau that Alwin Vogt suffered a cerebral vascular accident and died following a massive stroke. My father and his brother Herbert went to claim his body. He died at the age of thirty-seven, and we would never know if he died a natural death or if a Nazi physician killed him.

Overruling the objections of the majority of his generals, Hitler carried out the daring military occupation of Denmark and Norway on April 9, 1940. Denmark capitulated in two hours, but the Norwegians, helped by the British, held out in their mountainous terrain until June. England landed troops in the town of Narwik but were forced by the German army to evacuate. As the war started to spread over Europe, the early construction of air-raid shelters that commenced in 1939 had now reached its peak. From a simple fragmentation shelter, a high-rise concrete bunker was now in full swing, especially in densely populated cities. Most buildings in Berlin were solid brick and concrete structures with an underground cellar. With a minimum of construction effort and cost, the average cellar could be converted and equipped as an air-raid shelter to protect the tenants. A new organization came into being to educate and supply the public for protection against an attack from the air that was obvious to come. The people had a chance to prepare themselves for the bombing offensive, which, though it had not come when first expected, was nevertheless thought to be inevitable. Air-raid precautions were improved; prefabricated air-raid shelters, homemade fragmentation trenches covered with dirt, and converted basements mushroomed in the gardens and parks of the major cities. Shop windows were taped in a dazzling variety of patterns to prevent them from shattering as a result of bomb blast, and most noticeable of all, the blackout was strictly enforced. In shops, offices, and private homes, the windows had to be covered with black curtains so that not a ray of light showed from the outside. Many people constructed rigid contraptions to bolt on to the window frame, which considerably simplified the nightly ritual of "putting up the blackout." Those who were careless or late risked the humiliating experience of a warden's stentorian voice roaring for the whole street to hear the words that quickly became a catch phrase: "Put that light out." In case there was no reponse, any pedestrian was allowed to throw a stone in the window, or many times a policeman would pull out his pistol and shoot the light out.

Repeat offenders had to pay a fine or, in some cases, were arrested. A uniform system of civil defense was now organized and enforced by the government. Appointed party members were given police power as air-raid warden. They conducted classes for the public to learn all about air raids, firefighting, and equipment for protection. The minister of defense ordered the distribution of one gas mask for every citizen; it was made of thin rubber and a cheap aluminum filter filled with charcoal powder. It was now mandatory that nobody could appear in public without carrying the gas mask hanging in a bag over the shoulder. In several major parts in Berlin, huge concrete bunkers were built that could easily provide shelter for hundreds of people. Anybody living close by or happened to be in the area could take advantage of it. Traveling and getting stopped in an air raid presented more of a problem. The train would stop immediately next to the nearest air-raid trench, long and wide, extending far below the surface, covered with heavy timber with about one meter of sand over it. To protect you from flying fragmentation, these were excellent shelters. Unfortunately bomber pilots made railroads a selected target. A direct hit with a five-hundred-pound bomb would turn the deep trench immediately into a mass grave. Still, the best protection for most of the city dwellers was the basement of their house, provided that the walls and ceilings were reinforced to carry the load if the house should cave in. The conversion was relatively inexpensive and did save many lives during the war. The only problem was to get enough labor to complete the project in a minimum of time. Most of the manpower was already serving in the armed forces, the rest of men and women were conscripted to the war effort. There was only one option open—put Polish prisoners of war and volunteers of the Hitler Youth to work. Obviously, the heavy work was done by prisoners and the rest by the Hitler Youth. The whole project was organized and supervised by the Organisation Todt, a paramilitary construction unit.

One day in May 1940, our principal Boese called a meeting to order in the auditorium in our school. Present at the time were all the teachers, our *Stammführer* from the Hitler Youth, and the guest speaker, who was an officer from the Organisation Todt. The emphasis of his lecture was the opportunity of the Berliner Hitler Youth to serve the fatherland. I had never seen so much excitement and enthusiasm among my classmates in any other meeting before. I don't think there was anyone that evening not willing to sign up. From now on, all our weekly HJ meetings were only geared to prepare us for our duties; divided in several groups, we received instructions as to what we had to do, who our group leaders were, and when and where our first job would start.

Except for some single houses on the outside of Berlin, the city was a multitude of four-story or more of commercial or apartment house complexes. Each building had a basement with a strong supported ceiling and concrete foundation, but it was not designed to protect the basement for a total collapse of the structure. To make these buildings air-raid safe, it was necessary to install under the basement ceiling additional heavy beams supported with strong vertical studs. All doors had to be replaced with steel frames and heavy steel doors with strong rubber gaskets to make them gas proof. In a similar fashion, the basement windows were to be replaced, and in addition, a block wall had to be erected in front of them. The wall adjacent to the next basement had to be broken with an opening big enough to escape. The hole was then plastered over and the edges marked with a big white circle. A sledgehammer was placed on the wall next to the hole. Sometimes tenants of several houses had to share one air-raid shelter, but by the end of 1940, the project was almost completed, and every family was assigned a place. One of the delays of construction was not only the primary clearing of all basements but also the clearing of attics or under the roof storage areas, which were boarded up in small cubicles belonging to each tenant, loaded up to the ceiling with all kinds of extra furniture, boxes, and useless gear.

Before the Hitler Youth was integrated in the regular participation of air-raid protection, it was our job to clean out buildings in an area each group was assigned to. Many times tenants refused to cooperate, and our group leader had to call the air-raid warden in charge. Anything of value the tenant could take to his apartment or place in a public storage facility. The rest we sorted out for recycling or took to the dump. After the work was done in one building, we put up sandboxes and plenty of pails of water in the attic to put out a fire if needed. After a basement was converted and inspected, we had to go back in to place signs of instruction and paint lines on walls and floors with phosphor paint to indicate escape routes from one building to the next. Each shelter was also equipped with shovels, axes, flashlights, first-aid kits, chemical toilets, and plenty of drinking water.

Once again the Nazi conqueror had struck out and drove in a Blitzkrieg across the border of Holland and Belgium deep into France on May 10, 1940. The campaign was over in six weeks. Hitler had decided, unexpected by the enemy, to strike through the hilly, heavily wooded Ardennes Forest in Belgium with his great tank armies. An armored attack was deemed impossible by the French and British in a totally wooded sector of the front. German tanks reached the English Channel at Abbeville in ten days, cutting off British and French forces. At the same spot and in the same railroad car where the Germans signed the Armistice at the end of World War I, in the forest of Compiègne, Hitler made the French surrender to him on June 22, 1940.

The month of June, I spent every sunny day I could at Heiligensee and at the weekend, specifically of June 14, I stayed overnight with my friends the Schultzs. I felt very much at home in their house, and I called Mr. Schultz Opa Hugo. Since I had never seen my natural grandfathers, I was very attracted to him. Being with him in his little repair shop and the smell of leather, rubber, shoe polish, and solvents all became very familiar to me. He had a little radio in a corner shelf, and all of a sudden, the music stopped as a surprise message came over the air. The announcement was a news report that Paris had capitulated to the German troops. The regular program was further interrupted with march music and speeches by party officials. Opa Hugo jumped off his little bench and started to whistle: "Preussens gloria."

I could see how he was pleased with the outcome of the war in the West. He closed the shop for the day, and we went upstairs to tell his wife about the good news, but it did not make too much of an impression on her. Mrs. Schultz was the kind of woman that you might call a pacifist. Opa Hugo was my age during the war of 1870-71 when the Germans defeated the French the first time. He had a big book printed in 1885, which he showed to me, that was full of war pictures, displaying Ulanen and Kürassiere in their colorful uniforms, sitting on tall horses, pointing flags and sabers toward the sky. Paintings of attacking cavalry overrunning the French defenders, battlefields of dead soldiers, and wounded men on the ground with blood-soaked uniforms and missing limbs were the highlights of the book. Bismarck riding in a carriage passing by the suffering troops was greeted in jubilation. The opponent of Bismarck, the French emperor, was sitting on the ground overwhelmed and in disbelief of his defeat. But history repeated itself; after the German Kaiser lost World War I, it was Hitler now turning the table.

After Opa Hugo closed the book, I had the feeling that he was very pleased with today's news; after all, he suffered four miserable years in the trenches of France in World War I for nothing. In a way, he was also happy that the conflict between Germany and France took a short end with a minimum of casualties on both sides. It was a blessing that both Mr. and Mrs. Schultz passed away without knowing that there would be another and final bloodbath before Germany and France would be able to establish a permanent peace between them.

After Compiègne, Hitler, at the moment of his greatest conquest, celebrated victory with his troops in Paris. Visiting the grave of Napoleon inflated Hitler's ego, making him believe that he was the greatest commander in chief of all times. For nearly an hour, Hitler gazed at the tomb of the great French conqueror. Obviously, he now considered himself equal to Napoleon; perhaps he became obsessed to do the same mistakes.

On his return to Berlin, Hitler received the biggest victory parade that ever passed through the Brandenburger Gate in Berlin. All schools and most businesses were closed. Both sides of the main street Unter den Linden was packed with people and secured by the SS, SA, and HJ. The parade seemed to be endless, the bells of the downtown churches kept ringing. Our HJ Stamm Tegel was placed west of the Brandenburg Gate on the north side of the Heeres Strasse. Hitler approached slowly in his open Mercedes, and I could see him standing in his car not more than twenty feet away from me. That was the second and last time I ever saw Hitler in my life. Hitler was the hero of the day; he had conquered most of Europe. Only Britain held out against him, but with her armies driven from the mainland and her island virtually defenseless, she could easily be conquered.

The Beginning of German and British Air Raids

Hitler hesitated to occupy England, assuming that the British would give up too. Instead, armed British land forces regrouped to oppose any invasion with the help of new arms brought hurriedly over from America. The Royal Air Force was still pretty much in good shape and proving itself a match for the Luftwaffe in defending the skies over Britain. By now Hitler literally recognized that he missed the boat. In desperation, Hitler tried to force England into capitulation by constant bombing of London, Manchester, Coventry, and other British cities. That was how the Blitz over England started on August 13, 1940. In round-the-clock raids over the next several weeks, two thousand people died in the city of London alone, and more than ten thousand were wounded or entombed in the rubble. Scars spread across the face of the city, bringing in the wake of death a despairing ache to the hearts of all those who loved London's streets, churches, proud buildings, and historic monuments. But if people and ancient edifices were suffering, there was a compensation in it for the British nation. England became united, but even so, Hitler was exhilarated by reports of the damage being done to the British capital; he had become convinced that the more Londoners were killed, the more eager would the rest of the nation be to sue for peace.

He assured his generals that the Luftwaffe was now so clearly the master of the skies over Britain that it would not be necessary to prepare for an invasion; he would be able to pound Britain into surrender without a single German soldier having to fight his way up the British beaches. Göring had told Hitler to expect a turning point soon as a result of the onslaught. The turning point had certainly been reached, but not in the direction the Germans had anticipated. Back in school one morning, the teacher told me that Principal Boese wanted to see me in his office. I kept thinking if there was anything I did wrong. To my surprise, it was good news.

"Get ready, my boy, you are going for three days to Brandenburg to take the entrance examination for the LBA," he announced proudly with a smile on his face.

I could not hide my excitement, and after I calmed down, he started to explain things to me. First he gave me the date when I had to report in Brandenburg and the schedule of events for the three days. On the first day, there would be an orientation, followed by an individual interview. The second day was reserved for an extensive written examination, and the last day, perhaps the most important day, would be filled with sports activities, endurance, and competition. Since I was the only student from our school appointed for selection, he was very interested for me to succeed.

So he was eager to give me all kinds of advice. "Don't worry too much about the written examination; the most important thing is to show your loyalty to Adolf Hitler." With those words, he tried to impress me. "Furthermore, they will ask you where the Führer lives." Looking at me, he expected an answer.

I told him, "The Führer lives either in Berlin, Münich, or at the Obersalzberg."

Boese slowly shook his head and said, "Remember, Adolf Hitler lives in the hearts of all Germans." Before he let me go, he made one more remark: "On the third day, give it all you got; only tough boys will be accepted for the Hitler schools."

My parents were not as excited as I was, but they were accepting. My mother helped me pack a few things and cleaned my uniform. I shined my boots and my belt the night before the day I took the train early in the morning. A few marks in my pocket, a sandwich in my knapsack, and Brandenburg here I come. At about 2:00 PM on August the 19, I arrived at the train station in Brandenburg. As soon as the train stopped, I saw several guys my age in uniform getting off the train. They were all coming from Berlin, but I knew none of them. We were standing around talking to each other as a bus was pulling around the corner and stopping in front of us. The door opened, and out came a brown uniform, an HJ Scharführer from the LBA. He was blowing a whistle, trying to get our attention. We were now ordered to fall into formation, and he was taking a head count. Calling our names while he was checking his list, he seemed to be satisfied that everybody was present. Next thing, we were on the bus, and the driver was taking off for LBA-Brandenburg. The school was an old gymnasium for boys outside of town near the river Havel. Brandenburg itself claims to be the oldest city in the Mark Brandenburg, the birthplace of Prussia.

Once we were past the gate and off the bus, a comfortable dormitory and modern facilities awaited us. Each boy was assigned a bed and a locker for his belongings. At the dining room, we were given a brief routine for the next three days, and one hot meal was served. The first day started early in the morning. Out of bed and only dressed in a sweat suit, everyone rushed down the stairs to get to the yard. It was time for the mandatory morning exercise, the five-kilometer road running back and forth along the riverside. On the way back, I really had to press forward to keep up with the gang, but I just moved in time through the gate. I noticed that some boys did not make it, and they were washed out from the program. After shower and breakfast, we stayed in the dining room for the orientation meeting. The director of the school gave a short speech, wished us good luck, and turned the meeting over to the teachers. The rest of the day was taken up with physical examinations and individual interviews. The second day, we all had to take a written examination after the ritual running marathon and breakfast. In the afternoon, we were called in individually to face a panel of teachers for an oral examination. The last day was rather a fun day; there were all kinds of sports activities—swimming, jumping, sprinting, etc. The highlight of the third day was a boxing contest. We had to match up in pairs and fight each other like gladiators. I knew this was my last chance to make up if I should have failed in some subjects the first two days. As soon as I heard the bell, I jumped at my opponent and hit him as hard and as long as I could. He recovered and started to swing at me. I took cover, and the moment he slowed down, I opened another barrage. This time I must have landed a good one right in his face. He was bleeding from his nose, and the referee called the fight. After we removed our gloves and had shaken hands with each other, I told him I was sorry that I hurt him. He was a good sport and told me, smiling, "The next time I will beat the living daylight out of you." Unfortunately, I never saw him again. The three days went by really fast, and before I knew it, I was back at the platform of the Brandenburg railroad station, waiting for the train to take me home.

Something the people in Berlin never deemed to be possible was the first air attack on Berlin by the RAF on August 25 and 26. Not that it did much damage to the city, but the public was now waking up to the reality that the British were able to inflict the same suffering to innocent civilians as we were doing to them in London. It was still time for Hitler to come to his senses and stop this kind of brutal warfare. Instead he told the German people that from then on, the German Luftwaffe would drop three times as many bombs over London. This irresponsible escalation by Hitler resulted in the total destruction of all German cities at the end of WW II. This statement is not the opinion of the author; it must be seen for what it is—a historical fact. As a child, I had no mind of my own; only in later years did I develop a conflict of interest. Since I am no longer influenced by political teachings or any religious dogma, I am now trying to find the truth on my own. To me this is a luxury. I was not allowed to think for myself, only to repeat what I was told. Finally, after an idea is put into your head long enough, you not only believe it, you become so fanatic that you are willing to defend these ideas with your life. This is exactly what the Hitler Youth was all about. I embraced the Nazi philosophy with all my heart; I trusted in it without any reservation. Obviously, it reflected at the selection process in Brandenburg because I was notified two weeks later that I was accepted to enter the LBA-Neisse beginning October 1, 1940.

The second air attack on Berlin took place on September 23. This time the RAF came with eighty-four airplanes and bombed primarily Tempelhof, a suburban residential neighborhood. This was actually the first major air raid in Berlin, causing some substantial damage and the first human casualties. As soon as my parents listened to the broadcast on the radio, they were very much concerned about the safety of my grandmother on my mother's side who lived in Tempelhof. She had remarried, and she and her husband had purchased a condominium. He was also a WW I veteran but was never married before. In the old days, nobody had a telephone except business people or public offices. My mother was very anxious and urged my father that we take the train to go and see them immediately. What a relief it was to see them both unhurt and that their house was not damaged. We stayed overnight, and the sudden trip out of fear for their lives turned out to be a pleasant visit.

The next day on the way home, we could see some of the houses that were destroyed. People tried to salvage some of their belongings from the rubble, and uniformed men were helping civilians carry furniture they were saving from the fire. The impact of this incident made both the public as well as the government realized what they were in for and that drastic measurements were needed to protect the people, as much as could be done, against the impending threat from the air. A quick decision was made on September 27 to get all children under the age of fourteen out of the city of Berlin. Camps were organized without delay in all parts of Germany and also in the newly occupied countries of Poland and Slovakia. All the while, schoolchildren were evacuated in classes to take up a whole camp supervised by a Nazi teacher or a party leader. Women with small children were also sent to stay with families in safer areas, mostly the rural parts of West Germany. For the civilians who stayed behind and could not leave their jobs, the issue of civil defense became suddenly very acute. For me it was also time to get ready to leave Berlin behind and report for the departure to the LBA-Neisse (now Poland). The next three days, I spent my time saying good-bye to friends and relatives. The last day, I visited Gisela; no telling when I would see her again. She cried as I kissed her farewell and made me promise to write to her.

CHAPTER III

INDOCTRINATION AND HIGHER EDUCATION

Moving Away from My Parents

The last good-bye was with my parents, and they were depressed to see me go. My mother suffered very much knowing that she would not see me for some time. I told her that I would be back in less than three months for Christmas vacation; that gave her something to look forward to, and she managed to suppress her tears and produce a smile when she kissed me as I boarded the train. I stood at the window waving good-bye till they were out of sight and the train left the station. Now I was sitting down on the bench, looking aimlessly out of the window trying to sort out the thoughts going wildly through my mind. I was beginning to realize that this was the first time in my life that I was on my own and perhaps would never share the home of my parents again. Even at my eleven years of age, somehow I had the feeling that nothing would ever be the same again. Indeed, I was now entering a new chapter in my life as the war was tearing thousands of families apart.

My deep thoughts were suddenly interrupted by the sound of music coming from an accordion player next door. I could stand some more cheerful mood to come up to my normal gaiety, so I went over to see what was going on in the next compartment. When I entered, I saw four boys of the Hitler Youth singing to the tune of the melody by the accordion player. They were looking at me, and my being in uniform made them invite me to join them. Immediately it was clear that we all had the same destination, Neisse—the pedagogical academy of the government. We all got acquainted, and it made me feel good that I was no longer alone. As we were talking and singing, a *Gefolgschaftsführer* came to see us, and we all jumped up and greeted him with the proper salutation. He introduced himself as the leader of the group going to the LBA-Neisse. According to him, we would be in Görlitz (now the Polish border) at about 1:00 PM, and everybody must get off the train. At that time we would pick up some more students who were arriving from Frankfurt an der Oder to have lunch all together at the Bahnhofswirtschaft, the restaurant at the train station. When we arrived in Görlitz, there was a large back room reserved for us at the Wirtshaus. This time a *Stammführer* was calling our attention and calling our names as we settled down. He was satisfied that nobody on his list was missing. Now we were stepping up in single file to the hall room where everybody received a plate of potato salad with a pair of wienies, bread and butter, and a tall glass of milk. At 2:00 PM our train arrived; it would take us all the way to Neisse. It was the longest train ride I ever experienced, the countryside was almost level but beautiful. I don't remember what time it was when we got off the train in Neisse, but it was already getting dark. A huge bus came shortly after we got off the train and took us to our final destination. It had been a long day as we arrived at the cafeteria of the school.

Sandwiches and herbal tea were available, but most of us were rather more tired than hungry. Finally we picked up our gear and walked up the stairs to the top floor to bunk down the first night at our dormitory. Next morning I felt kind of strange in unfamiliar surroundings; the routine was more or less the same as it was in my three days in Brandenburg except that the territory of the school grounds and its buildings was much larger and more complex. To explore the whole institution would take more than a month. Every day I was discovering something new, and at the same time I was learning about the past of the original founders and the people that had lived here, served, worked, prayed, and died in these walls and were buried in their own cemetery. To give a fair picture of these magnificent compounds, I will bring up their purpose and history as much as I know.

Neisse is a small town in Upper Silesia, the city is located on the east bank of the river Neisse. Outside of Neisse is a large institution called Holy Cross. It was founded by the Roman Catholic Church and belonged to the religious order of the Society of Jesus, or better known as the Jesuits. Jesuits take vows of poverty, chastity, and obedience. They work for the glory of God, defend the Roman Catholic faith against heresy, engage in missionary work, and educate the young. Members of the society are either priests with full vows or lay brothers who perform the minor duties of the institutions. Those preparing to become priests are known as scholastic students, and those undergoing probation to enter the order are called novices. Supreme authority rests with the father general in Rome. The Jesuits have been generally regarded as the leading and most scholarly of Catholic educators. They have established many schools and colleges wherever they have gone. They have developed original and highly successful methods of teaching the classics. Their scientific courses have achieved high standards of quality. In the fields of education, the society had at one time controlled 728 colleges with about three hundred thousand students. The Jesuits have often been seriously attacked for their activities. Yet in spite of this, they have contributed effectively in the work of education, especially in the state of Prussia. According to the report from Rome, before the war, there were over thirty-six thousand Jesuits teaching in colleges or on foreign missions throughout the world. Unfortunately, some institutions became victims of political intrigue and were closed or confiscated.

Holy Cross in Neisse was one of them. In the process of selecting institutions for the purpose of turning them into Adolf Hitler schools, the Nazi government was very selective. Only the finest and most suitable places came under consideration. It had to be a large estate, a castle, or a huge secluded institution. Holy Cross in Neisse met the above criteria. It resembled a small self-contained village on about two hundred acres completely enclosed by an eight-foot brick wall. All the buildings inside had the same gothic architecture. On the other side of the main gate, the church owned another two hundred acres of farmland where crops were produced for their own consumption. Past the entrance were several administration offices, followed across a courtyard by a huge building laid out like a horseshoe. At the end of the five-story main building were two rotunda-type towers.

West side of LBA Neisse with vegetable garden in front.

Adjacent to it, separated by a garden and a swimming pool, were all the workshops, farmhouses, and the bakery. Reaching the center of the property was a tall cathedral rich in gothic ornaments. It was the biggest church in Neisse and open to the public to worship. Next to the church was a small cemetery where all the brothers and priests that had worked, lived, and died in the monastery were buried. On the west side of the property was a huge park with a man-made creek turning into a small bay. The cove at one point was crossed by a wooden bridge leading to a shady miniforest. Coming here, one was suddenly surrounded by an environment of peace and tranquility, an ideal spot for meditation and prayers. The minister of education recognized that Holy Cross was the leading center of the Jesuits in East Germany and Poland. In order not to interrupt their operation, the government was able to reach a compromise with the church. Since the institution was such a large estate, the property was divided into two parts. The east side with the main buildings was turned over to the government, and the west side with the cathedral was retained by the church. The large park was declared an open sanctuary for both the Jesuits and the students of the LBA to enjoy. The farmland of the order came under the jurisdiction of the department of agriculture. The students of the LBA had frequent contact with the brothers in their territory and were treated with courtesy, but I had never seen a Jesuit on the side of the property they had relinquished to the school of the NS Party.

The church had a small courtyard with access to the street for the public to come in or visit the priests in their office building. One of the brothers' job was to run a small post office for the convenience of the neighborhood, which included all the students who came over to buy stamps or deliver the outgoing mail. Such activity or going to the park was only possible during the few hours we had outside our daily schedule, which started early in the morning. Classes began after breakfast, with an hour off for lunch, then back to school till 4:00 PM. Dinner was served at 5:00 PM. After the evening meal, we were expected to do our homework but were more or less on our own. The curriculum was pretty much like any other college except that our school emphasized very much on sports activities. Also on the schedule were piano lessons or any instrument of choice to enable us to join the school marching band. What I enjoyed the most were the classes in English and history. Our teacher in English had lived many years in England between WW I and WW II. Our teacher in history was a party leader and also a retired navy captain. Most of the teachers had come out of retirement and had many years of teaching experience. They lived in the town of Neisse, and we didn't have any contact with them after class.

As a young cadet in LBA Neisse

Since the LBA-Neisse was a semi-military school, around-the-clock supervision was conducted by leaders of the party and the Hitler Youth. The student body was divided into two groups, juniors and seniors. The first three years, everybody was a junior; and the last two years, students advanced to the rank of seniors. At the same time, they also became leaders of the Hitler Youth and were in charge of commanding junior students. Teachers were selected by the minister of education and were only teaching one subject. Normally they didn't get involved in politics and did not participate in other activities of the institution. Classrooms and dormitories for juniors were located at the west side of the compound, and seniors had their quarters on the east side near the front gate. Next to the front gate was a booth, which was occupied twenty-four hours by a sentry of four Hitler Youth guards checking and watching every person going through the gate. One senior student was in charge, and three junior students were under his command. They were on guard duty for twelve hours and then were replaced by another team. Every visitor had to sign in and out at the gate. Students were given periodically a pass to go to town or on a limited leave of absence under certain circumstances. The gate closed at 10:00 PM, and any student with a day pass not checking in on time would be retained and reported to the director of the school. With no prior convictions, the student would find himself for the next two weeks peeling potatoes in the kitchen or cleaning latrines. But not all assignments were given out as a punishment, many duties were taken voluntarily or for the good of the community.

East tower of Academy with adjacent dormitory

Early in December a shipment of coal was delivered and dumped in the main yard, and it needed to be deposited in the coal bunker in the basement. A group of thirty students was fitted out with shovels and wheelbarrows to take and throw the coal down the opening in the ground to the storage chamber. Once a year, students were also employed at harvest time to bring in the crop from the farmland of the monastery. Jobs of more permanent nature were also given to students with a special interest. To mention a few, there were places like the library, the first aid station, and the wardrobe and uniform supply station also known in German as *Kleiderkammer*. Only a few hours of weekly participation was expected from each of the many volunteers in order not to interfere with their studies.

I had a special interest in medicine and applied to be taken for duty in the first aid station. There was an opening, and I was able to spend several hours a week as volunteer. The first aid station was permanently open and occupied by a crew of three. The attendant in charge was a last-year senior certified by the Red Cross, next to him were two juniors for assistance. Since I arrived in Neisse I had written my parents several times and explained to them about my daily life in my new home and school. My parents had always answered my letters and were telling me what was going on in Berlin. The news I received in their last letter was rather disturbing and worried me very much. The Royal Air Force had developed a nasty habit of bombing Berlin about every third night. No major damage had yet been reported, and Tegel so far was not on the list of their targets. Talking to my other classmates from Berlin, I got the same information about the ongoing air raids over there. Luckily, nobody in their families reported any casualties or damage to their homes. Also in other parts of Germany, especially in West Germany, there seemed to be an increase of air raids by British flyers.

Somehow I was beginning to grasp the seriousness of the war that had come over us. I felt that my country needed me, and I should prepare myself for whatever I could do to help win the war. If I was old enough, I would volunteer to join the air force, but as it was for now, I could only be a good student and get ready for when my time came. In less than a week, school would be closed, and everybody was going home for Christmas vacation. For the occasion, we had received a brand-new set of uniform. Needless to say that we were very proud to wear the special suit made only for members of the Adolf Hitler schools.

Finally, all dressed up on the morning of December 15, the school bus took us to the train station. Most of us were from Berlin, and it was the same group that entered the train once more. We were all happy to go home again to see our families. Three weeks' vacation was a long time and something wonderful to look forward to. In Görlitz, everybody got off the train. Some students caught another train to Dresden or Frankfurt an der Oder, but most of us continued our journey to Berlin. In two hours we reached the capital of Germany, and after a short good-bye, we were taking the U-Bahn in different directions to get home in a hurry. Reaching Tegel and coming home to my parents was a very happy event.

Class of Berlin Students at LBA Neisse.
The author is sitting second from right

My mother told me how glad she was to see me and how handsome I looked in my new gray uniform. There was a lot we had to talk about while I enjoyed my mother's homemade meal. The next day I slept in and got to visit Tegel. Walking toward the lake, suddenly I found myself in front of my old schoolhouse. Naturally I could not resist to go in to see my former classmates. First I stopped at the office, and there he was—my mentor, Rector Boese. He greeted me with a warm handshake and wanted to know how I was doing and how I liked my new life at the institution in Neisse. I told him everything, and he was very pleased about my satisfaction.

"Come on," he said, "let's go upstairs and see your old class." He opened the door, and as we entered the room, all the guys and girls went crazy to see me. I never had to answer so many questions, and they would not let me go. Anyway, Boese went back to his office, and I stayed with the class till school was over. Now it was my time to ask some questions. I looked around, and the person I wanted to see the most I could not find. Who else was on my mind but Gisela. When I moved my head over to the side of the class where the girls were seated, searching for her, one of my friends grabbed me by the arm and interrupted me.

Before I could inquire any information, he whispered in my ear, "Your sweetheart is no longer here, she transferred to another school."

It kind of surprised me because in her letter I received in Neisse, she did not mention anything about it. After school, one of the girls she was very close to gave me her new address. I made it a point in the few precious days ahead of me to go and visit her. Time went by fast, and I was trying to make the most of it. One day I went to the basement, and there I found my old ice skates. Lake Tegel was frozen, and I spent a whole day skating across the lake. It had already been snowing for the last two days, and from the way it looked, we would have a real white Christmas. Everybody was running around making last-minute shopping for the biggest feast of the year. Going to the stores with my mother, I noticed that there was now less merchandise for sale as in previous years. It was obvious that the war had priority over peacetime production. There was a shortage in groceries. No food items could be purchased without food stamps. Most of the Berliners were willing to take those restrictions in order to help the war effort, but the increasing air raids over Berlin were something else. Not only was the population terrified to get out of bed in the middle of the night to rush to an air-raid shelter, there was also the constant fear of being helplessly exposed to the risk of losing your life.

I experienced such a shocking event the first night in Berlin on December 16, 1940. At about 4:00 AM, I was torn out of my sleep by a nerve-shattering sound of a siren loud enough to bust your eardrums. My first reaction was to put the pillow over my head to stop the noise. In a few minutes, it was all over, and my father appeared at my bedside and urged me to get dressed immediately as we all had to go to the basement. My parents were very calm and had already two suitcases packed with the most important things we needed to survive in case they lost everything. I also helped them carry down some food and drinking water as in some cases, a shelter was buried under the house that came down and nobody was able to get out for days. Luckily, nothing happened in Tegel, and at 6:00 AM, the siren sounded again, this time with a less-alarming noise, meaning that the air raid was over. We all got out of the shelter and went upstairs to go back to bed. Some of the folks were not so fortunate and had to get ready to go to work.

As we were having breakfast that morning, my father turned on the radio to find out which part of town got bombed. No report of casualties was given, only that the RAF came with forty-five airplanes and attacked Spandau, Charlottenburg, Neukölln, and Wilmersdorf. None of these targets were near any industrial places. In the three weeks of vacation I was spending in Berlin, I got ambushed in three air raids, and all of them happened in the week before Christmas. On December 20, the RAF attacked with twenty-three Lancasters at nights from 10:00 to 1:00 AM in Reinickendorf, very close to Tegel. The following day there were two air raids, one from 5:00 to 7:00 AM and another from 7:00 to 7:30 PM. Their targets were the town centers—the Alexander Platz, Potsdam, Lustgarten, and Wedding. On the list of destruction were the museum at the Spreeinsel, the Zeughaus, and the Charité, Berlin's biggest hospital. According to a government statement, from the end of August to the end of November 1940, five hundred people were killed in an air raid and approximately 1,600 dwellings were totally destroyed. The last air raid in 1940 was on December 21. The British started to attack Berlin again on March 13, 1941. After the last air raid, my mother went to see my grandmother and her husband to find out if nothing happened to them. They were fine and invited us to spend the holidays with them. We had taken some food and drinks and stayed with them until early on Christmas Day.

It took about ninety minutes to get to Tempelhof by streetcar. As we were passing the center of town, we were shocked to see all the bombed-out houses, a senseless destruction of what was once a beautiful neighborhood. My grandparents were happy to see us and introduced us to some of my grandfather's relatives whom we had not met before. Everybody contributed something to make it appear like a peacetime Christmas dinner table. There were also some gifts for everybody under the Christmas tree. My grandfather from my grandmother's second marriage was a merry old soul, he survived WW I and liked the good life. He and his brother were self-employed, and they were running an independent repair shop for window shutters. My

Father's side

In Lindenhof

Mother and parents

Mother's side

My real grandfather Wilhelm Schmidt and my mother's father.

My grandfather top row second from left
in the Kaiser's army before WWI

Alwin Vogt sitting in the middle recovering in a hospital during WWI

My grandfather Alwin Vogt 1914

grandfather was also a hobby winemaker and always had a bottle or two open to the delight of his guests. His motto was, "Enjoy life while you can." Under Kaiser Wilhelm II, he spent four years in the trenches of France, was wounded twice, and had to start his life all over again after he came home defeated at the end of WW I.

As I mentioned before, both of my natural grandfathers got killed during the war. Taking that place made him the only person that I could call Opa, other than my honorary opa Hugo. He had the gift of getting people involved in lively conversation, and this Christmas was no different. The celebration went on past midnight, causing us to miss the last streetcar or U-Bahn to go home. My grandmother told us not to worry about it, that there was some room for us to stay overnight. We all slept well, and my mother got up early to help clean up the house and prepare breakfast. My father went to the bakery, purchased some danish, and got the newspaper. The headline this morning said that the air raids by the Luftwaffe, in progress since November 14, had almost destroyed the city of Coventry.

My grandfather just glanced at the headline and exclaimed in anger, "I don't like it. This is going to kill us all; the escalation of bombing your enemy's cities is nothing but a brutal competition to murder innocent civilians."

My father agreed and said, "At the end, there will be no winners, only losers."

"I wish there would be something more encouraging in the newspaper this morning," my grandmother replied.

"Here it is, on page 2," my mother announced. "As a bonus for the Christmas season, each Berliner would receive an extra ration of food, a bottle of liquor, and tobacco."

"These are my kind of news," my grandfather said, and everybody agreed by laughing wholeheartedly.

On our way home later that morning, we walked through my grandparents' little victory garden, and my grandmother proudly showed us her chicken coop. She gave us a dozen of fresh eggs to take home, and we accepted them gratefully.

Time went by fast, and in a few days we would ring in the New Year. In our neighborhood was a little forest, and the highest elevation was called the Steinberg with a small lake. Next to it was a colony of weekend houses, all fenced and nicely taken care of. They had a homeowners association, a restaurant, and a huge clubhouse. On holidays they had picnics, dances, and parties either outside or in the clubhouse. One of the biggest events every year was the New Year's Eve party. Our neighbors next door, Hans and Martha Jakubowski, were good friends of my parents', and they were members of the allotments. Both of them invited us to come along for the

1941 Sylvester Festivity at the Steinberg colony. Actually, the celebration on the thirty-first of December took place in all the streets of Berlin and started as soon as it got dark. Kids of all ages spent their last nickels and dimes on firecrackers. As the night went on, the noise increased; and, of course, at midnight all hell broke loose. So no matter what part of town you were in, or which party you attended, some drunk would kiss you at the stroke of midnight and wish you a happy New Year.

Finally, when it was all over, life went on as before, but we couldn't help wondering what would be in store for us in the new year. All I knew was that my vacation would be over in a few days, and I knew that I couldn't leave town without visiting Gisela. Looking at her new address, I noticed that she moved to Wilmersdorf. Her father got a new job, and the whole family relocated to the southwest section of Berlin. She was surprised to see me when I showed up in front of her house without letting her know in advance. Her mother asked me to stay for lunch, and they were very interested to find out how I was doing in my new school and so far away from home. I told them it was a very regimented lifestyle, no privacy but a solid education promising a successful future. I hoped that I was able to stick with it and eventually graduate from the academy. I asked Gisela how she liked her new school and if she already got acquainted with her new surroundings. She said she missed the gang at Tegel, but she had also made some new friends in Wilmersdorf. Her mother suggested that she take me for a walk through town, and we might catch a movie in the afternoon. I said good-bye to her mother, and we left the house.

Wilmersdorf was an elegant neighborhood and had a lot in common with Tegel. After walking for some time, we were getting cold and decided to go to the local cinema. I had enough money to buy two tickets, two Cokes, and a bucket of popcorn. At the moment, my finances were stocked up as I had received plenty of money for Christmas. Sitting in the heated theater, watching a movie with my girlfriend was a luxury for me that I enjoyed very seldom. The movie we were watching was fantastic, the longest movie I had ever seen—*Gone with the Wind,* written by Margaret Mitchell and played by Clark Gable and Vivian Leigh in a 1939 Hollywood film production. We got out of the cinema theater late. I had just enough time to take Gisela home and catch the U-Bahn back to Tegel. It was a quick good-bye for both of us, and we promised each other to keep writing till we saw each other again.

My mother stayed up waiting for me, warming up some leftover supper for me to eat. The next day was the last day of my vacation, and she begged me to stay home. "I would not have it any other way," I told her, and she was very pleased. I was not overlooking that she had all my shirts and uniforms washed and pressed. This time I had much more to pack, a bigger suitcase was needed to get all my gear together. My parents were not very emotional or passionate, but I knew that they loved me very much; I could tell by the little things, like the way they cared for me. They made the last evening very pleasant for me; then in the morning, they took me to the train. A last-minute advice and a final good-bye, and then I was back on my way to school.

My Return to LBA-Neisse

Traveling from Berlin to Neisse and back was to become almost a routine event for me. What made this particular trip so special was an interesting conversation I had with a soldier I was introduced to at the train. Walking down the train to stretch my legs, I passed an open compartment occupied by only one passenger. The person, a man, perhaps close to thirty years of age, was wearing the uniform of the German army. He asked me to step in and do him a favor. As I came closer, I could see that his right arm was missing, he had a patch over one eye, and there were some scars in his face. He introduced himself as Lieutenant Walter. His request was for me to take down his heavy suitcase from the overhead luggage rack. After doing so, I was ready to leave, but he insisted for me to sit down and talk to him. He wanted to know who I was and where I was going. He also noticed me wearing a special uniform and could tell that I was a member of the Adolf Hitler school.

We started a friendly conversation, and I told him that I was from Berlin and was back on my way to LBA-Neisse. He told me that he was going to Oppeln to visit the mother of his best friend, who was killed in Paris. Afterward he would return to his parents' house in Breslau. I told him that my father was born in Breslau, and he described to me what a clean and beautiful city Breslau was. He paused for a moment, changed the expression on his face, and then he went on exclaiming that the war for him was over; he might get an early discharge, or the army might keep him to be assigned to a desk job. He went on saying that just a few days before Christmas, he was discharged from an army hospital outside of Paris. I was polite enough not to ask him any questions, but I had the feeling he wanted to talk to somebody, and I was listening to the story of his life and his army history. His father was the owner of a successful hardware store in Breslau and had the money to send his son to the university in Frankfurt (Oder) to study engineering. After he graduated, he spent the mandatory two years in the Arbeitsdienst, the German labor force for young men and women. With his skills, he was employed in building the Autobahn. He proudly explained to me that the Autobahn was a technical marvel and the first freeway of its kind. He remembered engineers from all over the world who came to study and copy the construction method. After he left the labor force, he was automatically drafted into the army. Following the basic training, he was sent to the Army Engineering School near Cologne. When the war broke out, he received his order to report to a pioneer battalion in West Germany.

During the war against France, he was right up front, building bridges for the Panzer units to cross rivers and repair roads in their drive toward the Atlantic coast and the capital of France, Paris. "We made it," he said. "The French and British thought an armored attack through Belgium was impossible. But it wasn't. Against the advice of many of his top generals, the Führer decided to strike through the hilly, heavily wooded Ardennes forest. We worked day and night to clear the way for our great tank armies. Within ten days, German tanks reached the English Channel at Abbeville, cutting off the British and French forces. My regiment was right on their heels, and here was where my misfortune occurred.

"The French infantry tried to blow up a bridge in a desperate attempt to slow down the German troops. To cease the assault by the enemy, I took six of my men; and under heavy-fire protection, we went under the bridge to cut the wires leading to the demolition charges. We disarmed about half of the bridge when suddenly the rest of the charges exploded. Two of my men were instantly killed, and the rest of us were severely wounded. That is all I remember."

He further said, "Then I found myself in a surgical military medical unit discovering that I lost one arm and an eye. I was still in intensive care when France formally surrendered unconditionally on June 22, 1940, at Compiègne. After the German army occupied Paris, I was sent there to a special hospital for some plastic surgery to get my face restored. The army hospital had me stay there for almost six months. Actually I was ready to go back to Germany for follow-up treatment in Bavaria. A few days before, on September 15, 1940, a comrade, Sergeant Helmut Grabow, also from my unit and wounded the same day at the bridge near Abbeville, asked me to go with him to visit Versailles. The castle of King Louis XIV with Hall of Mirrors in Versailles is near Paris, and we did not want to miss the opportunity to see it. I managed to get a staff car for one day, and Helmut had to do the driving. We drove through Paris and crossed the river Seine, entering the Latin quarter on the left bank of the river. Passing a narrow street, we had to make a stop as some vehicles were parked right in the middle of the street. Our car was an open Kübelwagen, which is a converted

Volkswagen and the German version of the American Jeep. On the right side of the street was a small hotel and a café from which suddenly three or four men came out and jumped on top of the VW and attacked us with knives. Helmut and I were both unarmed and did not have a chance to get out of our seats. The first assault by two men was against Helmut who sustained stab wounds in his chest and neck. I tried to protect him by stopping one of the aggressors while a third man stuck his knife in my back from behind me. They left as fast as they came, and we were lying in the car, bleeding profusely without anybody giving us any medical help. I pressed my fist against Helmut's carotid artery in a desperate attempt to stop the bleeding. Finally somebody must have called the police, and an ambulance came to pick us up. Helmut died in my arms on the way to the hospital. I recovered from my back wound after they removed one of my kidneys."

A period of silence set in, and after the lieutenant took a break from talking, he looked out of the window as if he could find an answer out there that would make any sense. His turned his head around and said, "And here I am, on my way to see the parents of my best army buddy that I have known since the days we were together in boot camp. How can I face these people and answer all their questions without hurting them? I have no choice but to go and see them. In the long run, they will suffer more pain if they have to live the rest of their days not knowing the truth. We are soldiers, and some of us will get killed in the line of duty; we are aware of it since the day we put on the uniform."

After saying so, he changed the conversation, asking me a few questions. Then I noticed that the train was getting closer to Neisse and I was about to reach my destination. Before we said good-bye to each other, I wished him good luck; and he gave me his address, urging me to come and visit him if I had some time to spare since Breslau was not far from Neisse. Thanking him for the invitation, I told him that I would not come to Breslau without calling on him.

Getting off the train, I was greeted by some of my fellow students. All of us were standing around waiting for the bus to come. It was already getting dark, and after being in the heated train for hours, it was rather cold outside. The arrival at the school was the end of a wonderful vacation and the beginning of a new school year full of discipline and hard learning. On the first day of school in the New Year of 1941, a general assembly took place in the auditorium, where new assignments were given out. In the hall were posted academic curriculums for each class and age group. Some instructions and lessons were taking place in new classrooms, and new textbooks were given out. I noticed that our new timetable showed a heavier schedule on history and political science. Perhaps the word "political science" is not the right title as the orientation of the subject embraced almost exclusively the glorification of National Socialism. I found it very fascinating how nationalism made an end to the chaos that existed in Germany before 1933. In view of the political success of Adolf Hitler, National Socialism was the only thing that was good for Germany as it had reestablished what was true German, replacing misery and defeat with pride and honor. There was no denying that the Democratic Party under the Weimar Republic had promised to save Germany but had failed to do so and finally ended in corruption. National Socialism had given Germany a new identity and created a welfare system for every citizen in need.

When that generation of Germans retires, then, it would be the Hitler Youth who would provide the leadership of our nation of tomorrow. So we were made to believe. We trusted the Führer, and we would be ready to carry on his work in the future. Our lives were in his hands, and we were willing to sacrifice ourselves if Germany was in danger. We were at war, but Germany had conquered most of Europe from the Vistula River to the Atlantic Ocean, from the North Cape high above the Arctic Circle in Norway to the Pyrenees Mountains on the border of Spain. Only Britain held out against Germany. With her armies driven from the mainland and her island virtually defenseless, the Führer was sure the British would give up too. If not, and if they kept on bombing our cities, we could easily conquer them. The invasion of Britain was never attempted; instead, German troops landed on February 11, 1941, in Tunisia; and with the help of the Italian army, the Africa Corps was fighting to drive the hard-pressed British out of the Mediterranean and Egypt. During the campaign, Field Marshal Rommel came close to occupy the Suez Canal, a vital supply line for the British.

Operation Barbarossa

Our days here at school kept us very much occupied and exercised and also isolated from the rest of the world. The only connection we had with the outside were the radio, letters from home, and a day off to go to town every other Sunday. The bad news about the first air raid of the year in Berlin on the thirteenth of March had us guys from Berlin pretty scared. Schöneberg and Wilmersdorf were the main targets of the British bombers. Then again, on the twenty-third of March, they bombed downtown Berlin. I was relieved to know that my parents were out of danger as Tegel had not been attacked, but I was worried about Gisela since she was now living in Wilmersdorf. She must have known about my anxiety because she wrote me immediately that she, her parents, and their home were unharmed. On the sixth of April, the German army invaded Yugoslavia and Greece. Our history teacher told us that we had no choice; German intelligence had found out that the British made preparation to occupy these two countries. Once more the British suffered a defeat.

I had a feeling that out of revenge the RAF launched another attack in Berlin three days later during the night from the ninth to the tenth of April. This particular air raid was the first attack to destroy a historical landmark. The Staatsoper Unter den Linden, built by the famous architect Knobelsdorff, burned completely to the ground. On Easter Sunday, a furlough was given for everybody in our school for the weekend, unless you were assigned for guard duty. Most of us were too far from home and had time only to go to town or visit the nearby lake. It was a chance for us to explore Neisse and see what was going on Saturday night in town. On Sunday morning, I had the urge to go to church partly because it was Easter Sunday; and also, I needed to pray for my parents, family, and friends living in constant danger in Berlin. I did not feel any conflict of interest between nationalism and religion; both were diverse and presented many forms of goodness in their fields. The church had given me all the basic values of morality and spiritual strength when I needed it. The state educated me for citizenship, made me aware of my mission, urged me to unity, and harmonized in the interest of human solidarity. Socialism and nationalism were unique and original creations. The new state was not reactionary but revolutionary for it anticipated the solution of political problems without parties, parliaments, and the irresponsibility of assemblies.

Democracy and liberalism spelled individualism. Nationalism spelled collectivism based on solid foundation of popular support. As a total surprise, it was announced on the radio that Germany attacked Russia in the morning hours of June 22. The victories over the Russian army were staggering. After advancing hundreds of miles, the German armies were rapidly approaching Moscow and Leningrad. The fields of the Ukraine were quickly overrun by German panzer divisions. The military authorities in Berlin, London, and Washington believed that the Soviet Union was finished. Never before had Germany in all its history in any war gained so much territory. As a new and powerful nation, the German people had also, as never before since the dark days of 1918, regained pride and self-esteem. Unemployment was virtually nonexistent, and considering all the sacrifices needed for the war effort, the standard of living was relatively high.

A country that was victorious in a conflict with the enemy had not only displayed more bravery and higher skills on the battlefield but must be more convinced of the ideology it was fighting for. The spirit of the people was high, and everybody hoped that the final victory would be in the near future. Nationalism and communism were two opposing ideologies. Long before anybody was aware of it, Hitler had sensed the danger of communism not only for Germany or Europe but for the whole world. In modern history classes, we had long discussions about the subject. Stalin had killed or starved to death millions of his own people. Our teacher showed us pictures taken by the German army as they discovered mass graves of Polish officers who were shot by Russian firing squads and buried by the thousands in the forest of Katyn. We had also seen in the newsreel how the Russian people by the roadside greeted the German troops with flowers and refreshments. For them we arrived as their liberators from Stalin's tyranny. It also explained why in the first month the Russian army mostly surrendered with very little resistance.

In the beginning, Stalin could not counterattack as he had eliminated most of his senior officers. Operation Barbarossa, the code name for the invasion of Russia, was a successful surprise attack. The fighting units advanced faster as expected, and keeping them supplied turned out to be a problem. The legend of Germany invading an unprepared Soviet Union was a myth that was refutable. Several high-ranking Russian officers after their capture had stated that Stalin also planned an invasion of Germany.

The only reason that Germany attacked first was the fact that Stalin was not ready to attack. As early as the spring of 1940, a few months after the signing of the nonaggression pact between Germany and the Soviet Union, Stalin already started to make preparation for the invasion of Germany scheduled for September 1941. By the order of Stalin, the generals Shukov and Timoschenko submitted a plan whereby Soviet armies would, from the West Ukraine, advance into Silesia and secure the Krakau-Breslau area. Then Soviet forces would push north to reach the Baltic Sea in an attempt to confine the German armies in Poland and East Prussia in an encircling battle.

The operation was to be carried out as a surprise attack without a declaration of war. The whole plan was nothing but an operation on paper; it never materialized as the German government acted faster than the Soviet Union and turned the Red Army into chaos. Not quite convinced about the validity of the story, I asked the teacher, "How do we know that the prisoners are telling us the truth?"

The teacher replied, "It more or less does coincide with the information obtained by our own secret-agents. There are certain facts that speak for themselves. Let's look at some statistics that don't lie. At normal times, the Soviet Union maintained an army of not more than 1.9 million men. By introducing compulsory military service, the Red Army increased by July 1, 1940, to 3.6 million men, by January 1 to 4.2 millions, and had reached on July 1, 1941, a maximum capacity of 5 million men. In 1939 the Russian army had only 58 divisions and by early 1941 the number increased to 303 infantry, panzer, and motorized divisions. For an underdeveloped country like Russia, it made no sense to maintain such a big army unless the ruler of the nation had some conquering in mind."

Our classroom had a big map of Russia on the wall, and every time our school received some news from the battlefront, we followed up the events of major advances of our armies by putting little flags on a pin as marker on the map to establish a line of the battlefront. The war went on, and more men were drafted to follow the call of duty. To replace them, women and the Hitler Youth had to take their places in factories and farms. This year all students had to pitch in to secure the harvest at the school farms. As a result, our summer vacation was postponed by one month. It was fun for us even if it was hard work, but it gave us great pleasure when we came back and enjoyed the swimming pool in the evening. Finally on August 15, the school closed, and everybody was going home on vacation.

To my surprise, when I arrived in Tegel, my parents had not yet come back from their vacation. I relaxed for two days, then I went to visit my grandparents. They were both doing fine, and they were very happy to see me. Since they were living in Schöneberg, which was close to Wilmersdorf, I took the opportunity to go over and visit Gisela. Her parents were not home either, but the two of us had a lot to talk about, and we had to decide how we would spend our few days together. Meanwhile, my parents returned from their trip, and they told me what a wonderful time they had in Austria and how nice it was to get out of the city.

My First Major Air Raid

The few days out of the year that I was spending with my parents were suddenly interrupted on the night of September 7, 1941, by a British air raid over Berlin. It was the first major air raid for me, and I jumped about a foot high out of bed when unexpectedly, the screaming noise of the nearby siren went off at two o'clock in the morning. For me it was a new experience, but my parents went already through it several times. You get immediately dressed, take your bags, food container, drinking water, and a flashlight. After you turn off the lights, leave the house unlocked and proceed without delay to the nearest shelter. As described in the previous chapter, most houses in Berlin were built with underground basements, which were converted into air-raid shelters. This was done by sandbagging the windows, putting in steel doors to the outside and to the next-door basement, making it possible to escape from one shelter to another. More important than anything else was the reinforcement of the ceiling supported by heavy vertical beams. If a house was hit by a bomb and everything was destroyed above ground, the weight of falling walls was tremendous and must be supported by the ceiling of the basement. The inside of the shelter was primitive but functional. Bunk beds, tables, and benches were the basic furniture. Gas masks, firefighting equipment, medical supplies, and provisions were also part of the inventory.

As soon as the last tenant arrived, the steel doors were closed shut, and I could not fight off an oncoming feeling of claustrophobia. A few minutes later, a formation of British bombers crossed Tegel, approaching their targets in East Berlin. All of a sudden, hell broke loose. Two blocks from us was a large vacant field where every year the circus would come and put up a tent and park all their vehicles for the animals, equipment trailer, and mobile homes for the entertainers. Well, tonight it was a different kind of circus. I could not sneak in or out under the bottom of a circus tent; I was trapped behind steel doors in an air-raid shelter. Where the circus used to be was now a permanent parking place for a battery of six 88 mm Flak (antiaircraft guns) and 48 in searchlights. The moment they all started firing at the same time, it sounded like bombs were exploding over our heads.

Women got hysterical, and children cried in the shelter; the terrific noise and the constant vibration made us believe we were under direct attack. The air-raid warden tried to calm everybody down, explaining to us what really went on and that we were out of danger. The whole thing lasted not more than ten minutes, but it seemed like hours. Coming out of the shelter, we could see in an easterly direction large bright orange red fire clouds over Berlin. As we found out the next morning, Lichtenberg and Pankow suffered severe fire damage caused by thousands of *Brandbomben* (phosphorus bombs).

The Potsdamer Platz, the main traffic artery downtown, was also the target of several bombs. Nearby, at the Pariser Platz, a 1,800 kg *Luftmine* (heavy bomb exploding above ground) killed dozens of people. Air raids were now becoming a new chapter in the history of warfare. The attacks were not always against factories and military installations. Most of the time, the targets were the civilian population. The enemy was trying to win the war by terrifying and demoralizing unarmed women and children. It made no difference if the killing took place in London or Berlin; the people would not be pressed into submission. In a way, I was glad that my parents were now living outside of Berlin, thinking that Tegel might be less of a target for the British. To be on the safe side, my father suggested to start taking things we valued in several trips to Kremmen and storing them in the attic of Aunt Erna's house in the country.

Just a few days before the end of my summer vacation, we went out of Berlin to Aunt Erna's. It was nice to be together again after we had not seen each other for over a year. Cousin Ingeborg said that we must all come back and celebrate Christmas together in Kremmen. Everybody agreed, but in the meanwhile, I had to go back to Neisse for the last three months of my school year.

Our curriculum had not changed very much except that Greek mythology had been added to the schedule. The traditions and legends of the Greek people, which are embodied in their beliefs concerning their origin, gods, and heroes, were very inspiring. The commanding courage of Hector and Achilles in Homer's *Iliad* and *Odyssey* animated our current struggle for survival. The battle of Troy was a parallel of our times. The death of a hero dying for his country was the most admirable and supreme sacrifice. "Dulce et decorum Pro patria mori" (How sweet and beautiful it is to die for one's country). None of us young teenagers wanted to die, but all of us were willing to fight no matter what the consequences. Maybe one of these days there would be peace on earth. The world over, people were celebrating Christmas praying for peace, and it was not any different this year except that the war was constantly intensifying.

Once more the school was closed over the Christmas and New Year holidays, and as I was sitting in the train going home, these things were going through my mind. For many people, Christmas was no longer a religious festival, but rather, a convenient occasion to take a break from whatever they were doing, to relax and indulge in food and drinks.

On Christmas Eve, my parents and I arrived in Kremmen to be with Aunt Erna and Ingeborg as we'd promised. At midnight we attended the service at the little Lutheran church in Kremmen. Being in the country among farmers, wearing civilian clothes and not surrounded by cadets in gray uniforms, I felt like being in a different world. What would my life be if I could just be an ordinary twelve-year-old boy in a peaceful Germany?

Folks living in the country had not been touched by the war, yet they also had not seen any shortage of food. On Christmas Day, we exchanged a few small gifts but enjoyed mostly being with each other. For Ingeborg, I had a big surprise. She had always wanted a bicycle, and since I no longer had use for mine, I decided to give it to her. She was very happy and tried it out immediately. Aunt Erna's parents had a big farm near Schwerin in Mecklenburg and kept her supplied with smoked ham and sausages. When we returned to Tegel (Berlin), Aunt Erna gave my mother some ham and salami to take home, which we gratefully accepted.

To celebrate the New Year, we were invited to my grandmother's house. My grandmother's second husband, whom I sometimes called Grandfather, was an old winemaking buff, and he was very good at his hobby. His favorite pursuit was a tasteful and pleasing Elderberry wine. He was friendly and good to me, and for the occasion, he insisted that my parents allow me to enjoy a few sips of his savory creation. My grandmother, as always, with whatever little she had, managed to put a wonderful meal together. Some of the ham and salami we received from Aunt Erna we shared with them.

On January 3, 1942, it was time again for me to return to school. The academy by now was my primary home, and I had found my purpose in life, and I was embracing all the opportunities the academy had to offer. The LBA-Neisse had strong connections to all activities and courses the government had to offer to sponsor the Hitler Youth. One of these organizations was the NSKK, the National Socialist Automobile Corps. It was a motorsport group engaging in racing motorcycles and operating all kinds of cars, trucks, and tanks. One day in school, two officers of the NSKK came to visit our class to give us an introduction to the organization and showed us a film about all the different activities. It aroused my interest since I always wanted to ride a motorcycle. I signed up, and it gave me a chance twice a week in the afternoon to go to Neisse and join the group.

Riding a motorcycle is basically the same as riding a bicycle. Once you are able to coordinate clutch and gears, a full throttle will give you a speed you can only dream about sitting on a bicycle. Everyone's goal in the group was to eventually get a driver's license. Theoretical and technical courses were a prerequisite along with driver's education. During the war, the minimum age for a driver's license had been lowered to the age of fourteen. Under the age of fourteen, boys who were members of the Hitler Youth NSKK were used as motorcycle couriers attached to the police or any branch of the armed forces.

The Balance of the War in Russia

Still every day in class, we listened to the report of the OKW, the high command of the army, and adjusted the lines on the map according to troop advances. This week in June was the anniversary of Germany's first attack on Russia, and the Führer's headquarter had the lessons of the first year's victories and failures to help them in making their second-year plans. This week the clock struck. The time for Germany's great attempt to crush Russia had come. The Führer had no second year in which to conquer Russia. He had at most four months, perhaps only three, during which Russia must be conquered or the war would be dragged out and become a burden. From the Führer's standpoint, Russia must be liquidated as an enemy before the United States could throw its real weight into the war. Germany must beat Russia in time to allow the German war machine to turn and meet the enemy in the West. As our history teacher pointed out to us, we could not afford to make the mistake again we did in WW I by getting tied up in a two-front war and split our fighting power in half. The basic facts were known as our high command sat down to plan the German campaign of 1942. This time they had to pin down the Russian army in order to crush it, for the Russians could even retreat one thousand miles without even reaching the Ural industrial area. To push an army away without destroying it stretches your supply lines and leaves your flanks open for a counterattack. To crush the Russian army, the German troops had to be free to attack along the whole two-thousand-mile battlefront. For this we had to wait for good weather. Not until the end of June could the ground be counted on to be fit and hard in the north around Leningrad and in the Ukraine. With this starting time limit and the necessity of finishing before another winter, the general staff had to devise a plan for crushing Russia in a few months' time—a campaign as crushing as those against Poland in 1939 and France in 1940, a campaign better than the Blitzkrieg that failed against Russia in 1941. This had to be the greatest thunderbolt of all, and it had to strike on time. Failure would almost certainly be loss of the war. But the prize of success would be freedom to turn the German Wehrmacht loose on Britain and the United States—probably to take all of Asia, possibly to take most of Africa, and perhaps to take Britain itself. It would be exciting to see how the strategy would develop in the next few months. It was also obvious that this summer, the world would witness the biggest tank battle in history.

The day was July 19, 1942. It was my thirteenth birthday, and I was celebrating this day away from home, without my family. I was now a teenager, a step closer to adulthood in age; but in reality, all of us youngsters were growing up a lot faster these days, and the circumstances obligated us to act as adults. My parents sent me a letter with a nice birthday card. They also mailed me twenty marks, and my mother enclosed some coupons for bread or bakery goods out of their own restricted food rations. With these food stamps and some spending money in my pocket, I asked my friend Helmut to come along and celebrate my birthday with me. Helmut was a fellow cadet who came from Schulzendorf, a little village next to Tegel. We got acquainted at a Hitler Youth meeting, not knowing that we would be classmates in Neisse. He also joined the motorsport group in town, and today we left early. The most famous part of downtown Neisse was called the Ring; as the name implied, it was a huge circle of beautiful houses, stores, and restaurants. In the middle was the plaza, which was more like an open park with Sacred Heart the oldest church in Neisse. Another landmark at the ring was the café Heimatland, which had a pastry shop and an ice cream parlor. The corner was a preferred hangout place of most cadets on their days off, especially the seniors who came here with their girlfriends.

Today I was the big spender. Helmut and I sat in the garden under a big chestnut tree, and we were enjoying the specialty of the house, marzipan and mocca torte with a *schlag* and vanilla ice cream on the side. While enjoying this wonderful treat, we had a nice conversation and started to talk about our upcoming summer vacation and what we were planning to do with our days at home. Well, I said, besides visiting friends and relatives, I liked to spend as much time as I could on the lake in Tegel. I had not been sitting in a kayak for a long time. Helmut was telling me that he felt the same way and that he would take out his parents' motorboat every time he had a chance to use it. We had the boat tied down on the river Havel not too far from where we lived.

Of course, he kept on saying, "You are more than welcome to join me anytime you feel like it."

"It is a deal," I said, "I will take you up on it when the time comes."

And time would come soon for our summer vacation. In less than two weeks, school would close on July 31 and would open again on September 16.

Today was the twenty-second of July, the anniversary of Germany's first attack on Russia thirteen months earlier. Our history teacher, Colonel Kluge, was the chief officer of a regiment fighting the Russians in WW I. He knew all about strategy, and he was an expert of warfare and daily facts and figures on our map and in reality could not escape him. Relating to statistics and information we received, he could very much describe what had happened and predict the move our army would make. As it stood thirteen months after the outbreak of war with Russia, our army had only occupied about 7 percent (some 580,000 square miles) of Russia's land, but we had not conquered Russia. We had destroyed or captured upward of 4.5 million Red soldiers, 15,000 Red tanks, and 9,000 Red planes; but we had not destroyed the Red Army. German artillery men could see Leningrad through their telescopes, but they had not captured Leningrad—a city we had to take in order to cut off the enemy's Murmansk supply route coming from the Baltic.

To end the war for us in victory, it was absolutely essential to capture Moscow immediately. According to Kluge, it was more important to attack Moscow, the heart and capital of the USSR with its vast railway system that rayed out from Moscow and served most of Russia, than try to go for the oil in the Caucasus and besiege the fortress of Sevastopol, which controlled the Black Sea. German armies were poised on the outer borders of the industrial Donets Basin, but they did not have its mines, power plants, and factories, or its roads to Caucasian oil. With the limited time available for reaching these goals, Germany must make all possible preparations in advance before the start of the offensive. All along the two-thousand-mile front, from Murmansk to the Sea of Azov, innumerable local chores of the war had been done. Contrary to Kluge, our Führer decided to take Sevastopol, not Moscow. The question at Sevastopol was not whether we could take it, but how much we could afford to pay for it. Here was the situation the way a Red soldier captured by the Germans described it: "Now at Sevastopol there is no air fit to breathe because of the decaying bodies of German, Russian, and Romanians." The Führer wanted Sevastopol, not only for great strategic reasons, but because he particularly needed it as a triumph to stiffen the morale of the German people for the great campaign to come.

The German armies were ready. Yet the spectacle of death at Sevastopol was only the overture for what was to come. In spirit, in the will to win or die, the German army had no superior. Just how it stood in effective numbers and vital weapons, only the German High Command knew. Within broad limits, the general strength and distribution of the German armies were estimated in the following sectors:

1. On the northern front, from Murmansk to Staraya-Russa, below Leningrad, nearly one million men in thirty-five German divisions, including three panzers, twelve Finn divisions, two Italian divisions
2. On the central front (Moscow, Kalinin, Rzhev, Vyazma, Bryansk), over 850,000 men in forty German divisions including four panzers, two Italian divisions, and one Spanish
3. On the southern front (Kharkov to the Crimea), about 1.3 million men in fifty German divisions, including eight panzers, fourteen Romanian, and two Italian divisions
4. In reserve (in the occupied Ukraine, White Russia, the Baltic, Poland, East Prussia), more than 1.5 million men in seventy German divisions, including at least four panzers and probably more, six Romanian, and four Italian divisions
5. In the Luftwaffe, now mainly in the south, about six thousand frontline planes in three air fleets of two thousand each

The sad part of the first year's war in Russia were the 1.5 million casualties Germany had to pay for the invasion. The plan was ready, the spirit of the German soldiers was unbroken, and they would fight desperately, knowing that Germany would lose everything, at least in their generation's lifetime, unless they won. Gigantic problems were now facing the German army. The enemy had lines of prepared defenses in the rear, blocking every mile of the primary roads to Moscow and the objectives in the north and south. Against such defenses, the typical Blitz—the quick shock; the breakthrough; the spearing advance by planes, tanks, and mobile artillery; then the follow-up by infantry—would not serve as it did in Poland, in the Lowlands, and in Russia's first months. Now in depth and thorough preparation, the Russian defenses were stronger than those that slowed the German drive last fall then stopped it with winter's paralyzing help. But if Stalin and his staff had learned how to crack the 1940-model Blitz, Germany's generals had had many months to study Soviet's defense. Moscow's hardheaded commanders could only assume that the Germans had a plan, that the plan was ready, and that it was in scale with the German task. The German armies, in their preparatory spring attacks, had already shown a few new tricks. Essence of these new tactics was to choose a very narrow sector, smash the selected area with a maximum concentration of planes (the Russians counted one thousand on a fifteen-mile line below Kharkov), then strike with closely integrated formations of artillery, infantry, and tanks. Full-strength panzers had not attempted to dart through the enemy lines, swirled at will in the Russian rear. Instead, the Germans apparently kept their tanks in smaller groups, close to artillery and infantry. Thus, while the German pace might be slow, it was calculated to keep concentrated columns intact, always with enough strength to protect themselves from the surrounding Russians. At Kharkov, these tactics worked so well that Moscow had to admit a continued German advance. At Sevastopol, the German's brute concentration of men and metal brought that fortress to the verge of collapse in sixteen days. It was possible that the recent variations of German tactics had been merely a change of pace, perhaps partly caused by the desire to concentrate tanks.

Considering the size of the battlefield and the size of the Russian armies and the tendency shown in every previous campaign in WW II for the Führer to lay plans on a grand scale, the German plan for 1942 might well call for breakthroughs and encirclements on a huge scale. There were many opportunities for such attacks. A major drive in the center might take Moscow and, sweeping on, outflank the entire southern front. A major drive in the south might strike directly at the Caucasus or swing north to outflank the central front. A drive in the far north might cut the lines of Allied aid from Murmank and Archangel. A major drive through or around Turkey might cut off the Russian back door through Persia or swing south to attack Suez. There were possible variations upon these themes. Several such drives might be launched at once, some of them real, some feints. Any two adjoining drives could become a pincer movement. Whatever the plan, it was certain to be breathtaking. The Führer told the German army, the air force, and the navy where to fight. Sometimes he told them when to fight. But the high command and his small thoroughly professional group of generals told them how to fight.

Up to now, in WW II, the product of General Franz Halder's planning had always been a thunderbolt, the lightning that withered Poland, Norway, Holland, Belgium, and France, the shaft that staggered Russia last year. Thunderbolts should strike on time. The Führer's time in Russia—his only time—was now. The world had a right to expect something terrific, and our teacher said the German people should expect more days of glory ahead. These were the strategies we discussed with Colonel Kluge, and only history would tell the eventual outcome of the conflict.

Finally the day had come when school closed down for the summertime and everybody was heading for home. At 11:00 PM on August 1, I arrived in Tegel. I was very tired, and after greeting my parents and after a short conversation, my mother urged me to go to bed. The next day, after a good night's sleep, we had a lot to talk about. Somehow I noticed that my parents appeared kind of depressed. I asked them if there was something bothering them, and my father told me what was upsetting them. Unexpectedly, my father received a draft notice for the air force on July 30 to report for military duty on August 12 at the Herrman Göring Air Force Base in Spandau. I was devastated with the news—not that I was afraid my father would not be a good soldier, but I could not see my parents being separated from each other. All I could do at this moment was try to cheer them up by saying that the war would be over soon, and Dad would be back in no time at all. Deep down in my mind, I was not too convinced of what I was saying, but I ignited a glimmer of hope in my parents eyes. As always, in the short time we had together, the days were filled with visits to relatives and friends. They said hello to me and good-bye to my father who was departing in a few days, shipping off to be stationed at the Hungarian front. The air force base in Spandau where he was to report was only thirty minutes by bus from Tegel.

In the morning, my grandparents came for an early visit to see us before my dad had to check in at 1600 hours. We had plenty of time for a nice lunch and a beer at the nearest pub. My grandfather, an old veteran, had plenty of advice to give my father on how to survive the war. When the bus came, both my mother and my grandmother cried at the last good-bye. On the way home, my mother told me how afraid she would be in a few weeks when I would be going back to Neisse. To make her feel better, I told my mother, "Mom, a friend at school, also from Berlin, who's mother is all by herself got a transfer to the LBA-Brandenburg. If they also allow me to transfer, then I can be with you every weekend."

My mother said, however, that she would be fine and I should not leave the academy if I liked it there. "The only time I feel alone is at those terrible air raids. It is a most dreadful experience like nothing in my whole life," my mother said. I tried to change the subject, but in my heart, I was fearing for her safety. As a grim reminder of the war, my mother and I spent four frightful nights together in the basement shelter during my summer vacation. On August 27, the targets were Zehlendorf and Kreuzberg, and two days later Kreuzberg, Tempelhof, Tiergarten, Lichtenberg, and Treptow. Again, on September 9, Soviet planes attacked Mahlsdorf and Weissensee, and on the eleventh, the RAF bombarded Berlin with thirty-three planes. After that Berlin was left without any more attacks for the rest of the year. The reason behind it was simple; the British had overextended their air raids, and whatever planes they had left, they were using them for a new strategy by concentrating their attacks more on West Germany, especially on the Rhineland where all the heavy industry was located.

After the air raid, I had to go and see Gisela; she lived in the area that got hit the most. Gisela and her mother were not hurt, but the roof of their house was hit by two of those small firebombs. Luckily, the Hitler

Youth Bucket Brigade came and extinguished the fire before it could burn down the house. Firebombs were approximately three-by-twenty-four-inch hexagon aluminum container filled with a highly inflammable yellowish phosphorus substance that exploded and ignited on impact. The average airplane could carry up to a thousand of those tiny bombs and were designed to inflame and burn down highly populated cities. Once a part of town was burning, the fire created its own heat and wind, could no longer be controlled, and would spread all over town. It was useless to try to put out a fire started by a firebomb; in order to keep on burning, it needed oxygen and only sand would retard the fire. A house was a lot safer from firebombs if there was plenty of sand available in the attic beneath the roof. Gisela and I went down the street, and as we were walking through the neighborhood, Gisela showed me some houses completely destroyed, and some were still burning. Everywhere people were carrying furniture or trying to salvage some of their belongings. When I asked Gisela about her father, she told me that he was also drafted recently and was currently fighting in Russia. Many women were now living without a husband or alone with their children. I told Gisela that I considered, because of my mother being alone, a transfer next school year to the LBA-Brandenburg. She did not say anything, but the possibility of me coming home made her happy and the farewell at the end of my vacation easier. Before I departed for Neisse, I did encourage my mother to live with Erna and Ingeborg in the country, as my father earlier suggested, to escape the danger of becoming an air-raid victim. My mother did not answer me, but two weeks after I went back to school, I received a letter from her telling me that she had taken a full-time job at Borsig as an assembly line worker for pieces of machinery.

The war was no longer proceeding in a Blitzkrieg manner, but victories were still reported. Germany was concentrating on reaching superiority over the enemy by developing new wonder weapons. Our class burst out in jubilation when the radio announced the first successful launch of a long-range missle by the German scientist Wernherr von Braun on October 15 in Pinemuende. At the end of December this year, we were only getting a short Christmas vacation of ten days, just enough to visit my mother and celebrate the holidays with my grandparents. For the New Year, we were invited to stay with Erna and Ingeborg. Of course, the day before I left, I stopped by to see Gisela and her mother; they were both doing fine and were happy to see me. Since the last time I was in Berlin, there were no air raids, and all of us were hoping that the British were running out of steam. Living in an illusion that we had seen the end of air raids over Berlin, I decided to stay in Neisse. The new school semester started, but on January 17, 1943, Berlin was again another target of the RAF. This time they came with 111 airplanes, concentrating their attack in Dahlem, the place where I was born; in Tempelhof; and even Tegel. The damage was extensive, and it was now clear to me that we were in for hard times. To confirm my suspicion, on February 18, Dr. Goebbels, the German minister of propaganda, asked the Berliners at a rally in the Sportpalast if they would accept a total war.

The response, even as we lost Stalingrad, could only be described as a definite yes in a spontaneous outbreak of anger against the enemy. As a result, every person in Germany was now expected in one form or another to contribute to the war effort, and the Hitler Youth was no exception. A week after Goebbels's speech, an emergency act proposed by the ministry of war was signed by Adolf Hitler into law, declaring to draft all male students fourteen years and over to serve as Flakhelfer near their high school to help the regular crew of an antiaircraft battery. At thirteen and a half years old, I volunteered for the military service like most of my fellow students at the academy. Our assignment was to attend a basic seven-month course after school at the Luftwaffe (air force) base at the Talsperre near Neisse. The *talsperre* (valley dam) was the biggest water reservoir and hydropower plant in Upper Silesia. For the protection from the air, several .50 caliber and the famous 8.8 cm antiaircraft guns were placed around the dam and its installation. The whole complex was surrounded by a chain-link fence with barbed wire on top and placed under twenty-four hours' surveillance by MP guards with watchdogs. A big front gate was the only entrance where the guardhouse with the officer of the watch and his crew were located.

Every person, employee, or military going in or out must show proper identification. Two lanes were installed only for the inspection of incoming and outgoing vehicles. The air force base was located about forty-five minutes from the LBA, and our school bus took us there every morning. One of the barracks at the base was converted into two classrooms. All newly inducted LwH (Luftwaffenhelfer) were receiving theoretic instruction before they were allowed to get near the Flak for the first month. The next three months were a combination of classroom instruction and actual training at the battery side. Every gun had one crew, and every member of that crew functioned according to his assignment. It was all teamwork, and your position behind the battery was of equal importance. The heavy 318 Flak Battery consisted of four 8.8 cm guns, some .50 caliber guns, and several 2 cm guns for the defense of nasty low-flying airplanes.

For the Neisse Flak Battery, his primary commission was to protect the valley dam with its hydropower plant, but its base also served as a training facility for the air force. Before we started our training, each of us had to undergo a physical examination to make sure we were fit for premilitary service. Even though we were receiving special military training, we were not classified as regular combatants and officially were still members of the Hitler Youth. We were receiving the same meals as any other soldier, but when it came to rations of cigarettes and alcohol, we were going out empty as it was considered hazardous to our health. We had not received any Luftwaffen uniform yet since we were considered only part-timers for five hours daily at the base. We were checking in at nine in the morning and return to the academy at two in the afternoon. In the afternoon, we still had about three hours of classes of our scheduled curriculum.

Finally, the first month was now completed at the base, and the day we all had waited for so long had come; our training at the battery side was now beginning. Each of us was now issued some overalls, a kind of fatigue dress especially designed for gun crews. The bunch from our school appearing at the base was a mixture of students ranging from fourteen to eighteen years of age. The oldest ones were selected for training at the guns to relieve a regular Flak soldier that could be sent to the Russian front. The medium-aged group, if they were smart enough, were earmarked to operate optical and radar-measuring instruments. The rest of the dummies including me got stuck in the *Umwertung* (revaluation). Normally, distance and position of enemy aircraft was given directly from the observation operator to the battery. In case of communication breakdown, the Umwertung would give any received data immediately to the battery. The Umwertung was located underground close to the battery, and the main function was to keep the regional Luftwaffe headquarter informed about position and amount of enemy airplanes. In the middle of the dugout was a huge map table of Germany covered with a grid of map squares. Each province had its own map of grids, starting with the northwest corner being square A going alphabetically and horizontally one letter for each square to the northeast corner. Back to the northwest corner going vertically down alphabetically from *A* with the next letter for each square to the southwest corner.

Looking at the map of Brandenburg and locating the city of Berlin, you would find it in the square marked with the letters *FG*; the square below was marked *GG*. If I was in charge of the Umwertung, I would have to watch the map in front of me and report any movement of enemy aircraft to general headquarters through my head speakers. A typical message would be like the following: "Here is Kornblume, a bomber group of six Lancasters is leaving Friedrich-Gustav, flying in a southerly direction approaching Gustav-Gustav." I had no problem, and I was learning fast to be stationed in the Umwertung or be placed at observation. On a clear day, as shown in a slide projection, I could identify a bomber either as a Lancaster, Vickers Wellington, Halifax, B-17, or B-29. Low but fast-flying fighter planes I had to distinguish between Spitfires, Hurricanes, Mustangs, Thunderbolts, Focke-Wulf, and Messerschmitt 109. Everything we had learned would now be put to the test by going through a series of simulated alarms of enemy air attacks. Such a drill would only be complete and successful if every member of the team performed correctly at the right time. All of us kids were getting along with the regular gun crew, and they were very patient with us if we didn't get it right the first or second time. In charge of the whole battery was a drill sergeant by the name Klotz. He was a noncommissioned officer next in rank to Captain Lehman, the CO of the base.

In command of our detail from the LBA was an eighteen-year-old senior student from München by the name Max. He was a husky boxer, and we nicknamed him Schmeling. Even Klotz called him Schmeling, and if something went wrong, he always let it out on him. There were altogether four seniors in our group, and each one of them was assigned as gun layert at the four 8.8 cm Flak at the battery. The rest of us had a less responsible position, but not a less important function to fulfill. One of the key elements besides proper performance was speed. The moment the siren went off like a lubricated lightning rushing out of the barracks, we were running as fast as we could either to the gun emplacement, dugout, or wherever our battle station was. In one of the first simulated alarms, the second oldest gun layert was so much in a hurry that he made a mistake. The captain of the battery gave the following orders: "Enemy bombing squadron at 180 degrees" and "Sperrfeuer at one thousand meters." *Sperrfeuer* means "box barrage," or call it an iron curtain of exploding shells. To accomplish that, all shells before being loaded manually must be set to explode at the same altitude. To activate the timing was a simple procedure. Around the tip of the shell was a device called *Führungsring*, a detonator ring with an adjustable time fuse to set the numbers for the shell to explode at a certain altitude. The mistake the cannoneer made was a wrong number; instead of one thousand meters, he skipped a zero and turned the ring to one hundred meters. For exercise purposes, we were not using live ammunition, or the battery would have been showered with bursting shell splinters. The only thing that rained down on us was the cussing of Drill Sergeant Klotz. To make matters worse, at the next exercise, I screwed up. As we were scrambling into position, I jumped inside the dugout, put on my earphones, and started to make a report to sign in. "This is Kornblume calling headquarters, headquarters come in, over."

There was no answer, so I repeated, "This is Kornblume calling headquarters, headquarters come in, over." Before I could repeat my message, Sergeant Klotz was behind me and tipped me on my shoulder. I turned around, and there he was, holding with his other hand the plug at the end of the cord to my headgear. Red in the face, he pointed at the plug, speaking in a mad voice, "You might get a better reception if you plug it in." Klotz was trying to punish me, as he knew how much I liked my job in the Umwertung, by taking me out for another stupid assignment on the outside. From now on, I was what they called the Birdy. During an alarm, everything was performed in a chain reaction; even though it was only simulated, whatever you exercised was exactly the same thing you would do in a real air attack. The only thing that was missing was the enemy airplane. To correct the deficit, some genius had invented the birdy. Now everybody behind the gun sight of a Flak had an object to aim at. The birdy was a little model airplane with an approximate wingspan of twelve inches with a three—to four-foot wire underneath attached to a twelve-foot aluminum pole, which was held vertically up in the air. Somebody was holding the end of the stick, walking in a distance from fifty to one hundred feet away and around the battery to give every gunner a chance to shoot you down. I was the new dummy now to fly the birdy. The birdy I was flying was a B-24 Liberator. I was the pilot flying VFR (visual flight rule), cruising around the battery trying to locate the lake twenty kilometers away from Neisse. I was flying low and turning the plane over to the bombardier to blow up the dam. No matter how much Klotz would chase us back and forth between barracks and battery, he could not break our spirits; after all, we were Hitler Youth, and this kind of grinding had made us tough. Klotz was a pugnacious fellow but learned soon that we were able to endure hardship. One day, as we were not running fast enough, he stood in front of us and proclaimed, "We will practice this all day long till you clowns get the lead out."

Well, enough was enough. Schmeling got really angry and told him in his heavy Bavarian accent, "Blow it out your ass."

Klotz was shocked for a minute, turned closer to him, and asked him calmly, "What did you say, will you repeat that?"

Schmeling did not move a muscle, looked straight into the eyes of Klotz, exclaiming slowly, "I said we are out of gas." All of us had a hell of a time not to crack up aloud in laughter, but none of us altered a tone of voice when we were spoken to. Suddenly a sharp sound of a bell indicated that it was two in the afternoon, time to change uniforms and get back to the academy. On the bus, we finally let our emotions go, and Schmeling was the hero of the day. That day we were so tired, and some of us fell asleep in class. Most of us fellows from Berlin went to the director of the LBA-Neisse and asked at the end of the semester to be transferred to the LBA-Brandenburg.

Concurrent with the completion of our four-month training as Flakhelfer, in July we decided to be closer to the action in Berlin in case we were needed. In June, I also took my driver's test but was not issued a driver's license till July 19, 1943, the day I turned fourteen years old. I was granted the same month a transfer to the LBA-Brandenburg and at the beginning of the summer vacation said good-bye to the beloved school in Neisse forever.

CHAPTER IV

BERLIN: BOMBS AND BODIES

Back to Brandenburg and Berlin

Arriving in Berlin, I finally realized that today, the second of August 1943, was the beginning of a new chapter in my life. What I left behind in Neisse was not only an organized life and education but also security. In Berlin I had entered the war zone; at a tender age of fourteen I must prepare myself as a part of the fighting force at the home front. My mother did not know that I left Neisse for good. She believed I just came for the summer vacation and was glad to see me. Later I told her that I got my transfer from Neisse to Brandenburg and would come home to see her every weekend. The good news made her so happy she had tears in her eyes as she told me how much she missed both my father and me. A minute later, her eyes brightened up, and she told me that she got a letter from Papa. He was doing fine, stationed outside of Budapest and not in any danger.

Next day, Mother and I went to town to do some shopping. Somehow I was getting the impression that life had changed in Berlin. I missed the easy-go-lucky crowd of people hanging out having a good time. I could see that the war and its air raids had taken a heavy toll on the Berliners. You also couldn't see any schoolkids on the streets. Most schools were closed, and whole classes of children with their teachers were evacuated to safer places in the country. As we were visiting my grandparents, my grandfather told me that ever since January 31, 1943, the day the German Sixth Army under General-feld marschall Paulus capitulated to the Russians, we had lost the momentum of the Blitzkrieg. The invasion in Russia had slowed down, and we were taking more and more the position of defense. In his opinion, most of the German people didn't even believe anymore that Germany would win the war. I personally still trusted that Hitler knew what he was doing and would never give up fighting for Germany. This conversation was way over my head, and I could never have a dialogue with one of my teachers putting our victory in question. I respected my grandfather, not because he was much older than I was, but because he had lived four years in the trenches in WW I and knew that war had never solved any human conflict. The suffering on both sides was a needless misery not contributing to a lasting peace for the defeated survivors. He might be right, but what I learned from history, I challenged him with the this argument: "Under the Kaiser, the nation had a Reichstag in Berlin, the German Parliament, representing the voice of the people. If the German people did not see a reason to go to war over the Sarajevo incident, why was he not overruled?"

"Good question," he said. "And I can give you two good answers why the Kaiser succeeded. Number one, the Prussian militarism is so strong that they have the upper hand over the civilian government. Secondly, the German people have an abnormal respect for law and authority, and their impulse is to adjust themselves to circumstances rather than to revolt against them. To an extraordinary degree, Germans are in the hands of their leaders. After the Kaiser lost the war, Germany's responsible leaders were ruined by the Treaty of Versailles's postwar operations. Chancellor Brüning tried to show the Allies that it could not be obeyed by trying faithfully to obey it.

"Depression made Germany's creditors call their loans, leading inevitably to foreign exchange control, standstill agreements, the Hoover Moratorium, and the bankruptcy of Germany's international credit and internal politics." He paused for a moment and then went on. "Had not President von Hindenburg, the only German Germans could still respectfully look up to, been in an advanced state of mental senility, Adolf Hitler might have failed to call the cards. Franz von Papen, beloved of Hindenburg, spoke for Hitler to the aged president and, effective parliamentary government having been scrapped three years before, Hitler was in as chancellor. The rest you have witnessed yourself," he said.

"You are absolutely right," I replied. "I am a witness to Germany's resurrection. My generation will now take over and protect what the Führer has given back to us—our dignity, moral worth, independence, and respect among other nation. You must admit, the Treaty of Versailles all but wrote into its text the eventual arrival of Adolf Hitler or any other German freedom fighter to lift the shame from Germany."

Our conversation came to an end as we both agreed that he was the man of the hour, but he drew the line when Hitler got us into WW II. A silence came up between us, making me wonder what went through his mind. Once more he turned around, asking me, "Do you really want to die for your country, throwing your life away in a war that makes no sense?"

Without hesitating I answered him: "Dulce et decorum Pro patria mori." How sweet and beautiful it is to die for one's country.

All I heard him say was, "Yes! They gave us the same line of shit when I was your age. It sounds very familiar; you cannot say history does not repeat itself." Slowly, without saying anything, he got up and went out to his victory garden, checking if any tomatoes were ripe for supper. Little did I know that this was the last time I would ever see him.

The day we left Neisse, the group of Berlin students transferred to LBA-Brandenburg looked like a bunch of pack mules. We were instructed that in addition to our clothes and personal belongings, we were to take all of the schoolbooks and the blankets given to us to the new school in Brandenburg. We first dropped all our gear at our parents' home, and all we had in mind was to spend four weeks of vacation in leisure in Berlin before reporting back to school in Brandenburg on September 2. Practically up to the end of August, my mother and I had a good time together; the weather was fine, we went to see places around Berlin, visited some friends, and for four days we stayed with Erna and Ingeborg in Kremmen. At nights sometimes we went out to eat or would go and see a movie. It did not last very long, the good time, when on August 23, all of a sudden hell broke loose again. A visit of the British Air Force reminded us that the war was still going on. It was a massive air raid over Berlin, and the selected targets were Berlin, Mitte, Kreuzberg, Tiergarten, Friedrichshain, Spandau, Kopenick, Weissensee, Pankow, and Tegel. Downtown Tegel was hit pretty hard. After the air raid, I could see the fire in the near distance. Running down the street trying to make myself useful, I joined a group of Hitler Youth Bucket Brigade on the way to the city. On the corner of Berliner Strasse and Schlossplatz Tegel, an air-raid warden stopped us and told us to follow him to a six-story-high building whose top floor was on fire.

At the lobby of the building, he made each of us grab a steel helmet before we went up the stairs. As we were climbing higher, we could feel the heat; the man behind me pushed the nozzle of the fire hose into my ribs, motioning to me to pass the hose up the line. Bright light from the fire hit our eyes the moment the fire chief watered down the door to the attic, trying to confine the fire on one side and giving us a chance to get upstairs. The primary objective was to keep the fire from spreading to the adjacent buildings on both sides. We split up in two groups to check out the house on either side. Plenty of buckets with water and sandboxes were placed in the attic, ready to be used if needed. On the west side, where I slipped in past the major fire, no new fire had developed except for a few smoldering pieces of wood scattered on the floor of the attic that flew over when the next door beams burned down and collapsed. It was easy to put them out of action with water. Back on the east side, the fire seemed to be more progressive. An extra bucket brigade was needed to come up the staircase next door to reach the fire from the other side.

Come nine o'clock in the morning, the fire was finally put out or under control. Many places in Tegel were not so lucky, and nobody knew yet how many people were dead or homeless in Berlin. This particular day was my baptism under fire, and overnight I grew up to be a man. Needless to say that my mother was worried about me being out all night long. She wanted to know what I was up to. After a second cup of *Muckefuck* (that was what they called *Ersatskaffee* in Berlin, a form of substitute for real coffee beans brewed mainly from roasted barley), I told her everything and ended the conversation with what I have not mentioned yet. My mother did not exactly recognize the corner I was talking about, but when I said, "Schönborn Candy Store," she interrupted me, saying, "Oh, you mean the chocolate factory."

"Exactly, and I almost came home with a box of chocolates for you. Before we left the building and after we extingished the fire on the way down, the manager of Schönborn was waiting for us in front of the store. He and some employees were busy trying to nail some boards and plywood across the broken store windows, which had been blown out by the bomb explosion, to keep looters out of the unprotected store. As soon as the air-raid warden and we, the Hitler Youth, came down the stairs, he dropped the hammer, shook our hands, and assured us over and over again how grateful he was that we saved the corner building. 'Here,' he said, 'take home a big box of chocolates, each of you, as a token of my appreciation.' My eyes got bigger looking at those fancy boxes gift-wrapped in golden paper, but that was only how close I got to taking possession of one of those marvels. The warden stepped between us and the friendly storekeeper and vigorously objected to the idea of anybody taking any merchandise out of the store. The proprietor got upset and told the warden that he had no right to intervene. 'Yes,' said the warden, 'I have the right and the obligation to protect these boys. If on the way home the SS should catch them, they will take them for looters and hang them on the nearest tree without asking any questions. I have seen it before what the SS bastards are capable of doing, and I don't want the kids to take any chances.' Needless to say that the prospect to dangle from a rope scared the living daylight out of me. Well, now you know how we earned the chocolates and why we could not bring them home."

My mother just smiled and assured me that surviving the fire was more important than all the candies in the world. Never before in history had civilians been attacked, bombarded, and killed from the air as in WW II. I had one week left before I had to go back to school. Trying to have my mother go and live with Erna and Ingeborg in Kremmen was of no avail. Before I left, I visited Gisela one more time, and on the second of September, I reported back to school at the LBA in Brandenburg. Nothing had changed there, and the sleepy little town at the river Havel showed no signs of being involved in the war. The fact that I was able to go home every weekend, to see my mother, made our lives somewhat easier. The month of October and almost the month of November went by relatively uneventfully for us. However, every day one city or another in West Germany suffered mass destruction and heavy casualties. The favored targets of the RAF were the more densely populated areas of the Ruhr and the Rhine Valley; they were also the most industrial location of all Germany.

Berlin was free of air raids temporarily. Then the British and American air forces were starting a new intensive mass bombardment that lasted till the end of the war. Air raids were going on practically twenty-four hours a day. The British bombers would attack at nights, and in the daytime the Americans were unloading their deadly cargo with more precision. By the end of 1943, ruins were piling up from one end of Germany to the other, the effect of night raids by RAF Bomber Command and day raids by the American Eighth Air Force, joined by the Fifteenth Air Force from October 9 from their air base at Foggia, hastily brought back into action after its capture by the British Eighth Army on September 27. These round-the-clock attacks were the result of a plan adapted at Casablanca late in January 1943 at a meeting of the British and American combined chiefs of staff committee. A list of proposed objectives was drawn up, giving priority to the destruction of the German aircraft industry, transportation, oil plants, and other war industry. However, this order did not reflect the realities of strategic bombing. In fact, they agreed with the directives specified in the general objective of the strategic air offensive, which was the destruction of the German industrial system and the undermining of the German home morale. After the complete failure of a series of American bombing raids on selected German targets, followed by a similar British lack of success, it became clear to the enemy that bombing techniques would need drastic improvement or, at least, that less demanding targets should be selected. This made Germany's cities subject to even greater ordeals as enemy bombing raids grew in ferocity, and with the arrival of the American Eighth Air Force in Europe, the Allied bombing offensive would go from strength to strength. The Allied task was divided round the clock equally between the British and the Americans, the former taking off at nightfall and the latter by day, each sticking to his task with ruthless obstinacy and without complaining of his losses. From January 1 to December 31, 1943, in spite of the loss during the year of 1,261 four-engined planes and most of their crews, the growing strength of the Eighth Air Force grew from 5 B-17 Flying Fortresses in January to 5,618 planes in December. The American crews operating over Germany preferred the Boeing B-17 over the B-24 Liberator. Flying Fortress, of which over 12,000 were finally made, had a range of two thousand miles and an all-round firepower of eleven machine guns, which the Americans believed was all the protection they needed.

This optimism was proved false by experience. For example, on August 17, 1943, the Eighth Air Force lost 60 out of 376 Flying Fortresses on raids on the Schweinfurt ball-bearing factory and the Messerschmitt assembly plant at Regensburg.

On October 14, a new attack on the first of these objectives cost another 60 planes out of 291 that had taken off, and altogether the loss of aircraft on these raids over the month was running at the intolerably high level of 10 percent. Under these conditions, it could be imagined that questions by airmen were raised as to whether or not the advocated methods were failing. It was relatively easy to replace the planes; it was not the same thing for the crews, and after the second attack on Schweinfurt, some loss of morale was noticeable among their ranks. By the autumn of 1943, our Luftwaffe had won a major victory over the Eighth Air Force. On deep-penetration raids the German day fighters were shooting the U.S. Air Force out of the sky. It was during the period leading up to the bombing run that the Luftwaffe struck hardest. The German fighter pilots had discovered the American practice of formation bombing by order of the bombardier in the lead plane. Thus the lead groups in large formations suffered mercilessly from fighter attacks, as was the case on the "second" Schweinfurt raid where the lead formation was virtually wiped out. A bigger disaster for the Americans was the notorious raid against the Ploesti oil refineries in Romania; the casualty rate was nearly a third of all planes involved. Deep-penetration raids turned out to be costly for the enemy, and the Eighth Air Force changed their priority of targets and joined the British offensive. Bomber Command continued its area bombing against Germany's cities during 1943. Improved equipment was now making possible greatly improved standards of navigational and bombing accuracy. The RAF's night offensive was based on taking off at dusk, and the device for guiding bombers known as *G* then, after March 5, 1943, the Oboe blind-bombing targeting system device, gave the bombers their position at all times and then enabled them to locate their targets with considerable accuracy. The objective was also indicated by Pathfinders using colored flares. As soon as they came into service, they were fitted with the new H2S radar, which presented an image of the below rather like a fluorescent map. Carpet bombing at night was a very popular tactic of the RAF Pathfinder planes flying in front of the bomber formation would stake out four corners and drop a flare. Those bright white markers would hang in the sky for about up to ten minutes, and seen from the ground, they looked like burning Christmas trees. Should you be inside of those four corners, you better find yourself a hole in the ground in a hurry. Minutes later, the field between the Christmas trees would be saturated with bombs. Not only was radar used by the Allies for target identification, it was also used in jamming the German radar.

From July 1943 the British used a device called Window. This consisted of thousands and thousands of strips of metallic paper that confused the echoes of the German Würzburg apparatus for directing German fighters. For evident reasons, on their day raids, the Americans rarely sent in more than 200 planes on the same objective. By night, the British attacked the towns of Germany with three and sometimes five times as many and made the raids as brief as possible so as to saturate the active and the passive defense particularly the latter, which, within two hours after the raids had begun, was faced with hundreds of fires concealing delayed-action bombs. The theory was simple: the leading planes would drop high explosive with the intention of causing structural damage and keeping the firefighting teams underground. Incendiaries would follow, setting light to the buildings, creating fires of sufficient intensity to develop into an all-consuming firestorm. Such a case was the devastation of the city of Hamburg. In the last week of July 1943, Hamburg and its port were reduced to ruins by the concerted efforts of Bomber Command and the Eighth Air Force, a combined operation unique of its kind. The operation was called Gomorrah and started on the evening of July 24 with an enormous release of Window. On the following morning, 235 Flying Fortresses took over from the RAF and on the twenty-sixth started their attacks again, concentrating their efforts on the shipyards and port installations. During the night of the twenty-seventh to twenty-eighth, the British sent up 722 four-engined bombers against Hamburg and forty-eight hours later another 699. As weather conditions had deteriorated, only 340 reached their objective during the nights of August 2 to 3.

During these six attacks, nearly 3,000 British and American planes dropped nine thousand tons of bombs. The results, half the city was devoured by flames that ravaged 277,330 dwellings. Civilian victims totaled some 43,000 men, women, and children. All the British paid for their barbarism was 89 bombers shot down by German fighters and antiaircraft. The losses were not as light at the British offensive against the industrial complex of the Ruhr. From March 1 to July 1, 1943, when 18,506 night sorties were made, RAF paid for it with 872 four-engined bombers and a total of 5,600 crew members. A similar fate to that of Hamburg came over Berlin in the last days of November. In comparison to Hamburg and other cities in West Germany, Berlin was relatively safe as it was up till now considered a target of deep penetration. But in the end of 1943, increasing numbers of long-range P-51 Mustang fighters enabled the U.S. Air Force to renew its deep-penetration bombing and decimate the German fighter force. For its day operations over Germany, which consisted of harassment or diversionary raids, the RAF used principally the de Havilland Mosquito. Constructed almost entirely of wood, it weighed nine tons on takeoff, and its two motors delivered 2,500 hp, giving it a top speed of 400 mph, thus putting it virtually out of reach of any Messerschmitt or Focke-Wulf fighter. The Mosquitos took part in one thousand raids in 1943, attacking forty German towns, including Berlin, twenty-seven times. What started as just another nuisance attack in the morning hours of November 18, 1943, by some Mosquitos dumping pamphlets over Berlin turned out to be the biggest single air raid that lasted till November 26. In the first nine days of the beginning of mass bombardment over Berlin, 1,486 British and American airplanes killed 4,941 people, then injured another 10,054 and left half a million homeless.

Tragedy in the Family

The school in Brandenburg went on its normal pace from Monday to Friday, without interruption; but come Friday, everybody built up a certain tension, eager to go home. Morning of the twenty-third of November was not any different except that our breakfast was interrupted by the sudden appearance of the principal. It was obvious that something was wrong. Normally, any academic message would be disclosed after breakfast and before we were on the way to our classrooms. Today the news was rather bad as he announced that in the night from the twenty-second to the twenty-third of November, Berlin had been severely attacked by a large Allied bomber force. He said, "In view of the situation and since most of the students were from the Greater Berlin area, there would be no classes today, and I want you to go home and look after your family now. See you all Monday. If for some reason you cannot make it, call in and give your report to the school operator."

After the initial shock, we rushed to the dormitory to pack a few things for the weekend, and off we went to the train station. The ride from Brandenburg to Potsdam was less than an hour, and in another hour we would be in Berlin. As we got closer to Berlin, the sky was getting darker, and I became more nervous. I was worried about my mother, not knowing if she was all right. At Bahnhof Zoo there was an unusual heavy traffic; people were milling with kids and luggage in all direction. I pushed my way through the crowd, trying to get to the S-Bahnhof to catch a train to Tegel. A sign on the wall informed me that the railroad had suffered some damage and that the line in that direction was out of order. I had only one option left, take the train to Oranienburg, get off at the Wittenau station, and walk from there to Tegel. Bernau and Oranienburg were the only two destinations going north that were still in operation. This was the usual route that I took every weekend, but I had never before seen so many people trying to get out of Berlin. As the Oranienburg train pulled in, it was already packed with refugees. Just before the train left the station, I was able to open one door and squeeze myself in, with not one inch to spare as the doors of the train automatically closed. Every time the train approached a station, people were screaming, "I have to get off here, let me get out!" But nothing was moving; people were packed like sardines without the oil.

Luckily in Wittenau, the ramp was on the same side next to the door where I was standing, making it easy for me to get out. What a relief, the freedom from stress and being capable of breathing fresh air again. It was now 3:00 PM, and I was estimating that I should be in Tegel in three to four hours, provided that there would not be another air raid. I was also trying not to deviate too much from the major roads as it got dark early, and it was easy to get lost in the blackout. There were two things that helped me find my way home. A full moon let me see what was ahead of me, and I was meeting some people on the streets who were going my way. As it got darker, some fires from the previous night's air raids were still burning out of control. At the end of my journey, I was more familiar with the neighborhood, and I was beginning to see that Tegel got hit pretty badly. British bombers had lanced five-hundred-pound and eight-hundred-pound bombs into densely populated apartment houses (blockbusters), tearing huge holes and starting blazing fires. In most instances, the local firefighting teams were unable to contain the spreading flames. I could not believe my eyes; some of the bombs had passed clean through the roofs and landed in the basement unexploded, making it impossible for firefighters and rescue teams to do their jobs without risking their own lives.

As I could see, our house was still standing, but because of those time bombs all around it, the whole block had been evacuated. This I did not know when I walked into our apartment, nobody had seen me in the darkness going in. My mother was not home, but a letter from her on the kitchen table told me the whole story. She had left the place to stay with my grandmother and was asking me to follow her. She also reminded me to bring a few things when I came. It was getting late now, and I was hungry and dog tired. I had not walked that much in a long time. Where could I go in the middle of the night? A few bombs that could explode anytime were not going to scare me, so I decided to stay overnight and catch up on my sleep. At 2:00 AM, I heard the siren going off, but I paid no attention and slept through the whole air raid. The next morning, I found out that nothing happened to Tegel, and the primary target of the RAF was the Hansa Viertel, a residential area of diplomats and the upper class. I also noticed how hungry I was, but there was not a stick of food in the house. It was my good fortune to know where my mother kept her food stamps, and auspiciously some stamps were still left. As I got to the grocery store, there was already a long line of people trying to get into the store. I had no choice but to get in line and wait for my turn to get inside. Luckily, I got a loaf of rye bread sprinkled with "sawdust," a pound of cottage cheese, one half pound of blood sausage, and a jar of sauerkraut. After I got home, I found some potatoes in the basement and some schmalz in the pantry. Altogether it was enough to survive another day or two. In comparison to what the people in Berlin had to live on, I could only say that the meals we received at the school in Brandenburg were fit for a king. Slowly all the neighbors came back to their apartments; the warning had been called off since all the unexploded bombs had been disarmed. Also, I went to the train station and got the information that the connection from Tegel to Berlin's west end had been restored. One more night for me to stay in the apartment, and tomorrow I would catch the first train out of Tegel to go and see my mother.

According to schedule, I should arrive Sunday morning around 11:00 AM at my grandparents' house in Tempelhof. During the train ride, a daytime air raid interrupted my journey. The train made it just to Stettiner Bahnhof, and as soon as the train stopped, all the passengers rushed to the shelter next to the train station. By no means was it a bomb-proof shelter, but rather a hastily constructed dugout to protect the travelers from flying fragmentations of bombs and artillery. This time it was the U.S. American Air Force that was participating in the destruction of Berlin. Just before the doors of the bunker were closed, I could take another look at the sky and counted more or less fifty B-17 Flying Fortress. The American Air Command decreed a changeover to area bombing by mass bomber formations. The areas chosen were not particularly large, but they were hard to miss. The first chosen were the train installations and all the principal airfields to destroy German fighter planes on the ground before they had a chance to attack the Allied bombers. For ten days, practically the entire air fleet was engaged in attacking these and other targets in Berlin. The new tactics worked well. Enormous damage was inflicted, yet the cost to the Luftwaffe was negligible. Most of the remaining fighter planes were forced to evacuate Berlin. Factory work was brought to a virtual halt; even in the underground workshops, work was continually interrupted by power breakdowns and light failures. The airfields were kept barely functional by civil labor and the local troops, but in any case, the planes that used them were being slowly consumed by the battle above.

During the last four nights of November, the British and American bombers shifted their attention to secondary targets—camps, barracks, ammunition depots, and roads. Antiaircraft positions were subject to almost continuous attack particularly those in the eastern corner of the city. It seemed to the population of Berlin that the sky was rarely clear of the enemy for more than ten minutes. The scale of the air assault and the losses involved, naturally created enormous difficulties for the civilians and the political and military leaderships. None of the losses could be replaced. By this time the situation in Berlin was serious and was recognized as such by the Führer. The drain of manpower at the Russian front was also so severe that the military leadership decided to transfer all Flak and regular gun crews from Germany to Russia. As replacements, Adolf Hitler decreed to draft all members of the Hitler Youth from the age of fourteen and up to serve on the Heimat front and at the age of fifteen and up as helpers at the Luftwaffe.

Being locked up for hours in an underground air-raid shelter was an experience of its own, a feeling of claustrophobia, anxiety of the unknown, and the fear of being buried alive. The moment the first bombs exploded above and the shelter started to shake while dust and debris were raining down from the ceiling, you have all the ingredients for big-scale panic and heart attacks. Women and children were screaming, scratching on the door, trying to get out; others were praying out loud for God to help them. The oxygen in the narrow room was slowly fading away, and the air became more and more saturated with the stench of puke, urine, and all kinds of other strong, offensive body odors. I was ready to faint, but unfortunately, no such relief came over me. I had to take it all in till finally, after two and a half hours, the air raid was over and somebody from the outside pulled the door open and let us out. As soon as the Allied bomber formations had left, it was clear to me that they had doomed a large part of downtown Berlin. The B-17s were dropping their bombs from high in the sky in a hurry but with little accuracy on the burning city below. The daytime bombers arrived and found the defenses hard to penetrate. Many of them without fighter escort were piercing through the German Flak, and fighters were eliminated before they had a chance to unleash their deadly cargo. The British pilots found themselves plowing through the same dense Flak as had greeted their American comrades. The attackers did not escape unscathed. Though the antiaircraft defenses had little reason to congratulate themselves, the German fighters, once airborne, took a heavy toll on the Allied planes.

To catch another train to go south was almost impossible. From Stettiner Bahnhof to Bahnhof Friedrich Strasse everything was disrupted. By foot I had to go on and fight my way through rubble and burning streets. A hot wind was blowing ashes all over the place making it difficult to breathe. I didn't know how long it took me, but finally I got to Bahnhof Friedrich Strasse. My eyes were burning, and it felt good to get out of the smoke-filled air. The bombs missed the station, and the railroad was open going south. Late in the afternoon, I was able to board a train, taking me closer to my destination. It was already dark when I got off the train at Priesterweg, the nearest station to my grandparents' house. The damage around here was minor compared to what I'd seen downtown. I had to go to a long dark tunnel in order to get to the other side of Tempelhof. Watching where I was going, I almost stepped on two people on the floor in front of me. Not knowing if they were dead or injured, I reached down, trying to examine them, and at that time, they became alive. The moment I came in contact with them, they both stopped making clamorous movements, trying to rearrange and cover certain parts of their bodies without being too hasty or showing any signs of embarrassment. Feeling guilty for interrupting, I apologized and left the scene. In my imaginary mind and vision, the act of making love was normally supposed to take place in the privacy of a bedroom and not being a spectacle and exhibition on a dirty floor in a tunnel. But then I asked myself, what was normal these days of hunger, death, and destruction? Time, place, or circumstance in which anything occurs are part of the evil of war, including the display of feeling or passion between two persons in public.

Without any more delays, I arrived fifteen minutes later at Domnauer Strasse 6, the condominium of my grandparents at the end of the Lindenhof, a gated community right at the heart of Tempelhof. Both my mother and my grandmother were happy to see me but could not hide their surprise that I showed up so late. Over some food, which I had missed for over a day, I told them all about of what was going on in Tegel and the air raid I got stuck in in the city. Suddenly I noticed that my grandfather was not around. My grandmother was telling me that he was at the fire station. Today was his turn of twenty-four-hour duty, but he would be home at midnight. Being exhausted, we all went to bed early. It must have been not later than 11 PM when the air-raid siren interrupted my first deep sleep. I thought I was dreaming, but my mother kept shaking me into reality. Not quite awake, I got up and dressed in a hurry. Minutes later my mother, grandmother, and I left the house all bundled up with a few small suitcases and stepped out in the cold night of November 25, 1943. Grandma knew the shortest way to the nearest bunker. She was leading us in a fast pace trying to get a place to sit in the bunker. Getting closer to the bunker, people were coming from all directions, heading for the big concrete monster. Air-raid wardens were posted by the entrance, making sure that people were going down the narrow steps in an orderly single file. Inside the hallway, I could already smell the stuffy and sulky air that was ill-ventilated. In no time, the bunker was filled with people, and the big iron door shut with a bang and would stay close till the end of the air raid. Luckily, the three of us got a seat at one of the wooden benches. It turned out to be the longest time I had ever been locked up in any kind of shelter; the air raid lasted over five hours. It was not difficult to assume that Berlin was the target of a major bombardment. In comparison to the rough dugout shelter at Stettiner Bahnhof, the Tempelhof bunker was a large solid, concrete steel-reinforced two-story building. Periodically the bunker would undergo some vibration, or the lights would go out at certain intervals, telling us that Tempehof was the victim of massive Allied bombing. Even my grandmother could sense what was going on above us. In her discernment, she was not concerned about her house, but she very much worried about her husband. She did not have to tell us, but her anxiety was written all over her face. Her mind was already outside the bunker, and strangely she whispered and insinuated that her husband got hurt. My mother put her arm around her and was trying to convince her that he had taken refuge in some basement or shelter waiting till this was all over and for us to come home. Oma just smiled with tears in her eyes, not really convinced of what my mother was trying to tell her. The thunder of the bombs was suddenly over; the last bomber formation made a 180-degree turn, flying back to England. The sirens went off again, indicating the end of the air raid. My grandmother first hesitated to get up being afraid of the uncertainty awaiting us on the outside. The moment the doors of the bunker swung open, she was in a hurry to get up the stairs, pushing other people impatiently to the side.

The first impression from in front of the bunker was of shock and horror. With extreme dread, accompanied by excessive fear and great disgust, we were stepping into a landscape of shuddering destruction. A picture of inferno, fire, smoke, and tormented earth. We got on the road soon to be stopped by folds of debris, hollows, holes in the road, burning houses, and the spasm of terror under the hailing of annihilation in the bellowing death of nearby explosions. People coming back from the direction were telling us that a firestorm made it impossible to go through to the other side of Tempelhof. At the communication center by the railroad bridge, we were told to take the open fields at the other side of the tunnel. From there on, my grandmother knew every foot of ground. At the other end of the field was the Mathias Cemetery. A shortcut through the cemetery would get us to the far end of the Lindenhof Siedlung. All three of us were tired, hungry, and totally exhausted; but my grandmother kept pushing us to come along faster. Burning houses stood out like torches against the night, or was it morning already? The sky reflected each fire, simulating it as daylight. On the right side of the cemetery near the fence was a small chapel. As we got closer, I saw a huge hole in the ground that looked like a dump to me but were actually several bomb craters. Fragments of exploded coffins and body parts were all over the place. The graveyard was a mass wreckage. Coffins and corpses lay strewn about. They had been killed once again. The mortuary was destroyed; crosses, tombstones, and statues of angels were torn up, littering the cemetery. In the branches of the trees, dead men, or parts of them, were hanging. A woman in a white dress was squatting in the fork of a tree; there was only half of her sitting up there, and the top half and the legs were missing. My stomach turned over, and I felt like vomiting. The two women ran to the chapel out of fear, seeking protection. Once inside, we saw that there were already several homeless people looking for shelter. Most of them were sitting up or stretching out on the benches to catch some sleep. The back door of the chapel opened, and a Red Cross nurse came in with a bucket of hot *Hagebutten* tea (*Rosa canina*). Everybody grabbed a paper cup with red herbal tea to wash down the dust of ashes from a dry throat. At the same time, an air-raid warden appeared, giving us firsthand information of the situation in Tempelhof. The bad news was that besides other neighborhoods, the *Siedlung* (settlement) of Lindenhof was completely wiped out; the fire was still so intense that nobody could get near it.

Grandma was getting restless; she wanted to get closer to Domnauer Strasse 6 to see for herself what was going on. On the south side of the cemetery, we saw more craters. Out of the craters in the early daylight rose the mists. It looked as though the holes were full of ghostly secrets. The white vapor crept painfully round before it ventured to steal away over the edge. By now, what appeared as a ghostly group was a column of Russian POW bundled in rags, each armed with a shovel. They were slowly getting off a truck, forming a single line stretching from crater to crater, digging connections for one big mass grave. A second group of prisoners was busy unloading another large truck of corpses, some of them burned beyond recognition. They put the dead in the first large crater. In my estimation, there were three layers, one on top of the other. The stench of the burned corpses was a strong offensive odor. It was not the sight of the horror scene that was afflicting me; it was the nausea that I was fighting. My mother was feeling the same way; she was pulling my grandmother by the arm to go back and find another way to get out of the cemetery. However, Grandma was determined to go through no matter what. It took two soldiers of the guard to stop her while she tried to convince them that her house was just across the fence. "What house?" he was asking her. "Don't you see over there, the whole block of Domnauer Strasse from the corner of Eyth Strasse to Reglin Strasse is either damaged or destroyed. Even if we let you go, you would not make it; the heat of the fire is so intense you could not even get near your house." Helplessly, like all the homeless people from Lindenhof, we stood around, not knowing what to do and where to go.

However, our party leaders were always well organized, bringing every chaos and emergency situation under control. At that time of confusion, a high-ranking party member with a bullhorn appeared at the scene, telling us that trucks were on the way to drive us to the nearest refugee shelter. Being exposed to the cold November air lowered our body temperature, and the time spent waiting for the trucks was making everybody uncomfortable. Finally the trucks arrived, and leaving this place of horror was a big relief. On the way to the shelter, the road passed a long block where the fire was getting very close to us. Ironically, the heat of the flames were blowing over the open trucks, doing us some good by warming up our frozen bodies and making the blood circulate again. Actually, our destination was the Friedrich Ebert Stadion, a nearby indoor sports arena at the Aboin Strasse. It had been converted to a shelter with plenty of bathrooms, and the restaurant was now serving as a kitchen for the refugees. The arena was heated and looked like one huge superbedroom. Big signs with all letters of the alphabet were hanging from the ceiling, indicating the area where every individual was assigned to. The floor of the place was covered with wall-to-wall army cots, and each cot had a pillow and a blanket. The staff was friendly; there were Red Cross nurses and many volunteers. At the counter, they were giving out sandwiches, hot tea, and potato soup. After I dropped the bundle of my grandmother's last and only belonging on her bed, we all fell in line to get some food. Putting some food in our stomachs made us feel better, but then neither of us could keep our eyes open any longer. We stretched out on our beddings and went to sleep immediately.

When I woke up the next day, it was 2:00 PM. My mother was sitting on her bed, but I could not see Oma. Asking my mother where she was, I found out that she was talking to somebody from her church. My grandparents for many years were both active members of the New Apostolic Church. As Oma went to get some information, she ran into one of the elders of her church who was a coordinator for the volunteers. His name was August, and he and his wife, Lisa, were good friends of my grandparents'. They had spent a lot of time together privately helping the church in building a new parish. August had helped many young people in the congregation to find a job. The first thing August wanted to know was where Erich was. She told him that she had not seen him since yesterday when he left for the firehouse. "Don't worry," he said. "When I get off here at three o'clock, we will go and look for him." August was the proud owner of a 1940 Volkswagen; and being a member of the party, he managed to keep his car from being confiscated for service in the armed forces. Getting in the car, he first drove us to the fire station, only to find out that Erich and Emil Lemke, a next-door neighbor and also a firefighter, had left last night during the air raid to go home. Hoping that both of them took cover in some air-raid shelter, we then tried to get through to the Lindenhof. At the entrance to the colony was a huge stone arch with an iron gate. Next to it was the clubhouse and a type of restaurant beer bar where we had celebrated many birthdays and other holidays. Today, as I could see, not much was left of it. There was no way that we could drive through the gate. We left the car in the parking lot and decided to walk down on Domnauer Strasse to get to my grandparents' house.

Every house we passed was either damaged or totally destroyed; some of them were still burning. Lindenhof was built in the early 1920 in art decor by the well-known master builder Cropius. His architectural style, which he called Jugendstil, made him famous in Berlin and Leipzig. Tears came to our eyes when we had to witness the grisly picture of terror—a landscape of ruins, rubble, ashes, and burning timber. The image I have in my mind of the beautiful and peaceful Lindenhof all of a sudden no longer existed; it blew my mind, which would not accept the horror picture of reality. In about three hundred feet, we shall reach the home of my grandparents, or what was left of it. Despite all the obstacles in the street, my grandmother was beginning desperately to run the last few hundred feet, impatient to get to her house in a hurry. I followed her, and then instinctively, she came to a stop and grew rigid. We were now facing Domnauer Strasse 6. No question; what we are looking at was the front elevation of my grandma's house, next to the main entry was still the old porcelain shield with the number 6 visible. This was the only wall standing without doors and windows, nothing behind it except the stone smokestack of what used to be the fireplace. For my grandmother, it seemed like her world came to an end. From her initial numbness and stiffness, she plunged into a state of uncontrolled hysteria. Before anybody could restrain her, she jumped over rubble and smoking debris into the interior of the floor, trying to get to the trapdoor that led to the cellar. She insisted to get to it, and on her knees with her bare hands, she tried to remove everything that was in her way. She was determined to find out if Erich was in the basement. We had no choice but to give her a hand to find the door. After we were able to remove the last black beam, we eventually, among the ashes, found the handle and pulled the door open. As it was getting dark, with little daylight left, August and I went down the stairs. We could hardly find our way around, looking carefully in every corner, making sure there was no human body, dead or alive, in the basement. While we were downstairs, my mother was holding dear old Granny, who kept screaming and crying from the top of her lungs, "Erich, wo bist Du, Erich, kannst Du mich hören?" (Erich, where are you, Ehrich, can you hear me?)

At the end, we came up again and convinced her that nobody was in the basement, but the poor soul kept crying for her husband. August and my mother took her by her arms and, more dragging than walking her, they got her back to the car. The only thing left to do was to get the hell out of there. Back at the Friedrich Ebert shelter, a friendly nurse came to our help and gave Grandma a sedative. August offered for us to go home with him and to stay in his house till we got things straightened out. My mother said, "Thank you, we are in good care here." He said good night and promised us that he would be back in the morning to give us a lift wherever we had to go. We all slept well, and the enemy was nice to us too; there where no more air raids since the nights of November 25 to 26.

    My mother had decided that she would take my grandmother home to Tegel. The two would need each other when I was back in school. My mother was just thinking out loud to me based on a statement made by August to her, to be prepared for some bad news. As promised, he came this morning with his wife, Lisa. Lisa took my grandma and told her to go together with them to a special warehouse where the government was giving out clothing and other items to people who had lost everything to the bombs. On the way over to Tempelhof, we would stop by at the police station to find out if they had information about Erich. As soon as the two women left, August asked us to go with him to the emergency mortuary that was set up for all the air-raid victims of Lindenhof and Tempelhof at the high school gymnasium. We parked the car in the backyard of the schoolhouse. Stacked up against its longer side was a high double wall of unpolished, brand-new yellow coffins. They still smelled of fir and pine and the forest. There were at least a hundred. As we entered the building, we noticed that first, the school looked like any other schoolhouse, but then a volunteer came up to us and took us to the office that was now the center for information and registration. The interview was short, friendly, and directed to find out who in our family was missing. We told them that the name of the missing person was Erich Cislicki, living at Domnauer Strasse 6, Lindenhof. A quick look in the register revealed that no deceased person by that name was identified among the dead. For one moment, my mother let out a sound of relief from pain and grief. However, she was interrupted by the registrar, who said that her stepfather might still be among the not-yet identified victims.

    An assistant was now leading the way for us to the section of the mortuary showing only unidentified dead bodies. The moment we entered the hall, August and I took my mother in the middle, holding her closely in case she would faint on us. To our amazement, she was very much composed as we quietly entered the house of horror. Corpses were spread out on the floor row after row. Most of them were disfigured, limbs missing or burned beyond recognition. All corpses had a tag tied to their big toes with a number on it. We could not see Erich among the bodies that still had a normal face. We further eliminated all the burned victims except for two corpses, number 63 and 64, who, due to some shrinkage from enormous heat, had the appearance of a dried-up mummy. Back at the office, we were asked to sit down and have a cup of tea, trying to relax us again. August gave them a complete report of our grisly inspection and the uncertainty about numbers 63 and 64. To make sure, the registrar said, "I will cross-check with our file of personal belongings we have obtained from the victims and the exact location of where the bodies have been found." As we finished our tea, he came back with two envelopes. Both corpses were found in the basement of Domnauer Strasse 14, a room under the house that was converted into a shelter. The house took a direct hit from a bomb and burned—no survivors. The envelope number 63 contained only a key chain with several house keys. Envelope number 64 had only one item, a pocketknife. My mother could, with absolute certainty, identify the keys as the house keys to Domnauer Strasse 6; the pocketknife, she had never seen before. As it turned out, the pocketknife belonged to Emil Lemke, the owner of the house at Domnauer Strasse 14. Both men, Erich and Emil, left the fire station and made it home to take cover together in the shelter of Domnauer Strasse 14, the house of Emil Lemke. At that time the carpet bombing destroyed the Lindenhof, among the victims were Erich and Emil, also known as numbers 63 and 64. The registrar was satisfied that he had some names for numbers 63 and 64 and removed these two cases from his list of unidentified bodies. My mother signed some release forms, and August told him that he would make the arrangements for somebody from the church to come and remove the remains of my grandfather. On the way out, my mother told the registrar how much we appreciated his help, and he handed her the house keys to a home that no longer existed. Without saying anything, August drove us back to the shelter, but one thing was on everybody's mind: how were we going to tell Grandma?

The burden of explanation was taken away from us; she was overtaken by an intuition, an instinctive knowledge, that her husband was no longer alive. When she came home, she started to ask all the questions, and a long conversation cleared the air. She had tears in her eyes and wanted to know if he was suffering before he died. August assured her that Erich died instantly the moment the bomb hit the house. Lisa explained to her that she did not have to worry about anything; everything would be taken care of by the church. The pastor would come in the morning and get her out of the shelter and take her home to his house. "After the funeral," my mother said, "you will come to Tegel and stay with me permanently." Next morning, when the pastor came over at breakfast, my grandma told him she wanted her husband cremated and buried at the Mathias Cemetery. He agreed and told her that her husband would have a full church service and a ceremony at the graveside. After breakfast, we kissed Oma good-bye, and she left with the pastor. Before my mother and I got out of the shelter, I was able to call the academy in Brandenburg to let them know what my dilemma was, and graciously, they granted me a leave of absence till after the funeral. The trip back to Tegel was more or less easy; some of the damage had already been repaired to make local traveling possible. When my mother and I arrived back in our apartment, we were physically and mentally exhausted, but it felt good to have a place to come home to. The recent experience kept us in a state of denial, but the nightmare did not want to go away, and a feeling of helplessness had a stupefying influence on my behavior. Two days later, I called August from the corner drugstore as agreed, and he told me that my grandfather's funeral service would be on December 1 at 1:00 PM at the chapel of the Mathias Cemetery.

Flowers were hard to get those days and at that time of the year, but my mother went to the Steinberg and brought home some fir tree branches to make a beautiful wreath. The chapel at the Mathias Cemetery was filled with members of the Tempelhof congregation of the New Apostolic Church. The front row was reserved for the family and close friends. Only six persons from the family were attending the solemn service—my grandmother, my grandfather's brother and his wife, my mother, her oldest sister, and me. The interior of the chapel was decorated with garlands, but it was otherwise simple in appearance. In the middle of the altar was the urn containing my grandfather's ashes flanked by two big candles. In front of the urn was the Holy Bible, and on the wall over the altar was a plain wooden cross. After the opening hymn, "Praise Ye the Lord, the Almighty," the minister gave the invocation. He described death merely as a transition; Erich would have a new life as he left this world to enter the kingdom of God. The eulogy was given by my grandfather's brother. The service was ended with the hymn "Amazing Grace." After we left the chapel, an icy wind would accompany us to the burial side. At the grave, the minister read short passages from the Bible and ended with a prayer; and then the ceremony was finally, quietly closed.

My grandmother was now living with us, and my mother was trying her best to make her as comfortable as possible. They went out together; she kept her busy in an effort to put the past behind. On the morning of December 4, I went back to school. My recent situation was not an isolated case. Many of my fellow students from Berlin had the same experience or worse. The director of the LBA-Brandenburg decided that all students from Berlin would be transferred to the LBA-Dahlem in Berlin. I had two more weeks to attend the school in Brandenburg, and after the holidays, I must report on January 2, 1944, at the new school in Dahlem. *Weihnachten* (Christmas) 1943 was a very sober event for all of us. A long neglected visit to my girlfriend Gisela was also connected with some bad news; her father was reported missing in action a month ago at the Russian front. The only good news we received at the end of the year was a letter from my father telling us that he was out of danger and had not seen any combat yet. Nobody knew how much longer he would be stationed in Hungary.

CHAPTER V

MORE DEATH AND STARVATION

To a New School and More Hardships

With the beginning of 1944, my life was taking a turn to a more active involvement in the war. Over were the days of good food, carefree sport, and uninterrupted learning. Forever gone were the pleasant years of protective surroundings of LBA, Neisse and Brandenburg. I enjoyed tremendously the orderly life at both boarding schools. On January 2, I started to attend the LBA-Dahlem at the southwest part of Berlin, a very luxurious neighborhood. As for all Adolf Hitler schools, the National Socialist Party was always acquiring the best accommodations for the elite students. To have a new LBA in Berlin, two large side-by-side villas were purchased and converted to one new facility with classrooms, dining room, and dormitory. Most of us students were still managing to go home at nights and live with our parents, even though we had to get up early in the morning and catch the first train to go to school. If the train was on time and the trip was uninterrupted by air raids, it took me about an hour to travel from Tegel to Dahlem. My home and the school were close to the train station. I tried to keep this arrangement up as long as possible; my mother and my grandmother somehow felt safer with me in the house at nights. My mother came to visit me one day at my new school, and she was amazed at how clean and comfortable the academy was. What surprised both of us was the coincidence that the small hospital where I was born was only two blocks away from the LBA-Dahlem. People who lived in this community were mainly movie stars, diplomats, or high-ranking government officials. For one reason or another, the Allies had not bombed this part of town whatsoever. My grandmother half-jokingly said, "Perhaps the American and British are preserving the finest corner of the city as their future residence when they come and occupy Berlin." The Berliners were always known for having a *Grosse Schnauze* (a big mouth); sometimes speaking about our own government would get someone in a lot of trouble. I set my grandmother straight, telling her that Dahlem had no military or industrial targets. I did not know what to say as she pointed out to me that her husband was not a soldier and Lindenhof had no factories. She was not given to complaining; she was a mild-mannered, good-natured little woman, but her spirit was breaking. Now she was suffering a second harder war, and at the end of her life, she had lost everything, including two husbands.

Food shortage and inner crisis somehow pushed people to the brink of their war endurance. The war in Russia dragged on, and the effect on supplies for the German home front was immediate. The civilian meat ration had been five hundred grams per person per week. That amount was equivalent to about two small steaks each week. After the defeat of Stalingrad in 1943, a reduction of meat rations was announced by the food ministry to four hundred grams a week. Now early in 1944, another cut became necessary, and only three hundred grams were given out for each person per week. The solution to the meat problem was now compromised by shifting more to the production of sausages, which were mainly 50 percent fat and organ by-products, plus fillers like milk powder. In restaurants, for a one-hundred-gram-meat coupon, you might only get an eighty-gram piece of meat. Fat was also in short supply; the eastern front was draining away scarce fats like butter and vegetable oil so quickly that the German people only got highly hydrogenated margarine. Most food items were becoming worse and less available. The most serious shortage was the potato crisis. Potatoes are to Germans what bread is to Americans and spaghetti to Italians.

To housewives who had watched all their other shopping items dwindle, the sudden disappearance of the potato, which they thought they could always rely on, was a severe shock. Other vegetables were also becoming more scarce to find and were considered as luxuries. Tomatoes were rationed too for a while; now they were disappearing altogether to canning factories, where they could be preserved and sent to the eastern front. Lesser amenities of life were following the same pattern, a decline of quality and decrease in quantity. Some other commodities were beginning to disappear altogether also. Cosmetics were hard to find; even soap and toothpaste were in short supply. Cigarettes suffered the most rapid decline in quality. They were made with dry inferior tobacco powder and sprayed with chemicals that were severely damaging to the lungs. The government gave away the fact that a severe shortage was at hand by suddenly publishing propaganda in the press against smoking. Even at school we were lectured that a Hitler Youth must not smoke as it was harmful to our health. Our bodies must be preserved to serve the Führer and *Vaterland*.

The sudden departure of beer, wine, and schnapps from hotels, taverns, and shops were by far the unkindest cut of all to alcohol-loving Germans.

The army needed every drop of alcohol for drinks on the front for "internal heating" and for medicaments. Beer had always been the most abundant beverage in Germany. But as in the case of everything else, more reductions were ordered, and soon all taverns would be closed. Wine, which had been second only to beer in consumption, disappeared from shops abruptly in November and December last year, just before the holidays. For us it was the bleakest and driest Christmas ever. I want to emphasize that all these scarcities and absolute disappearances came all at once, and the supply situation was changing with a swiftness that was staggering. Clothing offers one of the best examples of this rapid decline. The government was giving out allotted number of points as allowed by the annual ration card, but in reality the supply of clothing and shoes simply ceased to exist. My grandmother, who had lost everything, was walking in shoes held together by a packing cord and with the bottoms stuffed with cardboard. These were her only shoes, and she could not find a store anywhere in Berlin that would be able to sell her a new pair of shoes. The third traditional category of things essential to man after food and clothing was shelter; it too had become a serious crisis. In Berlin the problem was most severe due to the fact that a major part of the city was already destroyed and because of the paralysis of the building industry. It was extremely difficult to get a single room and impossible to get an apartment for rent anywhere in the entire city. Berlin had become, with appalling suddenness, a city at war; and circumstances left not a single feature complete. Weary and not in good health, Berliners were also low on resistance to infections. This winter 1943-44, there had been the most severe epidemic of colds and influenza in Berlin, and doctors predicted it would get worse. If something could not be done about food and clothing, illness and malnutrition might probably assume more dangerous proportions. People's faces were pale and unhealthy with red rings around their tired, lifeless eyes. From lack of food and vitamins, the average person suffered from fast-decaying teeth.

Bad transportation was also a factor for the breakdown of production and distribution. It was known that Berlin had one of the best municipal transport systems in the world. Constant air raids and lack of spare parts had crippled the network severely. Many buses and streetcar lines were going to be discontinued. Due to years of hard labor and poor maintenance, trains and buses stopped running. Parts and gasoline were in short supply, and most of the skilled mechanics were now in the army. Any train that could not be fixed, once it came to a dead stop, would be hauled off to the terminal, to be repaired after the war. The underground metro was still the most reliable transportation, but all the engineers and drivers were now being replaced by inexperienced women. The only thing these days that was not in short supply was money, and the reason for that was very simple: there were not very many things left to buy anymore. One weekend after school, my mother and I went downtown to do some shopping. To buy something useful, the best place had always been the KaDeWe department store. To our surprise, besides a few staple foodstuffs, Berlin's biggest shopping center looked like a big empty old barn. Any tangible goods or luxury item could only be purchased at the black market. My mother and my grandmother were sometimes in the mood for a real cup of coffee, but KaDeWe could not sell us one hundred grams of coffee, not even of the cheapest brand; but the saleslady was friendly enough to tell us that across the street from the store, at the Wittenberg Platz, was a black market going on. It was causing the government a serious headache, but the black market succeeded in stabilizing its activity due to the law of supply and demand. Rocketing prices had become painfully evident everywhere in Berlin. People were willing to pay any price. For a pound of roasted coffee beans, we paid eighty marks, and my mother was happy not to go home empty-handed. The economic situation inside Germany had become dismal; all the little things that made life pleasant and that were necessary to continue everyday life had practically disappeared or drastically deteriorated. Especially when it came to food, some items had fallen below the level of fitness for human consumption. The result was a low standard of general health condition of the public. The stress of the war and its hardships had also created a great burden on mental health. I could see it in their eyes that the very young and old people were desolate. Sitting night after night in an air-raid shelter and then going back to work in the morning dead tired could grind down the strongest character. I could hear more and more voices saying, "What is there to look forward to, what have we got to live for?"

Low standard of life and low morale were beginning to surface. Morale had slipped badly because the constant drain of energy was making people sickly and irate. Production was going down, and no Gestapo in all Germany could make an unhealthy and demoralized person work as efficiently as a healthy, high-spirited one. In the past, the record of the German people as producers had been, technically viewed, an outstanding one. The drop in production in the occupied countries was also taking a disastrous proportion more than in Germany, mostly pronounced by the exhaustion of their food supplies. Production, so I heard, had dropped as much as 50 percent in some industries in the occupied territories. There were now more cases of sabotage by communist workers, especially in Northern France. Malnutrition among the Russian prisoners inevitably reduced the efficiency of laborers. Between old and new Tegel, right behind the train station, was about a square mile of vacant field. The kids in the neighborhood used to go and shoot rabbits; now the vacant territory was occupied by the military. Because of its central proximity, the field was presently taken by a large antiaircraft, an 8.8 cm Flak Battery, and a Russian prison camp. All the barracks were side by side; the prisoners supplied the labor for the Luftwaffe installation and were used to haul ammunition during air raids. These prisoners were undernourished and running around in rags. Under the danger of being arrested and punished, I had seen women at nights going up to the fence and throwing bread over the barbed wire. It was surprising to me that despite the inevitable strain of war, smaller and insufficient number of meals, and being engaged in a life-and-death struggle in which absolutely everything was in the scales, the German people found it in their hearts to share a meager bread ration with a defenseless enemy. The same people were also able to cut your throat in a heartbeat. There were reports that British and American airmen, after they parachuted to the ground, had been beaten to a bloody pulp by civilians for destroying their homes and killing their loved ones. The urge to personalize hate by revenge is a quirk of human nature, for it is strong in the best of men. The decision of the RAF to increase regular air raids on Berlin in January of 1944 resulted in serious material damage and higher human casualties. Multiple raids night after night shocked civilians' morale more effectively. In the morning after long hours of raids, people were in a miserable mood from lack of sleep and nervous strain. Transportation was destroyed and traffic was jammed.

Berlin was in a state of chaos. Many days, on my way to Dahlem, I would arrive late at school and miss all the morning classes. It would be a big relief when, starting on the first of February, we would only be allowed to go home on weekends and sleep at the school's dormitory from Monday to Friday. But the order to stay after school also had another reason we would soon find out. In January, the British dropped 2,961 bomber loads of high explosives and phosphorous incendiaries. The five-hundred-pound and eight-hundred-pound bombs lanced into the roofs of downtown apartment houses, tearing huge holes and making it easy for the following incendiaries to start blazing fires. Some of the bombs had passed clean through all floors to explode in the basement of the building. These triggered off more explosions as the fires spread to the gas lines. Fuel lines ignited, sending rivulets of flames washing across the floor to spread the fire. The heat of multiple fires was so intense that the asphalt cover in the street would melt away like butter in a frying pan and start burning by its own ignition.

Last night was the severest bombing as of now. The British dropped a considerable number of fire bombs, and there were quite a few big fires. Hundred of incendiaries fell near the Pariser Platz, Brandenburger Tor, and the Hotel Adlon. The office of the minister of munitions between the Adlon and the embassy also was hit. Actually the British were trying to destroy the Potsdamer Bahnhof. They had bad luck and missed it altogether even though they took nearly a perfect run. Their first bombs hit the Reichstag and the rest fell in a direct line toward the Potsdamer station. The last bomb exploded about three hundred yards short of the Bahnhof. The two-hour alarm last night from the twenty-ninth to the thirtieth of January alone killed 1,131 people and injured another 1,775, bringing it to a total of 2,114 killed and 3,792 injured for the month of January. A great number of the victims were the boys of the Hitler Youth firefighting teams who were risking their lives and in most cases were unable to contain the spreading flames. Burned boys were lying screaming in agony amidst the charred corpses of their dead comrades. Collapsing buildings were killing them before they had a chance to get back to safety. Some groups of Hitler Youth were going out to look for survivors under the rubble when suddenly they got blown to bits by the explosion of a time bomb.

From the School Bench Into the Fire

In the month of February, the enemy was giving the people of Berlin a short break to recuperate from the everlasting air raids. Of course, everybody knew that this interruption was not intended for our benefit but rather, for the British to regroup and prepare for bigger attacks to come. Only on the fifteenth of this month the RAF attacked with 806 bombers the center and east part of Berlin, causing 169 people killed and 512 injured. Obviously something was in the making; the Allies must be in the process of changing their strategy. In the month of March, the RAF was temporarily disappearing from the skies over Berlin and taking shorter flights to targets and cities in West Germany. As their replacement, the U.S. Air Force was taking over the bombardment of Berlin. For the first time, enemy bombers were under the protection of long-range fighter escort minimizing casualties inflicted by German fighters. On our side again, not the military but the civilians paid with their lives for it. In bright daylight 2,697 U.S. B-27 and B-29 bombers attacked Berlin in the month of March and killed 312 people and injured 578; the property damage on the ground was horrendous. Germany was also desperately short of manpower. Our leaders told us that the finest, most honorable hour of the Hitler Youth was yet to come. It was payback time.

In Germany the Führer strengthened his grip on boys and girls, following the "get them young" strategy by making membership in the Hitler Youth compulsory in 1939. (This author was not quite ten years old when he joined.) For those whose physical and mental abilities were higher, he set up Adolf Hitler schools (LBA and Napola comes to my mind) to train this elite group for service in obeying and fighting for the state. Every German boy who belonged to the Hitler Youth organization, and that included 98 percent of all German boys, was eligible for candidature.

Hitler wanted a big elite, not a small one; for this reason, the Führer took good care of the German youth. Of all the elements of the population, certainly the youth (apparently) was benefiting the most and should be therefore the most loyal segment to their Führer. We had been well fed and received special rations of food and clothing not available for the average citizen. We received healthy vacations at the expense of the state, and our training and schooling had been physically and mentally good. Adolf Hitler schools were a good idea, so we were told. The LBA (loosely translated) Leaders Training Academies, and Napola, (National Political Academies), had given their students undeniably the highest curriculum of all academic institutions.

So we were convinced that we the LBA students had the responsibility to respond. Now the Führer was calling and counting on us to help Germany in its desperate time to fight and win the war. For some time now, the older boys of the Hitler Youth had already been engaged in wartime activities. They would be ordered up to labor camps in the eastern front to dig ditches and build defense lines for the retreating German army to hold off the Russian advance. The civil defense could not be effective without the help of the Hitler Youth as firefighters, dragging hose lines and forming bucket brigades. They were serving as air-raid wardens and dispatch riders, but most of all, the Hitler Youth had become famous for being Luftwaffenhelfers; that was why they called us the Flak crew generation. Since I had been in Dahlem, I noticed the change in education toward more political science and war-oriented topics. Lessons in history emphasized the glory of Greek and German heroes. Discipline and military drill were on the agenda. We didn't ask any questions, we only carried out orders. My generation was growing up in a Prussian military culture. In our world, the words "reason" and "think" did not exist.

The Hitler Youth could only obey and fight. The school was slowly preparing us to be transformed from boyhood into full-swing warriors, and our theater of operation would be Berlin. All young men at the academy were hoping that we see some action before the war was over. Our class of 1929 (born in) was now the oldest group, our ages between fourteen and fifteen, and the class of 1928 had already been inducted as firefighters. They would join the Luftwaffe as Flakhelfer soon, and we would be the new firefighters. We hoped that we would be as brave as they were and became heroes. What is a hero? A hero is just a symbol of what is good in all of us. We really don't know who we are and what we are till we are tested.

The average school day in Dahlem was getting supplemented with lectures given by high-ranking members of the NSDAP geared to solicit Hitler Youth volunteers for war duty. Frequently the academy was visited by army officers highly decorated for bravery, who were sent straight from the front to come and talk to us. What could be more inspiring to a boy of the Hitler Youth than a true combat story of a war hero? Last week came a guest speaker from the SS Division Hitler Youth telling us how brave our comrades were and urging us to join them.

Today was the twentieth of April; it was Adolf Hitler's birthday, and in honor of the Führer, we were assembled in the school auditorium. The celebration was highlighted by several NS Party dignitaries who in their speeches praised the Führer for saving Germany and reminding us of our obligation to obey him. At the end, everybody sang the national anthem, and we were dismissed to go back to our classrooms. Shortly thereafter, the door opened and in came the secretary of the Party—Gauleiter Martin Bormann. Immediately we all jumped up and snapped into attention. He raised his right arm and screamed, "Heil Hitler!" This was followed by another loud "Heil Hitler!" from all of us. Before we had a chance to sit down, he continued in a one-sentence bellow, sounding like the roar of a bull. He said, "Is anybody in this class not volunteering for war duty?" A few minutes of lasting silence was the answer to his question. The complete absence of any sound made us all, the entire class of 1929, instantly a close group of volunteers to fight in the war for Adolf Hitler. In order to get into the right spirit to fight, one must be, without reservation, completely convinced of a certain ideology and ready to die for it. In a term paper at the end of the semester, I expressed my feelings as to why and how the Hitler Youth embraced National Socialism as their purpose in life. Life was conceived as a struggle in which man is trying to get a really worthy place in modern society by fitting himself physically, morally, and intellectually, and have the necessary qualities for winning it.

In the eyes of capitalism, democracy may be an ideal form of government, but it did not show much interest for the welfare of the underprivileged individual. Being liberated from the Kaiser, the German people had high hopes for the success of the Weimar Republic to ease their burden of unemployment and starvation. Unfortunately the first German form of democracy was corrupt and anti-individualistic. The National Socialist Party was the only system of life that stressed the importance of the state and recognized the liberty of the individual. Under Adolf Hitler, the state was expressed in a living ethical entity only in so far as it was progressive. Inactivity could not be tolerated as it meant death. Not only did the state stand for governing authority conferring legal form and national pride on individual wills, but it was also power that made its will felt and respected beyond its own boundaries. National Socialism could be viewed not only as a lawgiver and a founder of institutions but also as an educator and a promoter of a higher standard of life. The Führer did not merely aim at remolding the forms of life but also its content and, for man, his character and his faith.

To achieve this purpose, he had a special interest to sponsor German boys and girls. We were the next leaders, and leadership enforced discipline and made use of authority, entering into the mind and ruling with undisputed sway. Therefore, the Hitler Youth had chosen the name of the Führer as its emblem—the symbol of unity, strength, and justice. We had taken an oath of loyalty. We must rush forward. The old regime was superseded; we must take its place. The right to the succession was ours; Hitler was calling us to enter the war, and we would lead the country to victory.

As air raids increased, the students of LBA-Dahlem were now fully incorporated in the Hitler Youth civil defense program. My class of 1929 was divided into two groups. The first group would move out at night for one week to stay till in morning to be attached to a command post in Steglitz. During this time, the second group remained at the academy as a ready reserve. Alternating on a weekly basis, each group would be active or standing by. Every other weekend, the reserve group was permitted to go home Friday night, to see the family, and be back Monday morning. I was part of the second group and stayed at school the first week the operation started. On April 28 at 8:00 PM, a dozen boys of my group jumped on a truck, and for the first time, we were going to see some action. Our destination was the command center in Steglitz. Somehow we expected to be taken to a fancy army place; instead, we were entering a primitive air-raid shelter in the backyard of an old schoolhouse. The classrooms of the school were emptied out and served as quarters for the several detachments on duty. Kitchen and bathrooms were on the first floor. Each room had several bunk beds, tables, and chairs; shelves on the wall were loaded with blankets, steel helmets, overalls, and army gas masks. An old air-raid warden was our troop leader, we called him Hindenburg. His age and stature reminded us of WW I Field Marshal Paul von Hindenburg. He was in charge of the compound outside the command bunker and the distribution of equipment. The first day on duty, each of us received a pair of overalls, a blanket, a gas mask, and a steel helmet. The helmets were Dutch army helmets looted by the German occupation forces. They were all one size and much too big for us. Luckily, if we wore our uniform cap underneath, we were able to see out. Hindenburg was easygoing; he wanted us to relax and be rested up to be ready for the next big air raid to come. We were lying on the bunk beds or sitting at the table having snacks and playing cards, no drills, exercises, or any of that nonsense. At the beginning of each shift, two of us were routinely ordered up to the command center as standby dispatch riders to bring messages to other units in case of a communication breakdown. Since I had my driver's license, I was on the list of selected candidates to hit the road with a motorcycle in an emergency situation.

Today was the day! The twenty-ninth of April 1944, no air raids the whole month, but surprisingly tonight, the U.S. Air Force decided to pick Berlin for a massive bombardment. Up till now, my group had not seen any action; as usual, we were leisurely hanging out at the compound listening to the radio when suddenly the shrill and piercing sound of the overhead siren made an end to our comfort. It was exactly 11:11 PM; we were all dropping whatever we were doing and getting ready to be shipped out. Heinz, the junior group leader, was tuning in to the UKW (ultra short wave) sender to get information about the enemy position. The anouncement was clear and repeated every two minutes. Major American bomber groups had left the area of Hannover and Brunswick and were now entering the outside of West Berlin. The distant but rapidly increasing noise of Flak fire left no doubt about the message. At precisely 12:08 AM, the siren went off again, letting everybody know that the air raid was over, but the suffering on the ground was just beginning. A few minutes later, Hindenburg was coming in, dressed up in full battle gear, telling us to get on the truck that was waiting for us outside the compound. Everybody was looking at him, and as the truck was pulling out, he described to us what went on during one of the shortest air raids over Berlin that only lasted fifty-seven minutes. Without any particular target, over eight hundred super Flying Fortresses had saturated with carpet bombing the area from Hallesches Tor all the way up north. The center of Berlin and all the downtown section of government buildings were damaged the most. Our orders were to go and join a rescue team that was operating near the Potsdamer Bahnhof.

From Steglitz the driver was taking the Haupt Strasse. As the Haupt Strasse became Potsdamer Strasse, we could see already red fire clouds in the sky, and bright lights were spreading in front of us almost to daylight. At the corner of Potsdamer Strasse and Lützow Strasse, we had reached our final destination, the Elisabeth Hospital. The hospital was severely damaged by several bombs. When we arrived, the rescue operation was already in full swing. One side of the hospital was destroyed; one wing was still burning, but the main section only suffered minor damage. The firefighting team was desperately trying to bring the fire under control. The heat was making it almost impossible to get near the flames. Hindenburg was explaining to Heinz that it was our job to go to the west wing and look in the ruins for survivors. We were forming a line, spreading out twenty feet apart and slowly approaching the west wing. As we got closer, I could see that one section of the building was only partly destroyed, and one corner was still standing, but ready to collapse anytime. The structure was sliced in half, exposing the interior from the ground to the highest floor. Beds, furniture, and an open staircase were visible from the outside. The picture reminded me of a dollhouse I had seen little girls playing with.

While the rest of the group was searching the basements under the rubble for survivors, Heinz was asking me if I wanted to go with him to check the still-standing section of the west wing. Heinz was the oldest in our group, a daredevil and fearless fellow. I felt kind of honored that he was asking me to go with him, and of course, I immediately agreed. Climbing on our hands and feet over a ruin obstructing the entrance of the staircase, we finally got to reach the inside of the building. Nothing was detected on the first floor, but the second floor was a house of horror. A long wall was lined up with hospital beds. Each bed was still occupied by a dead patient killed instantly by the lung-bursting explosion of the blockbuster bombs used by the U.S. Air Force.

In a hurry, we checked each corpse to make sure none of them was still alive. As we checked the last few bodies, I could not hold it any longer; I turned around and puked my guts out. "Come on," Heinz said. "There is no time for that, we have one more floor to check." It was almost impossible to reach the top floor, a five-foot section of the staircase landing was missing. The connecting part was hanging in the air, but Heinz was able to jump across. Now it was my turn to fly to the other side; for a moment I hesitated, but if he made it, so could I. In a successful leap, I also made it to the other side. On the top, floor beams and debris were blocking our way. Part of the roof up here was missing; at the far corner the roof had collapsed, covering the floor like a wooden tent. Looking around, we had not seen one body yet. Ready to descend to safety, I almost stepped on a naked arm sticking out under the caved-in roof. Automatically I reached down, trying to detect a pulse on the wrist. The moment I pressed on the skin, the arm started to move, and its hand firmly clinched my fingers. Shocked by the incident, we now knew that this arm belonged to a living person pinned down under the roof. Immediately it came to our mind, how could we get this person out from underneath? Lifting the roof was impossible; it was too heavy, and we didn't have a crane or any other equipment. There was only one solution: we had to remove all the tile shingles one by one and create a hole big enough to go down from the top to rescue the person if possible. This was accomplished in a relatively short time. I was holding the flashlight, and Heinz was squeezing himself through the narrow opening of the rafters. To our astonishment, there was a young girl, a Red Cross volunteer, semiconscious, unable to move, but still alive. Not knowing if she suffered any internal injuries, we had no choice but to get her out of the trap if we wanted to save her and before the building came down and killed all of us. I went out of the hole again and pushed her arm back under the roof. Luckily, the girl's body was not clamped in by the weight of the roof. Heinz was able to move her forward, lifting up her torso, trying to push her out between the rafters. As soon as her head was sticking out, I was taking a strong hold under the arms, pulling her body from the top to the outside. In a joint effort, pushing and pulling, we were able to get her out. At a quick glance at her body, we saw that there was no evidence of any external injuries. Retreating down the stairs, the girl opened her eyes, trying to say something we didn't understand; obviously she must be in pain. By the part of the broken stairway, we were happy to see two comrades waiting for us. Together we managed to bridge the gap with some strong and long lumber to carry the girl down the stairs. The extra help made it easier to get us out of harm's way. Hindenburg dispatched them looking for us; he was very much concerned to get us out before disaster struck. Minutes after we cleared the rubble, the rest of the west wing came tumbling down. An ambulance transported the girl to the nearest hospital. For the rest of us, we were calling it a day, or a night, I should say.

The truck was taking us back to our quarters, and Hindenburg was insisting that we catch a good sleep before we returned to Dahlem. At noon we got out of the sack; a shower and a hot meal made us feel better in no time. In the evening the next group arrived, and we were taking the same truck back to Dahlem. Next morning we listened to the grisly report on the radio. In the one-hour air raid of April 29 over Berlin, 369 people were killed and 538 injured. All of the victims were civilian casualties, mostly women and children. On May 1, our group went home for a short visit; all of us were concerned as to how our families were doing. I was relieved when I saw my mother and my grandmother, and I was very happy that they survived the terrible air raid. It was very comforting to me knowing that the two women lived together and supported each other. Whenever possible on my visits, I brought them some wrapped bakery goods I'd saved in my locker. Thank God, we were getting plenty of hot meals, and I could do without sweets. School hours were still the same, but homework consisted only of a few reading assignments. Another allotment had been made for the group not on active duty to leave the academy after school, but strict curfew at ten in the evening was observed. That meant practically, for all of us, not enough time to go home, but there was a chance to get away for a few hours to do some shopping or whatever.

In my case, it gave me the opportunity to visit Gisela and her mother since Wilmersdorf was very close to Dahlem. Surprised by my unannounced visits, they were happy to see me. Mother and daughter were doing fine; we had a lot to talk about the first day we saw each other again. I did promise to see them soon whenever I had the time.

On my next visit, Gisela introduced me to some teenagers in her neighborhood. It was a small friendly group, and Gisela and I were making it a habit to hang out with them. They usually got together on Wednesday and Saturday nights, but I could only make it every other Wednesday. Our get-together took place in an underground air-raid shelter that was not occupied, unless there was an air raid. One of the boys' father was the air-raid warden in charge, and he had an extra key. The shelter was clean as it was not for the general public and looked more like a large living room. Anyway, the gang called it the Clubhouse. An old gramophone and a radio contributed to our entertainment. Singing and dancing was our biggest amusement. Sometimes we smoked or get high on torpedo juice, a mixture of root beer and vodka. I know, we were not allowed to smoke, drink dance, and even listen to the English radio, but who cared for tomorrow we might all be dead? Germany's propaganda minister, Dr. Goebbels declared that it was the duty of all Germans not to listen to foreign radio stations. Those who did so would be mercilessly punished. In reality the effect of the new wave of propaganda and threats against listening to foreign radio was making those who had been afraid so curious that it converted them into regular listeners of enemy stations.

 The people knew that it was almost impossible to catch a person actually listening to foreign stations. Should somebody ring the doorbell, all you had to do was switch the dial on your radio to another station. Almost all those who had been arrested were apprehended not while listening but while telling others, in public places, what they heard. I had to admit that I was one of the offenders, not because I was interested in enemy propaganda, but simply because us youngsters liked to listen to the music of Glen Miller. We could not receive jazz or any American swing music on the Deutschland sender; that was an absolute no-no. We had no choice but to turn to BBC, either very low so the neighbors could not hear us or, if we could find a battery-operated radio, full blast in the woods.

 The week of leisure went by, and my group was back on active duty on May 8. As we got off the truck in Steglitz, Hindenburg was waiting for us with the duty roster in his hands. He was pointing at Oscar and me, telling us that we were selected this week to stand by in the command center. We took our gear and went over to the bunker to report for duty to the CO. The room was filled with telephones, radios, and wireless broadcasting equipment. Maps and charts were all over the place; on the walls and on the table in the middle of the room was a map of Greater Berlin divided into map squares. A small anteroom served as our temporary quarter. At 10:00 PM, we received a radio message that an American bomber formation of about six hundred B-29 was heading for Berlin. Ten minutes later, the German radio sender announced that they would stop broadcasting. The moment the Reich's sender got off the air, we had only one way of communication left, and that was by wireless broadcasting. Drahtfunk (cable radio) communicated over the telephone network. An enemy plane could not receive the broadcasting, nor could the navigator in an aircraft use the sender as a direction finder. At 10:34 PM, Berlin was receiving a full air-raid warning.

Minutes later, Flak batteries from all over Berlin were putting a curtain of exploding shells in front of the bomber formation.

No specific targets were located, another air raid of carpet bombing. Specific targets were only selected in daylight raids when better visibility offered more accuracy. Since the German fighters were no match for the American P-37 Thunderbolts and the P-51 Mustang's escort fighters, the German Ministry of Air Defense made Berlin a city with a high concentration of Flak batteries. The British and the Americans lost heavily and were able to claim only a limited success in getting Berlin out of action. The air raids over Berlin in the month of May were now an uninterrupted day-and-night affair. In the night alone, from May 7 to 8, one thousand U.S. bombers killed 317 people and injured 525 more. The inner city, from the Tiergarten up to Unter den Linden, carried the brunt of the attack. Steglitz was not far from downtown, and our group was one of the first commando units to arrive. Oscar and I remained at the command center till the air raid was over. Shortly after midnight, both of us received the order to take the motorcycles and report to the Steglitz police station. Oscar and I took our helmets and an overcoat, stepped out in the night, and got each a 250 cc NSU street bike started. A full moon gave us good visibility on the road we were taking. Oscar knew the way to the police station, which was located right on the end of the Haupt Strasse in Steglitz. When we arrived at the station, two fireworkers were waiting for us. In a quick briefing, we were instructed to drive them to a location they knew in order to defuse two one-thousand-pound time bombs. Both men were experts in their field and operated as carefully as a brain surgeon. Time was of the essence, and our destination was Stadtmitte. If we didn't encounter too many obstacles, we should be there in about twenty minutes. Some streets might be obstructed with rubble and not accessible by car. Those two time bombs were deeply lodged in an apartment house about two hundred feet apart. A rescue team of Hitler Youth had already completed with the evacuation of the whole city block. At the same time, a group of Russian prisoners was busy exposing both bombs to make them accessible for the fireworkers. Most time bombs had a fuse delay of four, eight, or twelve hours; the fireworkers explained to us. Two hours were almost gone, so with good luck, the two time bombs might not explode for the next two hours. We were making a shortcut driving through the Tiergarten to reach Unter den Linden, a broad way with less rubble on the street. At Friedrich Strasse a policeman stopped us; apparently he must be already waiting for us. The two fireworkers instructed us to wait and take cover while they followed the policeman. Pulling the motorcycles off the road, it felt good to stretch out on the ground. Looking to the north, we could see red clouds high in the sky; that was in the direction of Wedding, Reinickendorf, or even

Tegel. For a moment a painful image went through my mind, but then I told myself that nothing happened to my mother and my grandmother. Oscar and I must have fallen asleep because at about 3:00 AM, the two fireworkers came back, tired but smiling, and told us that everything was taken care of and it was time for us to go home. We were driving back the same way but much more relaxed. Back at the command stand, a hot cup of chocolate was waiting for us. The rest of the company had also returned. There would be no school in the morning; instead, everybody in Dahlem would get some well-deserved shut-eye.

Next day, Hindenburg asked Oscar and me how we made out last night. "Mission accomplished, but the carburetors on both bikes are sluggish, we don't get enough speed. As a matter of fact, it may be a good idea to check the rest of the motorcycles," Oscar told Hindenburg. "It would be embarrassing if somebody in an emergency gets stuck with a bike that quits on him."

Since Hindenburg was also in charge of the motor pool, he suddenly realized that it was his responsibility to make sure every vehicle was functioning. His argument was that he had only one mechanic who had hardly enough time to take care of the cars and trucks. "We had nothing but old equipment at our disposal. Everything manufactured now goes straight to the Russian front."

"Well, maybe we can help out," Oscar replied. "Suppose we take one bike at a time to school with us and work on them in our spare time?"

"Who will do that?" Hindenburg wanted to know.

"I can do that," said Oscar. "Remember, I am the son of an auto mechanic; my dear father has a workshop, and he even knows where to get spare parts."

Hindenburg agreed under one condition that there be no compensation or charges for any parts as he had no funds available. "Of course not, this is strictly volunteer work, our contribution to help win the war." At the last week of active duty in May, Oscar and I took the first motorcycle back to Dahlem. A good cleaning, an oil change, a new sparkplug, and the bike was as good as new.

"What is in it for us?" I asked Oscar.

"Very simple," he said. "Every other week, when we are off duty, we routinely fix another bike and take it for a test drive. At the same time, we are going to town, do our shopping, or catch a movie. I also understand that the days by the lake are very nice this time of the year."

"Oscar, you are a genius," I exclaimed. "I am sure the Führer wants us to have some leisure time in order to keep on fighting on the home front." We were now independent, no more buses or streetcars that were not always on time or did not show up at all. Tomorrow was Wednesday, and I was inviting Oscar to come with me to visit the club. I was telling him about our private speakeasy, the drinking, singing, and dancing to jazz music.

"That's just what I am looking for," he said. "Exactly what I need for one day to escape the rotten reality of war." After tomorrow, we would be back again in the Bucket Brigade or on our hands and knees sifting through rubble and ashes removing corpses or trying to rescue injured or alive people from burning houses.

It was a surprise for Gisela to see us come to visit her on a motorcycle. As always, the welcome mat was out, and her mother served us some cool lemonade; she loved to have company. We were talking about everything and the latest developments and trying to forget about the war. In the evening, we went to the club to meet the gang; they made Oscar feel at home. Some of the girls kept him occupied in a lively conversation. Somebody started to get the old gramophone going, and pretty soon the torpedo juice was circulating. Oscar was a good dancer, something that I had to learn. Gisela was very patient to teach me the first steps. After I stepped a few times on her toes, I was beginning to get the hang of it, but I was still far away from being a regular hoofer. I could not remember when I ever had such a good time. As the night went on, some of the couples got lost in the dark corners of the underground to do some innocent kissing or whatever. Who cared, we might be all dead tomorrow. As the party came to an end, it was time for everybody to break up; boys and girls were going back to the gray and bleak world of reality. Oscar and I were still in a good mood; we took Gisela home, said good-bye, and hit the road. How could we get to Dahlem at this time of the night without the motorcycle? We would have to wait till morning to catch an early streetcar and be probably late for roll call.

One weekend in May, when I came home, my mother handed me a letter from the military service board with calling-up orders to report on June 1, 1944, to the Wehrertüchtigungs Lager (premilitary training camp) at Angermünde. My mother and my grandmother were up in arms telling me that I was too young for military service. It was taking me some time explaining to them that this was only a four-week course, a boot camp; I would not be drafted for military service at this time. Since I was already serving under active duty in the air raid emergency squad at the home front, I might be suspended. The women had calmed down as I had promised them that I would take up the matter with the director of the academy first thing Monday morning. As it turned out, the director told me that there was nothing he could do about it for me. "As a matter of fact," he explained to me, "you are not the only one, practically every boy in school born in 1929 has received the same orders."

Premilitary Combat Camp

The first of June, I was taking the S-Bahn from Tegel to Bernau; it was the northern end of the Berlin electric train system. From here on, I would be catching a local train with a steam-powered engine going over Eberswalde to Angermünde in the Uckermark. Angermünde was only eighty kilometers from Berlin, but it would take two hours to get there The train was going so slow that one was almost able to pick flowers along the way. It was a beautiful sunny day, and I enjoyed the ride and especially the blooming meadows. I was in no hurry to get there, and I was not particularly thrilled by what was waiting for me. At the train I met a few guys and found out that we all had the same destination. Early in the afternoon, all of us were getting off the train, a happy young bunch not knowing what we were going to do next. It did not take very long, and a big army sergeant appeared at the Angermünde train station. He stepped up the platform, took a deep breath, and kept blowing a whistle till his lungs ran out of air. The shrill sound was getting everybody's attention, then his loud voice was taking over, telling us to fall into formation and follow him. What he was not telling us was that there was no transportation, and we would have to walk an hour to get to camp. Angermünde was a little sleepy medieval town, but we didn't see much of it; instead, we marched along a dusty road next to a forest. What appeared as a dust cloud in front of us was actually a marching column of boys our age heading for Angermünde. They had completed a month of training; they were combat-ready and were going home waiting to be called for active duty. The same thing would happen to us a month from today. The camp was away from civilization, isolated outside in the country. A huge tract of land was covered with prefabricated barracks. The whole thing was surrounded by a chain-link fence. As we entered the camp by the front gate, I had the feeling like I was going to prison. Several members of the army were calling our names, and we were disbursed to different barracks. My first impression was that I didn't belong here. Forty bunk beds were in each building, and open latrines were behind each barrack.

At the first roll call next morning, I and two other boys were already having a confrontation with the sergeant in charge of our barrack. His name was Sergeant Fleisch; we called him meathead. He was a professional soldier, twenty years in the army and never made it past the rank of a drill sergeant. His purpose in life was to cool his frustration by drilling newly enlisted recruits to his satisfaction. For openers he posted a time schedule at the barrack outlining the events of training for the first week. A footnote at the bottom of the note said that all college students had to report the following day at 0800 at the office of Sergeant Fleisch. Well, there were only the three of us who showed up, assuming that he had some academic job in mind for us. Instead, with a sadistic expression in his face, he told us that we were selected every day for the first week to clean the latrine with a honey bucket. We were taking it with a smile, assuring him that we would do a good job. He expected a reaction of insult, scorn, and contempt, but that was one pleasure we countered with noncompliance. We were not here for four weeks to be drilled into submission; we had plenty of that in the Hitler Youth. It seemed like this kind of behavior was rather a private chicanery of some sergeants. More obvious was the fact that the army needed some urgent replacements, otherwise they would not bother giving us youngsters a quick training of basic weapons from a pistol to a machine gun. Heavy emphasis was placed on the instructions of hand grenades and Panzerfaust. The German version of the U.S. bazooka was the Panzerschreck. Firing an 88 mm rocket, this launcher was an early copy of the bazooka captured in Russia. It was an improved rocket launcher highly effective against the Russian tanks. The blast of flame and smoke from the rear caused it to be nicknamed Stovepipe by the German soldiers. In comparison to the Panzerfaust, the Panzerschreck was clumsy and obsolete, and that was why here at the camp, they only trained us how to handle the Panzerfaust. It was less awkward and heavy, basically a small recoilless gun firing a large oversize bomb. We had given it the name Toilet Plunger. The Panzerfaust was the most remarkable antitank weapon ever developed. Its hollow-charge warhead could penetrate any tank in the world. The production of the Panzerfaust by now must be in the hundreds of thousands. In the field of the camp ground was an old Russian T-34 tank, which we were using for training purposes. The secret was to get as close to the tank as possible without being detected by the crew of the enemy tank. If the observer behind the machine gun caught you, you were dead meat. All of us had to practice this approach over and over again.

With the Panzerfaust ready, you jump from cover to cover and crawl on your belly if necessary, but never lose your cover. Place yourself in the direction of the oncoming tank hiding behind something. Wait until the tank is as close as about one hundred yards, aim at the tank's belly, and fire your weapon. At the battlefield, it must take nerves of steel to stay calm and hit a tank that close. In several days, I went through the exercise about ten times and got killed twice. It does not matter how many times you get killed at the camp; in reality you can only die once.

After the first week at the camp, we were beginning to feel the pressure of the military officers influencing us to become volunteers for the different branches of military service. Every other day or so, members of two barracks were assembled for lectures in the dining room. All of these lectures were given by officers decorated with iron crosses hanging from their necks. No question, these officers were real heroes; each one of them was telling a venturesome story using boastful language to get us excited to join the army. In the barracks at nights, during a conversation, I heard from some boys that they decided that the army was the life for them and signed up. How many had volunteered had never been revealed to us. The recruiting process took place in strict privacy. Individually, all of us were given an appointment at a certain time to appear for an interview at the offices of the officer in charge of enlisting of recruits. If the particular officer did not succeed to sign you up for his branch of the military, then the prospective candidate was called in some other time for a second interview. Usually at this time, you were facing a Gruppenführer of the Waffen-SS. If you resisted him, he would take his gloves off and tell you that you were a member of the Hitler Youth, and if you didn't join the SS Division Hitler Youth, you were a coward. When the time came for my interview, I was called in to see a middle-aged army major. He had my file in front of him, and he asked me to sit down. I was impressed about his manners; before he got to the subject, he was asking me about my parents and how I was doing at the academy. I told him that I had one more year to go and after graduation I would follow any orders wherever they sent me.

"Then I take it," he said, "that at this time you will not serve your country."

"Oh no," I replied, "that is absolutely wrong. I am already under commitment to the Führer. Next month at this time, I will turn fifteen and join the Luftwaffe as Flakhelfer in Berlin, for which I have already previously trained for in Neisse. Being attached to a Flak battery in my hometown gives me a chance to finish my education."

The major, I forget his name, agreed with me and wished me luck, and I saluted him. At the end of June, I found myself marching again on the same dirt road this time toward Angermünde. As the train headed for Berlin, I was leaving a nightmare behind me.

Back at school and back at the command post. All my comrades and Hindenburg were happy to see that I survived the notorious Nazi boot camp. I asked the gang what happened while I was gone, and to my surprise, they told me that I only missed five major air raids in the month of June. The biggest attack was on June 21 when 876 U.S. Air Force bombers made north and south Berlin their target and killed in one night 474 civilians and injured another 756. Oscar told me that among the dead were over 20 Hitler Youth rescue workers.

As I told my mother and my grandmother about the casualty of June 21, they were very upset about it and urged me to be very careful when our detachment was called into action. I kept telling them not to worry about me, to take good care of themselves, and to make sure they had enough to eat. Whatever was available of food items on ration cards kept the people of the city barely from starving to death. But the Berliners were tough; they were fighting every day to stay alive, their spirit could not easily be broken, they were able to endure hardships with a strong, firm, and tenacious will to survive. Every park and every strip of greenery was now converted for growing potatoes or any kind of vegetable. Even the large and beautiful Tiergarten designed by the famous eighteenth-century botanist Lene was now a big cornfield. All the old trees were removed and cut into firewood. At night people snuck into the zoo and slaughtered animals for their own consumption. Most balconies in Berlin were barricaded with lumber and poultry wire to serve as cages for raising rabbits and chicken. My grandmother was a farmer's daughter; she had a green thumb and made behind our apartment house the most productive victory garden. I also helped her to convert our big balcony into a *Kaninchen* farm (a rabbit shelter). This reminded me so much of Lindenhof and my grandfather who was so proud of his garden and the backyard with the chicken coop. In addition to supplement their food supply, the two women would often go by train to the farmers in the countryside to exchange cigarettes for food. Tobacco products were also in limited supply and given out on coupons. Since both of them were not in the habit of smoking, it made it a desirable commodity for bartering.

In the month of July, for one reason or another, U.S. bombers had disappeared from the sky over Berlin. Taking over the daily air raids were the Mosquitos of the RAF. They were not causing any serious damage, but they were certainly a nuisance by blowing up trains and shooting with machine guns at anything that was moving on the ground, mostly civilians. My grandmother told me how my mother came home one day screaming and running hysterically all covered with blood. It happened one day in bright daylight while she was standing in a long breadline to buy some food, when suddenly, out of nowhere, several Mosquitos came flying over the rooftops and emptied their machine guns full blast into a mass of standing women and children. The cowardly attack of the British pilots created a bloodbath and killing field of innocent people. Thank God, by a miracle, my dear mother was not hurt; she could wash off somebody's blood, but she could never erase the traumatic shock she suffered. My mother did not want me to know about it, but Oma told me confidentially. The war had become too brutal on both sides, right or wrong; there was no way out. I was convinced now, without reservation, that I must actively join the war and fight back even if it killed me. One day after my birthday this month, I would go and volunteer for the air force. Several boys at the academy had elected the same option; nobody wanted to quit school before graduation. Once you were drafted for the army or the Volkssturm, that was the end of your education. On August 1, we would be assigned to a Flak battery near the academy. I would be together with my comrades; Oscar and I would still visit the club. As long as Oscar could keep up the deal with Hindenburg, it was our private pleasure to have a motorcycle. Most of all, my mother and my grandmother were happy that for the time being we were still all together in the same town. Somehow I felt that at this junction I was undergoing a drastic change, a new dimension of events started coming my way, and life would never be the same again.

CHAPTER VI

TO HELL OR SIBERIA

Getting Ready for the Inferno

In Berlin there were more Flak batteries than in any other city. You could see them now on top of buildings and in open fields in the suburbs. The three deadliest Flak towers were the zoo bunker within two hundred yards of the Theater Center on Kurfürstendamm in the big Tiergarten, in Friedrichshain, and in Humboldhain. There were 12.8 cm antiaircraft cannons and dozens of 2 cm automatic guns mounted on a 40-meter high bunker with 2.13-meter beton walls. Each bunker was a fantastic monstrosity of a fortress, just frightening to look at. An enormous square clod of steel-reinforced concrete about five or six stories tall. The bunker with all its guns on the roof and every corner was painted a dark green to make it invisible from the sky among the trees on the ground. All guns were fired by remote control from another similar but smaller tower about a hundred yards away farther on in the woods. A huge umbrella of a radar screen would tell you that here was the command center not only for the zoo bunker but also for the rest of the Flak towers in Berlin. These monsters were bigger than a city block and completely equipped with a power plant, hospital, deep water well, and amazing reserves of food and ammunition. No artillery or bombs could do them any harm. I looked at the zoo bunker, and it reminded me of a space station from a lost world or another planet. Most of the 8.8 cm Flak batteries were placed on the open fields in the city, and Berlin was known to have plenty of open fields and parks. To the contrary, the lighter 2 cm automatic guns were usually placed in populated areas on rooftops of high-rise buildings. An ideal weapon to fight low-flying enemy aircraft. On the last day of July, the academy in Dahlem closed up for summer vacation, and we, the new Luftwaffenhelfers were closing up for good. We were cleaning out our lockers and taking everything, especially our books, to the new barracks. Tomorrow we would report to our new assignment, the 147 Flak battery in Schmargendorf next to Bahnhof Hohenzollerndamm. The battery and its barracks were located on the

Last picture in uniform as a Flak helper in January 1945

A 2 cm light flak. Deadly for low flying aircraft.

Fifth flak battery school in Konigsberg near Neisse

A small ammunition dump in Schmargendorf

My friend Oscar as a Luftwaffe regular Flak soldier

A 8.8 cm Flak battery in action

This picture was taken during the period
I volunteered for the home front

In front of the main ammunition bunker showing 8.8 cm shells.

The most famous Hitler Youth Flaksoldier now known as Pope Benedict 16th. In utmost respect to the Holy Father

Picture of unknown Hitler Youth in blue Flak uniform

Bombed out building in East Berlin. People are still living upstairs

The Kaiser Wilhelm Gedächtnis Church destroyed in WWII has never been restored.

open fields of the old Berliner Sport Verein 1892. The first day we were indoctrinated, receive our gear and new uniforms. After inspection, we lined up in front of the battery to meet our CO, Major Schneider. He was wounded as a young Luftwaffen officer in the Russian Front and was now the commanding officer of the 147 Flak battery in Schmargendorf.

In a short speech, he told us how proud he was that we all volunteered but reminded us of our responsibilities to serve the fatherland. The highlight of the day was the oath he took from us. All forty recruits, first and second platoon, repeated after him, "I swear, as Luftwaffenhelfer, to do my duty at all times, faithful and obedient, brave and ready as it is expected from a boy of the Hitler Youth." Our training would only take thirty days; by September 1, we had to be ready to replace the old crew of regular soldiers who were desperately needed on the Russian front and now also on the west front. Besides the CO, only sergeants in charge of the barracks, the gun captains, and loading gunners would remain at the base. The new recruits would be disbursed according to their abilities into three groups. The more robust type would serve as members of the 8.8 cm Flak crew. The intellectual boys were assigned to operate the surveying equipment. These instruments were vital for the fire control to estimate location, speed, and distance of enemy planes. In Neisse I was trained on the B9 Kommandogerät 1936 which was now, as I found out, obsolete. To shoot in the right direction, data were given now to the gun crews with two more modern surveying instruments.

First there was the Kommandogerät 40, an optic instrument that calculated numbers; provided there was clear vision. The second instrument and more often used was the Funkmessgerät (Fu MG), which was operated by radar. The K6 was the Richtkanonier; the crew member responsible for aiming at the target, he kranked two wheels till the command he got from the Funkmessgerät showed up on his scale. The third group and the rest of the LW helpers were sent to the Umwertung, a dugout shelter that gives operational reports to several outside battle headquarters in regard to enemy strength and direction. Every boy of the Hitler Youth wanted to be behind a gun and shoot at the enemy, but to become a member of the 8.8 cm Flak crew was strictly by selection. Before receiving a permanent position, all of us were tested more than once for our abilities. If you wanted to be assigned to a 8.8 cm Flak, you had to undergo first an enormous endurance test. Each ammo box contained three grenades and had a total weight of thirty kilograms, which was about sixty pounds. Only boys who could carry such a box running fast, for not less than three hundred feet, made it to be one of a six-member 8.8 cm gun crew.

I could not move fast enough and flunked the test. The only position I was able to take as a member of a gun crew was the Zündereinstellung of the Führungsring (setting the timer of the detonator to go off at a certain altitude). I remembered this from my Neisse days, and nothing had changed since. It was almost impossible to learn everything in thirty days, but since everybody had only to learn one job and do it right, it made it easier; things fell into place, and the success of the battery was accomplished by teamwork. A few minor air raids were taking place in the month of August, and we had not seen any action yet. Everything besides our military training was on schedule including our five-hour schooling every day. Two or three of our regular teachers from Dahlem were arriving every morning to set up half-day classes in the dining room in one of the barracks. Should alarm be given, then all of us took the steel helmet and the gas mask and ran to our battle station. In the month of September, there were suddenly even fewer air raids. They were telling us this must be for two reasons. The Allied Bomber Command was busy supporting the invasion in Normandy, which took place on June 6, and the British were also trying to interrupt the constant bombardment of London by the German VI missiles, which started on the same month. Since our battery was not very active, we took turns enjoying free afternoons. We were also getting weekends off, and only a skeleton crew took watch at the battery.

Wilmersdorf was next to Schmargendorf, and Gisela's house was only fifteen minutes in walking distance from the base. I took advantage of the situation by visiting her as much as I could, and my two women (mother and grandmother) in Tegel on weekends. However, the war went on, and on September 16 we received our baptism of fire. It was early in the morning, and we were just in the middle of an English lesson as the siren went off, and we rushed to our position at the battery. A formation of RAF Mosquitos approached Berlin. The ammunition bunkers were now open, and the Zebras (Russian POW) were piling up the ammo boxes next to each gun. Each of us reported to the gun captain to be in position, and the gun captain announced to fire control that battery was ready to receive fire orders. The interpretation room informed the command stand of a group of twenty very low-flying Mosquitos toward Wilmersdorf and Schmargendorf area. Captain Schaefer, in charge of the command stand, gave the battery of 2 cm automatic gunfire permission on enemy sight. The moment the first fighters were in range, the boys from the other side of the field gave the British everything they got. The enemy was also strafing the barracks in the less than sixty seconds it took them to fly across the base. Nobody got hurt, but we crippled two of the Mosquitos in the process. As it turned out, the next 2 cm battery in Steglitz finished them off and got the credit. It was kind of disappointing for the rest of us that we did not have a chance to fire one single shot. I guess the 8.8 cm Flak was designed for bigger, slower, and higher targets. Our chance arrived when the bells got us out of bed the next day at one o'clock in the morning. Not really awake yet, we automatically went to position. A loudspeaker from the command bunker told us that a large enemy bomber formation was now entering Spandau heading for Berlin. Sergeant Kummer was in charge of surveying, ready to communicate with Major Schneider, the leader of the battery fire control. The gun captain Feldwebel Raabe made sure his crew was ready by calling each station. He looked at me and said, "Ignition device?" I replied, "Ignition control ready." Minutes later we could see the first pathfinder planes staking out a territory in the sky with smoke bombs showing the armada of bombers behind them where to do the carpet bombing.

The five-meter long barrels of the 8.8 cm Flak were turning now into the direction of the oncoming bombers; all guns were loaded with brand shrapnel, more effective for barrage fire. The bomber formation would ignore the Flak fire and fly through the air chamber marked by the Pathfinder. Zebras were ordered to bring high-explosive shells for the second barrage. The new projectile was equipped with a dual detonator; in addition to the time fuse, it also had a detonator that exploded on impact. Huge searchlights were sweeping the sky and had found a squadron of Lancaster bombers. Suddenly an unexpected nerve-shattering thunder roar was shaking us up. Simultaneously all the 8.8 cm Flak, the big 10.5 cm gun at the Tiergarten and the biggest of them all the 12.8 cm cannon on top of the zoo bunker, were shooting at the enemy. Minutes later there came from our own command stand over the loudspeaker the order, "Battery fire." Sergeant Kummer and his men were constantly checking the fire control. So far we were still on target at six thousand feet. I didn't have to make any adjustment on the Zünder machine, but that could change any minute.

Apparently the British had not given up flying formation or changing altitude. A few planes, after they had been exposed to the searchlights, were trying to dive out of it, but most of them got shot down before they had a chance to escape; after all, there were much more guns on the ground than planes in the air. Visibility was good, and the enemy was paying a high price for the attack. The targets of the enemy airplanes for tonight were Treptow, Schöneberg, Friedenau, and Wilmersdorf. A second group and a third group were flying over our base to unload their bombs in Friedenau and Wilmersdorf. We were shooting now at the enemy uninterrupted for over an hour, hitting three or four of them without suffering any casualties of our own. As soon as they were out of range, there came the order to "cease fire." We might get a second chance to shoot at them when the enemy was on the way home. We didn't have to wait too long; this time they were no longer flying in formation and much higher. The Focke-Wulf and Messerschmitt night fighters were on their tails and had successfully shuddered or destroyed a good portion of the Lancaster groups. Our battery could still catch some of them as they were trying to reach the coast, but our limit on the time fuse was now reduced to five thousand feet since our own fighters were still operating above at six thousand feet. We were not scoring any more hits, and at 3:30 AM, the show was over, but not for us. Every gun in the battery did fire an average of about 150 rounds. Even though all of us were dead tired, we could not hit the sack immediately.

Our ammo bunker at the battery was empty and needed to be restocked. The main reserve ammo bunker was a good three hundred feet away from the battery. It took about five hundred boxes to refill an empty Flak bunker. The job was shared by all of us—LW helpers, regular soldiers, and Russian POW. The Zebras had volunteered for war duty. They had their own barrack, did all the maintenance work and cleaning. We treated them nicely, but otherwise we were instructed not to have any contact with them. During an air raid, their sole job was to haul ammunition but must stay away from the battery. After an air raid, if needed, they were loaded into trucks and became part of an emergency rescue squad, mainly to do the clearance and digging. They were also assigned many times to the bomb disposal squad. In other words, they were doing all the dirty work the Hitler Youth used to do and still did. The truth was that the Third Reich was running out of eligible Hitler Youth. The boys whose ages were from fourteen to eighteen years old were now filling the ranks of the regular soldiers, and the ten—to fourteen-year-old boys were serving on the home front. Der Volksmund (vernacular), or the Berliner Schnauze used to call us LW Helpers, "Kinder flak," but that changed very quickly. First we earned the respect of our fellow soldiers, and finally the appreciation of the civilians we protected with our lives. The irony was that we were not treated as equals. We died like regular soldiers, but we were still considered as Hitler Youth. LW helpers received army food supply number 3; that was the lowest food provisioning without any extra combat ration. Every soldier in any branch of the armed forces received a regular supply of cigarettes and a fair amount of alcoholic beverages. LW helpers received nothing of the kind; as a matter of fact, if they saw any of us smoking or drinking, we would be punished. The Führer had declared that consuming alcohol or smoking cigarettes was detrimental to the health of the Hitler Youth.

Nobody knew exactly the extent of damage from last night's air raid over Wilmersdorf till I talked to a policeman. He lived in the area, and according to him, the section of Bahnhof Wilmersdorf, Bahnhof Friedenau, and Bahnhof Schöneberg were severely damaged. Most of the civilians got killed around Innsbrucker Platz. He knew for sure that the neighborhood at the Fehrbelliner Platz, the northern part of Wilmersdorf where Gisela lived, have not been attacked. The news I received certainly made me feel better. My next step was a trip to see our barrack leader, Sergeant Backe. I was telling him my story and asking at the same time for a short leave. He told me that an overnight pass was out of the question, but he might let me go provided I would be back by 10:00 PM. In a hurry, I ate all the lunch I could hold, and half a loaf of black bread disappeared in a brown paper bag. My uniform was clean, and in no time, I was passing through the front gate. Even though I knew my way around in Wilmersdorf, the last air raid turned most of the familiar streets into chaos. Reaching the north part of Wilmersdorf, everything looked almost normal.

It made me happy to see Gisela and her mother, the two women I cared the most about next to my own family, being unharmed. Gisela was very excited, telling me that she had good news. She said, "My application to enter the nursing school at the Frankfurt (Oder) Hospital has been accepted. I will move in as a student nurse on October 1, 1944."

"That sounds very good and, like your mother, I am also happy for you, but if you live there we might not see each other that often," I replied.

"I promise," she said, "I will come home every chance I have, and please, since you will be closer to my mother, I would ask that you come and look after her every day if your time permits."

"Don't worry," her mother replied. "I have my job. I am very busy taking care of all the clients that need my help."

Since Inge, Gisela's mother, became a widow, she had been working again. Her former employer, a major insurance company, rehired her as a caseworker. Her job was to check and adjust the claims submitted in her district. All the claims of war and air-raid victims were investigated by a few selected big insurance companies. The damages were assessed, and certain emergency funds were paid out. The actual money was subsidized by the government. The decision to go back to work in the field, she knew, was a smart move, otherwise the government would have called her to work on an assembly line or at an ammunition factory. Inge did not have to punch a clock or wait for a streetcar to go to work; the company provided her with a VW car to visit as many cases a day as possible.

Now Gisela wanted to know if we could get together this Wednesday, but I had to tell her that my next scheduled two days to stay overnight were the following week on the last Wednesday in September and on the week after. The sixth of October was my mother's birthday, and luckily I could stay one day overnight in Tegel. "That works out," Gisela said. "The gang wants to give me a farewell party, and we can do that the last Wednesday in September."

"If I may make a suggestion," Inge declared, "let's have a bite to eat and catch the early six-o'clock movie. They are playing in all theaters the color film *Kolberg*. The film is a cinematic masterpiece but mainly designed for Dr. Joseph Goebbels's propaganda. It serves as a contemporary analogy inspiring the German people to keep on fighting and win the war as it is in the case of Kolberg. I have not seen a good movie in a long time."

I agreed with Inge, and so did Gisela. The only problem was that I had to be back at base at 10:00 PM or I would catch fire and brimstone. "Don't worry," Inge was trying to convince me, "the movie is over at 9:00 PM, and Gisela and I will drive you from the theater straight to the barracks." Question remained, what were we going to eat before we left the house?

"I got you covered," I said. "Open the brown bag, and there is your abendbrot."

"Great," Inge announced. "I have some Schmalz [lard with burned onions]; Gisela will brew some tea, and we are all set."

As we sat around the table, I raised the cup and said something stupid like, "Long live the Führer's revolution."

Inge looked at me with a strange face, she put her cup down and whispered slowly, "You have to be out of your mind."

"Don't take him seriously," Gisela said. "You know he is a student of the Adolf Hitler academy; he does not know any better, but the old soldiers at the battery will straighten him out."

At 5:30 PM, we left the house and drove to the Wilmersdorf Kino. We just got our tickets on time before the movie started. The story was action filled, but none of us saw any correlation to modern times. Only a miracle could make Germany win this war; that was the reason why the NS Party had a widespread rumor going around that Germany had almost perfected some secret weapons that would destroy our enemies. We stopped this forbidding conversation as Inge parked the car outside the base. I hated long good-byes, so I just kissed them and got off the car.

The following day, I called the command post of the Steglitz rescue squad, leaving a message for Oscar to call me at Schmargendorf Flak Battery second platoon. Two days later, Oscar returned my call, telling me that he also would be free on Wednesday till the next morning and that he would pick me up in front of the base at 4:00 PM. The remaining days before the party, many things were going through my mind about the relationship of Gisela and I. Our interest in each other was now far beyond the point of what you might call a friendship between a boy and a girl. In the eyes of society, we were still two good-behaving teenagers as long as there was no sexual contact. Speaking for myself, I was sincerely in love with her, and my feelings were deeper than just being platonic. Has anybody ever come up with a true definition for the meaning of love? What I experienced was a dual desire of spiritual and physical togetherness. Many philosophers had given us their own version, either sagacious, profound, or difficult to understand. Most of the explanations had a romantic overtone. At the extreme opposite would be a statement given by F. Nietzsche: "Love is the failure of the mind to understand nature." Anyway, in our case, I could see a definite conflict of interest. Nature told me that we were mentally and physically ready for love; society said we were both too young (we were both fifteen years old). Economically we were not ready, there was a war going on, and our future was uncertain. I agreed that marriage would be out of the question, but how was I going to tell my brain to stop pouring out hormones till there was a more suitable time ahead? The church said you could not have sex till you were married, and my father said, "I don't give you my permission to be married before the age of twenty-one." Under these circumstances you could not blame any young and decent girl to preserve her virginity. Fortunately, nature had given young women an advantage over young boys the same age.

As planned, Oscar showed up with his motorcycle at the gate on time. Ten minutes later, we were at the house of Inge and Gisela. Gisela looked beautiful in the dress Inge had fixed for her. Oscar also appeared sharp in his sporty outfit. I was the only one in uniform, and I might look out of place at the party. Inge took me by the hand and asked me to follow her to the bedroom. She opened one side of a wall-to-wall wardrobe, and I was facing a complete need section of men's suits and shirts. "Inge," I said, "these are your dead husband's garments."

"Exactly," she replied. "He has no use for them anymore, so please help yourself."

I hesitated till Inge gave me a hand, selecting a few items for me to wear.

"Here, try this on, I believe it is your size." Indeed it was; even the shoes she picked fit me—well, it was a little large. When I entered the living room again, Gisela and Oscar complimented me. This was the first time I was wearing a suit since I made my first Holy Communion. I had not been out of the uniform for the last five years. Another hour of lively conversation, and the three of us were leaving for the party.

Oscar was going by bike, and Gisela and I were leisurely walking over to the clubhouse. "I am so happy we can be alone together; one more day, and I have to go," Gisela said. She embraced me in the middle of the street, and her kisses put my brain on fire. For a few minutes, I heard bells ringing. All day long I had this feeling; I could not care about anything else, I just wanted to be with her.

"Hold it," I whispered. "We don't want to be the first people at the party. A block from here is a beautiful park, let's sit there and talk for a while." The look in her eyes was one of agreement. A bench under a willow tree by the pond was a perfect setting for our mood. We were talking between kisses and promised never to stop loving each other. I looked at my watch and discovered that it was a few minutes past seven o'clock. "Kiss me one more time," I heard her say, "And then we will go."

A mighty welcome was given us when we arrived at the club. Actually the party was combined for Gisela farewell and another older girl who was graduating from premed school. All the rooms were beautifully decorated, and if there was no air raid, we had the whole underground complex at our disposal. The boys and girls must have set up a committee to make all the arrangements. Tables, benches, and chairs were set up inside and out in the garden. Here we were, five years into the war, three million people in Berlin were starving, and these kids, God knows how, put out a buffet of food that was unbelievable. Hot potato salad, black bread, cucumber salad, rhubarb and pumpkin pie; and somebody had the great idea to make some popcorn. In the same corner, as always in the big room, was the open bar. Tonight one of the boys was playing bartender. He would serve you schnapps, homemade apple wine, beer, lemonade, or *Hagebutten* tea. Singing and dancing were the main entertainment of every meeting or party. Usually the orchestra was nothing more than a radio or an old gramophone. Today there was some live music, a guitar player was invited for our pleasure. Whenever he took a break, a disk jockey took over, operating an electric record player with amplifier and two loudspeakers, one for the main room and one for the garden. His repertoire of records was simply amazing. Most of them were even in English; don't ask me where they got them.

While I was dancing with Gisela and I was singing along in English, she wanted to know where I learned to speak English. "No secret, I am taking English lessons every day at school for the last four years."

"Come on, why would they teach you English at the Adolf Hitler school?"

"For two reasons: the whole world speaks English, and the Führer likes the English people. He thinks they belong to the Germanic race, that's why he was trying hard to make peace with them."

"Now I heard everything," Gisela said, "I think you had too much apple wine."

"Talking about apple wine, shall we sit down and have a refill?" I asked her.

"If you can handle it, but let's also get some of that delicious potato salad and sit down in the garden."

"I would like that very much," I said, and I followed her to the table. Sitting close together under the full moon, listening to the romantic music, and being influenced by the wine, both of us were getting exceedingly amorous. As we listened to the beautiful sound of Peggy Lee's voice from the other room, it made us get up again and dance as we follow her song.

Just as we danced past the warden's small office, I noticed behind the open door a leather couch with some pillows in the corner of the room.

"Let's go in and sit for a few minutes," I suggested. At first she was a little unwilling. "Don't worry, I will close the door, and nobody will see us or know we are here." My heart was pounding with anticipation as we went in, and I locked the door behind us. Gisela looked very attractive as she sat on the sofa. "You look great tonight, I will never stop loving you." After I said that, she put her arms around me, and we started kissing as I was moving quickly closer to her. We remained locked in a kiss for quite some time with our eyes closed, but suddenly as if she was coming out of a deep sleep, she screamed, "No no, stop it, not here, not tonight." At that moment, I was taking fast hold of myself, and after a couple of minutes, we both were leaving the room silently.

Back at the table, neither of us was asking any question, and I felt kind of uneasy to start a conversation. The suspense was broken the moment Oscar showed up. "I could not find you, you disappeared. Don't you think it's time to go home?"

"Yes, Oscar."

"Any time you say, we are ready."

"Here, Gisela, take my jacket. Oscar will drive you home, and I will see you both at the house." I needed to be alone to think everything over, but nothing was making sense to me. I was running most the time, and shortly thereafter, I was also at the house. Oscar was waiting for me with the bike outside, and without making any noise, I got in the house and put back on my uniform. As I was ready to leave, Gisela came, kissed me good night, and apologized for freaking out as she called it.

"Believe me, my love for you is genuine, and I will write you a letter from Frankfurt [Oder]. Please take care of my mother, and I will see you soon."

Another kiss and I had to go; Oscar was already waiting impatiently.

Escape from an Air-raid Shelter

After all the air raids over Berlin, the Allied Bomber Command was so far not able to interrupt the life of the city. Somehow emergency crews were always available to repair any vital damage in an offhand way. With the beginning of autumn 1944, this was all changing as Berlin again became the target number 1 on the hit list of the RAF and the USAAF. The prelude of the new massive attacks was on October 6, 1944. The day before, everything appeared routine at the battery, and I was leaving the barracks for Tegel on my scheduled weekend furlough. The sixth of October was my mother's thirty-fifth birthday. There wasn't much I could bring her, but I managed to save a few foodstuffs for her and my grandmother. I found them both in good spirits. Oma was proud of her victory garden and showed me everything she was growing. But that was not all; she already made a big crock of sauerkraut, and her pride possession were two rabbits she'd captured out in the field. The best news was a letter my mother received from my father. He was doing fine, and his regiment was still stationed in Hungary near Budapest.

After a long evening of talking, we all went to bed at 10:00 PM. At ten minutes to midnight, the ugly sound of the siren interrupted my first deep sleep. I jumped in my uniform and helped the women with their luggage. The whole ritual was now a silent routine practiced over and over again. Nothing was added to it, and nothing was taken out. The luggage was taken automatically each air raid to the shelter, and if you came out of the shelter alive, you took it back to the apartment and placed it again in the same corner in the corridor. You put your gas mask with your flashlight on top of it; you went to bed and thanked God that you were alive and still had a roof over your head. If not, then your few bundles that you had saved became and remained your only worldly possessions. Sometimes people couldn't save anything, not even their own lives. Our air-raid shelter was two houses down the street. A few people had already taken their places when we arrived. The shelter was about forty square meters big with two airtight steel doors. The ceiling had several iron beams resting on two reinforced load-bearing walls to keep the shelter from collapsing. The shelter was equipped with benches, tables, and bunk beds. Everyone knew his place, and the people you saw here were the tenants you knew as your neighbors. The last people had entered the shelter as the air-raid warden and block warden Lindeman ordered to shut both security doors. I liked to know what we were up against tonight, so I turned on the radio, trying to tune in to the UKW (ultra short wave) for information from air command head quarters. I was getting the right band, and the same message was repeated every two minutes: "Hier meldet sich das Oberkommando der Luftwaffe, feindliche Bomberverbände von 375 B-17 und B-29 U.S. Langstrecken bomber sind jetzt im Anflug auf den Planquadrat Gustav-Gustav." (Air command reports the approach of 375 B-17 and B-29 US bombers to the Gustav-Gustav area).

"That is us," I said. "The question is only what part of Berlin our enemy has in mind, or is it a trick maneuver only to get the German night fighter looking for enemy bombers all over the sky in Berlin while the enemy decided a last-minute 180-degree turn and bomb the hell out of the unprotected area of Potsdam or Brandenburg on their way home to the coast of Britain?"

The warden told me to hang on to the radio for further messages. The latest broadcast transmission announced that Spandau and Charlottenburg were under attack. "Well," I said to the warden, "I hate to destroy your illusion that it is all over for tonight and one more time we got off easy."

"What makes you think the air raid is not over?" the warden wanted to know.

"Two reasons: number one, the bombers entered Berlin from the north at Spandau flying in a straight northeasterly line directly into Charlottenburg and raise havoc among women and children; they could have done that in both parts of town with 200 airplanes. Secondly the enemy will never undertake a major air raid without trying to destroy at least one industrial or military target. Therefore, in my estimation, they will attack Reinickendorf and/or Tegel, since it is only five more minutes extra flying time. The enemy always first starts a diversion of panic on the ground before the rest of the bombers go to attack the real target. As soon as the first bomber group has dropped their bombs, they climb at a higher altitude to escape the Flak; that's when the German night fighters get after them to shoot as many of them down before they get away. Meanwhile the second smaller bomber group is flying lower not to miss their target."

The warden was shaking his head and saying, "Well, I guess we are underestimating the enemy; we will see if your hunch is right."

"We can find out right now," I told him. "As they keep telling us at the battery, observation is better than speculation."

"I like to know how you accomplish that," he replied.

"Very simple, just open the door and give me five minutes; I will go on top of the roof, investigate all sides of the sky as far as I can see and come right back and give you a full report of what I have observed."

"That is against my orders. I cannot let a civilian out of the shelter during the lockdown time before the air raid is over."

"Look at my uniform," I told Lindeman. "I am not a civilian, I am a Hitler Youth member of the air force. This is a military action, and you give me such an order in the line of duty as air-raid warden in charge."

"OK," he agreed. "It is your party, you volunteered, but be careful." He opened the steel door for me, and I slipped outside.

Even though I knew my way around in the block, a half moon gave me enough light to distinguish objects between shadows in the darkness. I only used my flashlight very briefly as I got up the stairs, and as I reached the attic, my eyes were already adjusted to the darkness of the night. Immediately beneath the roof was a long open garret rendering access continuously from house to house. Every twenty feet, the roof was interrupted by a two-by-three-meter skylight. With the help of two sand buckets put on top of each other, I was able to open one of the skylights. Pulling myself through the opening of the window, I was now sitting on the edge of the roof. What a wide 360-degree view, and the visibility was illuminated by some distant fires in the north. I compared the sight in my conception as red-tinted daylight. The burning side, estimating the location and distance, was definately the Spandau-Charlottenburg area. Suddenly I saw two Christmas trees igniting in the sky, one not far from me, somewhere over the S-Bahnhof Tegel (railroad station), and one to the right in the direction of the Lake Tegel. These two markers hanging in the sky could only mean the forthcoming carpet bombing of Tegel. Not wasting one second, I jumped back in the building and ran down the stairs as though I was in a house on fire, knocking furiously on the door to the shelter.

Lindeman opened the door; and after I entered and still out of breath, I motioned him into a corner to make sure nobody could hear us. After I told Lindeman the whole story, there was no need for him to explain the situation to everybody. The silence was interrupted by the sudden ear-shattering bellow of the six guns of the 8.8 cm Flak Battery, stationed less than half a mile from here at the railroad field. The ongoing barrage was telling me that the battery was firing in a salvo tact to create a shellfire curtain in front of the enemy bomber formation. This was the best defense against a massive air attack as long as the enemy was still flying in formation. No state of panic had set in among the people, but I could see the fear in all the frozen faces. Mrs.

Lehman was sitting in the corner, busy pushing the beads of her rosary. My mother and my grandmother were sitting very close together with a blanket over their heads, trying to keep the noise out. I was going slowly toward them, bending over my mother, removing the blanket from her head and speaking into her ear, "Happy birthday, Mom. I love you." I kissed her, and she had tears in her eyes. I gave a kiss to my grandmother too, and she squeezed my hand. Under the circumstances, there was no other way to communicate. I looked at my wristwatch, and it was one o'clock in the morning. The Flak had been firing uninterrupted for the last thirty minutes. By now they must be up to their armpits under empty shells. I felt so helpless, and I wished right now to be back at the battery to help shoot some of the bastards down. I could not complete my act of thinking because two huge explosions blasted my thoughts away; both bomb explosions occurred two seconds apart. I was standing, and the tremendous impact threw me across a nearby table. The lights went out; people were screaming, and a bunch of plaster fell down from the ceiling. The first flashlights provided some light, and Lindeman was able to get a carbide lamp going to set up some emergency light. Women were busy trying to calm down their children, telling them that everything was OK, and, indeed, nobody got hurt. In fact, the Flak ceased firing, and the shelter was filled with the silence of the grave.

The electricity must be out in the whole neighborhood, no siren was indicating that the air raid was over. At this point, there was no communication with the outside world. Lindeman decided that nobody was leaving the shelter for now. He wanted to go out on his own first to see if the situation was safe. The trouble was he had a problem trying to open the steel door. I tried to give him a hand, but the handle was not moving. "Let's try the other door," Lindeman said. This time we had more luck; the door opened, but right behind it, the hall was tightly packed with rubble. There was only one explanation: the house above us or beside us got hit by a bomb, and our shelter was buried below it.

"What are we going to do now?" I asked Lindeman.

"Well," he said, "we have only two options: we can wait for the rescue service or start digging our way out of here." Everybody was in favor of doing something, even if it was wrong. As Lindeman put it, "It is a good choice, our lives are on the scale. If we don't try to get out on our own, we have already three strikes against us. Number one, even if every shelter is registered with the police and the Luftschutz Organization, we don't know how busy they are and how long it will take them to get to our shelter. Secondly, the reinforced ceiling may be overloaded with debris and could collapse anytime. And the last point, that will happen no matter what; if we don't get out on time, we will run out of oxygen, perish gradually, languish with faintness, and expire in a death by asphyxiation."

"But we are not going to die. I want to know where do we start digging?"

Lindeman knew everything about this shelter, he watched the construction crew when they reinforced and rebuilt the shelter. He took me and a few other males to the west wall of the basement. This was the only wall of the shelter that was part of the outside wall of the building. "If we knock a hole in this wall, we will face the outside and hopefully get some fresh air. Here," Lindeman said, "give me a hand, and let's remove a few bunk beds." The original wall was about eighteen inches solid concrete, and in the upper part was an opening left for a four-by-three-foot window. On the outside, the window was just a foot above the ground. During the war, the window was canceled and filled out with bricks to make it a solid wall. Looking at the wall from the inside, you could never tell that there at one time was a window under the plaster, except for a frame made with an oil paint to outline where the area of the brick wall was. That was done purposely to create an emergency escape like it was in our case. With a sledgehammer, a pick, and an ax—that was all we had—we removed the wall brick by brick. It was certainly easier than going through solid concrete. As we removed the first few bricks, we were hoping to reach the outside; instead, some sand came our way. A few more bricks and more sand. I pushed a table underneath the opening, climbed on top of it, and started hitting the bricks right below the window header. After I removed two bricks, there was still sand behind it, but I was not about to give up on it.

I took a long steel bar to keep pushing toward the sky, but so far, nothing but more sand; now I was removing the last bricks in the right upper corner to get the shovel through the hole. It was easier to cast up dirt from the top as most of the earth was falling into the room without force. Between excavating, I thrust the bar, hoping to reach outside above the ground. I was ready to take a break and let someone else do the digging when I gave it another good poke, and somehow I felt less resistance at the end of the bar. I tried again, and this time I pushed the bar as hard as I could, and it went to the outside like crap through the goose. To make sure it was not just an air pocket, I followed it up with the shovel; I stuck my head into the hole, and here was what I saw: a real patch of sky. How can I describe the reaction and temper of my fellow friends and shelter tenants when I broke the good news to them? Jumping for joy, embracing, kissing, laughter, praying, and expressing merriment. And what was I doing standing on the table? I screamed as loud as I could, and then I started singing with a full chest of air Ludwig van Beethoven's beloved Ninth Symphony, "Freude schöner Götterfunken." Verse after verse, we were all singing together till dutiful Lindeman stopped our jubilation by reminding us that we were not out of the woods yet. We started digging again, and as the hole got bigger, we worked harder; finally we reached the point where the exit was large enough for everybody to escape. Full of eagerness, people were already lining up to get out of the shelter.

"Not so fast please; all of you be seated till further notice. For all we know, the basement may be, for the time being, the safest place for us. I will send out some volunteers to scan the neighborhood, scrutinize all the damage, and have them return in ten minutes with a complete report," said Lindeman. Since there were only four eligible men (on those days we boys didn't think of ourselves as nothing but "men") available in the entire group, we all four volunteered, and each of us was ready to investigate in one direction. Lieutenant Lindeman, former officer of the Kaiser's army, was an experienced soldier of WW I. Too old now for the Russian front but good enough to serve on the home front as a civil defense air-raid warden. He took his responsibility very seriously, he reminded me of my deceased grandfather. Nobody said anything, and disciplined as we Germans were, everybody retreated quietly. A stool on top of the table, and the four of us were slipping into the night.

In the center of the apartment house square, we had a good view of the surrounding damages. Behind us, the houses on Dietrich Eckert Strasse 72 to 74 were down to the ground and burning. Looking back toward Tile-Brügge-Weg, the upper portion of number 76, with our shelter underneath, was missing. Number 80, my house, had front damage, but neither house was burning. I asked Mr. Lehman, one of the volunteers, to come with me; I wanted to check the extent of damage on the east side of Tile-Brügge-Weg. He agreed, and the other two fellows went south to north on Bolle Street. In Tile-Brügge-Weg, two houses, numbers 75 and 83, were down and burning. The flames of the bombarded buildings cast strange shadows and a red glow on the otherwise dark streets. Without getting any closer, I could see that our apartment was severely damaged. Across the street, an exhausted group of Hitler Youth and some Russian prisoners were desperately trying to bring the fire under control or keep it from spreading. We had seen everything that could possibly be observed in a time span of already over ten minutes.

Arriving at the shelter, some bad news was waiting for us. The other two observers were spotted by a policeman who went back with them to the shelter and told Lindeman that the whole block was evacuated. A one-thousand-pound time bomb went to a house on Havelmüllerweg, misfired, and was buried in the basement. At least for the night a shelter was made up by the Red Cross of the large Lyzeum, a high school for girls at the farther end of Marzahn Strasse and Tile-Brügge-Weg. Lindeman had been ordered to take all of us immediately to the new shelter. Everybody was taking their bags, sacks, and bundles; and one by one, each of us was crawling to the outside. An early-morning wind full of smoke, dust, and ashes was blowing in our faces. A faint twilight before sunrise mixed with the reflection of the red flames by the burning fires illuminated our way to the shelter. At the corner of Bolle Strasse and Tile-Brügge-Weg, the group came to a halt. The five-story house was literally blown away, and its rubble covered both sides of the streets. Some rescue troop must already have searched the area because some people had gathered more than a dozen corpses and piled them up in a remote spot. Actually there were more body parts than corpses. Lindeman said, "This is a job of a one-thousand-pound air mine." Then he told Lehman to take the group of women and children to the Lyzeum, and the rest of the men to follow him.

Every air-raid warden must know the location of all the air-raid shelters in his district, government and private. Following a hunch, Lehman was trying to find in the back of the rubble one of the steel doors to the shelter. He picked a certain spot, and with not much effort other than removing some bricks, we exposed the door he was looking for. We knocked on the door twice, but there was no response. With combined effort, we pulled the long handle up, and the door was open. It felt kind of spooky as we entered the hallway, no light and no noise of any kind. Using our flashlights, we saw that we were now in the middle of the room with a bunch of people sitting around a big table in front of us. One of our men broke the silence by saying, "Come on, let's get out of here; the air raid is over." At the same time, he pushed the person next to him by the shoulder. This triggered a domino effect, and all of them pushed each other to one side of the bench before they all fell to the floor. More by surprise but panic-stricken, I screamed like an idiot before I realized what just went on.

It must be at least forty corpses either sitting or lying in bunk beds—men, women, and children—all with their eyes wide open, a sign that they all died instantly of air compression in the lungs. This kind of death was caused by special high-explosive bombs (Luftmine). Lehman urged us to get out of there since there was still one bomb of this particular brand that had not exploded or been defused yet. As we entered the shelter at the Lyzeum, I noticed for the first time how tired I was. My mother had saved me a cot and a glass of tea; I stretched out on the cot, and before I could finish the tea, I was already asleep. It must have been around noon or so when I woke up. "Let us go for lunch," my mother said. The Red Cross put up a small kitchen for all the refugees. The largest classroom served as a dining room; my grandmother was already standing in line, saving us a spot to catch some food. Potato soup and a slice of *Kommissbrot* (black army bread). Kommisbrot was not exactly gourmet food, but when you are hungry anything that will satisfy the need will do. Once you get past the outer heavy layer that tastes like sawdust, it's not too bad anymore. My grandmother had dentures, so she could not eat it unless she soaked the bread in some liquid.

We were meeting all kinds of homeless people from Alt-Tegel, Neu-Tegel, Wittenau, Freie Scholle, and the St. Joseph Siedlung. By listening to all their stories, I got a pretty good picture about the intensity of yesterday's bombardment.

From a military point of view, we received a severe blow by losing Borsig, a factory in Tegel, and Mauser a factory in Wittenau. Both factories were known worldwide for making weapons and ammunition. The suffering of civilians was much more tragic. The beautiful and historic Alt-Tegel was practically wiped out. Next to Něu-Tegel were the settlements of St. Joseph and Freie Scholle. Both colonies might be destroyed up to 50 percent. I heard every firsthand horror story that survivors were telling us. The church of St. Joseph, where I received my first Communion, and the chapel of the Martin Luther Friedhof (cemetery) were completely destroyed. According to one eyewitness, the cemetery was ploughed over from one end to the other. "I will never forget as long as I live seeing an open coffin on top of a roof and the dreadful image of human limbs and organs hanging on trees and fences," the woman said with a disturbed look on her face. Equally horrible was the report given by people living around Havelmüllerweg. There, homes were bombarded with tons of incendiary bombs. When such bombs explode, the phosphor they contain is sprayed all over the place, and that phosphor ignites a new fire, wherever and whatever it comes in contact with. The only way an incendiary bomb can be stopped from burning, provided you catch it in time, is by putting enough sand on top of it; without oxygen nothing can burn. Some people in their effort to put out multiple fires were not careful and had spots of phosphor all over them. Unless you get some immediate help, the phosphor will keep on burning. In their pain and fear of death, several people had jumped in the water of the industrial canal in front of Havelmüllerweg. But water does not stop phosphor from burning, as a result, they died an agonizing death by being burned alive with the help of the oxygen in the water. Every survivor had a different story to tell. One women was still in shock; she lost her baby in the fire, and the good sisters of the Red Cross had to take her to the hospital.

Early in the afternoon, it was a relief for some of us to hear over the radio that the last bomb had been defused and we were free to go home. My grandmother, mother, and I were picking up our luggage; and silently we were getting out of the shelter with a burning question on our minds: do we still have a home to live in and how much is it damaged? As we carefully walked along the rubble-filled Tile-Brügge-Weg, I could see that our house was still standing, and the roof was intact.

The house with our shelter, two houses down the street, went down to the first floor because of the explosion of the house across the street. The house was totally destroyed, and two people were killed, unable to reach the shelter. The damage to our house was the result of a five-hundred-pound bomb that destroyed a house three hundred feet across the street. Looking at our house, I saw that all doors and windows had been blown out. We didn't have to open the door, we walked right into the house. The air pressure of the explosion went right through the house. All load-bearing walls were still standing, except for one dividing wall between the living room and the bedroom that fell apart and left just the studs standing. Most of the upright furniture with everything in it was on the floor. The total picture was a disaster, and I'd seen more than one. My mother was crying, and my grandmother was trying to cheer her up by saying, "This is a sudden and unexpected misfortune, but look at it from the bright side. All of us three are still alive, and we'll have this place fixed up in no time."

"That's right," I reminded my mother. "It could be a lot worse, most of it is just cleaning and some carpenter work. We will straighten out one room at a time and make this apartment a place to live in again." I was more concerned about security, I had to get the front door back in place. Till I got some window glass, I might just nail some boards across and provide some open spaces for the light to come in. I didn't see any problem except that I might not have the time to do all the work alone. I did not have to worry about it too long. Early next day, an emergency crew, organized by the party, showed up to help me put the door in. As a matter of fact, they assessed all the damage and told us that they would bring some windows they'd salvaged at another place. I even found some plywood pieces I could nail across the studs and, with some paint, make the inside wall look like a wall again. All of this could be done on another weekend; right now I had to get to a telephone and explain to Sergeant Backe why I did not show up at the base this morning. He was very understanding and gave me another day or two to take care of my affair at home. I was just back in the house, and my grandmother kept on saying, "Come on, let's go and eat." My reaction was, eat what, where? On the way out, she told me that a woman from the party stopped by and gave them some tickets for one hot meal a day for air-raid victims as long as they had no gas or electric power to cook their own meals.

"That is us. Where are we going to dine, at the best hotel in Berlin?"

"Don't be silly," my mother said. "You know we are going back to the soup kitchen at the Lyzeum shelter." Today there were less people at the diner, and the food was better. Navy bean soup, boiled potatoes, sauerkraut, and a one-by-three-inch slice of rubber sausage, also known in English as bologna. I liked navy beans, good food that stuck to your ribs. Telling the young server—she must have been about my age—what a beautiful girl she was and how tasty her beans were earned me an extra portion.

Talking to a woman at the table, my mother found out that a shipment of food had arrived at the grocery store on the corner of Zikow Strasse and Tile-Brügge-Weg. That was good news. I don't remember all the items we purchased, but certainly everything the store had available we traded in for ration stamps. At home we put the scarce items in the pantry, and the shelves didn't look so empty anymore. It would be nice if we could cook, but for now the little food we had must be eaten cold; we had to comfort ourselves, saying that at least we had water, that was the most important thing. It made me feel kind of guilty to see my mother and grandmother still being in a mess and I had to go, but I promised them that I would try to get a leave of absence under the circumstances.

Capitulation Is No Option

On my way to the base, I got off the train in Wilmersdorf; I was anxious to find out if Gisela had written me a letter. Inge, Gisela's mother, came home from work early that day, and she was happy to see me. "There is so much we have to talk about, and I am really in need of somebody I can talk to." The first thing Inge did was hand me a letter from Gisela. Her description of the hospital at Frankfurt (Oder) and her daily work was rather interesting, and she was telling me about the wounded soldiers arriving every day from the Russian front, and she had to take care of them. She had a nice room in the dormitory, which she was sharing with a girl named Helga who was also from Berlin. Closing her letter, Gisela told me how much she missed me and hoped to see me soon. Giving the letter to Inge, I asked her to read it. Inge read the letter and handed it back to me, saying, "That is about the same thing she wrote me."

"Why on earth did Gisela have to go all the way to Frankfurt to become a nurse?" I asked. "Don't we have plenty of hospitals in Berlin?"

"That is true, but not very many hospitals have nursing schools. Gisela wanted to get into the Charité and Robert Koch Hospital, but none of them had any openings. Besides, Frankfurt (Oder) is only one hour away by car," Inge said.

"Correct," I replied. "And Frankfurt (Oder) is also only one hour away from the Russian front."

"I tried to talk her out of it," Inge said. "But Gisela has a mind of her own, she wants to become an RN like her mother." For a moment we stopped the conversation, and I looked around in her living room, telling her what a beautiful house she had; it reminded me very much of the house in Lindenhof my grandmother used to have, and then one night it was all gone. Now it was Inge's turn to ask me questions. "You appear disturbed today, tell me what is the trouble."

I told her the whole story, what we went through the last few days and that I was very worried of what was going to happen to all of us. "The way Germany is surrounded and defeated, it enters my mind for the first time that we might lose the war. Is there any way out of it, and what will the end be like if we keep fighting to the last bullet?"

"I will rather fight and die in the streets of Berlin before they drag me to Siberia. If capitulation is no longer acceptable, I like to know what other choices we have left given by the enemy as to fight till we are totally destroyed. We are no longer in this war to fight for an ideology; we are only fighting to prolong this war from one day to the next, and at the end, we will only face two options: death or slavery." Obviously Inge noticed that something of my innate NS Party integrity was beginning to crumble. "All of us in Germany have been deceived by Adolf Hitler and his party, maybe you because of your upbringing, more so than I am. We are all deluded, but we must not give up hope. There is, and will be, a third way out. Remember, three months ago on July 20, 1944, heroes like Klaus von Staufenberg and others came real close to saving Germany from Hitler's madness. Furthermore," she said, "do yourself a favor and try to stay alive; it makes no sense to get killed last minute before the war is over. I don't know how, but Germany will survive. There will be hard times ahead, but the savage and cruel killing will be over."

"Well," I said, "the way you put it, there may be some light at the end of the tunnel."

"Trust me, as a woman, I never give up." And that was how she changed the conversation by asking me to follow her to the kitchen.

Out of a brown bag came a flask of Slivovitz, genuine old plum brandy. I asked her, "How did you come across something so rare and excellent to drink?"

"My job is to help people to find housing. They know I cannot and will not accept money, but it makes them feel good when they can show their gratitude by giving me something on the side. Rather than insulting them, I graciously accept their little trinkets."

Inge was about to open the bottle when I asked her, "Don't you want to keep the bottle for a special occasion?"

"In times like this, we live in the here and now; there is no better occasion than today to drink to our health and friendship. We don't know what will be tomorrow. Here," she said, "if you drink, you must have something to munch on. Take this tray with cheese and crackers and put it on the coffee table in the living room. I will bring the bottle and two glasses."

After we had the first drink, our conversation shifted from the dull present back into the more pleasant past. Inge took out the old photo album and showed me the pictures of her family. I was especially interested in looking at some pictures that were taken in Tegel with Gisela in it. We kept on drinking the delicious Slivovitz and had a good time reminiscent about the good old days. Perhaps we were dwelling upon the past, having recollections, hoping that the image of the memory would come alive again. There was one picture I remembered vividly because I was also in it; I think it was the year 1937. The photo was taken in front of the old Catholic schoolhouse in Schöneberger Strasse at the beginning of the new semester. That was the time when I started to get sweet on Gisela. We were together every day, and I would go with her after school and carry her books. What I would give to have her closer to me again. "Please, give me another drink before I start crying."

"You think you got problems, look at me," Inge said. "First my husband gets killed in this damn war, and now my only child left the house. You have still your parents and your grandmother. I come from work every night, and there is nobody home. Every night and weekend I am alone, that's why I am happy when I have visitors."

I was trying to apologize for being so childish, but Inge did not want to hear any of it. "You must ventilate your feelings. Don't keep it bottled up inside of you, it will make you sick. That is what friendship is all about, to cry into each other's Slivovitz; it is therapeutic."

"You know, Inge, for the first time in my life I am beginning to understand the meaning of the word 'friendship.' It would be very selfish of me to call you my friend if it would only serve my own interests. Sure, I am influenced by your wisdom and life experience, and there is so much I can learn from you; but primarily, my biggest attraction to you as a friend comes from my own instinct that tells me we can trust, help, and protect each other."

"If you feel like I do, then let's seal the coherence of our friendship with another drink."

"OK, but that is the last one; you are getting already drunk, and I am in no condition to drive you to the base."

"Inge," I said, "I am very happy to be with you. You don't know what I went through the last few days; being in your company and being in your home, I feel sheltered from the chaos of the outside world, and right now I feel no pain."

"I am glad you feel that way," Inge replied. "But I am afraid tomorrow you may not feel so good."

"Don't worry, I can handle it. A little headache will not make me regret drinking with you. Remember, every good medicine has a little side effect. Right now, if you don't mind, I'd like to take a short snooze and sleep it off. In an hour, I will be fresh as a daisy and on my way to the barracks."

"Of course not, just stretch out on the sofa, and I will get you a blanket." Inge tucked me in, gave me a kiss on the forehead, and whispered pleasant dreams.

A few hours later, I woke up to the smell of real fresh-brewed coffee. "I cannot believe it, I must be dreaming."

"No, you are not; I saved these beans for a special event. Luckily, I had enough left to brew two cups of coffee." Both of us enjoyed the coffee, and before I said good-bye, Inge reminded me to come and see her on Wednesdays, her day off. It felt good to step out in the fresh air. I enjoyed the walk to Schmargendorf, and at about 10:00 PM, I walked through the gate of the base. Nobody noticed me when I walked into the barrack, but in the morning I would have to answer some questions.

Sergeant Backe was a family man, and he fully understood my problem. Besides, he had a complete report of all the damages in Spandau, Charlottenburg, Tegel, and Wittenau. He mentioned a figure of about 450 being killed and 825 people severely injured. Now to the good news, as of October 1, 1944, the Führer declared that all the Hitler Youth of the year 1929, if not already engaged in war duty, could now be drafted as Flakhelfer or could now become a member of the Volkssturm (militia). "The days you were gone, we already received reinforcement; an extra platoon of new recruits will now be assigned to each gun to learn. The rotation for on and off duty will be more relaxed. Even as school time is now shorter, we are trying to keep up with each student's education the best we can. A directive from the Adolf Hitler schools has given us a new schedule for all students ready to graduate in 1945. Special classes will be available beginning in October for those eligible to take their not abitur in February and March 1945. You look into it and let me know before I prepare the new duty roster." These were the Sergeant's last words before he dismissed me.

My first step was to contact Dahlem, and I enrolled for special classes at the LBA every Monday and Wednesday. These were the days I would be, with the sergeant's permission, absent from the battery; plus every other weekend, I was also allowed to go and see my mother. Early in November, our battery also received reinforcement on smaller guns.

An absolute necessity for any 8.8 cm Flak Battery was a defense against low-flying enemy aircraft. Some batteries with heavy guns only were wiped out as their long barrels could not be adjusted to a low degree of altitude. The number of daytime air raids, mostly carried out by P-40 Warhawks and RAF Mosquitos, were now at least equal to nighttime bombing. Many of the Allied daytime fighters picked a certain target in Berlin to complete the destruction of vital installations, which were missed the night before by carpet bombing. As a result, we were tied up days and nights either at the barracks or at battle station. On many air raids, we were hanging on to our guns without being able to fire one shot. Fatigue duty and *Budenangst* (claustrophobia) were widespread among us. The daily classes in the morning were either cancelled or interrupted by an air raid or time-out to get some shut-eye. The goal of the NS Party was to keep up our education, but in reality, the pressure of the escalating war was more and more consuming the lives of the Hitler Youth. One morning in the middle of November, we were instructed at breakfast to remain in the mess hall as the CO would come and talk to all the LWH (Luftwaffen helpers). Soon Major Schneider and Captain Schaefer entered, and we all snapped to attention and saluted them.

"At ease," he said, and we sat down. Major Schneider started his speech by saying, "The briefing this morning is about some reassignments. As you all know, we are now fighting a war on two fronts, and there is an ever-increasing demand on manpower. As a direct result thereof, each home front battery is losing more and more of their regular Luftwaffe soldiers. As it stands right now, we are only left with two regular soldiers per 8.8 cm gun, the gun captain and the K6 the loading gunner. Obviously these are the two most important positions. The captain being in constant communication with the command stand and the K6 responsible for exact time frequency between percussion cap setting and firing. One difference of a second, up or down, could result in missing the target by one hundred feet or more. As far as the smaller guns are concerned, we are left with one regular soldier per gun. As you can see, every Flak battery is slowly taken over by the Hitler Youth. Our immediate problem right now is to train some of you more experienced 8.8 cm gunners to serve the newly arrived 2 cm twin guns and the 3.7 cm Flak. In the beginning, we don't want to take more than one of the old LWH away from each 8.8 cm gun and replace him with a new LWH. Anybody of you interested to make a switch, please let your sergeant know. I believe we might occupy the vacancy of the new guns just with volunteers and newcomers. That's all, and good luck to you."

After the brass left, we went over to the barracks and started to talk about our new option. I didn't have to think about it very long; my liking was toward a smaller, more flexible gun. Not uncertain about it, I went to the sergeant's office, telling him how I felt to make a change. My only reservation was I didn't want to switch barracks. "I like it where I am, being very close to my comrades, and let me be honest to you, I appreciate all the help and advice you have given to me, and that is another reason to stay."

"Don't worry," the sergeant said. "You will not go anyplace; the only place you will change is your battle station. You might have to run a little faster to get there because all the smaller guns are placed on the perimeter of the base." Being satisfied with my decision, I told him to put me on his list for the new assignment. Next day, in the morning, I went to school in Dahlem. The course for the *Abitur* preparation was pretty streamlined, but it still covered the subjects of German literature, English, arithmetic, history, geography, chemistry, and biology. In the afternoon, I was heading for Wilmersdorf to see Inge. We had a few hours of happy conversation; unfortunately, there was no letter from Gisela. Inge wanted to know if there were any news on my end, and I told her that I was on Mondays and Wednesdays back to school in Dahlem for a refresher course. My goal was to graduate in February and become a part-time teacher. "Well," Inge said, "that sounds good provided there will still be any children and schoolhouses left in Berlin."

I was taking her sarcasm, knowing that she was trying to bring a point of uncertainty across, and I agreed with her that Germany would not win this war unless we were saved by a miracle. "All of this is pretty clear to me that it makes no sense to keep on fighting. The question still remains, how do I get out of this war, take off my uniform, and stay home? The SS would have me hanging from the nearest tree so fast it would make my head spin. I have one option left, keep on fighting and kill as many of the enemy before I get killed. Seeking to be captured (by the Russian enemy) is no option, then I will wind up in a gulag in Siberia where they work you to death anyway."

"Just one minute," Inge said. "You missed out on one more important option."

"Oh great, I'd like to know what you have in mind."

"Germany must capitulate," she exclaimed. "Excellent, it is such a simple task it did not enter my mind. I think you should take the idea up with the Führer first thing in the morning." Now I was beginning to be sarcastic, but Inge did not get mad; she just smiled and countered with a question, "How many times have they tried to kill Adolf Hitler?"

"It must be a dozen times by now, but even if somebody would succeed before the end of the war, by now the Allies are so close to win the war they will not accept any terms less than an unconditional surrender, and that is suicide if the West is going to deliver us to the Russians."

"The Russians are coming to Berlin anyway; I see no reason why we should prolong this stupid and senseless war if there is a way out of it and save thousands of lives on both sides," Inge said.

"Even, if I would agree with you, I still don't see how our government can put a plan together to accomplish such surrender."

For a few moments, neither of us said anything, then I looked at her seriously, and I spelled out what was more a request than a question. "If you know more about the situation and what is going on in Germany today, please tell me confidentially, and I will be on your side."

"I will trust you, and I will tell you, but please wait till I know for sure."

"Fine by me, and I will also know then if the decision I have made recently is the right one." We parted as good friends with deep respect for each other.

Getting into the barracks, I went straight to bed, hoping for a good night's sleep. Having more LWH on the base made it easier to have one platoon on standby for minor daytime air raids, and another group could follow their classroom routine in the morning. Should there be a major attack, day or night, then everybody at the base would hit his battle station. Till I completed my training in the classroom and at the gun side of the 3.7 cm light Flak, I would still be setting detonators at the 8.8 cm Flak. It took four men to operate the 3.7 cm gun—a gun captain, gun layer, range finder, and loading gunner. At all times, the gun would be in telephone contact with the command post. The firing of the light Flak was more rapid and easier to load; the cassette contained ten 3.7 cm cartridges, ideal for low-flying, fast-moving planes. Out-of-range flying bombers were not a right target.

CHAPTER VII

MORE HAPPENINGS OF 1944

A Strange Funeral at Midnight

I always welcomed the weekends I could go home and see my mother and grandmother. I was anxious to find out how the two women were managing to survive in their dilapidated living quarters. Coming home was full of surprises for me. Before I entered the house, I could see already from the outside the new windows; actually they were salvaged but in good condition, and even the paint looked relatively good. After I hugged both of them, I started to look around, and I was really amazed to see everything having been repaired, cleaned, and orderly put together. It was certainly not the image I had in my mind of the last time I saw the apartment. Here we were; it was the end of November and already cold outside, but in the house it was cozy and warm. "How do you manage to accomplish all this in such a short time?"

"Well," Oma said, "we had nothing else to do, and it is a great relief to have some sense of normalcy inside the apartment. It was also good for us to work at it together."

"What about the utilities?"

"Everything is in except gas, so we cook on the wooden stove."

"Where do you get the wood from?" "Just look around, wherever you go there is rubble and broken lumber."

I told them both that I was prepared this weekend to do some repairs, and now, except for a few minor things, it was all taken care of. "You are not getting off that easy," my mother said. "If you feel like it, you can cut us some more firewood."

"That is a deal," I said, and we retired for the evening. Saturday I got up early to go to Alt-Tegel to see the extensive damage of the sixth of October. It would be a long list if I would write down all the destruction of the beautiful resort town of Tegel; neither did I have the time to go and see what the St. Joseph Siedlung and the Freie Scholle neighborhood looked like. All I knew was that my mother went to see the total destruction of the peaceful Christian village including the community church of St. Joseph. The priest who gave me my first Holy Communion also got killed that night. Now back to Tegel, the railroad station was severely damaged; going down the Bahnhof Strasse on the right-hand side, the new post office building where my father worked was burned down. Next corner, Berliner Strasse, I was making a left turn going toward the Borsig-Werke; I saw the big brown ornamental brick gate still standing, but behind it there was nothing but rubble and twisted metal beams that used to be part of huge halls for machine tools. Many acres of waste and rubbish all the way down to the lake. Lake Tegel, an extension of the Havel River, was a prominent place in the summertime with restaurants, hotels, and by the promenade were several landing places for elegant excursion riverboats. Nearly all of them had burned down and turned into unusable wreckage.

The famous Tusculum and the Strand Schloss, just to name a few of the fancy resort clubs, were no longer on the map. It was pitiful to see all of that being so senselessly destroyed in a matter of two hours. On the way home, I took the Schöneberger Strasse, noticing that the tall old gothic Roman Catholic church was still standing. Most of her windows had been blown out, but she survived. Not so lucky farther down the street was the old Catholic schoolhouse I used to attend for many years. All that was left was the foundation and part of the front elevation with its massive concrete staircase. In the back of the schoolyard was still the old stone bench next to the fence. I went over and sat down there for a few minutes. It was very quiet around me, and everything was free from any motion; the calmness and freedom from noise or disturbance made my mind regress into the past. Looking at the staircase, I had a reference point from the present back to the past. How many times had I climbed these stairs going or coming from school? Like most primary school students, I was expected to go to school on my own carrying a heavy brown leather backpack. There were no school buses in those days, and it was a forty-minute journey across the railroad tracks from Alt-Tegel to Neu-Tegel twice each day. The practice of sending children off by themselves began when most children attended neighborhood schools and crime was not an issue. The only perils we had to fear were wind, rain, ice, and snow. Educators believed that unattended commuting fostered healthy independence. We discovered the thrill of traveling with friends, especially after school, stopping for an ice cream cone or browsing around at the open marketplace. Sitting at this bench also brought back sweet memories when Gisela and I would sit here talk to each other over lunch. I snapped out of my dreams when a big black crow broke the silence by flying over the old schoolhouse's rubble, making a racket and looking for its nest that no longer existed. In a way, I felt like the blackbird; I wanted to cry out for something that was forever gone.

Coming home to my mother and grandmother, I told them about my grief, that I no longer had respect for the enemy and that I would fight them tooth and nail if it killed me. This upset my mother very much, and my grandmother screamed at me with an angry voice, "Nonsense, the war is lost, it is almost over, what do you accomplish by throwing your life away? You don't want to die for a handful of criminals sitting in the government trying to save their own skin by sacrificing innocent people."

"Those are strong words," I reminded her. "And for saying that in public, they could hang you for treason."

"I have lived my life, lost everything, and don't care what happens to me," she said. "The only thing I am concerned about is making you see the truth. I know you are intelligent, but regardless of the education you received at the academy, start to learn thinking on your own. I am just repeating what your grandfather told you years ago." My grandmother had me in the corner, and I just changed the conversation. She was right about one thing, I needed some more time and evidence to think about it. I was depressed walking the next day to the S-Bahn station, it might make sense to the reader to understand that for two reasons. First of all, it hurt me very much seeing my beautiful Tegel in such a mess or ruins, and secondly, I felt betrayed if my belief in Adolf Hitler had been violated by the fraud and unfaithfulness of him and his government. As the train pulled out, I experienced a certain degree of temporary relief for the change of scenery. In reality the images did not change; riding the train across Berlin was like watching a movie. The whole panorama was composed of only two alternating picture frames, showing one section of town destroyed and another part of the city still standing.

Getting off the train in Schmargendorf, I was delighted not to see any destruction. There were many people seeking the stairway down from the platform. Everybody seemed to be in a hurry except for one old lady catching her breath and supporting herself on a cane with a small suitcase next to her. I stopped in front of her and said, "It looks to me like you need some help, do you want me to carry your suitcase down the stairs?"

First she looked at me, not saying anything; a few seconds later, her face became alive, and she was telling me, "Since you are in military uniform, I guess I can trust you."

We got started, and in a slow pace, we walked the last few steps up the stairs and got out of the station at the street level. An empty bench gave us a chance for her to relax and to get acquainted. I introduced myself, telling her that I was stationed here at the air force base serving as a Flakhelfer. She shook hands with me, saying that her name was Gertrud von Rathenow. "My husband died a year ago, and now I am living here alone in a big house in Schmargendorf. Most weekends, I go to visit my daughter in Bernau. She is married, and together with her husband, they own a restaurant and a small hotel. I have four grandchildren, and it keeps me young every time I am around them. I also have a son who is a doctor and the chief of the surgery department at the charité."

"Look," I said, "it is getting dark now; if you don't mind, I'd like to walk you home. Just show me the way; I am not in a hurry, and I really think I should escort you home."

"I do appreciate your help," she said. "But it is really a very short walk. You see over there the Heidelberg Platz, I live two blocks behind it on the corner of Johannesberger Strasse and Nauheimer Strasse."

I took her arm and suitcase, and we started walking; in less than ten minutes, we were in front of her house. I told her that it was a pleasure to meet her, but before I could say good night, she interrupted me, insisting that I come up and have some tea with her. How could I refuse the lonely old lady to have a chat with me? I was very impressed with the interior of her penthouse, lovely antique furniture, and a Bechstein grand piano—something my parents could never afford to have. Somehow she must have detected my amazement and was beginning to tell me that she already downsized her belongings and that this was all she had left. "We had a villa in Dahlem, and I gave it to my son after my husband died, and I took his penthouse." Enjoying the hot tea and the chocolate cookies she served on a silver tray, I learned more about her departed husband. According to her, he was one of the best attorneys in Berlin. His law office at the Friedrich Strasse still existed and was now run by the senior partners. "I will come right to the point," Mrs. Von Rathenow said. "I am about to ask you to do me a big favor; of course, I will reward you for helping me."

"Sure," I replied. "Anything that I am able to help you with."

She pointed to the fireplace across the room from us, asking me if I could see the big round vessel on top of the mantel. "Yes, I do see the ornamental vase under the big mirror, but pardon me for saying so, even though it is very pretty, it resembles an urn."

"You are absolutely right. It is an urn containing the ashes of my dead husband, Gilbert, and I am going to bury the urn as soon as possible, but so far I did not find anybody to assist me. Gilbert died of lung cancer; his last wish was to be cremated and his ashes to be buried in a certain place, not in a cemetery."

"May I ask what place he had selected as his last resting place?"

"Let me explain from the beginning. My husband and I, we are both natives of Berlin; we went to school together and have lived in this part of town ever since. We both love the Grunewald and the Wannsee. Some fifty years ago, when Gilbert finished law school, we decided to get married. During the time we dated, our favorite meeting place was a special big oak tree at the highest hilltop of the Grunewald. Sitting on an old wooden bench, underneath the one-hundred-or-more—year-old tree, the view is spectacular. Overlooking the Wannsee watching the many sailboats crisscrossing the lake is an exciting wonder of scenic effect. This is the same spot where Gilbert proposed to me, and under the old oak tree between kisses and embraces, we promised to love and to be true to each other forever with a full moon as our witness. We were very fortunate also that our preacher agreed to climb up the hill to marry us under the old tree with the reception taking place under the blue sky at the hilltop of the Grunewald. Do you have any idea by now where I intend to bury my dead husband, Gilbert?"

"Right next to the old oak tree," I said. "And I also know who is going to take him up there and dig the proper hole."

"Don't tell me you are going to do it," she was asking me with an uncertain tone in her voice.

"Yes, I will do it, maybe next Wednesday at night when we have a full moon. My girlfriend's mother has a car, and I have to ask her if she can drive us up the hill. Please let me have your phone number to tell you when we can make it," I asked. Overwhelmed with joy, she gave me her number, hoping to hear from me soon. On my way out, she shook my hand and thanked me again for my offer to help her.

After school Wednesday early in the afternoon, I had lunch at the cafeteria and took some sandwiches with me. From Dahlem I took the train to Wilmersdorf. Getting to Inge's house, she greeted me with a smile that could only mean one thing: she received some mail from Gisela. Indeed, there was one letter for each of us. The good news was that Gisela would get one-week vacation from December 13 to December 20. Gisela explained that only a few nurses could actually go home for Christmas; the rest would have to take turns before or after the holidays. Gisela and Helga decided to go together as soon as possible before something came up and they stopped, left all together. The good news in both letters certainly put us in a cheerful mood. Now Inge was changing the conversation over to something else.

"I don't know if I ever told you, but in my younger years in nursing school, my roommate's name was Hildegard Seifert. After our graduation, she married a high-ranking party leader by the name of Eckard. In all these years, we remained good friends, and she lives now in Dahlem with her husband Otto Eckard who recently was promoted to *Gauleiter* (district top official). Every year they invited us to the Christmas party in their house. Since my husband died, I haven't gone to see them. A few days ago, I received a call from Hildegard asking me please to come to her party and to bring a male escort. I really like to see her because we have a lot to talk about. Hildegard and I always had a very confidential and trustworthy relationship. I would be glad to go if you will come with me."

"Dear, Inge," I said, "you know I would love to go with you, but don't you think I would be a little outranked among all the party bosses?"

"Not at all, you would have a lot in common with the Gauleiter's son; as a matter of fact, he is a cadet at the Napola in Spandau."

"OK, that sounds good, you got yourself a date provided they let me out of the barracks."

"I already looked into that. The party is on the twelfth of December; that is a day you go to school in Dahlem, so you can come over here after school, take off your uniform, and get dressed up for the party. I think both of us will have a good time doing something else for a change." Inge finished by saying, "I am sure you have something to tell me that occurred lately in your military career."

"I have taken advantage of an option given to us by the CO to switch from the 8.8 cm Flak to either the 3.7 cm Flak or the 2 cm Zwillings gun. My choice is to go over to the 3.7 cm Flak, more rapid firepower and added flexibility. For personal reasons, living longer by hitting your target first."

Inge did not express an opinion; she just said, "I hope you know what you are doing, but tell me what else is new."

"Relax," I said. "Make yourself comfortable and listen to what happened to me last Sunday at the train from Tegel to Schmargendorf." I told her the whole story just like it happened. As I ended this lifetime human event compacted in a short report, I did not say anything more, and neither did Inge; but I kept watching her face for any emotion. Finally Inge broke the silence by saying, "You know, I try to feel sorry for the old lady, but I cannot. If I meet her, I will tell her that she is a lucky soul being happily married to a wonderful man for so many years and that she is blessed with a family taking care of her. One more thing, I will tell her at the Grunewald when we are watching you digging her husband's grave, 'I am envious of you knowing where your husband final rest. You can visit him here anytime, rest for a while, and come spiritually real close to him.' This is a luxury God never granted me. God only knows where my husband died in Russia or what kind of animals picked the flesh from his frozen bones." Inge could no longer talk, tears were running down her face from emotions too long bottled up. I hugged her in a gesture to comfort her, telling her to let it go.

"It's OK, you will feel better in a minute." As I embraced her, she slowed down, and after a few sobbing, she became composed again. I kept holding her, and she looked at me with a forced smile but she was still crying profusely. I purposely kept quiet, waiting till she was ready to talk. The first thing she said was, "Oh God, I needed that." I was not exactly sure what she was talking about, so I asked her, "What do you mean?"

"I am talking about a catharsis; I have seen it on some of my patients in crisis. I would not assume this could happen to me. I am not the type that cries very easy. I guess that's why I became a nurse; usually I can control myself pretty good. I did not even cry when they handed me that well-known infamous letter informing me that my husband died as a hero for the Führer, Volk, and Vaterland. Of course, I was at that time still in the state of denial."

"Look," I said, "you did fine. We are all human beings, and everybody has a breaking point; it was long overdue to purge yourself. Maybe it would have been better if I did not come across the old lady, and in time you would heal on your own."

"I don't agree," she said. "Self-pity is a poison. It slowly eats your guts, and I am glad it is out in the open. If you want to know if I am still going with you to do the job you volunteered for, the answer is yes. I am absolutely sure about it, and I want you to be here next Wednesday right after school. In the meantime, I would like to call Mrs. von Rathenow from the office and tell her that she can expect us next Wednesday. I will also make it clear to her that she never will have to worry about that we will ever talk to anybody about our undertaking."

"Inge," I said, "that is very nice, and what we are doing for the old lady might make us feel good for a long time. Since it is decided how we take care of it, I have another problem. I must tell you that I am hungry. Will you please do the honor and split a sandwich with me?"

"Sorry," she said, "I don't have any bread in the house, only some soup from yesterday."

"Great, warm up your soup, and I will provide the sandwich each made with Schmalz (lard) and Swiss cheese on rye bread." After supper we both noticed how fast time went by and that it was time to say good night. I hugged her good night, and somehow I'd never felt so close to her before.

As it was planned on Wednesday, I showed up at Inge's house to do our good deed. She was driving to Schmargendorf, and I was showing her the way to get to Mrs. Rathenow's place. The old lady was very happy to see us. I introduced the two women, then Mrs. von Rathenow invited us to the dining room to have some Kaffee und Kuchen with her. It smelled so wonderful how could we not accept? "I am honored to be your guest," Inge said. "But may I ask you respectfully, how can you afford to bake such a rich cake and share it with us when everybody lives on tight rations?"

"Normally I don't, but my daughter lives in the country, and I am so fortunate that she always helps me out. I am not a big eater; it is a pleasure to have my friends come over and eat with me. The real coffee from the coffee beans is something my son insists that I have one cup a day. He is a doctor, and he buys it for me."

"Yes, he is right," Inge agreed. "I am a nurse myself; when we get older, coffee is a great stimulant for a tired heart." The two ladies had a lively conversation, and I was just listening. Inge told Mrs. von Rathenow that Gisela was a student nurse in Frankfurt an der Oder and told her that she could not find a hospital in Berlin. "Sooner or later Frankfurt (Oder) will be evacuated, and then your daughter will return to Berlin. Being already a student nurse, I am sure my son will help her to find a hospital to go on with her studies."

"I would be very grateful," Inge said.

"Oh, think nothing of it, that's why we are friends helping each other."

"Ladies," I said, pointing at my watch, "I hate to break up this conversation, but we better get going."

"You are right," Mrs. von Rathenow said. "We'll talk more when we get back, but tell me, what do you need?" "Four items: a shovel, a pick, a flashlight, and a blanket to wrap the urn."

"Follow me downstairs, and we can put everything in the car."

I wrapped the urn in the blanket and put myself in the backseat, holding the urn. Mrs. von Rathenow was sitting in front next to Inge, telling her how to get to our destination. As we entered the Grunewald, there was very little traffic. Inge was almost able to drive up to the very top and park the car close to our place on a small dirt road.

When we got off the car, not one person was visible on the whole hilltop. A cool winter wind was blowing from the lake over the Grunewald. Mrs. von Rathenow was showing me the spot where she wanted me to dig the grave. I urged the women to go back and take shelter in the car; this was going to take me at least thirty minutes. Luckily the ground was not frozen, yet after I was about one foot deep, I started feeling hot and had to take my jacket off. As I was more or less three feet into the ground, I hit a big root of the old oak tree. Enlarging my hole on one side, big enough to get the urn past the wood, I dug another two feet. By now it was getting more difficult to get the dirt out. According to the length of the shovel, I judged the hole to be about five feet deep. Putting my overcoat back on, I walked back to the car for a short rest. "Are you all done?" I heard them say.

"Yes, we can now proceed with the burial." Inge was helping the old lady walk over to the graveside while I carried the urn. Pausing at the grave shortly, I waited for a signal from the widow to go ahead. Carefully I lowered the urn down the hole, manipulating it under the root to the ground.

The big root was stretching out like an arm to protect what was underneath. The widow deposited the first three handfuls of earth on top of the urn, and while we did the same, she finished her prayers, saying, "Good-bye, Gilbert, rest in peace."

"Wait for me in the car, I still have to backfill the grave," I whispered to them. It went fast; a little compaction and a heap of dry leaves on top, and nobody would ever know what happened here tonight. We were all sitting in silence as Inge was driving us back to Schmargendorf. As I put the tools away, Mrs. von Rathenow requested that we all go upstairs. We followed her wish, and again we were relaxing in her comfortable living room. I could tell by their faces that everybody seemed to be relieved that the task we gathered here for was accomplished. Mrs. von Rathenow appeared to be on top of it again as she was trying to get our attention to make a speech. "Words cannot describe how happy and grateful I am that you have helped me to fulfill my obligation as a wife, but you two total strangers came to actually help me carry out my husband's last wish. Your kindness makes you a friend to our family. Gilbert also reserved a bottle of wine for this solemn occurrence. Now let us open the bottle of 1929 Rothchild Cabernet Sauvignon and drink to the spirit of Gilbert and our new friendship."

The crystal-stem glasses were already on the table, and she was asking me to open the bottle of rare red wine. We raised our glasses, toasting each other by saying, "To your health, Mrs. von Rathenow."

"The same to you," she replied. "It is custom among friends who drink together to call each other by the first name, and since I am the oldest one in the room, I propose we do the same. Also", she said, "please give me a few minutes, and we will have Abendbrot [dinner] on the table." Inge went out with her to the kitchen to brew some black tea and put hot potato salad, bread, and butter on a tray. Together we set the table while we waited for Gertrud to come with the hot wieners *Würstchen* (hot dogs). We were now five years into the war; everybody was starving, and to have a meal like this was a special event. After supper, Gertrud showed us some pictures of her family. She was very proud of her children and grandchildren. Her son the doctor knew about our Grunewald adventure and left a token of his appreciation for Inge and me with his mother. Gertrud told us that he would be very insulted if we refused his gift.

"A rich high-ranking Nazi patient must have given it to him, and since he is not drinking, he hopes he can do you a favor with it, knowing that money cannot buy you anything anymore." Finally, at the end of the day, we thanked each other again, promised to stay in touch; and then Gertrud was showing me the big wooden box I had to put in the trunk of the car. After we left and Inge stopped in front of the base to let me out, she asked me if I knew what was in the box.

"Yes, I do," I said. "Twelve bottles of genuine French five-star Hennessey cognac."

"Oh my god, what are we going to do with it?"

"Nothing right now, take it home and hide it in the basement. This is better than gold; at the end, we might need it to barter for some food to survive." Inge agreed, and as we said good night, she reminded me of next week's Christmas party at her house and not to be late.

The first weekend in December was my turn for the two-day furlough; as usual, I was on my way to Tegel. Before I left the base, I packed a few things I'd saved, and then I went over to the mess hall to pick up my forty-eight-hour ration—one black bread and one can of wunderwurst, the German version of Spam. Walking to the railroad station, looking above, I saw a blue sky, clear and bright—a perfect weather condition for an air raid. At the ticket counter at the station, I saw a long line of people. One good thing was that when you were in uniform you didn't pay for transportation. Entering the S-Bahn, I saw that the car was already packed with people; the air stunk, and the interior was littered with filth and trash. What shocked me the most was the red-paint graffiti sprayed on the walls and windows. Slogans like Down with Hitler and Long Live Stalin didn't seem to elicit any emotions from the passengers one way or the other. As Christmas 1944 was just around the corner, I could sense it that most Berliners already knew, by a strange gut feeling, that this was their last Christmas before Germany's doomsday. Any way you looked at it, there was very little to celebrate and to celebrate with. Ultra short rations, constant stress, and much of the Capital being reduced to rubble in never-ending air raids were not putting people in the mood for the upcoming holidays. The theme of Christmas is peace on earth, and when you are about to face death, then this noble message is nothing but a joke. This kind of gallow's humor was circulating, saying, "Enjoy the war; the peace will be unbearable." Most Berliners spent more time in cellars and air-raid shelters doing nothing than upstairs in their own beds. Being helpless and the lack of sleep resulted in a form of trust in your underground neighbor sitting next to you. By talking to each other, you ventilated your feelings and thereby suppressed anxiety, fatalism, and hysteria. Wherever you went, there was a pervasive atmosphere in the air of impending downfall in personal lives as much as in the nation's existence.

An unexpected surprise happened in Tegel: as the train came to a stop, all the doors were simultaneously opened from the outside, and members of the SS guard were demanding in a loud voice to have the passport ready for inspection. Several people were taken out for further interrogation to the station master's office; they might not have any papers or were arrested under the suspicion of being deserters. The rest of the passengers were free to go, and the train was moving on. My mother and my grandmother were just having supper when I walked into the house. "Come on and join us," they were saying, and I put my meager contribution on the table. "You like vegetable soup; it is out of my own garden," Oma said. After dinner, the women sat down in the living room and did some needlework. I pulled a chair next to them to have a conversation with them. Oma was telling me of an invitation; they had to visit her youngest daughter, Senta, my mother's half sister. She got married recently, and they rented a house where we all could stay overnight.

Acquaintance with a Fighter Ace

Senta and her husband, Heinz, were now living in Oranienburg. Heinz was a fighter pilot at the nearby Jagd-Geschwader 16. I had not seen Senta since the Lindenhof days in her parents' house when she was still going to school. "Should Senta really be serious about our visit, it would be my pleasure to go and see them."

"Of course, they will be happy to see us, so let's get going tomorrow morning," Grandmother said. Next morning, after we got up, had breakfast, and packed a few things, we went to the other side of our block to catch on the corner of Bolle and Gorky strasses the bus number 14 to take us to Waidmanslust, which was only three miles from our house. Here we were, waiting for the S-Bahn that would go all the way to Oranienburg. Oranienburg was at the northwest, outward end of Berlin. Arriving in Oranienburg, Oma opened her purse to look for Senta's letter. In the letter was the address and a short direction how to get there. Not far from the city center, we found her house at a dead-end street. It was an older two-story Victorian house with four bedrooms. The visit with Senta was a friendly reunion after almost five years. There was so much we were talking about from the bad times, from the good old days, and the good things of the presently bad times. Senta was telling us about her husband and my mother interrupted the conversation, asking her when we were going to meet Heinz. "Right now he is at the base, but he will be here this evening," Senta said. When it got dark, I heard a motorcycle pulling in, and here he came—Heinz Koehler on a shiny Triumph. The moment he got off the bike, I jumped up, saluting him, saying, "Good evening, Lieutenant, sir."

He saluted me with a smile on his face, saying, "Please don't give me this Hitler Youth crap; you are in the air force now." He made us feel at home with his pleasant manners. I was very impressed with his good behavior when he asked my grandmother respectfully if he could call her mom. At Senta's question of what were we going to have for supper, he replied, "Fresh fried fish from the Baltic Sea caught this morning, and all you can eat."

"What kind of miracle is this?" Senta wanted to know. "Did the fish fly over here?"

"Exactly, you said it, baby, special delivery by a group of Me 109s." Now Heinz explained to us that some of the fighter groups from the coast were relocated to new sectors around Berlin; they were urgently needed for the better protection of the city. "As always, our group captain was on the ball; he called the other CO up north asking him to stuff the planes with all the fish they could carry. The new fighter group assigned to our base just arrived before I left; I helped them unload ten pounds of fish for every family. Here was our share, and Heinz handed Senta a big brown parcel. "Give it to me," Oma said. "I know what to do with it." Thirty minutes later, we were all sitting at the table. Heinz opened a bottle of Riesling, and we all enjoyed a most delicious fish dinner. As the women did the dishes, Heinz invited me to sit with him in the living room in front of the fireplace. Completely relaxed, he pulled out a pack of cigarettes and offered me one. "No, thanks," I said. "I am not smoking."

"Very well, do you have any other vices?"

"Yes, I do, I like to drink when I am with company. I learned it from my grandfather; he was a winemaker."

"Ya, Senta told me about him. Too bad he lost his life in such a horrible way. You must be very fond of him."

"Yes, indeed I am; he was my mentor. I learned more from him than I learned from my own father. He'd seen it all coming; he went through it all in WW I. He tried his best to open my eyes not to follow a regime that is taking us to hell."

"How do you feel now about it?" Heinz wanted to know.

"At best I have mixed feelings; you have to understand where I am coming from. Four years living in an academy under the name of Adolf Hitler did not leave me much room to do my own thinking. Throughout history, the scale of human tragedy," I was trying to explain to Heinz, "at the end of any bloody war was beyond the imagination of everyone who did not live through it. Any generalization concerning the conduct of individuals on both sides must be avoided. Extremes of human suffering including degradation can bring out the best as well as the worst in human nature. The almost unpredictability of life or death reflects human behavior to a large extent, even below the most aggressive animal."

"Are you trying to come up with a defense for the barbarous killings going on in Germany?" Heinz interrupted me.

"If you are referring to our prison camps, then I must remind you about the gulags in Russia and the detention camps in America."

"Let me tell you," Heinz said, "there is a hell of a difference between a prison camp and a death camp. What I am talking about are death camps you find all over Germany built by the Nazis, where human beings, including women and children, are driven in by the trainloads."

"I never heard of anything like that."

"I believe you," Heinz said. "Neither do 80 million decent German citizens know anything about those atrocities committed by the Nazis, SS gangsters, and Gestapo criminals of the Third Reich."

For a moment I was speechless, shocked, and in disbelief. Heinz must have sensed it when he said, "I know it is hard to understand, but just ten minutes from here, outside of Oranienburg, is a death camp; and people living in this city don't even know what is going on behind the walls of Sachsenhausen. All of this will come out by surviving witnesses in a war tribunal at the end of the war. The guilty ones will be given in a court of justice a swift death sentence, but generations of innocent Germans will suffer and pay for the crimes of the Nazis."

I adjusted my chair a little closer to Heinz and asked him, "Can you answer one more question for me? What in the hell's name are we all fighting and perhaps dying for?"

"To save lives," he said. "Whose lives? The Führer's life and those of his hangmen for a few more days in his bunker."

"That too, but what is more important, we can slow down the Russians to give millions of refugees a chance to escape. As far as you and I are concerned, every enemy plane we shoot down may save that many more people on the ground."

"To be very honest with you, Heinz, I never did believe in all the wonder weapons Hitler promised us, but the legend of it makes it a great propaganda tool of Dr. Goebels to spread hope among the German people and to keep on fighting."

"No, not exactly, from an engineering point of view, the VI and the VII missiles are mechanical marvels, unfortunately, to change the course of the war the missiles came out too late, and since the British destroyed the production in Penemünde, they are not much more than a nuisance over London. However, the concept of jet propulsion is the most revolutionary development in the history of aviation. Even two years ago if we would have started the mass production of jetfighters, we could have stopped the enemy from destroying our cities. Instead our glorious Führer insisted on building a fleet of jet bombers, which never got off the ground anyway. What we have left now are a few old Me 109, which are too slow and some Focke-Wulf 190 altogether no match for the armada of enemy fighters. Things are so bad that we are instructed not to engage in dogfights anymore but to get after the Flying Fortresses the best we can. The situation is so desperate that we are beginning to set up a group of *Rammjager* (commando of suicide fighters) which are willing to sacrifice their lives by flying straight into a Flying Fortress. These German suicide pilots are mostly young Hitler Youth fighters trained in a hurry who see it as the greatest honor to die for the Fatherland. One of the first bases for such volunteers is the JG-3 Jagdgesohwader Udet outside of Stendal. According to our intelligence, there are thousands of American bombers sitting on the east coast of England waiting to be assembled. Even if every pilot in Germany would today sign up for suicide duty, we would long run out of pilots before the Allied Bomber Command would suffer a shortage on bombers."

Before we were able to end the conversation, Senta came in to tell us that it was time to go to bed. "Yes," Heinz said, "let's call it a day; but before that, I have to call the base and see if the air is clear."

I said good night, and Senta was showing me to my room. Next morning, somehow a lazy Sunday, I slept in. Over breakfast Senta was telling us that Heinz had already left for the base; she also told us that because they lived within five kilometers from the base, he was allowed to go home and sleep with his family, but that he must be constantly in radio communication. "We are so lucky we got this house."

Since this was such a clear day and just a little cold, everybody wanted to go for a walk, and Senta would show us the beautiful old town of Oranienburg. We were going north from Lindenring, the street of Senta's house, toward Bernauer Strasse to see the Schloss Oranienburg (castle), the former residence of the Kurfürsten von Brandenburg. Below the castle was the monument of Louise Henriette. The castle was built from 1651 to 1655; today it was used as an SS barracks. A few steps behind the beautiful baroque buildings were the huge Schloss park. On a cold day in December, there was not much activity in the park, but a few tables and benches invited visitors to sit down and relax, or even have a picnic under the shade of the trees. Grandmother motioned us to sit a spell and to enjoy the beautiful landscaping before we went home. My mother wanted to buy a few things in town, but unfortunately, on Sundays all stores were closed in Germany. Back at Senta's house, she brewed some fresh coffee, and we had some oatmeal cookies. The conversation went on about many things you talk about when you have not seen each other for such a long time, but finally Grandma said, "It is getting dark we better get going." As we were getting ready to go, Senta insisted that she would walk with us to the train station. Now that we were living so close to each other, she was suggesting that we get together more often. "Say good-bye to Heinz for us and tell him fortune favors the brave," I said.

At Waidmanslust we all got off the train together, then walked over to the bus stop. Waiting for the bus, my mother was happily telling me that

Senta gave us all the rest of the fish to take home, almost five pounds. She did not want to take it, but Senta said, "You have to take it home. Heinz is bringing so much food from the base; we cannot eat it all."

"Good for them," I said, but to myself I was saying, *What a price to pay when the medium life expectancy of an active fighter pilot is only ninety days.* Here came the bus; I helped them in, say good-bye, and the next stop for them would be Neu-Tegel. Going back to the S-Bahn station, I entered the waiting room to get out of the cold. Checking the train schedule, I found out that there was one more train tonight going to Westkreuz. How lucky could I get? I was thinking, if there was no air raid tonight, I should be in Schmargendorf in less than an hour. Everything went perfect; reaching my base, I entered the barracks just five minutes before lights-out. I had a good night's sleep and next morning, I went after breakfast to school in Dahlem as I did every Monday and Wednesday. Then after school, I would be going straight back to the base to do my homework till bedtime, which I had neglected lately.

But, there would be no bedtime; a major air raid tonight was going to come down over Berlin. Every time a bomber group crossed Leipzig or Magdeburg, Berlin received a prealarm warning, regardless if the enemy group was flying home or on a bombing mission. If there were several groups, it could be confusing. In the past, home-flying bomber groups had changed their course, setting up markers over Berlin, pretending to get ready for carpet bombing. The German command center ordered all the nearby fighter groups to intercept the Flying Fortresses before they were able to unload their deadly cargo. Suddenly, undetected by German radar, out of the clouds from ten thousand feet above were interacting a U.S. fighter group of P-51 Mustangs engaging the German Me 109 and Fw 190 in a dogfight. The new combat took place at four thousand feet, but the Flak on the ground had to stay out of it as long as our fighters were at the same altitude. While this battle was going on, as precisely planned, a second U.S, bomber formation was flying several bombing runs to destroy a major oil refinery in East Berlin by instrument targeting. The Americans were playing the old shell game "now you see it, now you don't." The vacuum they created in the German defense gave them the chance to destroy a major strategic target with practically no casualties of their own. The outcome of the battle over the center of the city was a different story.

Looking back, none of us were really aware of what happened till next day at the briefing. As far as our battery was concerned, we could truly say we had a great night, and for many of us, it was our first action under fire. It all started about 9:00 PM when this message from the command stand came over the radio: "Attention, attention, an enemy bomber formation of about nine hundred to one thousand U.S. B-17 and B-29 Flying Fortresses are now entering the Heinrich-Dora area."

"That is it," I said. "They are now in Magdeburg; in an hour they will be in Berlin." Right after the announcement, the battery bells were ringing, giving us first alert. We were sitting in full gear in the barracks, helmets and gas masks handy, ready to jump at a moment's notice. At 10:28 PM, there was full alarm, the sirens were going off in most parts of Berlin. This was no drill, but it still meant hurry up and wait. Everybody was running to his designated battle station, taking position at the gun under the open sky. At the same time, most Berliners with children and luggage were on the way to seek protection at the nearest bunker or air-raid shelter. The success of a Flak battery depended on the dexterity and coordination of each gun. It was all teamwork, and the performance of each individual member of the gun crew made it all work.

Unconsciously, we were trying to kill time, not showing to be nervous by making last-minute adjustments, turning dials, hooking up equipment, and checking the earphones. My job was to keep loading the gun; you didn't ever want to run out of ammunition in the middle of a battle. Behind me I had already a good supply of ammo magazines, but to have an adequate reserve, I asked two of the Russian POWs to go back to the main depot to bring me a few more boxes of ammo. All that was left to do now was wait for the gun captain's order and watch the sky. Several searchlights were now going back and forth, scanning the sky. At about ten thousand feet, two B-29s were nailed down by the light fingers of the searchlights. Most likely they belonged to the 600 Fortresses reported over Weissensee, East Berlin. Many times you'd see bombers not flying in formation you could assume that they were already hit by Flak or night fighters and trying to limp home. Neither of them was trying to get out of the light stream. Seconds later our 8.8 cm Flak started to shoot at them point-blank. One of the B-29s got hit in the belly and exploded. At the second salvo, the other plane lost a wing; it made a barrel roll to the right before it tumbled to the ground. No crew members of the two planes had a chance to bail out.

More planes were coming, this time in a small formation without fighter escort. They sure picked the wrong way to fly back to England; our battery had a field day. I counted at least six more B-29s being hit and going down. Some of them Fortresses were trying to fly low in order to escape the 8.8 cm Flak. This was the moment we were waiting for. From the command stand came the order: "Small-caliber fire at random." Every gun was now busy firing at any bomber flying above us, even the 2 cm Flak with its great flexibility had plenty of targets flying below three thousand meter. There were still more bombers flying above the battery. One came in very low, attacking us with his 50 mm board guns. Bullets were raking up the dirt next to us, but nobody got hurt, and luckily, the gunfire missed the ammunition boxes next to me. It all happened very fast, and as the pilot made a pass, our gunlayer had his gunsight pointed at the bomber's tail. A long burst of fire from our 3.7 cm Flak ripped the bomber's tail unit right off; at the end of the field the Fortress hit one of the Russians' barracks and exploded.

At 11:38 PM, the air raid was over; it was still early, and there might be another air raid, but for now we were closing down and returning the leftover ammunition to the main bunker. At the end, we hit the sack; at first I was more shaking than sleeping.

A Visit at the Eckard Mansion

Two days after the last major air raid, I arrived at Inge's house in Wilmersdorf. It was still early in the afternoon, and we had time to talk; naturally we were talking about the event and casualties of last Monday night. According to the official report, Inge told me, East Berlin was the target of the night, 406 people were killed and 303 were injured. In reality these figures could be a lot higher. I was telling Inge how our battery had repaid the enemy in a small version, but she was more interested in the conversation I had with Heinz Koehler. The German air command told them of the dwindling of planes and pilots through July and August, of the month of September when the count of pilots fell below the survival minimum, of the desperate pessimism in the Luftwaffe all throughout October, of Berlin burning, civilians dying in large numbers and no night fighters available, and of the Allied bombers still coming on and on, setting fire to residential districts and bombing and spreading the fires trying to break the city's spirit.

The Luftwaffe was anticipating a new, larger onslaught in the New Year and the spring. The remaining German planes were grounded for lack of fuel. "I don't want to be a crape hanger, but to prolong the war is suicide; somebody has to approach the United States and Britain to arrange some terms for surrender. Tonight," Inge said, "I will find out who in the Nazi hierarchy will have the guts to do it behind the Führer's back." While Inge was taking out some civilian clothes for me, I went to shower before getting dressed. On the way out, she gave me the car keys, asking me to do the driving to Dahlem today. I followed the Hohenzollern Damm as far as Kronprinzen Allee, driving south with the Grunewald Forest to my right toward Dahlem Dorf. "Slow down," Inge said. "And when you come to Hütten Weg, make a left turn." A few minutes later, at the end of the road, was a parklike clearing where I parked the car. Among all the villas in Dahlem, the residence of the Eckards was one of the largest suburban estates. At our arrival, a butler opened the door and led us into the vestibule. With the exception of some potted palm trees, it was furnished more as a large comfortable sitting room with a couch and two easy chairs positioned around a low coffee table. I thought the decanter of Gordon's gin and dry cherry on a silver tray were a nice welcoming touch, but the stay in the foyer for us was only momentarily. As soon as the butler got a hold of Mrs. Eckard, she came at once to greet us. The two women embraced each other like real friends who had been separated for some time. Inge introduced me to Hildegard, and with genuine openness, she gave me a hospitable welcome. Walking into the house, I found myself in a huge living room with an open beam ceiling. In one corner, a lady in a black dress was sitting at a grand piano playing soft music and some Christmas songs. What caught my eye the most was a ten-foot Christmas tree with all its beautiful decorations and flashing lights in a bay window. My fascination was shared by Inge, but then Hildegard invited us to the dining room for some refreshments. Actually the dining room was converted for the party with long tables to serving as a buffet. "Help yourselves," Hildegard said. "But now you have to excuse me; I want to see if I can find my husband." The last time I had seen so much food was before the war when my mother and I had lunch at the upstairs restaurant at the KaDeWe, the world-famous super department store like Harrods in London. With great gusto, Inge and I filled our plates. Among other guests, we found a place to sit down in the large solarium. For dessert we had butter cream torte and real Bohnen coffee and topped it off with the traditional Christmas drink of eggnog, known among the English as Tom and Jerry. Where did all the food come from? Well, we didn't ask any questions, but it certainly was not purchased with ration food stamps.

    It was almost as if Mr. and Mrs. Eckard did not want to disturb our meal; they both came to see us later with Mr. Eckard apologizing for not being able to see us sooner. Inge was telling him who I was while he was reaching out to shake my hand. I clicked my heels, saying, "Thank you for inviting me; it is my pleasure to meet you, Herr Gauleiter."

    "Oh please," he replied, "let's not be so formal, this is a Christmas celebration and not a NS party rally." He looked at me, and I could tell that there was a question on his mind. He paused for a moment and then he said, "If your name is Vogt, are you by any chance related to Obersturmbannführer Rudolf Vogt?"

    "Yes, I am, he was my uncle, a brother of my father."

    "This is a small world," he said. "I have fond memories of Rudolf Vogt; he was my liaison officer for North Brandenburg in charge of the election campaign. You can be very proud of him; he was a German patriot, too bad he was killed in such a tragic accident. You must meet my son Peter;

I am sure the two of you have a lot in common. Let me take you upstairs to his room." The two women endorsed his statement, seeing a chance to talk to each other in private. Peter had a small apartment on the second floor, giving him a lot of privacy—something that I never had. I envied him for not having to sleep on the couch in his parents' living room. Talking to him was a pleasure; he did not act like a kid of rich parents. I suppose what we mainly had in common was our mutual upbringing and education in a national socialist boarding school. He was asking me how I liked the three years at the LBA-Neisse, and I told him that those were the best years in my life, and I wouldn't have missed them for anything. "I feel the same way about the Napola in Spandau, a decent Prussian military academy. Our teachers are modest and believe in German nationalism even if they have to find a new Führer." The junction where our opinions differed was the question on what to do about the war. My opinion was to capitulate at any cost to stop the terror by the Nazi Party. Peter was strictly against it and wanted to keep on fighting to the bitter end.

He had not left the walls of Spandau, and it was easy for him to make such statement not being part of the war and not seeing people bleed and die around him. "I might change my mind," I said, "if you give me one good reason why we should keep on fighting."

"I will give you five good reasons," Peter said, and he went on elaborating on his thesis. "Facing an unconditional surrender will deliver us to the enemies of Germany without any mercy. A good example are the atrocities at Nemmersdorf, when Red Army troops had invaded the southeastern corner of East Prussia and raped and murdered inhabitants of this village. The Russian propaganda minister Ilja Ehrenburg and Stalin are openly declaring that the German people have to be destroyed. On the other side of the Atlantic, our chances to survive are not any better. Theodore N. Kaufman, a friend of Roosevelt, insists by saying, 'Germany must perish.' Many Germans don't see a chance for peace anymore, but what really puts them in a state of paroxysm of rage, despair, and desperation is the statement of Morgenthau that at the end of the war all Germans will be mandatorily sterilized and sent to labor camps in Russia and Africa. Now, the good news, if we can prolong the war for another six months, we might be able to bargain for an advantageous peace treaty."

"That is interesting," I said. "Perhaps you can tell me what we got left to make an offer with. The Americans know that we are close to put an atomic bomb together; we already have it on paper. What is setting us back is the valued heavy water we lost in Norway. The Americans are also working on the atomic bomb in their Manhattan project, but the most important item they have not developed yet is the trigger mechanism. There are two reasons why the Americans would like to get their hands on our papers.

First of all they are anxious to force Japan to surrender, and secondly they would hate to see our scientists being captured by the Russians. All this makes sense to press for negotiation with the West while we are still under arms. Tell me, Peter, realistically speaking, do you know how close we are to put such a bomb of mass destruction together?"

"All I know is that we have to overcome a minor uranium problem, and this monster will be ready to fly. Dr. Lange and his colleagues are working around the clock to extract pure uranium metal from the mineral pitchblende to separate isotope U-235 from the more common U-238. With the help of Martin Borman, Dr. Werner Heisenberg obtained all the uranium ore he wanted from the Joachimsthal mine in Czechoslovakia. Furthermore, Borman had also ensured that he would receive the lion's share of the heavy water produced by the Mormek hydroelectric plant. When that installation was destroyed in February 1943 by Norwegian commandos, he had ordered the IG Farben works at Merseberg to make good the loss."

"How do you get a hold of all these secrets?" I asked Peter.

"Well," he said, "sometimes it helps when your father is a Gauleiter. Life must and will go on; the worst thing we can do is give up hope."

At this point, I was trying to change the conversation by asking Peter, "Do you have a hobby or a favorite pursuit of recreation?"

"Physically," he explained, "I get plenty of exercise in all the sport activities the academy in Spandau had to offer, being on the football team is my highest achievement. I don't have a particular hobby, but when I am stressed out and especially when I am alone, I turn to good music. I enjoy American jazz more than anything else."

"You mean you listen to the BBC radio?"

"Hell no, I got my own record collection. I don't want to hear any British propaganda; Winston Churchill is a bigger liar than our glorious Dr. Joseph Goebbels. Here, take a look." And he showed me a big glass cabinet on the opposite wall of his studio. "Here you will find recordings from all the big bands, from Benny Goodman, Count Basie, Glenn Miller, Duke Ellington, Tommy Dorsey, Woody Herman, Artie Shaw, Harry James, Benny Carter, and Gene Krupa. I wish I had the time; I would play some of these records for you."

"I understand; they want to see us again down at the party, but answer one stupid question for me before we go, how did you obtain such a complete collection of American musicians in a country like Germany where American jazz music is outlawed?"

"My father has connections with a colonel of the German occupation army in Copenhagen where you can buy whatever you want in any music store."

As we went down to rejoin the party, many people had already left, but the Gauleiter was still busy entertaining his guests, mainly members of the NS Party. Inge and Hildegard were sitting on a small table near the fireplace enjoying their conversation over a glass of wine. They saw us coming and waved us over to sit down with them. Inge was telling Hildegard and Peter that Gisela would come tomorrow for just a short one-week vacation from Frankfurt an der Oder. Both were briefly acquainted with Gisela and liked to see her again one day if time permitted. Hildegard was suggesting that we all meet again at her house next Wednesday. She said, "If for any reason you cannot make it give me a call, and we set it up for another time." That sounded good, everybody agreed, and we had a tentative appointment for a get-together. We were still talking for another hour about the war and the good times past. The piano player was now packing in and on her way out, and that made us realize that the party was over; we were about the only one group left. Thanking the Eckard family for their friendship and hospitality, Peter was taking us to the car. On the way to Schmargendorf base, I told Inge how impressed I was and how good it felt just for one day to live a normal life.

"Don't forget your uniform and boots in the backseat, or they will put you in the brick, and please come early next week when Gisela gets here." A quick peck on the cheek and her car took off for Wilmersdorf.

History was my favorite subject, but today I was not able to concentrate, just sitting here in class chewing fingernails. All that was on my mind was Gisela. My civilian clothes were in a package under my desk, and I was ready to grab it and leave school. The last class was after lunch from one to two o'clock, which I was going to skip today. Taking the train to Wilmersdorf was only a fifteen-minute ride. Finally I was at Inge's house, and Gisela was coming out to greet me. We embraced each other. She was smiling while she had tears in her eyes, saying, "I'll never let you go."

"Well," I replied, "in that case you have to stay here and take care of me."

"I will, it won't be long, and I'll be back for good."

"Honestly, I missed you; ask your mother how we are worried about you being so close to the Russian front. We have to sit down, and you have tell us all about the hospital and what you are doing there."

"I don't want to interrupt you, but right now I think we should get ready and drive over to see Hildegard and Peter," Inge reminded us and handed me a clean shirt to put on after I take a quick shower. She also suggested to wear a different suit today. The moment we were getting out of the house, Inge tossed me the car keys, saying, "OK, we are ready; you can drive us now to Dahlem." Arriving at the Eckard estate, the beautiful villa looked even better in the daytime, and I could park the car right in front of it. The housekeeper opened the door for us and took us to the veranda. I could have found the large enclosed patio with my eyes closed just following the smell of fresh-brewed coffee. At the same time Hildegard was coming down the staircase to greet us. After the mutual salutation, we were invited to sit down in comfortable sofa chairs around the coffee table. The friendly housekeeper, a young blond girl from Poland, was bringing in a tray of *Pflaumenkuchen* (plum cobbler) and some other pastry. She was serving hot coffee and cake topped with whipped cream on fine sets of china. The coziness of the heated room, the tasty sweets, and the presence of friends created almost instantly the atmosphere of a genuine *Kaffeeklatsch* (gossip over a cup of coffee). The participation of the conversation was mostly among the three women, all nurses, and they were asking Gisela all kinds of questions. I did listen and learned a lot about her new life and environment. As the women were catching their breath, I inquired about Peter. "Oh, I am sorry," Hildegard said. "I forget to tell you, Peter will be home at six o'clock for dinner, and Otto is out of town for two days, party business, you understand. I hope you all will have abendbrot (supper) with us, then stay a little longer and have a glass of wine with me by the fireplace."

"We will stay," Inge said. "Too bad Otto is not here today; I was hoping to have a chance to talk with him about my problems. He was very busy at the Christmas party, and I did not want to impose on him while he was talking to his guests. You know in my position, I am responsible to get off the street to the people that are bombed out and have no home to go. There are by far more families drifting from shelter to shelter than there are apartments or rooms available where I can put them in. Otto, in his capacity as Gauleiter, might be able to pull some strings and motivate people to move closer together to give up a spare room or a suite in the basement that could comfort those unfortunate people that lost everything."

"I am sure Otto will do his utmost to help you," Hildegard said. "Just give me your office number, and I have him call you."

Right on time Peter walked in and said, "Hello, how is everybody. Next question, when are we going to eat? I am hungry."

"Give us ten minutes to set the table," his mother said, "and we will be ready to sit down in the dining room."

"Anything new in Spandau?" I asked him.

"Yes, there is," he replied. "Today the announcement came down from the Anstaltsleiter (academy director) informing us that every young man over the age of fifteen will have to join the home front war effort or enlist as Flakhelfer beginning January 1, 1945. The school for those students affected will be open on a part-time basis."

"What shall I do?" Peter said.

"First of all, think about the options you have and then make a decision. If you wait till you get drafted they might send you to a place far away from your home and parents. On the other hand if you volunteer, you have the luxury to make a choice of your own. In my case, I am just fifteen, but I decided to stay in Berlin to continue my education and primarily to be close to my mother and grandmother. If I have to go and fight, I want to do it right here in my hometown," I said.

"Last call for Abendbrot." Hildegard was calling us, and everybody went to be seated. Once more here came the Polish girl bringing to the table various dishes of butter, cheese, salami, ham, and other cold cuts. A platter of fruit and a basket of pumpernickel, white bread, black bread, and dinner rolls completed the selection. Inge, Gisela, and I, without saying anything, were very fascinated to see so much food on one table. I could not help but to make a comparison in my mind of how much the average Berliner was getting on his food ration stamps for a long time. Current daily calorie rates were reduced to a minimum of one thousand per person. That was too high to die on and not enough to live on. Besides the quantity, the quality of the food was also a major factor. On the bread I was eating tonight, I didn't taste any sawdust. The wurst (sausage) was not stretched with milk powder or any other fillers of carbohydrates. We had not seen butter in ages; instead, we received margarine that looked like butter but tasted like axle grease. "What are you thinking?" Gisela said, which brought me back to reality, and I was joining again the conversation inspired by the great company and food.

After the evening meal was completed, Hildegard and Inge moved over to the fireplace. Peter put his hand on my shoulder and said, "Come on, old chum, you and Gisela will relax for a spell in my private chambers."

When we reached upstairs the first thing he said was, "Oh boy, I had a rough day; what I need is a good drink." He opened his liquor cabinet, asking us what we would like to drink. "Nothing for me," Gisela said. "But I'll take a glass of water if I may."

How about you?" he asked me. "I have a good bourbon, or better yet, I can make you a Scottish whisky and soda on ice."

"Surprise me," I said, and he got busy mixing the drinks.

"Now," Peter remarked, "I did cut you short the other day; today you must listen to some of my records." And he started to play some soft jazz music. Lifting his glass, he said, "Cheers, good luck, and a better life to all of us."

I couldn't help myself, I said, "Your life could not get much better."

"That is right," he replied. "But it could get worse, so I will enjoy it as long as it lasts; that brings me to the point of what I worry about. I have the strange feeling that as of today, I will start a new chapter in my life. I do not see how I could stay out of WW II any longer."

"Relax," I said. "Living in Berlin, you are already in the war. Your chances of getting killed in Berlin are almost equal as fighting on the Russian front."

"I wish I could have stayed in Berlin," Gisela said. "But it was not in the cards for me." Then she kept on saying, "It seems to me it would be a logical choice for you Peter to stay in Berlin and volunteer for the home front; that way you could go on with your education, and at the same time you would not have to give up the privileged life you presently enjoy in the home of your parents."

For a few moments there was silence in the air, and then Peter took a deep breath and started to talk. "You guys have me convinced of what is good for me and thereby actually made a decision for me, which leaves me with two more options. I can sign up for the Hitler Youth firefighters or volunteer for the Luftwaffe as Flakhelfer; I think I will join the latter."

"If you ask me," I interjected, "pick a battery somewhere between Dahlem and Spandau, possible closer to home, because you will spend most of your time at the base, and teachers of your school may follow you there."

"Thank you for your advice," Peter said. "And I will keep that in mind; maybe I could join your battery in Schmargendorf."

"I am sure your father could arrange that" was my answer.

"Since that is decided, let's have another drink." And Peter mixed a fresh refill. This time Gisela accepted a glass of wine.

"One more for the road is OK," I said. "After that we have to think about going home. I have to be at the base by 10:00 PM." The women downstairs were also wrapping it up. Hildegard blessed all of us, and we wished each other a Merry Christmas and a Happy New Year. Inge thanked Peter and Hildegard for us and told them to stay alive. "And God's will," she says, "if after the war I am still around, I will make it up to you." Inge did not drink as much as I did, so she would do the driving.

Reaching the base, she parked the car, and we talked for a few minutes. Gisela asked me if I could come and see her tomorrow. Unfortunately, I had to tell her that I would not be able to see them before Friday night, but I would do my best to stay with them Saturday and Sunday. There was so much we had to talk about and such a short time to be together.

It broke my heart to think about Monday when Gisela had to take the train to go back to Frankfurt (Oder). I wished I could go with her or keep her in Berlin, but neither was possible. Not to get sentimental, I grabbed my bag with the uniform, gave each of the women a kiss, and went to enter the base.

Friday night I approached dear Sergeant Backe. He said nothing was in the forecast; and knowing that my girlfriend was in town for a few days, he was nice enough to let me go to Wilmersdorf till midnight. Gisela and her mother were like family to me, and that's the way we treated each other. This weekend was my regular furlough; normally on Saturdays and Sundays you would find me in Tegel, but since these were the last two days Gisela was in Berlin, I would be with her in Wilmersdrorf. Early Saturday morning, I had breakfast at the base and collected my two-day ration to take along, which was generally more generous, not in quality but in quantity. The first thing I did when I got to Inge's house was to undergo a regular metamorphosis: take off the uniform and put on some civilian clothes. It was an unwritten law primarily because Inge wanted to uphold the privacy in her home and not be reminded of the war. I totally agreed with her, and all of us felt more relaxed. Our conversation was mainly focused on Gisela's new life in the hospital. Ironically, we could not escape the war because we were all involved one way or another, and certainly we wanted to know about her contribution and foremost her safety being so close to the Russian front. Gisela was telling us that more and more wounded soldiers were coming in and that there was not enough room to put them. "In addition there is an overwhelming flood of refugees coming across the river Oder to get away from the Russian army. The kind of care we are able to provide is not the best, and a lot of meatball surgery, as we call it, is going on just to get the severely wounded ready for a transport to the rear area. At times a crew of us has to get out to the other side of the river to give first aid treatment to those that could not get to the hospital on their own, usually one physician, two medics, and two nurses. Sometimes emergency procedures such as blood transfusion and minor surgery have to be performed in the field or next to the roadside. The military only takes care of their own, but we treat both, military and civilians."

My Last Days with Gisela

To give Gisela a break, I raised the question: "Since it is Saturday night, we all should go and see one of the movies."

"Great," Gisela said. "I have not seen one in a long time."

"You two go," Inge replied. "I have to catch up on some of my paperwork." Personally, I thought it was just an excuse of Inge to give us a chance to be alone, which I had to admit was nice of her. Gisela's favorite theater was right here in Wilmersdorf, not far from the house serving now as a cinema at the present time but was built originally as a stage theater. It had a high ceiling, and upstairs was a balcony arranged like a horseshoe. During the war, to go and see a motion picture had become the number one entertainment for the average Berliner. Coming in from the cold, it felt good to be in the well-heated theater. Going upstairs, we were lucky to find a love seat in a private box at the balcony in the back. It was so cozy and warm up here that we had to take our jackets off. Punctually the lights dimmed down, and as it got dark, the film started rolling. First they showed the News Week followed by the main feature. Gisela and I were very comfortable and relaxed. I held her hand and put my arm around her. Moving closer together, we had not been so tightly embraced in a long time. Gisela put her face next to mine, and I kissed her softly. Every time I kissed her lips, she squeezed my hand. Should I go on? I hesitated to go any farther. Considering how I overstepped my boundaries the last time, I tried to cool off. She must have sensed what was going through my mind as she whispered in my ear, "Don't ever stop loving me."

I could not describe my happiness with her affirmation. We both promised to love each other, taking this as a commitment to be faithful before and after marriage. Knowing with certainty that we belonged together, we trusted each other completely; but only a dummy like me could ask such a stupid question as "Gisela, do you really love me?"

"In reality I don't know what love is all about," she replied. "But I know this much: I will never let anyone else ever kiss me or come close to me. If this answers your question, I will tell you confidentially that I dream of the day when we can make love and of the time we can be together always." Her open and sincere statement made me realize that I had to survive this war to be together with her in a better future. A new purpose in life was giving me hope. It was getting late; we were still embracing, but the movie was over, and we had to go home. When we got home, we saw that Inge had already retired; and without making any noise, we sneaked into separate bedrooms.

Sunday we stayed home since this was the end of Gisela's visit. There was still a lot we had not talked about. I was telling them what I had learned from Peter, and Inge must tell us what Hildegard knew about any ongoing peace treaty with the West. "It is a long story," Inge said. "It goes back to the days when Rudolf Hess flew to England on May the 10, 1941, to submit Hitler's peace offer to the British. Hitler, after he occupied France, believed they would accept his offer. The Führer supposedly saw the English as a Germanic nation; and found no reason to fight them. The real reason might have been that he already had in mind to attack Russia on June 22, 1941, and he did not want a war on two fronts. The time was ripe for a negotiation; Germany was practically the ruler of all Europe, and England was with the back against the wall without any Allies. The reception Hess received in Scotland was rather cool; Churchill refused to see Hess, and he was kept as a prisoner. Hitler's message was given to Churchill. The Führer promised to remove all German troops from Western Europe in exchange of Britain's neutrality in Hitler's crusade to save Europe from Bolshevism. Churchill was not a friend of the Nazis, but he was fully aware of Stalin's ambition to conquer the world. Churchill would have accepted Hitler's offer, but he had another option on the table. Churchill was Roosevelt's confidant, and they were good friends. Roosevelt's political priority was to get the American people involved in a war against Germany. Roosevelt pledged to the British an all-out support if England kept on fighting the war against Hitler. America did not have to declare war on Germany. Two days after Japan attacked the American fleet at Pearl Harbor on December 7, 1941, with Germany being in alliance with Japan, Hitler declared war on the United States of America."

"I have one question," I said to Inge. "Who knows or has seen Hitler's proposal for the British before Hess left Augsburg in a Messerschmitt 110 on his secret mission?"

"The Gauleiter of Magdeburg, Rudolf Jordan, is an intimate friend of the Hess family and received the information from Ilse, the wife of Rudolf Hess, and anything top secret circulates fast between Gauleiters."

"It really does not matter anymore," I replied. "It is all snow from yesterday. We are going to lose the war, and it is anybody's guess who will fight communism after Germany is defeated. The way I see it, the Russians and British will only accept a total surrender, that means a capitulation without any terms. I agree with Peter. Our only chance is to sell out our atomic secrets to the Americans, and if they don't want to buy, let's finish the atomic bomb and use it as leverage against them. I just hope we don't run out of time. As it stands now, we have to keep on fighting. Tell us, Inge, there is a rumor that Himmler and Goering want to arrange for a peace treaty behind Hitler's back, is that true, and does the Nazi Party leadership has any knowledge about it?"

"I would not say that it is common knowledge, sometimes people make up their own fairy tales. All I know is what Hildegard told me, and if any of this leaks out, we could all be arrested by the Gestapo. After the attack by Colonel Claus von Stauffenberg on Hitler's life failed on July 20, 1944, everybody connected with the assassination plot, either from the military or the new underground government, were arrested and killed. Earlier in 1944, Reichsführer-SS and Gestapo Chief Heinrich Himmler tried to make contact with leaders of the West through a Swiss diplomat. His offer was the destruction of all war prison camps, saving the lives of thousands of prisoners, plus the election of a new government without Hitler. Tentatively the offer was accepted by Eisenhower and Churchill subject to the elimination of Hitler and the approval of the new-formed German government by the West. As it turned out, the whole approach is academic now; because of the missing conditions, the separate peace agreement never reached the point of ratification. A large number of lives would have been saved on both sides.Currently, peace talks are not dead yet but become more difficult. NS Official Heinrich Himmler is also trying through his Swedish connection with Count Folke Bernadotte, the president of the Swedish Red Cross, to bargain for a separate peace treaty with the West. To dispose of a dictator that is a killer and a maniac is one of the most difficult undertakings. I wish I had some better news for all of us," Inge said. "But let's hope that the New Year will be more kind to us."

In the afternoon came Helga, Gisela's roommate in the dormitory for nurses of the hospital. She would stay overnight, and Inge would drive her and Gisela early in the morning to the train station. This reminded me that this was the last evening I would be together with Gisela till next year. At 10:00 PM, I had to be back at the barracks; that gave us just a few hours. Gisela and Helga were taking over the conversation, telling us more about the situation on the river Oder. Most disturbing were the reports of thousands of refugees from East and West Prussia. Everyone who fled for protection from the Russian army had a story to tell. The Red Army (Russian troops) were invading village after village, raping and killing innocent women and children. The Berliners were suffering from an atavistic and visceral fear of the Slav invaders from the East. Fear easily turned to hate. As the Red Army approached, Goebbels's propaganda used the atrocities of the Russians to his advantage, inspiring the people to fight.

The time had come where I had to say good-bye to Gisela. I didn't want to make a long farewell speech, all I said was, "God be with you." Knowing that we would not see each other for some time, I embraced her and kissed her tenderly, showing her a sweet and sincere expression of my love for her.

Christmas of 1944

When the next Wednesday came, Inge and I were alone again, but she said, "We should go and visit Gertrud von Rathenow. We will make it a short visit just to wish her a Merry Christmas. I have phoned her from the office, and she is happy to have us come over."

"I am all for it," I said to Inge. "But I hate to go and see her with empty hands—"

"I have already taken care of that," Inge interrupted me. "For years I have a beautiful decorated pillow sitting in my closet that I have never used. I think it will look nice on her sofa." She showed it to me and, smiling, I said to her, "Inge, that is nice of you, that solves the problem."

The reception at Gertrud's house was like always, sincere and sympathetic. With Gertrud, there was no small talk; our conversation was cordial and cheering. She wanted to know everything we did recently. It was obvious that the good old lady was desperate for some company. You could tell by the way she was showering us with tea, cake, and Christmas cookies. Gertrud invited us to stay for dinner, and we didn't have the heart to say no to her. She was very surprised and overwhelmed with happiness as Inge presented her with a gift. Meals at Gertrud's house were like prewar times; she admitted to receiving help with the groceries from her family, especially from her daughter who lived in the country. Gertrud told us that they all would celebrate Christmas in Bernau, including her son, the doctor, and his family.

"I am very happy you are not alone for the holidays," Inge said. "As far as I am concerned, I am not in the mood to celebrate, and it will suit me fine to be alone for two days to relax and sleep in."

"Not completely," I objected. "I will see my mother and grandmother for two days, but on Christmas Day I will come to see you."

"That is sweet of you," Inge said. "And I will be ready for your visit."

The day with Gertrud was coming to an end, and Inge was insisting for Gertrud to call her if there was anything she needed help with. When I got off the car at the base, I gave Inge a kiss on her cheek and told her, "Merry Christmas, see you in three days." Going home to Tegel was never without any mixed feelings, but this time more than ever. It must be the lack of Christmas spirit that put a damper on my mood. I hoped my mother and my grandmother would help me to overcome my depression. Anyway, I was going to do my best to show a happy face in their presence. Indeed, it cheered me up to see them alive and to get the genuine welcome I received. Except there was one thing that made me sad: both of them were sitting bundled up in a cold apartment. It was Friday night, too late and too dark to do anything about it; but first thing in the morning, I would gather some firewood. My old sled was still in the basement—a saw, some rope; and I was all set. Reaching the inner forest, I was able to pack a great load of wood. It was a good workout for me, traveling and pulling the carriage over ice and snow. On my way out of the woods, I came across a petite but neat and trim-looking pine tree, begging me to take it home. Now I knew that this was the missing link for a merry Christmas. The reception I got from both women showed this to be a fact. My mother took out the old Christmas ornaments, and while she was busy trimming the tree, Grandmother attended to the cooking.

My grandmother took me to the kitchen, telling me that she had one more job for me to do. She took a long knife with a six-inch blade and sharpened it. "What is this for?" I asked her.

"I want you to kill the rabbit to make some rabbit stew for our Christmas dinner."

"Oh no," I said. "I don't have the heart to do it."

"Why not, you are a soldier, trained to shoot at people."

"That is a bad analogy. We are shooting at the enemy to protect you from getting killed by the bombs they dump on us. Why should I kill the poor little animal, it has not done me any harm?"

"I accept your philosophy," Oma said. "But if you were really starving to death, you would not think twice." After all, we reached a compromise; I would hold the animal upside down, and she would cut the rabbit's throat. My mother assisted as she came with a big dish to catch the animal's blood while grandmother severed the jugular veins of the neck. In a few minutes, the rabbit stopped shaking, and it was all over. While the blood was still draining, my mother poured vinegar into the dish and kept stirring the blood to prevent it from coagulating. With some diced onions, bacon bits, and spices, you had the finest blood sausage you ever tasted. To strip the skin from a rabbit was an art Grandmother learned when she was a little girl on the farm. "Nothing is wasted," she said. "If you have enough pelts, you can make a nice fur coat." Christmas Eve in my mother's place turned out better than I expected. We did not exchange any gifts; the big-tiled stove kept the living room warm, and best of all, we didn't have to go to bed hungry.

The little Christmas tree gave us some joy and reminded us of previous years when the whole family with all the children together celebrated Christmas in peace and harmony. "I did almost forget," my mother said. "I received a letter from your father. I'll let you read it. He is doing fine, and his regiment is going to relocate in January from Hungary to Austria."

Grandmother also told us that she received a letter from Heinz and Senta inviting all of us to come to Oranienburg to celebrate New Year with them. "That sounds good," I said. "But should I not be able to get out of the barracks and don't show up next week, you will have to go alone. Tomorrow," I mentioned, "I have to leave early to see Inge. She is alone at Christmas. Gisela went back to Frankfurt."

"How is Inge doing?" my mother wanted to know. "The last time I have seen her was at a PTA meeting when they were still living in Tegel and you and Gisela went to school together."

"They are both doing fine. After her husband got killed in Russia, Inge went back to work for the government as a housing director for the homeless. Gisela is now a student nurse at the Frankfurt (Oder) General Hospital. She just left after a brief visit to see her mother in Wilmersdorf."

"Gisela is a respectable girl, the decent kind of girl that men want to marry," I heard my mother say.

"I agree with you, Mother, that will come later. We are only fifteen years old, and besides, right now both of us are involved in a nationwide conflict of fight and survive, trying to get out of this war alive."

"All you young people were robbed of the best years of your lives. The Hitler Youth, beginning at an early age, has made puppets out of you," Grandmother said. "And at the end, when the war is already lost, a criminal bunch of fanatics are sacrificing you to die in order for them to live a few days longer."

Christmas Day was clear but cold, and the snow that came down overnight covered everything under a white blanket. As I got ready to depart, my mother gave me a pullover she made for my father but he never had a chance to wear. "Here, take it and try it on. I think it will fit you and keep you warm." I thanked her and kissed them both and felt good stepping out in the cold.

Taking the train to Wilmersdorf, I noticed that very few people were on the road. Must be that they were all staying home trying to be together with the family. Christmas this year was not what it used to be; there was hardly one family that had not lost a loved one during the war. I admired Inge how she managed her life living all by herself, but her job compensated her by being able to help other people that were less fortunate. She received me in a very happy mood, telling me that Gauleiter Otto Eckard called her and that he had requisitioned about fifty residential dwellings for the homeless families living in a public shelter. "That is good news," I said. "Now you are going to play Santa Claus, putting those poor people back into some decent housing."

"It is only a drop in a bucket, but the lucky ones out of the shelter are given a new lease on life."

"I know what it is like to live in a shelter. I had a taste of it for a few days when my grandfather got killed, but I have to admit without the shelter and the friendly help of the volunteers we would not have survived. Any moment all of us could be the next victim, and God knows what it will be like when the Russians come in and unleash their revenge."

"It is an anxiety among us we have to live with from day to day. Live one day at a time, enjoy it if you are still alive, and focus on positive thinking, that is my motto," Inge was trying to convince me.

"To cheer you up, there is nothing better than some classical music for Christmas."

"Please, no more 'Holy Night,' 'Silent Night,' or 'Oh come and adore him.' That stuff gives me a case of depression."

"I was not going to play you that kind of music. What I have in mind is Mozart or Beethoven. They are always lifting my spirit."

"Talking about Christmas spirit, do you think we should open a bottle of that French brandy?"

"No, I believe we should keep it for a rainy day, as you said the other day."

"To make you feel better, I have a bottle of original German-style peppermint schnapps that was given to me at the office Christmas party. Let's try it while I start fixing dinner for us. What did you eat for dinner at your mother's house last night?"

"Potatoes, sauerkraut, and rabbit stew."

"That sounds good, did you like it?"

"I don't know. I did not eat the rabbit."

"I don't understand, was something wrong with the meat?"

"Yes, there was." And then I was telling Inge the whole episode.

"That's a sad story," Inge said. "All I can offer you for supper is Bratkartoffel and homemade Suelze." Fried potatoes and headcheese.

"Really, you are not kidding me, that's my favorite dish. It is amazing how the world looks better on a full stomach."

"You sound like the guy in *The Threepenny Opera* who screamed out, 'First a big meal, then the morality'"

"I did not see that opera," I told Inge. "As a matter of fact, I've only seen two operas, *La Boheme* and *Carmen*."

"I like *Carmen*, it has more action. *La Boheme* is too sad."

"I have the long-play record of *Carmen*, would you like me to play it for you?"

"Please do," I said. "I enjoy very much the Latin rhythm." Listening to the music and drinking schnapps made us relax after a dinner. Then Inge got a deck of playing cards, and she taught me how to play poker, which was very similar to skat that we played at the barracks all the time. She had a jar of pennies and divided them evenly, but as we were playing game after game, her pile of money was getting bigger and my pile was getting smaller. Then came the time again where we had to break it up.

"Thanks for coming over," Inge said. "I have to thank you for everything, and I will see you soon."

Air raids over Berlin in the month of December had slowed down to two minor air raids after the big attack on December 5. On the contrary, West Germany became more of a target especially in the industrial Ruhr and Rhine areas. At our battery, we stayed ready and alert, but the break the enemy was giving us provided more time to observe the holidays peacefully with our friends and relatives. I was very lucky to be off duty for the New Year's celebration. Arriving late at my mother's house, I stayed overnight; and in the morning, the last day of the year, we started our journey to Oranienburg. We knew the way how to get to Senta's house, and she received us with a happy embrace, telling us that we were just in time for lunch. If that was not music to my ears, then I didn't know what would have been. Senta served us her own oven-baked ham-and-cheese sandwich and hot black tea to wash it down. "Would you like some rum in your tea?" Senta was asking us; her eyes were resting on me.

"Very much so," I said. "But let's save it for tonight when Heinz can join us."

"What time is he coming home?" Grandmother wanted to know.

"Usually between seven o' clock and eight o'clock in the evening on Saturday, but after he gets out of the base, he is still on call till he returns Monday morning." To our surprise, Heinz showed up unexpectedly shortly after six o'clock. He entered the house with a big knapsack full of good things.

"What do you have in there?" Senta asked.

"Enough food and drinks for all of us that will last us till next year."

"You are very funny, do you care to tell us how you managed to get all the rare food items?"

"You got to have connection these days, and I happen to know a few farmers that are always in need of some secondhand items like batteries, tires, and things like that. We throw things out from time to time at the base when it shows too much wear and tear. You cannot take a chance in the air, but whatever we dispose can still be used on the ground. I don't take any money for my effort to keep the food production going, but I do accept samples."

"For openers," he said, "tonight we are going to feast on three kilos of pork chops, and here we have some fresh-baked bread and a pound of butter to go with it. My good friend, the farmer, also gave me a bottle of homemade Slivovitz (plum brandy) for fixing his tractor. So like the emperor said, let the games begin." As the women took initial steps for preparing the New Year's Eve dinner, Heinz asked me to help him bring in some firewood. This old Victorian home had a huge fireplace that heated the living room in no time. A large pocket door connected the living room with the dining room, keeping both rooms heated. Soon dinner was served, and everybody in the small family group was enjoying the last supper of the year. To relax after such a splendid meal, all of us got comfortable around the fireplace. Heinz served us some after-dinner drinks, and a vivid conversation full of laughter swarmed the room. I was sure the women would carry on the lively talks till midnight, but Heinz and I were also getting involved in our own dialogue about the war. Heinz wanted to know, "Did you see any action lately?" And I told him how our battery had successfully engaged in the battle of the big air raid on the fifth of this month.

"I was up there that night firing at the Flying Fortresses and damaged one badly, but then my wing commander made an Immelman coming down, blowing the B-29 to pieces. Naturally, he got the credit for the kill. Any day now our squadron will get the new Me 262, the world's first jet propulsion airplane. With its two engines, it will go over five hundred miles per hour, outrunning any conventional aircraft. Should we be able to produce enough of these jetfighters, we could clean up the skies over Germany again. All we need is time, and we might win the war or at least bargain for a peace treaty."

"That is exactly what my friend Peter told me. He believes the atomic bomb could be our lifesaver."

"Hope is the mother of all nations," Heinz said. "Besides all speculations, we must keep on fighting. At the end we either live or die. Since we have no control over our destiny, what is the use to worry about it? Let's live one day at a time and make the best of it. Come on, let's have another drink, you don't want to enter the next year sober. It is ugly, it is offensive to my intellect. This war is the utmost outbreak of human dung and psychopathic schizophrenia." As he said that, Heinz paused for a moment and filled our glasses. The hour had come, and at twelve o'clock midnight, we celebrated the New Year by kissing and embracing all family members, accompanied with best wishes for the future to survive and stay alive. Thereafter I remembered waking up on January 1, 1945, at noon with a slight headache. Heinz was already at the base, and Senta, before we left, fixed us a hearty brunch and walked with us to the train. Happy New Year 1945!

CHAPTER VIII

THE BATTLE OF ARMAGEDDON

1945 Summary of Disasters

The Führer's early military successes gave him delusions of grandeur. Advice and criticism of his generals enraged him. He dismissed or overruled anybody who advised caution. Our armies were sacrificed in consequence. The attack on Russia sealed the fate of Germany. Hitler's own weaknesses contributed greatly to his downfall. He misjudged the British after Dunkirk. He likewise failed to understand the people he conquered in Russia. Indeed, millions of Ukrainians hailed the German soldiers as liberators. Had Hitler recognized their aspirations for independence, he might well have destroyed the Soviet Union. Instead, the conquered people were treated so brutally, not by the regular army, but by the SS that they resorted to guerrilla warfare and sabotage on a huge scale.

For a while we were still victorious, but when we attempted to gain control of Stalingrad, a vital industrial and railroad center, we began to lose in the struggle. November 19, 1942, was the turning point of the war when powerful Russian reserves swept down from the hills to forge an iron ring around the German Sixth Army besieging Stalingrad. Enraged by the resistance of Russian assault troops fighting through the rubble of Stalingrad and infuriated by the request of his generals to retreat, Hitler made a great strategic error. He stubbornly refused to retreat, sacrificing twenty-two divisions either to be killed or become prisoners. Meanwhile the Allied successes in the West were matched by equally great gains in the East. After D-Day on the sixth of June 1944, while the Battle of Normandy was in progress, the Red Armies were invading East Prussia and Poland. Hitler's Reich was now caught in a gigantic vise with the Red Armies pressing from the east and south and the Americans, British, and French from the west. In mid-December Hitler ordered a last desperate counterattack to throw the Allies back before they reached the Rhine. A German panzer division struck a thinly held sector in the Ardennes forest and succeeded in driving a wedge (the Battle of the Bulge) of some fifty miles in the Allied lines.

When the skies cleared after Christmas, 6,500 planes roared into the air to blast our advancing columns, killing 120,000 men and eliminating vast quantities of equipment. Our last resources, desperately needed to hold off the Red Army, were now destroyed. The Allies were now crossing the Rhine, launching drives that became a series of military disasters for the remaining German armies. Equally overwhelming in the east were Russian tanks pouring across Poland, rolling on to the gates of Berlin.

Today was the twelfth of January 1945, and the Russians were fifty miles away from Frankfurt (Oder). In my estimation, in about two weeks or less, the Russians would have established bridgeheads along the river Oder by February 1 this year. As I was trying to explain the danger to Inge, she held a letter from Gisela in her hand. In her letter, she was telling us that she was very busy as mounting casualties were coming in from the battlefield in the east. There was one sentence in her letter that made Inge feel better: she stated that in the event that the Russians should come dangerously close to Frankfurt, the entire hospital would be evacuated. As good luck had it—or ill luck, or no luck at all—Gisela was a child who had little sense of danger. Not a shade of suspicion had crossed her mind when she decided to make the move to Frankfurt (Oder). "I shall have a chance to become a registered nurse no matter where it takes me." These were her exact words. It appeared that Inge was more confident about Gisela's safety than I was. Inge's self-assurance and trust with the hopeful outlook of a mother made me also think more positively about the situation Gisela was in.

On the last day of January, Soviet troops, after the fall of Posen, had reached the river Oder. They crossed the Oder by Küstrin and established the first bridgehead on the west side of the river. It was the last chance for the German army to keep the Russians from coming into East Germany. Unfortunately, the Russians had five times as many soldiers as the Germans and were better supplied with new trucks and equipment they received from America. The German government was desperately trying to send more troops to the eastern front. As a last resort, they were drafting all the Hitler Youth born in 1928 and making them join the infantry. Those who were already serving at the home front or as Flakhelfer were also sent to the east front and replaced at home by the Hitler Youth born the year 1929. At my battery, I could see it immediately that overnight all the familiar faces of the older comrades were fading away. Instead, we saw more and more new faces of the year 1929. All the regular Flak soldiers, with the exception of a few officers and sergeants, were removed with some of our 8.8 cm Flak guns to the Russian front to shoot at the oncoming flood of T-34 Russian tanks. From now on, the German army was no longer planning any major attacks but strictly geared for an all-out defense action. The Volkssturm militia, a replacement army, was organized locally by NS Gauleiters. Since almost all German males between the ages of fifteen and fifty-five had already been called up, the Volkssturm was a combination of teenagers and old men. After swearing the oath of allegiance to the Führer in massed ranks, the Volkssturm detachments received Panzerfaust rocket-propelled grenades and rifles confiscated in six different nations. Most members of the Volkssturm guessed that they would be thrown senselessly into battle for symbolic purposes and had no hope of making any impression on the Soviet onslaught. No rations were being allocated for the Volkssturm, so they had to be fed by their families, whose food budget was already strained.

The fighting spirit in the Volkssturm, in comparison to the Wehrmacht, was practically nonexistent. Only the Hitler Youth and veterans of the First World War were showing a sense of duty. Most of the rest were slipping away whenever they had an opportunity. I thought it was futile to throw children into combat without enough training and sacrifice them for an already doomed war.

Since the beginning of the year, Allied Bomber Command ordered continuous raids by small groups of planes. Such tactics, they felt, would give the defenders of Berlin no rest. But the enemy overlooked the fact that the raids did not do much damage either. New tactics were called for, and in early February, British Bomber Command decreed a changeover to area bombing by massed bomber formations. The areas chosen were not particularly large, but they were hard to miss. The scale of the air assault created enormous losses on both sides. At ten o'clock in the evening on February 3, the Gatow antiaircraft battery in the outskirts of Berlin made the first observation of the oncoming armada of 937 US Flying Fortresses, mostly Liberators, and six hundred fighters.

Alarm was given for every Flak battery in Berlin at 10:39 PM. The targets for tonight were the *Stadtmitte* (center), the district of Wedding in the north, and the Kreuzberg in the south. It was a massive bombardment, perhaps the biggest air raid Berlin had seen so far. No specific targets were approached by the enemy, an in-and-out high-altitude carpet bombing that lasted only till midnight, and the last bomber left Berlin by 12:16 PM. The casualties were estimated at over four thousand civilians, with injured people in the thousands. I remembered that night as we were very disappointed at not being able to fire a single shot at the enemy. After the U.S. Fortresses unloaded their deadly cargo, they were no longer flying in close formation but taken in smaller units the shortest way out of Berlin. Our luck had changed as one of their groups coming from the Kreuzberg area passed the near territory of old Schmargendorf. Our battery claimed one of the low-flying Liberators, but there was no time for rejoicing. Scores of others flew overhead as the accompanying fighters zoomed down on our 8.8 cm antiaircraft positions. As the assault came on, Sergeant Backe and his comrades just had enough time to take shelter in the dugout. Usually after an air raid, the crews of a battery would retire to the barracks. Such was not the case tonight; too many people were still in need to be rescued, and too many houses were still burning. The home front needed all the help it could get as time was of the essence. Three thousand tons of Sprengbomben (high-explosive bomb) had been dropped on the city tonight of which many had not exploded yet. Several trucks were ready to take us to our destination. In the center of Kreuzberg tonight, the flames in bombarded buildings cast strange shadows and a red glow on the otherwise dark streets. From time to time there was the thunder of masonry collapsing. This is the picture as we were arriving; at the same time, more trucks with Hitler Youth and soldiers were at the scene. As we were getting closer to where the action was, we replaced an exhausted group of firefighting Hitler Youth who were seeking shelter from the burning heat after being too long exposed to the scorching flames. One of them explained to us that the fire was too far gone, there was not enough water to control it, and there was too much smoke with no oxygen to breathe. As they all came down and removed their gas masks, I had the surprise of my life.

Who was I running into? My old friends from Steglitz—Hindenburg, Heinz, and Oscar. Oscar and I still saw each other as we were still going to school in Dahlem, but to meet the rest of the gang here in the rubble of Kreuzberg was really something. They were happy to see me, and we were toasting with some bottles of drinking water to our health. As we were talking about the latest events, a NS Party boss showed up, stopping our reunion by telling us that there was still a war going on. He was giving us instructions on where to search the next block of houses for survivors. Hindenburg did not like the idea that somebody else was telling his boys what to do, but the Gold Pheasant outranked him. Most of the houses were still burning, and there was no way to go inside or even get near them to search for survivors. Many houses were destroyed but not burning; they were the ones we were checking first. I didn't recognize the Kreuzberg area anymore the way I remembered it from my early childhood when my parents and I were living there. It was not that my memory was failing me—no, it was the ugly picture of total destruction. House by house, room by room, we were looking and hoping to find somebody alive.

Much rubble had been removed, but all we came across were dead people. Never had I seen that death could appear in so many forms as I did tonight. It was indescribably horrible and gruesome what we were digging up at this hour. Cadavers that were two hours ago still regular human beings—talking, walking, and living a normal life. These corpses, or what was left of them, were now reduced to dead pieces of flesh, lumps, burned, charred, and no longer resembling a human being.

If the bodies still had a head, their faces were cramped, clenched, rigid, unnatural, and pain-distorted. We found them naked, dressed in rags, twisted, and deformed. Or sometimes there was just a small pile of ashes with some bones sticking out. There was not one guy in the group who did not feel like vomiting. Finally, completely drained and dog tired, at five o'clock in the morning, the trucks from the base came to take us back to the barracks. Too damned exhausted, I just hit the sack without eating anything or taking a shower. Going to school the next morning was out of the question; instead, we had some classes after lunch at the base. We were getting last instructions for the *Not Abitur*, which would be conducted on March 15 and 16 in Dahlem.

Death in Cold Blood

In her last letter of February 15, Gisela informed us that she and Helga had been transferred to a Hauptverbandsplatz (MASH Unit) outside of Frankfurt east of the river Oder. The assignment was only temporarily as more nurses were urgently needed in the field to take care of the wounded soldiers and civilians. The MASH unit would stay east of the river till the rest of the German army and the vast amount of refugees from East Prussia and Poland had been evacuated to the west side across the river.

A rear guard would protect them from the advancing Russians till the process of the operation was completed. That was the general plan when we received the last letter from Gisela; thereby, Inge and I were more or less convinced that she would make it safely back to Frankfurt on the west side of the river. On the third of March, Hitler visited General Busse of the Ninth Army and inspected personally the east front. He instructed General Busse to fortify the entire Oder front and have all bridges destroyed by the Luftwaffe, except the main Oder bridge in Frankfurt. He declared Frankfurt to be a fortress and promised to send more troops and equipment. The destruction of all Oder bridges slowed down the evacuation and created a traffic chaos at the last remaining bridge at Frankfurt.

As scheduled on the fifteenth of March, I took my final written exam, and the next day in Dahlem, I was up for an oral defense in front of a five-member academic committee. I had a feeling that I would pass, but then you never knew for sure. At the end of March, I was on my way to seeing Inge, but I did not find her at home. That made me kind of suspicious that something might be wrong. I called her office, and they told me that Inge was under medical care and had been admitted at the Westend Hospital. Immediately I rushed over to see Inge. Entering her room, I saw that she was sleeping, and Helga was sitting at her bedside. Not making any noise, Helga motioned to me, and we stepped out to the hallway. Slowly closing the door behind her, Helga explained, "Inge has been heavily sedated after she suffered a severe nervous breakdown when I came to see her this morning in her office bringing her grave and painful news."

"What is going on?" I was losing my temper, demanding to know what she meant by painful news.

"Compose yourself," Helga said. "Let's find a place where we can sit down, and I will tell you everything from the beginning."

Between the many building complexes of the hospital was a large garden with trees and benches. We sat down, and I wanted to know what she was doing in Berlin. "Where is Gisela? Is she hurt?" These were my next questions.

"It all started in the morning, February 16, when Gisela and I worked at OP-2 and we just finished dressing a boy from the Hitler Youth who stepped on a land mine and lost both of his legs. At that time, a young doctor walked in the operating room asking for two nurses to go with him in the *sanka* [ambulance] on an emergency call. Gisela and I volunteered for the event. As we left the military surgical medical unit, he told us that about ten miles from there, a German staff car coming from the frontline was hit on the road by a Russian artillery shell, and all four officers were badly wounded. When we got there, two of them were bleeding profusely, and Gisela and I started an IV to give both of them some plasma. The third one had a piece of shrapnel in his head, could not breathe, and the doctor was performing a tracheotomy to save his life."

"Damned, I don't care about your Nightingale activities, I want to know what happened to Gisela!" I shouted.

"Well, give me a minute, and I will tell you what happened to both of us. Being preoccupied in what we were doing, we did not notice that a Russian search patrol of twelve Mongolians had approached and encircled us. They captured us, shot the four wounded soldiers, and made the doctor and us two girls march with them behind the Russian line. In a small unoccupied and mostly destroyed village, they locked us up in a basement. Tired from the long walk, we rested on some dirty mattresses. A few hours later, it was already dark outside, and the same filthy bunch came down to the basement. This time the rotten bastards were stinking drunk. They did not waste any time to rape us. As two of the beasts were beginning to tear our clothes off, Gisela and I kicked, bit, and screamed as loud as we could; but it did not do us any good. In an attempt to protect us, the doctor jumped between us and the attackers, trying to stop the assault, only to have to pay with his life for it. One of the Russians pulled a pistol and shot the doctor on the back of his head. The blood and brain squirting out of his forehead was spraying our faces too. Thereafter everything happened real fast. As soon as they had us stripped naked, they raped us one by one, all of them. Gisela and I, we were both virgins, and without any mercy the monsters literally ripped us open. I cannot describe the hellish and terrifying pain we suffered. As the biggest insult and degradation, as we were already floating in their filthy fluids, they formed a circle around us and pissed on our violated naked bodies. After the savage gangsters left us, we barely had the strength to cover our freezing bodies. Any movement we made would still give us agonizing pain, and our vaginas kept on bleeding."

"Stop it stop it stop it!" I kept on screaming. I could not take it anymore; this was too much. I could not believe that such kind of evil ordeal could be afflicted from one human being to another. I was getting blue in the face; all the blood was rushing to my head. "This is impossible to believe, where is God when you need him?" Helga was patiently waiting till I'd calmed down. "Tell me, how did you girls survive and get out of this ugly situation?"

"First of all, we were lucky the Russians did not kill us, and secondly, it was our good fortune that a German counterattack rescued us the next day. We returned to the military surgical medical unit again, this time as mental and physical casualties. Recuperation as far as our bodies were concerned did not take more than a few days, but mentally speaking, we may never be the same. I am trying to put it behind me, but I cannot forget it, it is constantly on my mind. Gisela's suffering was more than mine, a deep state of depression affected her will to live. She spoke very little, and at nights she would wake up screaming, her whole body shaking as she was having nightmares reliving the ugly gang rape over and over again. A week after the rape, both of us noticed a discharge. A Wasserman test turned out positive, showing that we are infected with gonorrhea. The biggest disaster occurred when Gisela discovered that she was pregnant. Rapidly her depression and anxiety got worse. An abortion is out of the question as it is punishable by law. On the twenty-fourth of March, Gisela missed her monthly period for the second time, and she was beginning to have morning sickness. Three days later before she went to bed—" Helga stopped her report at this point; she put her arm around me and said, "For what I have to tell you now, you have to be very strong and well fortified."

"Go on," I said. "I can already feel it in my stomach what you are going to tell me."

"That night," Helga continued, "Gisela committed suicide by swallowing a large dose of Veronal tablets, a very strong barbiturate."

Enraged with anger, shock, and frustration, I found myself on the brink of madness; I am on the edge of losing my mind, and yet I was unable to cry. Helga was trying to ease my pain by saying, "Gisela is an angel, she went straight to heaven. Her troubles are over, she is now in a better world than ours."

A few minutes went by till I was really composed and able to see straight again. My first question was, "How did Inge take it?"

"Being a mother, she is suffering about her daughter's death more than all of us together. I don't think a mother will ever completely recover from the death of a child. You are the closest friend to her and the only person left that is near to her heart."

"That is right," I said. "And believe me, I will take care of her and do everything that is in my power to help and protect her. Tell me one more thing, what happened to Gisela's body?"

"We buried her on the twenty-ninth of March on the east side of the Oder in a small military cemetery. The grave has a white wooden cross with her name on it. I also have a small bag with her belongings—a wallet, ring, watch, and others that I will leave with you, and you can give it to Inge at the right time."

"I will, but what about you, are you going back to Frankfurt?"

"No, it would not make much sense, they told me. First I have to report to the Robert Koch Krankenhaus [hospital] tomorrow morning to start a treatment program for my venereal disease. By the time I am clean again, the fortress Frankfurt may be completely surrounded by the Russian army. I am sure they can use me here when Berlin becomes a fortress. Come on," Helga said, "I have to go upstairs and say good-bye to Inge. I want you to stay with her. I believe they will discharge her today." When we entered the room, Inge was already awake. Not saying anything, I just rushed to embrace her. She had tears in her eyes and was trying to talk to me. but just a slow sobbing came out of her chest. I was still holding her firmly, and a few minutes later she was beginning to breathe normally. The first thing she said was, "I have lost everything, I don't want to live anymore."

"Hold it," I replied. "I have lost Gisela too. I need you more than ever, we need each other. Together we will overcome our tragedy, and the mutual grief over the fatal event will be easier for us to carry."

Inge presses my hand gently with a slight smile; I was happy to see her getting more composed. As soon as we knew that Inge was getting discharged tonight, I went downstairs to the pharmacy to pick up some medicine that the doctor prescribed for her depression while Inge got dressed to go. We were all taking the U-Bahn, but Helga was going in a different direction. Before Helga caught her train, she promised Inge to visit her as soon as she was done with her treatment. Arriving at Inge's home, she seemed to be a little more relaxed. Misery seeks company, that's why I decided to stay the first night with Inge; I just could not leave her alone in her condition. Both of us didn't feel like eating, but I made some tea for us and gave her a sleeping pill for the night. We talked for a while, but slowly she was going to sleep. I took the armchair next to her bed and grabbed a blanket to cover myself, but I was not able to go to sleep. Too many things were going through my head; I had to think constantly of my dear beloved Gisela, whom I had lost forever. I would never find another young girl that I could love that much. Finally, after a brief sleep, I got up early in the morning to get back to the barracks before roll call. The first thing I did after breakfast was to see Sergeant Backe in his office.

He was like a father to me, and he had always been capable to appreciate my dilemmas with understanding and sympathy. This time he really surprised me when I told him the whole story from beginning to end. He had a daughter too, and he could not imagine how he would suffer if that would happen to him. He was very moved and told me that Inge should not be left alone; she could attempt suicide too, and who was going to stop her? For a moment he really scared me, and I didn't know what to say. "I tell you what," he said, "I am assigning you to special duty. For one week, you will stay and take care of a widow in distress bereaved of her husband and daughter, both of whom were killed on the eastern front. I will make out your furlough papers and give my regards and deepest sympathy to the lady. Oh, one more thing, go and take your rations for one week and call me to let me know how things are going." I was shocked and ever so grateful for his noble and good-hearted gesture. I did not reach Inge's house one minute too soon. I found her again in the dumps and sulking.

"No more tears," I said. "You have to listen to the good news. I am at your service for a solid week. I will take you places, and we will do anything to get us into a better mood."

"That is wonderful," Inge said, and immediately I could see it in her face that she approved of the idea of me staying with her.

"You just relax," I said. "And tomorrow morning I will serve you breakfast in bed." She enjoyed the breakfast I prepared for us from my rations. "Guess what we are doing today," I asked her. "We have an appointment with the monkeys, we are going to the zoo." Indeed, it was a sunny day, and the fun we had did us a world of good. I intended to keep her busy, and I knew that Inge liked the outdoors, so I suggested the next day that we go for a long walk along the Wansee. The crisp air breeze coming from the lake and the smell of fresh blooming flowers wafted to us as we walked along the Grunewald; it was a unique experience. Unparalled also was the natural soothing effect it had on the nerves. Today was the third day I was spending with her, and for the first time, she was going to bed without taking a sleeping pill. The next day I was reading the newspaper, and I could not believe it, that some musicians so close to the end of the war in a city bombarded day and night could find the ambition to perform in a concert. I showed Inge the advertisement in the paper, and she was as much amazed as I was. I didn't want to run Inge's life and tell her every day what to do, but she was the one asking me if I would go with her to the concert. All I could say was that it turned out to be, for both of us, a most memorable evening.

The orchestra presented a remarkable performance. I was telling Inge how much my mother and my grandmaster would have liked the concert. "By the way," Inge suggested, "why don't we go and visit them?"

"Oh, that would be great."

"How about tomorrow?"

"That is fine by me," I seconded. "Before we go, I have to warn you, the Tegel you remember does not exist any longer." We started the trip next day early in the morning. My mother was really surprised to see us. She apologized for being unprepared and not having anything to offer. "Yes, we do," my grandmother said, and she came and opened up a tin can with home-baked cookies. "Great, let me make a pot of coffee." And my mother went to the kitchen. As we sat down and enjoyed the Coffeeclatsch, my mother looked at me, asking us, "Well, what do you hear from Gisela?" Inge looked at me with tears in her eyes, which were begging me to tell them the horrible tragedy. Immediately my mother and my grandmother sensed that I was going to tell them a dreadful event. It took all my skills to report the terrible disaster without dramatization; I must omit painful details that would inflict more suffering. To talk about it, no matter how delicately I was trying to describe the death of Gisela, stories of such ugly magnitude would challenge anyone's endurance. All the women were crying, but my mother and my grandmother were trying to console Inge the best they could. After everybody dried their eyes, my grandmother, who was born and raised in the countryside, really got mad. She raised her fist and started to cuss, "Those godforsaken Russian bastards, may they go to hell to pay for what they have done."

Knowing that the Russian forces were advancing rapidly toward Berlin, my mother said, "It won't be long, and you can tell them that yourself."

"Keep in mind," Inge said, "they cannot kill us all. After the initial revenge for what our forces have done to them, time will again begin to normalize." These words of hope coming from a woman who had been driven to the ultimate breaking point was remarkable. At the end of our visit, my mother gave me a letter from the school in Dahlem. I opened it at once and found out that I had passed the final exam. A diploma was also included, certifying that I had reached the college and university entrance level. The bad news was that the academy was permanently closed and was now the headquarter of the local Volkssturm.

Destruction of a Flak Battery

The last two days we stayed at home, and Inge took over her domain again; she wanted to serve me and made things comfortable for us. More casual than official, Inge told me, "I have to keep occupied to be able to put all this behind me and stop grieving my heart out. It has been nice to have you here, but you cannot be around here all the time, so it's better if I go back to work."

"I heard that work is good therapy if you want to forget something, so I am all for it if it makes you feel better."

"Have you ever considered sharing this house with me?" Inge wanted to know.

"No, I have never given it much thought, but on the other hand, I am getting too old to live with my parents much longer. Soon I will be sixteen. Time will come that my father will return from the war, then the one-bedroom apartment will be too small for all of us, and I would rather look for a place of my own and let my grandmother stay with them. Should I go to college after the war, I will have to rent a room in town anyway. I appreciate your offer, and I would love to take you up on it as soon as I am out of this uniform. I hope it will not be too long till the war is over and we are all free again. Let's stay alive, and hopefully we will remain good friends as long as our good fortune allows it."

"Thank you, those are kind words. I will keep them in my heart." I could see that Inge was slowly recovering and beginning to live for a better future.

It had almost been a perfect week if it was not for the last day that pushed us back into the ugly reality of a more-than-ever ongoing war. The early evening was suddenly interrupted by a radio announcement that a British and American two-thousand-bomber formation of Flying Fortresses had now crossed the German border at Aachen. "They are not coming to Berlin," was Inge's first reaction. "The shortest way to fly to Berlin would be the route over Hamburg."

"You never know," I said. "But I am afraid I have to go and report to the base. Please make sure to go to the shelter in case of an air raid."

"I promise you, but please you also be careful and come back soon." I saw tears in her eyes again as we said good-bye. "I don't want to lose you too," were her last words before I left the house.

8.8 Flak Battery

At the time I reached the barracks, the bomber formation had already entered the Hannover-Braunschweig area. Ten minutes later, the enemy was picked up by radar in Magdeburg. All batteries in Greater Berlin were now receiving a preliminary air-raid warning. First the *Gefechtsstand* (battle headquarters) was going into position. The standard equipment of a heavy Flak battery were the *Würzburg Gerät* (direction finder) and the *Commando Gerät* (rangefinder). Meanwhile the gun crews remained in the barracks in full readiness. The moment the sirens gave the air-raid alarm, then everybody jumped into action by taking position at the designated battle station. The *Gefechtsstand* (command center) and the four 8.8 cm guns were in proximity with each other. I had to run past them across the field to reach the smaller 2 cm and 3.7 cm guns on the other side. As loading gunner at the 3.7 cm gun, I made sure I had enough ammo behind me. The main ammo bunker was now open, and I saw the Russian POW bringing the ammo boxes. We were a small crew of five including the gun captain who made sure we were ready before he called the Gefechtsstand. The whole procedure we were experiencing night after night was always hurry up and wait, but tonight everything was totally different; what followed now was a total surprise coming out of the dark region of clouds in the sky above us.

There was nothing to see but plenty to hear from the direction where the Flak battery was located on top of the zoo bunker. Our Gefechtsstand was completely misled trying to get a fix on the bomber formation already under fire by the zoo bunker battery. At the same time, a second wave of bombers appeared undetected in a gliding flight, unloading their bombs over the Schmargendorf Flak Battery as a selected target. The impact of the explosions behind me threw my body against the gun, and as I became conscious, I found myself pinned between the floor and the base of the gun. I managed to get up and noticed that the Gefechtsstand was gone, and two of the 8.8 cm guns were blown to pieces. All around me a picture of destruction. The barracks were burning; dead bodies were everywhere, and wounded soldiers are screaming. Two of my fellow gun crew were killed by bomb fragments. The gun captain suffered a wound above his left knee; the number one gunner was unharmed, and with his help, I put a tourniquet above the knee. Then the two of us walked through the rubble looking where we could help some other wounded comrades. We were coming across some other survivors who were automatically doing the same thing. The group was getting bigger, and one of the new boys sitting in the dirt with one arm missing was asking us if we had seen his mother. He was not screaming or complaining about pain; apparently, the kid was still in shock and did not know yet what hit him. We took him to the dining room in one of the barracks that were still standing and now serving as a first aid station. Hours had gone by, and I was dead tired, but we continued looking for people still alive out there. It seemed like that this was my main occupation looking for survivors in the rubble. In the meantime, doctors and nurses had arrived to take care of the wounded and the most critical cases were already evacuated to the nearest hospitals. As daylight broke, the Russian POWs were beginning to collect the dead bodies, and the main ammunition dump was converted to a temporary morgue.

Finally, I could no longer stay on my feet, and I must find a place to sleep. My barrack, with my few meager possessions, was burned down to the ground, including my only pair of boots. I went over to the only barrack that still had a roof. Luckily I found an empty bed to rest my tired bones. I was sure the guy who usually occupied this bed was not objecting; he was sleeping tonight in the hospital or in the morgue.

Next day when I woke up, I was hungry and had to find someplace where they served some food. All the wounded were transported out of the base, and the dining room still served again as mess hall and living room. At 2:00 PM, the CO, Major Schneider was scheduled to speak to all the surviving members of the battery. The kitchen in the brick building was a mess, but the crew managed to serve a hot lunch as usual. Major Schneider was right on time, and everyone who had survived the attack was crowding the room. First of all, he was expressing his deepest sympathy to all of us who had lost so many comrades last night. He declared, "We don't have the exact figures as some have not reached the hospitals yet. To mention a few that we all know were dead, Captain Schaefer and his crew of the command stand, Sergeant Kummer and his men of the surveying group, Gun Captain Feldwebel Raabe, and base and barracks leader Sergeant Backe. For all departed, we would have a few moments of silence, and the base chaplain, Lieutenant Reuter, would lead us into prayer."

Thereafter Major Schneider went back to his speech saying, "What occurred to us last night has become the destiny to most of the open-field batteries in Berlin. Luftwaffen Headquarters feels that we are strategically better equipped if we leave the air defense of Berlin up to the Flak towers. My orders are to close this base and unite with the rest of the Flak batteries that are to be relocated to the eastern front. To be exact, we are going to build a second line of defense right behind the Oder front. Our destination will be the Seelower Höhen. This time we will not shoot at airplanes, our new targets are Russian T-34 tanks. If we don't stop the Russian army, then Berlin will be the next fortress. Before we set up the new defense line, we will salvage all the guns and equipment in Berlin and Brandenburg and put new and old gun crews together to form new and fully functioning Flak batteries together. As far as your individual assignment is concerned, go and see one of the sergeants sitting on the end of the table right now. They are waiting for you to explain all the details and your options before you sign up."

As it was my turn to be interviewed, I asked the sergeant in charge, "What are they doing with the old base?"

"After it is all repaired I guess the home front and the Volkssturm are moving in. Basically you have two choices, you stay here and move out with the battery when the time comes to the eastern front, or, if you have a valid reason to remain in Berlin, you must sign up for an SS special course for one week."

"I do have a special reason to remain in Berlin. There are three women—my mother, my grandmother, and my deceased girlfriend's mother—that depend on me for their survival. Now, tell me what is this all about the special course with the SS?"

"You will go to a camp in Marzahn, outside of Berlin, where they teach you commando raids and sabotage action behind enemy lines."

"That sounds like partisan violence and terrorism," I said.

"You got that right, and the name of the operation is Werewolf."

"Yes, I heard about it, and what am I going to do after the one-week course is over?"

"Then again you have two choices, you either join the SS Division Hitler Youth, or you go back for what you are trained for and report for duty at one of the Flak towers nearest your home." I did not have to think about it too long to make up my mind. I told the sergeant that I would take the second option of a Flak tower near my home.

"OK," he said, "where are you living, your last home address."

"I am living with my parents in Tegel." I gave him the full address, and he prepared the papers for me to sign.

"Now, here is the scoop. After the course, you will report to the Flak bunker at Humboldthain, that is the nearest Battery from Tegel. The time you must sign in is the twentieth of April at ten o'clock. Remember, that is the Führer's birthday."

"How can I honestly forget that day?"

"Here is the copy you signed. It shows the address of the camp, and you will also report there in the morning on the eleventh of April."

"That is all," the sergeant said. "You are free to go, wash up and see if you can find a clean uniform and some rations to take home."

Going over to the clothing depot, I rummaged around till I located a brand-new uniform and a shirt all my size. Taking a shower was more of a problem; the central boiler exploded in the fire, forcing me to take a shower with cold water. I also found two clean pillowcases, one for my dirty uniform and one for my rations to take home. The cook was very generous, telling me that they have no refrigerator and that I could take out whatever I could carry, or they would have to give the leftover food to the Russian POWs tomorrow before it would spoil. Walking through the gate for the last time and leaving the base, never to see or enter it again, gave me some mixed feelings. First of all, it felt good to be free and alive, to breathe some fresh air on the outside. Also, it felt good that by walking away from the base, I was closing a chapter of my life behind me, and at the same time, I was opening the next chapter; but would I be so lucky again and walk away alive from the next chapter?

On the way over to Wilmersdorf, I had to think about all the events of last night. I saw all the wounded and dead boys over and over again. What hit me the most was the death of Sergeant Backe; he was like a father to me and a dear friend at the same time. The stuff I carried was getting heavy now, and I was happy to see Inge's house around the corner. Needless to say, how happy we were being alive and meeting again. Inge told me, "I have been awake all night long, hoping and praying that you are not among the dead."

"I was worried about you too, but I have to confess that I did not find the time to pray." Inge wanted to know the whole story, and I told her everything I went through and how close I came to being killed. "I am sure now, your prayers must have helped save my life."

Inside a Werewolf Training Camp

Before the day was over, I must tell Inge the bargain I had made to stay in Berlin. For a moment, Inge was thinking about the details I had given her, then she concluded in her opinion, "Surely, you have opted for the lesser evil." I was relieved to know that we were in agreement. "Under no circumstances would I like to see you going to the eastern front."

"Here in Berlin we can play it to the bitter end one day at a time."

"Together, we will survive this war, even if I have to hide you from the Russians till this is all over." We had a lovely evening, but Inge noticed that I was very nervous and overstressed, telling her that all those ugly pictures kept flashing through my mind. "You went through hell last night."

"Not only that, but I am so tired, and I cannot go to sleep."

"You will go to sleep. I'll give you two of my sleeping pills, and you will sleep like a baby, and tomorrow is another day." And so I did. Deliberately and leisurely, Inge and I stretched the morning listening to soft music, enjoying a wonderful breakfast.

War makes for awkward friendships; here I was not even sixteen years old, feeling like an equal with a thirty-five-or-so-year-old woman and communicating with her on the same level.

For a moment, I wasn't saying anything, and Inge noticed that I was thinking. "What is on your mind?" Inge wanted to know.

"I wonder how my mother and grandmother are doing and how last night's air raid affected them."

"Well," Inge said, "there is only one way to find out, go and see them."

"Oh, you are not making it any easier for me. I really want to stay here with you this weekend. Remember, Monday I have to be in Marzahn."

"True," Inge said, "but one week will go by fast. You will be busy, and I am going back to work Monday morning myself. I have an idea, you take off tomorrow morning, stay overnight in Tegel with your mother and grandmother, and Monday morning you are already halfway in Marzahn."

I said, "That makes sense, why didn't I think of it? By the way, I cannot find my dirty uniform. I want my mother to wash it for me."

"You don't want the poor woman to have a heart attack with all those bloodstains."

"I never thought of it, but you are right." I filled my backpack with a few clean things needed for one week, and Inge gave me a paper bag with some of the food I carried away from the base. With the first glimmer of light in the morning I got out of bed, but Inge was already up before dawn. I said good-bye and promised to be back soon.

In Tegel, to my great relief, I found everything the way I left it. My mother told me about the last air raid and the big American plane that crashed behind the house in the Steinberg. "That sounds interesting. I have never seen the inside of an American airplane. I think I will go and investigate the crash site."

"Sure," Grandmother said, "go and stick your nose in it, as if you are not in enough trouble already."

"Nothing to it, it is my business to learn everything about airplanes. I will be back in no time at all. Who knows, I might even bring you a souvenir."

"You know what you can do with it."

"Simmer down, Mother, the boy is old enough to know what he is doing. After all, he has been doing the job of a man for some time now," my mother said.

I had no problem finding the plane; it was a B-17 hanging with the nose in an almost forty-five-degree angle between two tall pine trees. The plane came down with full flaps, telling me that the pilot was breaking the airspeed trying to land the plane in a small clearing in front of the forest. The position of the nose and the flaps indicated that the pilot was trying to stall the engines and land the plane at the same time over the small patch of land available. Unfortunately for the pilot, he miscalculated and could not clear the trees. The rest of the crew apparently walked away from the crash while the pilot broke his neck. I had to climb up on one of the trees in order to reach the inside of the B-17. I was amazed about all the modern equipment I found onboard of the plane. The radio and navigational system were the latest, and so was the new bombsight, giving the aim of the target more accuracy. On my way out of the plane I took a last look at the pilot, and I could not withstand the temptation to lift the .45 out of his holster. An even greater urge of possession I felt toward his beautiful new shiny flying boots. Compared to my shabby shoes with the soles coming off, I could not feel guilt to take them away from the dead man.

As usual, I got out of Tegel early in the morning, but that day I was not saying anything about my next endeavor. As of the first of April, the eastern riverside along the Oder-Neisse was completely in the hands of the Russian army. The German army headquarter was aware that it had reached the last line of defense to stop the Soviet invasion on the eastern front. On the second of April, out of desperation, Hitler ordered to set up a resistance movement by the code name Werewolf. It was organized by the SS general inspector for special defense. In a broadcast, Joseph Goebbels appealed to the German people to join the Werewolf. Every Bolshevik, every enemy pilot on our soil must be a target for our movement. A single motto remained for us: "Conquer or die." I was joining the Werewolf partly out of necessity, as an alternative to the eastern front after the destruction of the Schmargendorf Flak Battery, and for a personal reason as a second motive. We Germans were not a nation of partisans; we waited for orders from our leadership. Being a terrorist was the last act of desperation; you must be motivated by the death of a loved one. To live or to die depended on winning or losing. Since we were as a nation condemned to lose the war, we were all, according to Adolf Hitler, deserving to die; but we were supposed to die fighting and must at the same time kill many of the enemies before they could kill us. Such equation of the scorched-earth policy I wasn't ready to accept. My mind told me there must be a third solution. Instinctively I felt I was too young to die. I didn't think that the rest of the German people went for the suicide mentality of the Nazi Party either. This was how I was reasoning for the last few months. However, I was no longer concerned about my own life after I learned what a miserable death Gisela suffered. I was hoping to stay alive and have a future together with her. Now it really did not matter if I lived or died. My purpose in life shifted from living to fighting. I had the strong urge to avenge Gisela's death by killing as many Russians as possible when the battle of Berlin began. Let my destiny decide if I should live or die.

At that point, as a last resort, I would be one of the most tenacious and fearless defenders of Berlin—"the Hitler Youth," those whose homes had been ripped apart by enemy bombs and family members killed and their women raped by the Red Army.

Today was the eleventh of April; I was entering for one week the Werewolf training camp near Marzahn. In theory the training program covered methods of sabotage using tin cans packed with plastic explosive and to be detonated with captured British time pencils. Werewolf recruits were instructed to operate in small groups and select targets of greater importance to inflict higher damage. Special emphasis was put on railroad junctions, ammunition dumps, and gasoline supplies as targets. All attacks were underground operations and coordinated by a regional *Kreisleiter* in charge; he would also disburse weapons, ammunitions, explosive charges, and rations. The secret was to carry out a mission without being detected or captured. You dress in civilian clothing and go home after the assault as if nothing had happened. Under no circumstances were you to face the enemy or engage in any kind of combat; you would not win, you would only jeopardize your life and the secrecy of the underground operation. Play it cool, attend to your job or business, and act like any other ordinary member of the community, family, or church group.

Sunday night on the seventeenth of April, the Werewolf training camp closed, and all recruits were instructed to stand by till someone contacts them. I was anxious to go back to Wilmersdorf to see how Inge was doing. I worried about Inge being alone. But first I had to stop by in Tegel for one day and find out how my mother and grandmother were doing and if they needed anything. Sunday night I arrived late at my mother's house. Answering my question if she needed anything, she told me that they were running low on groceries. "What is the matter, are you running out of food stamps?"

"No no, not at all. The trouble is we cannot get out of the house. The moment a few people stand outside the stores, the Mosquitos (small British fighting airplanes) come out of the blue sky and fire at the bystanders."

"I know, Mother, you had a bad experience. You may be a little phobic about it, but first thing in the morning, I will get you something to eat." My mother asked me how things were at the base, and I told her that the Schmargendorf Battery would be closed, and in a few days the men and whatever equipment was to be moved to the Seelower Hoehen. "I have the option to go with them or stay in Berlin," I said, but I decided to stay in town; that was why I was transferred to the Flak bunker in Humbold Hain, which was even closer to Tegel. The rest of the story I kept from her; no use to scare her about my future.

Next morning, I asked my mother to give me the biggest basket and all the food stamps she had left, and I said to her that I would not come back till I traded all the stamps for real food. I kept trying successfully to get inside the bigger stores in Tegel. Surprisingly I was able to buy all the food I had tickets for in less than two hours. Talking to one of the customers, I found out that a small factory for preserves and confectionery in Wittenau burned down the night before. I knew the place, and it was not far from my mother's house. When I came home, I put the basket on top of the kitchen table, telling them, "This is all the food you get for the rest of the month, don't eat it all in one day." They were also listening to my story about Wittenau and that I was going back to check it out. "Be careful," my grandmother said. "If they catch you, they will hang you."

"That does not scare me anymore. If you are hungry, you have to eat."

As the woman said, the place burned down all right, and I was not the first one standing around trying to salvage some cans. There was not much left from the two-story factory except for some metal beams hanging in the air. Another man and I were walking across the heavy concrete floor looking for an opening of some kind that would indicate that there was a basement or storage room underneath. As the rubble cooled down, more people joined the search till somebody in the back of the platform discovered what seemed to be the edge of a staircase. It took some digging before we created an opening to go underneath. Another man and I were the first ones to reach the basement. We saw rows and rows of all kinds of five-gallon buckets of honey and different kinds of marmalade. I didn't want to be greedy; besides, all I could carry would be a one five-gallon bucket of honey. The crowd on the outside was getting bigger, and I had a hell of a time to get past them. I barely made it one hundred feet away from the bombed factory when suddenly, two Mosquitos came out of nowhere, spraying the people with their 20 mm machine guns. I was very lucky I did not get hit. How fast could you run with a five-gallon bucket of honey? Knowing that the two Mosquitos would come back for a second approach, I took shelter in a nearby doorway. Sure enough, the bastards made a second run, killing and wounding more innocent civilians. Anyway, I made it home with my precious cargo to the delight of two hungry women. I could not describe how happy I made them. They concealed the bucket in the broom closet. I was convinced that the nourishing honey would tide them over till the end of the war or beyond.

I wished I could stay longer with them, but they understood that I had to see Inge before I report for my new assignment at the Humbold Hain Flak Bunker. Arriving at Wilmersdorf, I found Inge in good spirit; apparently, going back to work was doing her a world of good. I told Inge about the incident I had with the Mosquitos, and she said she had the same experience wherever she went. "I have the feeling we must be now very close to the end," Inge said. "Where did you get those shiny new boots from?" she wanted to know. "I am certain it is not a product of Germany."

What could I say but tell her the whole story. "I can understand about the boots, but what do you want the gun for?"

"That is the most important thing. I took it for your safety. I don't want the same thing that happened to Gisela to happen to you. If at the end the Russians come in and you are in danger of being attacked, please shoot them or scare them off before they molest you. Do you think you can do that?" For a moment, Inge did not say anything.

"I appreciate your concern for my safety, and for that, I'll be forever grateful."

Being at the camp in Marzahn for one week, I was not up-to-date with the latest developments. Since the fifteenth of this month, the battle of the

Seelower Höhen was now in full swing; but already three days later, one sector of the defense of the Seelower Heights was broken. The beginning of the Battle of Berlin had now been officially declared. On the Oder front, Frankfurt still remained a fighting fortress. "In my estimation, the war on the eastern front should be over in one month." And Inge agreed. Tomorrow was the last day I would spend with Inge before I would report for duty at Humboldthain Bunker. There was no telling if and how many days I would be allowed to leave the battery. "I hate to see you go," Inge said. "But on the other hand, I am happy to know that you are more protected in a Flak bunker. It is a miracle that you survived the battle of Schmargendorf where your comrades died left and right helplessly standing in the open air in the middle of a hailstorm of bombs."

"I am beginning to be anxious myself to find out if I'll make it to the end of the war," I said.

CHAPTER IX

BERLIN: THE EYE OF THE HURRICANE

The End of War at Humboldthain Bunker

The moment the eight-centimeter-thick steel door of the Humboldthain Flak Bunker closed behind me, I had the feeling of entering a spooky dream world. What I left behind at the other side of the door was a city of chaos where millions of people were facing death and destruction. Life inside the three Flak towers was comparable to a peacetime atmosphere. The location of the major three Flak bunkers were Friedrichshain, Humboldthain, and the zoo. The upper portion of each bunker was a military installation; the lower part was reserved for the people, the wounded, and the dispersed military. The Flak batteries, mainly 12.8 cm and 8.8 cm guns, were located on top of the bunker and on the corner of each tower. The zoo bunker was the biggest one in Berlin. Directly below, under the gun platform, was the Luftwaffen Hospital where doctors and nurses were working day and night to take care of the never-ending stream of casualties. The lower portion of the zoo bunker had the capacity to shelter thirty thousand people. The Beton giant at Humboldthain was the first bunker to be bombarded around the clock by heavy Russian artillery. The result was a waste of ammunition.

Neither did any of the Allied bombs ever created more than a scratch on a big Flak bunker. The only Achilles' tendon in a Flak bunker was the upper deck, the gun platform. The big shield in front of the gun offered little protection. The situation was especially hopeless during carpet bombing. Since the Soviets have already put an iron ring around Berlin, with the exception of an opening to the west, Allied Bomber Command attacked Berlin for the last time on the twenty-first of April. Under the bombardment of Russian artillery, the city of Berlin was by no means any safer. The daily *Appell* (roll call) took place every morning in the communication center at the fourth floor. The second lieutenant reported to the battery chief the strength of the crew and other daily events of importance. The CO in turn gave orders of changes to be made. In the last air raid, the enemy was able to destroy the general *Gefechtsstand* for all three Flak towers located in the Tiergarten. As a backup, each Flak tower had its own *Commando Gerät* (communication equipment). Except for a few Russian bombers, the new targets were the Russian T-34 tanks approaching the outside of Berlin in increasing numbers.

Berlin needed an army to defend the city of 8 million people. The Volkssturm and the Hitler Youth alone were not able to defend Berlin against the onslaught of 2.5 million soldiers of the Red Army. On the twenty-fifth, Hitler agreed to retreat to the Frankfurt Garrison, or he would have another Stalingrad on his hands. Colonel Bieler managed in the last minute to get out of the Frankfurt encircled pocket to link up his troops with the Ninth Army. The next day, General Busse broke out of the Halbe ring leading the Ninth Army, not to relieve Berlin, but straight toward the river Elbe to capitulate to the U.S. Armed Forces. General Busse knew he could not save Berlin, that was why he decided to save the lives of his men. Marshal Tschuikow, no longer in need of reserve troops, concentrated all his men power for the fall of Berlin. It was now a race between Marshal Tschuikow and Marshal Konyew, whose troops would be the first to put the red flag on the Reichstag, the symbol of German authority in the center of Berlin. The battle of Berlin was decided, but by no means over yet. For the next few days, a ferocious house-to-house battle and savage killings on both sides were going on in the center of Berlin. The only military installations that could not be penetrated were the three green islands of Flak bunkers. Marshal Konyew noticed how ineffective the field artillery was against the bunker walls of concrete and steel. The aim of the Soviet artillery was the upper gun platform on top of the forty-meter-high Flak tower. This was the spot where the gun crews of the 8.8 cm and the 12.8 cm twin guns were constantly exposed to the artillery fire. The targets of the battery were the Russian T-34 tanks. The only problem was that the gun barrels could only be lowered to a certain point, and the target must be attacked by direct vision. Casualties by the upper deck crew must constantly be replaced. I was assigned to one of the 2 cm guns at the northwest tower. Our action, compared to the 8.8 cm, was not significant; we were not fighting enemy tanks. In our spare time, we were also helping out with the ammunition replacement. Yesterday the upper gun deck suffered a direct hit in one of the reserve ammunition piles. The 8.8 cm gun blew up, and there were no survivors of the gun crew. Six of us Luftwaffenhelfers went upstairs and removed the still-bleeding pieces of what was once an eight-man gun crew. The other five guys of the cleanup team, apparently new in this business, could not hold their stomach or were emotionally freaked out. I did not suffer any of those symptoms. Was it possible that I already adapted to brutality and saw the removal of cadavers as a routine job? On the outside, Berlin was bleeding to death, but the three Flak bunkers were not willing to give up. We had our own power generator, a deep water well, plenty to eat, and lots of ammunition to keep on fighting.

On April 30, 1945, Adolf Hitler and Eva Braun committed suicide at three thirty in the afternoon; both bodies were put in a crater near the back door of the Führer's bunker and cremated. The Flak towers were still fighting after Hitler and Goebbels committed suicide, and the red flag was already flying over the Reichstag. The commando center for all three Flak bunkers was located at the top floor of the zoo bunker. From here all orders were given to each Flak bunker. The Russian headquarter was sending at the dawn of light on May 2 several bearers of a flag of truce to the defender of the Flak bunker. On the German side, shortly before, an order was given to the bunker garrison to attempt a breakthrough to the north. In the hospital, the wounded and the civilians were to be left behind; some other soldiers also did not leave the shelter. In the middle of the night from May 1 to 2, all the Luftwaffenhelfers of the Humboldthain Flak Bunker assembled at the G-Tower (*Geschützturm* also known as gun tower), waiting to get instruction on how to attempt an escape. Our commanding officer explained that all military personnel would be given the last chance to escape before the Flak tower hangs out the Red Cross flag, to save the civilians and wounded soldiers, before the bunker will be turned over to the Russians. He said, "The Humboldthain Bunker is completely surrounded by the Red Army, ready to launch an all-out attack if we have not surrendered in two hours. As you all know, the G-tower is connected with the *Leitturm* (command tower) via the cable tunnel. This is the first tunnel of your escape route. When you get to the command tower, another underground tunnel will take you to the basement of the electric equipment factory on the other side of the Gustav-Meyer-Allee. You are now out of the Humboldthain area and should disburse single or in small groups before daybreak. Be careful, wherever you go there are Russians all over the place. Hide and sleep in the daytime and travel at nights. One more advice, leave any of your weapons in the bunker and get out of the uniform the first chance you have. Take some food for the road, and God bless you."

Minutes later, in a single file, we were entering the cable tunnel heading for the Leit-tower. There was very little light; the air was stuffy, and rats were running away from us. Getting out of the damp cable tunnel and into the Leit-tower was a relief. A strange picture was capturing my eyes as I entered the Leit-tower; what I had in mind was a highly sophisticated control and command center, the brain of the Flak bunker. Instead the whole tower of operation could rather be described as an officer's bordello.

Most of the regular Flak crew had already left the tower, but a number of officers had decided to outlive their lives with a bullet in the head right here in the Leit-tower. The last days or hours had to be filled out with as much gusto as they could grasp. All the worldly pleasures of food, alcohol, tobacco, and sex were still available to them. There were plenty of young nurses, secretaries, and telephone operators eager not to miss out on what could be the last chance to enjoy the pleasures of the flesh. The scenes that all of us Flakhelfers were encountering in every room were shocking to us. An erotic fever seemed to have taken possession of everybody. The breakdown of normal respectable behavior of the Luftwaffe may have been initiated first by the SS officers who had been out searching cellars and streets for deserters to hang, which had also been tempting, hungry, and impressionable young women back to the bunker with promises of parties and inexhaustible supplies of food and champagne. The air in the lower bunker was filled with smoke so thick you could cut it with a knife, mixed with the smell of alcohol and body odor. Men and women had discarded all modesty and were freely exposing parts of their bodies. More so, I was having a queasy sensation in my stomach by just looking at the SS officer talking to the leader of our group; he could retain us or shoot as on the spot as deserters. All of us were still in full uniform, and the argument that we wanted to break out was only to join the fighting SS Division Hitler Youth at Stadtmitte. That must have convinced the drunken SS officer, and he gave us a free pass to retreat.

 Discomfort with restlessness and the longing to escape this stage of apocalypse and underworld of hell were driving us to enter the next tunnel. This narrow tunnel was much longer and completely dark. A few of our flashlights gave us enough light not to run our heads against the walls. It must have taken us thirty minutes to end our walk in the basement of the factory. Momentarily we were protected in this underground warehouse, but there was not much time left till dawn, and everybody had to decide which direction he wanted to go. Before the group disbursed, the group leader sent two boys to go upstairs to see from the factory window and watch any activities on the southside of Gustav-Meyer-Allee. They came back reporting that most of the houses were destroyed, some of them were still burning, no fighting or gunfire was observed in the sector of the other side of the street, no traffic except for a Soviet supply column of horse-drawn carts and a few motorized vehicles. Two guys at a time took the dash across the street to disappear in the rubble. Waiting for my turn to get lost, I had to make a decision which way to go. Instinctively, I first wanted to go to Tegel, but I discarded the idea as it was too far north and now already completely occupied by the Russian army. Going south would take me straight into some pockets of resistance, and Wilmersdorf was just as far and dangerous to reach. As an interim solution, the thought came to my mind that Kieler Strasse was only two kilometers from here. I figured that if everything went well, I could be there just before dawn. Knowing the neighborhood would help me to find my way, and, if my luck held up, one of the old tenants might still be around to give me some shelter for a day or two. So what was I waiting for? Time was of the essence.

Walking west on the sidewalk of Gustav-Meyer-Allee, constantly with my eyes opened and ready to jump back into the ruins should I detect any noise coming up or down the street, I was taking cover several times before entering the Liesen Strasse. Trying to cross the broad Chausse Strasse was more of a problem; it was a major traffic artery toward the center of Berlin. One Russian convoy after another was going south to reinforce the advancing downtown front line. For some reason, the convoy stopped for a few minutes, and in the cover of the night, I jumped across the street. Here I was now at the Boyen Strasse, ten minutes away from my old playground. This sector of town was a poor neighborhood and showed less traces of war damage. There were certainly no more defenders of the German army left. How did I know? Very simple. On both sides of the street were hanging white bedsheets out of the windows, the symbol of surrender. If the SS troops were still around, they would have blown up the flags and killed the occupants of the house. Now I remembered walking down the same street with my parents when I was a little boy, seeing nothing but swastika flags hanging out of the same windows. Boyen Strasse terminated into Scharnhorst Strasse almost at the corner of Kieler Strasse. I had reached my first destination standing in front of Kieler Strasse 2. The house to the left side where the greengrocer used to be was burned out, but the corner on the right side with the bakery was still there. The bakery was locked, but the door to the house was open. As I noticed daylight coming up, I also heard the sound of a big but distant explosion. I looked at my watch, it was 7:55 AM, May 2. No longer hesitating, I opened the door, walking down the hall and up the stairs to the apartment of Egon's parents. I rang the doorbell once, nothing moved. I rang the bell again; after a few minutes, the sound of some footsteps told me that somebody was coming to the door. The door opened a few inches but was secured by a chain in the inside. The face of a woman appeared next to the chain, asking me who I was. Recognizing the face and voice of Egon's mother, I told her who I was. It was about nine years ago when she had seen me the last time; I didn't expect her to remember me immediately. A few seconds later, it all came back to her. "Oh my god," she said and was nervously trying to unlock the door. "Let me look at you, I can still not believe who is standing there. Please come in, come in." She was leading me to the living room asking me to sit down.

"Times are hard. We all are trying to survive the best we can, and I don't really want to impose on you as a burden, but I am desperately in need of a place to hide for a day or two."

"Nonsense, my boy, nonsense, you stay here till there is no more shooting. You look tired and hungry, let me fix you something to eat."

"Really, I am not hungry. I have still plenty to eat in my rucksack, a glass of water would be fine." She went to the kitchen and came back with a glass of cold water and a big cookie.

"Here, try it. I remember you always liked sweets. I tell you what," she said, "you look very tired. There is no use to ask you all kinds of questions right now, we have plenty of time for that later. Let me take you to Egon's room so you can catch up on your sleep. I even have a nightgown for you."

I accepted her invitation most graciously. I could not remember when I went to sleep that fast the last time. After I got up, I was asking Egon's mother if there was anything I could do for her. "Not at the moment," she said. "But maybe later. Right now I would like you to take off your uniform and put on some civilian clothes. Put your uniform in a bag, and I will take it down to the bakery to be burned."

"Thank you. I will be very happy to oblige." As I was getting dressed, I asked her about her family, "Where is Egon and your husband?"

Sitting down, she started telling me about Egon. "He joined the German Navy and was captured by the British Royal Navy. He is now a POW in England. We got all the information from the Red Cross. My husband and his younger brother, Albert, were still running the bakery till my husband was ordered to take over the job as a supervisor at the army bread factory in Düsseldorf. Albert and a Polish worker kept the bakery going, with me working behind the counter till about a week ago when we ran out of flour and sugar. The Polish worker went home, and Albert was forced to join the Volkssturm. Now that the war is over, I hope and pray to God that my husband, Egon, and Albert will be coming home soon. I hate to be alone, I want us to be together again and have a normal life."

"Be patient," I said. "It will get better soon, consider yourself lucky that your family is one of the few families that have not suffered any casualties; millions of families have lost one or more members" I did not want to get into my family history, but she was also interested to find out what happened to us since we left Kieler Strasse. Looking out of the window in Egon's room, I could see the waterfront just like it was years ago, and I saw us kids sitting there on the wall watching all the boats go by. Somehow she did read my mind as she was asking me if I remembered the old gang. "I certainly do, and those were the best and only years of my childhood. I wonder if all of them are still alive."

"I can tell you that at the beginning of the war, they all got scattered into different directions, and I have not seen or heard from them since. The only exception is the leader of the gang, Atze. I met his mother one day at the NS women's club, telling me that her son got killed at the battle of Stalingrad." At this point, Egon's mother was putting her hand on my shoulder, telling me how lucky I was that I got out of this war alive. "It seems like I got it made, but they are still fighting downtown Berlin. Suppose General Busse with his two hundred thousand men army would break the ring around Berlin and join General Wencks's defending army in Berlin, and together they could push Chuikou's army back to the Seelower Höhen. We can guess all we want, what we really need is a radio to find out the truth."

"I have a radio, but it is not working, maybe you can fix it." She brought the radio and put it on the kitchen table. First I switched on the light to see if we had electricity, then I plugged in the radio, waiting for it to warm up; but there was no light on the dial. Checking the cord, I did not see any damage; the problem must be in the radio. I unplugged the radio again, turned it around, and removed the back panel. Carefully I removed all six tubes, checking them for broken filaments. Nothing wrong here. Replacing the tubes, I noticed that the last one was not fitting tight in the socket; one of the terminals was not making any contact and thereby breaking the power in the circuit. With a paper clip, I was able to restore the path of the electric current. Keeping my fingers crossed, I plugged in the radio, and she lit up. All I got was some static noise, a disturbing electromagnetic wave interfering with a clear reception. By moving the set and the antenna, I finally managed to get the dial to tune in on a West German radio station. I was hoping to receive the BBC, but this radio did not have the power to bring it in. Playing with the radio for hours by the end of the day, I had a pretty good picture of what was really going on. Separating rumors from facts, it was now confirmed that Adolf Hitler committed suicide on April 30, making Admiral Doenitz his successor. It was also a fact that General Busse did not come to help General Wenck; instead, he took his Ninth Army to the river Elbe and surrendered to the American army. General Wenck had not capitulated yet to the Russians, and the rest of his army, mostly Hitler Youth, had linked up with the SS Division Flandern. A bloody battle with high casualties on both sides was still going on at Stadtmitte, around the chancellery, and the Reichstag. A large group of fanatic Hitler Youth was giving the Russians a bloody nose by bitterly defending the Spandauer Bridge over the river Havel to keep it open for the Berliner refugees to escape to the west.

I was so busy with the radio that I did not notice that Egon's mother had left the house to get some food. She had her connections to get some food and to obtain some news. In the daytime, the Russians didn't seem to bother the civilians. She told me that at Scharnhorst Strasse, on one side the Russians were trying to get into Berlin, and on the other side of the street, the Berliner refugees were trying to get out of the city. The information she was coming home with was new to all of us; it must be true because all the refugees coming out of Berlin were telling her the same story. It was the blowing up of the S-Bahn tunnel under the Landwehr Canal near Trebbiner Strasse and S-Bahnhof Gleisdreieck. Everybody kept saying the explosion occurred at 8:00 AM, which coincided exactly with the observation I made at 7:55 AM today. In any case, the explosion, as I found out later on, led to the flooding of twenty-five kilometers of S-Bahn and also U-Bahn tunnels once the water penetrated through the connecting shafts. Estimates of casualties were ranging up to fifteen thousand based on the fact that there were soldiers and many thousands of civilians in the tunnels as well as several hospital trains, which were subway carriages packed with the wounded. After the explosion, the water did not rise quickly since it was spreading in many different directions. Women and children were forced by the SS to evacuate the bunker at Anhalter Bahnhof and driven down the S-Bahn tunnel all the way up to the S-Bahnhof at Friedrich Strasse. Most of the people who made it up to this point survived by taking the higher U-Bahn tunnel up to Stettiner Bahnhof. The rest of them drowned on the way or left the tunnel at Friedrich Strasse and got killed in the cross fire between the SS and the Russian army. Some recounted seeing exhausted women running through the dark tunnels looking for their lost children screaming, terrified as the floodwater rose. Wounded soldiers who were not able to get up and out of the hospital trains near the Stadtmitte U-Bahn station would slip beneath the water. According to some witnesses, the order to blow up the tunnel below the Landwehr Canal was given by Dr. Joseph Goebbels to be carried out by the SS to hold the Russian army for a few more hours from entering the Reichs Chancellery. Goebbels also was the only one to refuse to sign a statement of unconditional surrender. General Zhukow replied, "Tell Goebbels and Bormann, if they do not agree to unconditional surrender, we will blast Berlin into ruins." Zhukov set a time limit of 10:15 AM of May 1. No answer was received. At twenty-five minutes past the deadline, the First Belorussian Front unleashed a barrage of artillery fire on the remains of the city center. General Weidling, the commandant of the fortress Berlin, made an end to the carnage by agreeing and ordering his troops to an unconditional surrender the next day. The actual fighting did not stop till May 3 when the last pockets of SS resistance were destroyed. All East Germany, including Berlin, up to the river Elbe, was now under Soviet occupation.

I no longer had to worry about the SS; my only problem left was to stay out of any conflict with the Russians. It was time now for me to move on to Wilmersdorf. Planning my way going south, I would avoid major traffic roads, use side streets, and walk across the Tiergarten. Before I left Kieler Strasse, I decided to go to Wilmersdorf first as it was without any transportation from here, only half the distance to walk. Today was the fourth of May, a strange, almost-frightening silence was hanging over the city; there was no more artillery or gunfire. Civilians were slowly coming out of cellars and basements; refugees were getting out of shelters, tunnels, and underground protection that saved their lives. Homeless people coming from as far as East Prussia filling once more the streets of Berlin or were trying in tracks to reach West Germany. My time had also come to leave again and say thanks to Egon's mother.

Cease-fire and Back on the Road

To show my appreciation, I gave Egon's mother my salami sausage, which I had saved; I wished I could give her more. In return, I could not refuse the two loaves of bread she offered me to take along. She also insisted that I put on one of Egon's short pair of pants; it would make me look a lot younger (I'd be sixteen in July). On her advise, I also destroyed all military identification papers and just kept my driver's license. As a last request, she asked me if I could stop at her sister's house, which was along my way to Wilmersdorf, and deliver a letter. It shall be done, and I also promised her that I would stop by again. Stepping out in the open, this beautiful morning was an indescribable experience of its own. The sun was shining, and despite all the ruins around me, a feeling of happiness to be free was coming over me. The war was over, and I still believed being alive was a triumph; who cared about victory this moment? Walking across the Kieler Bridge, I followed the Heide Strasse along the canal side all the way till I reached the Invaliden Strasse. So far I had seen very few people and no Russians, but here at this junction, the traffic was increasing. I was still a little shy, but with some other civilians, I crossed the street in front of a column of Russian soldiers marching toward town.

On the other side of the street, I kept on walking south along the Humboldt Haven. It was a shortcut but obstructed by huge piles of rubble; sometimes the riverside was my only orientation. Traffic was now getting intense as the *Moltkebrücke* was taking me across the spree. Before I crossed the bridge, I sat down, watched the traffic, and thought about the last few days of the war. Battle-hardened Berliners had come to believe that it must all end in death. Any other outcome appeared unthinkable after they had seen everything around them destroyed. People trapped in a bomb-ravaged encirclement were sitting in cellar holes among rubble, ready to be killed like rats. It was a hard school indeed for us young boys of the Hitler Youth to face reality. At the end, we had no longer fought for Hitler; we fought for ourselves to die in Berlin and not in Siberia. Few of us had any illusions about what lay ahead. And now that the war was over, everything on the ground was in chaos. Most of the civilians you could see on the main street were refugees. Soviet tank columns forced them off the road or simply crushed any refugee carts blocking their way. Some refugees had to abandon their carts and belongings and stagger with their children and their old folks through the debris on the sidewalks. From Alt-Moabit to the Moltke Bridge over the Spree was only six hundred meters. A distance of another eight hundred meters beyond the bridge was the Reichstag.

The Reichstag was the biggest building in the inner city, but it was not visible as it was still surrounded by fire and smoke from burning houses outside the Königsplatz. I could walk over there in a few minutes, but now it was impassable—covered with shell holes, railway sleepers, pieces of wire, trenches, and burned-out vehicles and tanks. The ground was littered with hundreds of dead bodies from both armies. It was obvious that I was walking on grounds that had seen the biggest and bloodiest battles of the last few days. Wherever I went were barricades that had been blasted open, and over tank ditches, partly filled with rubble and empty fuel barrels dropped by advancing tanks. Along the route, I encountered some young Red Cross nurses pulling a hay cart, taking badly wounded soldiers to the rear, many of whom had unbandaged stumps from limbs that had been shot off. In particular, I remembered the case of a Hitler Youth soldier who cried out for help. Neither of us could see him, but we followed his voice till we found him in a crater. The boy was bleeding from his abdomen. Taking his pants off, we could see his scrotum ripped wide open with both of his testicles hanging out. A shrapnel from an exploding shell hit him from the rear as he was trying to take cover. The girls were asking me to help them to lift the boy into the cart. I explained to the young nurses that we could make more damage by doing so if we didn't find a solution to repair him first. A bandage won't help much, and a cutting needle with catgut or some other suture material were not available. "How about some safety pins?"

"Yes, we have some," said one of the girls.

I untwisted the arteries and pushed the undamaged testicles back into the pouch and let one of the girls hold everything in place while I closed the skin of the scrotum with three safety pins together. With the scrotum taped to his left upper leg, the boy was able to stand up with our help. The girls asked me to help them push the cart back to the Tiergarten not far from here. One of the girls gave me her Red Cross badge to identify me as one of them.

Along the way, in every house still standing, I saw sheets and pillowcases hanging from windows in a sign of surrender. In one of the main streets, we were passing an endless column of German soldiers guarded by Red Army soldiers marching east as POWs to be shipped to a gulag somewhere in Russia. Less than half the way to the field hospital, we stopped to check on the wounded on the cart we were pushing, to see how they were doing. One of them passed away, it was the soldier with the leg missing. He'd lost too much blood, went into shock, and died. Earlier we could not put a tourniquet on him as the wound was too high up. I had to think back on my days at the LBA-Neisse of all the surgical instruments we had at our sick bay. If I had just one hemostat, I might have been able to save his life. All we could do for the dead soldier was to take him off the cart and put him on the sidewalk under a big tree. A woman must have watched us unloading the body, she came out of the house and put a newspaper over his face. The girls and I went on with our trip; this time it was somewhat lighter to push the cart. These brave young nurses reminded me a lot of my dead girlfriend, Gisela.

Surprisingly, I saw very few Berliners on the street. The smell of decomposing corpses from the piles of rubble, which had been buildings, and the smell of charred flesh from the blackened skeletons of burned-out houses kept them underground. Since most of the houses in Berlin were destroyed, there must be over a million people without a home. They continued to live in cellars and air-raid shelters. Smoke from cooking fires emerged from piles of rubble. Women were trying their best to create something that looked like a home for their children amid the ruins. Mothers emerged into the streets to search for water only in the early morning hours when Soviet soldiers were sleeping off their alcohol from the night before. They were desperate to keep their daughters from being raped by the Russians in some invisible hiding place.

We were now finally reaching the edge of the Tiergarten. The girls were completely exhausted, and I asked some of the male refugees, who camped out in the Tiergarten, to replace the nurses and give us a hand. We kept on going, and the girls were showing us the way. It was only another five hundred feet to the field hospital. I helped the nurses at the hospital to take the three wounded soldiers to the operating room; they all survived.

It was getting dark now, and I could hardly keep my eyes open. I was about to return my Red Cross badge before I was going to look for a place to sleep when the head nurse asked me to stay with them. "We are all volunteers. Nobody gets paid, but you get three meals a day and a warm place to sleep. Besides, our hospital is about the safest place in Berlin to be right now. You can go anytime you feel like."

"Sister," I said, "in my situation, I cannot refuse your offer. Please show me where I can put my head down."

"Very good, but first you must eat something before you go to bed. By the way, the girls are telling me that they think you must have some medical experience, is that true?"

"Well, not much practical experience, but I worked at the first aid station at the academy after I took some basic medical courses."

"That is good enough. We can use you in surgery. We are desperately short on help. We started as a Wehrmacht MASH Unit when Berlin became a war zone and keep now working for everybody under the protection of the Red Cross. All the doctors and regular nurses stayed on the job and will remain with the Red Cross as long as we are needed. One of our best sponsors are the Russians, they send us cases they are not equipped to handle. We have the finest surgeons on our team, some of them are from the Charité Hospital."

Next day I started to work in surgery, circulating in the operating room and transporting patients in and out. The second day, I noticed that we were getting a lot of fresh gunshot wounds. "What is going on? I thought the war is over," I asked one of the doctors. He told me that Stalin promised the Red Army that if they would deliver Berlin to him, surrendered by May the first for the victory parade at the Red Square in Moscow, he would let any Russian soldier celebrate victory over Germany for three days and drink all the vodka they could find. At the same time, they would not be punished for molesting, injuring, raping, or killing any of the German people. "That is the biggest war crime I ever heard of. Besides, the three days are over."

"I agree with you," the doctor said. "But that does not make any difference to the average Russian soldier. They have done it before the three days, and they will keep on doing it. There is no animal in this world as furious and vicious as a Red soldier when he is drunk." The doctor went on, "The worst mistake of the German military authorities had been their refusal to destroy alcohol stocks in the path of the Red Army's advance. This decision was based on the idea that a drunken enemy could not fight. Tragically for the female population, however, it was exactly what Red Army soldiers seemed to need to give them courage to rape and kill as well as to celebrate the end of such a terrible war. The Russians' victory celebrations did not signify an end to fear in Berlin. Many German women and young girls were still being raped as part of the extended celebrations. The young and old men we were trying to save here on the table were the victims that were shot when they were trying to stop the raping of their wives, mothers, or daughters." I estimated that in three days, I had seen more anatomy of the human body than a medical student would learn out of books in three years.

Unfortunately, my affiliation with the improvised field hospital in the Tiergarten was suddenly terminated. Late in the evening, two intoxicated Soviet soldiers armed with submachine guns entered the dormitory for the recovering patients, prodding each man in the chest threateningly. "Du SS?" they asked. My stretcher partner and I were coming in at the same time, bringing back a patient from surgery, when one of the Russians prodded my partner hard in the pit of the stomach, asking him the same question. My partner kept telling him that he was just a hospital orderly, doing his job.

"Da, da. Du SS!" the Red Army soldier insisted. My partner, who, like me, had destroyed his papers including his Wehrmacht passport, pushed the stretcher really hard against the Russian and ran in panic out of the door. The two Russians did not have a chance to shoot at him, but both of them followed the escaping man in a hurry, giving me enough time to disappear. In the cover of the darkness, I found shelter for the night in a cluster of bushes. Among them were several uniforms discarded by members of the Wehrmacht changing their identity. I took some of the overcoats to become more comfortable for the night. In the morning I found myself in the middle of a refugee camp on the southside of the Tiergarten. It seemed like all the wagon trains were stopping here to camp out; it was not as hectic as on the road where Russian tanks had crushed their carts for moving too slow. Crawling out of my hiding place, I was greeted by a bunch of civilians having breakfast. I mingled with them, and I couldn't understand how they were able to have large steaks for breakfast. One of the men helping with the grilling over an open fire was asking me, if I wanted to eat with them, to follow him. He pulled out a big knife and took me about two hundred feet down the road to a dead horse. As I was looking with mixed feeling at the rest of the cadaver, he told me, "Sorry, all the center cuts are gone as people have been hacking on it since the Russians shot the horse last night, but there is some good meat left on the ribs." He cut a good portion for me to take back to the group of civilians. I had never eaten horse meat before. Naturally, I was starting to eat it with some antagonistic feelings, but then I discovered that it had a taste like any other fried red meat.

Berliners, seeing campfires in their streets, shaggy Cossack ponies, and drunken filthy soldiers, tended now to believe Goebbels's propaganda. They didn't need to convince themselves anymore; reality showed them that their city was mostly occupied by raping and marauding Mongols. This was not my world any longer; on one side of the street, I saw Soviet soldiers making fire in the entrance hall of a house, rattling their cooking pans, and opening tins of meat or condensed milk with their bayonets. On the other side of the street, a whole block of houses was destroyed and used as a dumping place for cadavers nobody cared to bury.

My First Encounter with the Opposite Sex

Undoubtedly, what I saw today was Germany's collapse in the smoke, among the blazing ruins, and among hundreds of corpses littering the streets of Berlin. Street after street I passed was the same picture of destruction. I had now reached the corner of Hildebrand Strasse and Tirpitz Ufer. Some woman looking for firewood was telling me how to get to Lützow Platz, and not far from it was the Nettleback Strasse, which was the street I was looking for to deliver the letter from Egon's mother. Getting tired of walking, I was happy to find the right house number on a building still standing. As luck had it, I found Egon's aunt at home. She opened the letter, and she was so pleased to know that her sister was alive. She was so happy that she put her arms around me, giving me a friendly kiss. I answered all her questions and told her how nice it was that her sister gave me shelter. "That was nice of her," she said. "And since you are a friend of my sister and nephew and I could use some company living alone, I offer you my house to stay and hide for a while. My name is Gerda, and I am the younger sister of Egon's mother. I used to babysit Egon years ago. Tell me more about the years you and Egon spent together."

I was beginning to tell her that I was only three years old when my parents moved to Kieler Strasse right next to the bakery around 1932. Egon must have been three years older than I, and he introduced me to the gang of kids on the waterfront. Egon and I became real close friends as neither of us had any brothers or sisters. "It would take me the rest of the month to tell you all the crazy things we did together."

"That is all right," Gerda said. "I am a good listener."

"Egon and I had many things in common; traditionally, we would sit every morning on the sidewalk of the bakery and start the day by eating cake crumbs. We went to the same public school in the district of Wedding.

I joined the Jungvolk when I was nine years old, but Egon only signed up for the Hitler Youth much later when membership became compulsory. When we were kids, I was not aware of it, but it makes sense to me now when a few days ago, his mother told me that the whole family were members of the Communist Party till Hitler came to power in 1933."

"That's right," Gerda said. "And we still are, except that for twelve years we had to keep our party membership book hidden. Now we can operate in the open again and have a voice in the new government that will soon bring law and order back. Marshal Zhukov is trying to restore all utilities and food supplies for Berlin as soon as possible. Walter Ulbricht, a German communist leader, has lived many years in Russia and was trained to form a new government in Berlin after the fall of the Third Reich. My family's acquaintance with Walter Ulbricht reaches back to the years before he went into exile. I contacted Walter Ulbricht through the Russian military government twice, and we had long conversations; and at the end, he asked me if I would like to work with him as one of his secretaries. I accepted his offer, and I will go to work for him as soon as he is installed. I will tell you more about my job offer later," Gerda said. "But now let me offer you a bite to eat, you must be hungry after all that walking."

"I am always hungry, but today I had a superbreakfast." And I told her how I literally ate almost half a horse this morning. "Please, don't go out of your way to feed me." Gerda took me over to the dining room corner next to the kitchen. She was preparing for us hot tea, rye bread, braunschweiger, and some cheese.

"It is nice that you are here," Gerda said. "I alway have to eat alone. I hope you are not in a hurry to go someplace else and accept my offer to stay some time with me."

"My destination is Wilmersdorf to see the mother of my tragically killed girlfriend. Thereafter, I have to go to Tegel to see how my mother and grandmother are doing. Under different circumstances, if Berlin was not in such a state of destruction and ruins, I could have made all the visits by now."

"Be patient, it will not be long and you will see all the difference in Berlin. As early as tomorrow, Marshal Zhukov will have soup kitchens all over Berlin to stop the starvation of the people in the city. All utilities will be restored as soon as possible, and by the end of the month, the most important U-Bahn and S-Bahn lines will be reopened. The children will be back in school, and with the new ration cards, the stores will be able to sell you some food."

I responded, "For what we went through and what Berlin looks like today, that sounds like mission impossible."

"Believe me, I know Walter Ulbricht. He is a great organizer, and he has the full support of the Russian government."

"There is only one question, with hardly any men left in Berlin, how do you remove all the rubble?"

"One stone at a time, and they will be cleaned and reused by all the able-bodied women in the city. I am very optimist, and I can hardly wait to start working for the new government." I could detect that she was trying to sell me on the communist government idea.

"If you are really convinced that this new government will be able to achieve all of it, I would even kiss you right now."

"Why don't you?" Gerda, to my surprise, challenged me and came really close to my face. I kissed her lips, a little clumsily, not knowing if I did the right thing. I was not sure how to act; never had I encountered this situation, a mature woman (she must be thirty years old or so) insinuating herself in more than a simple friendship or need for my help like I had done for a lot of those women living without a man in Berlin, since our men were sent to the Russian front. Gerda told me about herself. "I hate to live alone, and it's not by choice. I am not a hermit. Three years ago, I was engaged to be married to a man I loved very much. Like so many other men, he was killed in Russia. Now if you don't mind me asking you, I would like to know how your girlfriend, being so young, lost her life." I told Gerda the whole story, and she was very sympathetic, trying to hold back her tears as she saw me fighting with the resurfacing pain.

"I know how you feel," Gerda said, "better than anybody else, but trust me, time will heal your wounds." She took out two glasses and filled them up with brandy. "Let's drink to better times. As long as there is life, there is hope. Forget the pain and behold the sweet memories when you were making love to her."

"That is exactly where we got cheated. She was saving her virginity for our wedding night. I keep thinking if those bastards have not taken her by force and raped her, she would have not committed suicide when she could not see another way out."

Gerda said, "I don't think she would want you to continue being bitter. I think she would like to see you being happy again."

"You may be right, but when it comes for me to make love for the first time with any woman, I may feel wrong as long as I am still in love with Gisela."

"Again," Gerda said, "time will help you. You cannot be in love with a dead person in a physical sense forever. Whenever you'll have the desire to have sex with a certain person, you will mentally and physically know so, then you either give yourself completely or walk away from it. Don't put any restrictions on your sexual feelings."

"Gerda, please give me another drink. I am amazed at how openly we are talking about sex. We know each other less than twenty-four hours, and here we are, discussing sex like we would talk about the weather."

"What is wrong with that?" Gerda wanted to know. "They are both a natural and marvelous phenomena. The only thing wrong that I see here," she kept on saying, "is our Judeo-Christian upbringing that has turned sex into a taboo."

I was very confused; what was Gerda leading up to? All this talk about sex, and she knew by now that I had never been with a woman before in that sense. We had one more drink, and then she showed me to the room where I would sleep. Sleeping in a clean bed was a luxury I had missed lately.

When I got up next morning, Gerda was already busy typing in her office. She did all her secretary work at home, and as she explained to me, it would be picked up by messengers for the time being till the new provisional German government had its own building. Gerda stopped her typing when I showed up and wanted to know how I slept. "Very well and comfortable too," I replied.

"You have to excuse me for the next thirty minutes. I have to finish my report for today, but if you hurry up, there maybe enough hot water left for one shower. When I am done with my work, we will sit down and have breakfast together." The breakfast Gerda was putting together reminded me very much of a perfect Sunday brunch with all the family in Kremmen, and I shared this comparison with her. "Tell me more about your past. I'd like to know how you grew up."

"That is one of the fondest memory I have being with my grandparents from both sides of the family. I don't have too many good memories to remember, just one or two. My childhood was kind of short-lived, but to be honest, the years at the academy at Neisse were the best times of my life. The boarding school became my second home. I received the best education, one that my parents could have never paid for, but of course, the political indoctrination was part of it. I tremendously enjoyed all the sports activities, knowing that we were groomed to be soldiers. In the end, I volunteered as a Luftwaffenhelfer, trying to do my best to protect Berlin. The last days I spent at the Flak bunker in Humboldthain shooting at Russian tanks when Hitler was already dead and the red flag of the Soviet army was flying over the Reichstag. Getting out of the bunker alive and escaping the day-by-day possibility of joining the long line of POWs marching to Russia is a small miracle. We have lost the war. I want to pick up the pieces and go on with my life."

Gerda understood that I would like to end the conversation, but she wanted to know how I felt about Hitler's regime now. "First of all, I feel like all of the surviving Hitler Youth, that we are *Hitler's last victims*. He betrayed our trust, and we will never forget what he has done to us, to Germany, and the rest of the civilized world. Now a new regime is on the horizon, the Communist Party is taking over. At this time, history is repeating itself. They are liberating us from the Nazis, proclaiming freedom for everybody, and at the same time, they are filling up the same old concentration camps with people that are against them. Like I said, history is repeating itself, and I will never in my life join another political party. I simply refuse to be fooled again. I do feel sincerely sorry for all the people who honestly and idealistically are working for the new cause and then be utterly disappointed. By no means am I attacking your noble work and effort to revive Berlin and to renovate the broken systems to make the city function again."

"Then what is your point to compare the Communist Party with the war criminals of the Third Reich?" Gerda said.

"I see the same pattern and method of operation all over again. When Germany was suffering after World War I, the early members of the Nazi Party were just as dedicated as you are today to help the poor people. Little did they know what Hitler's dictatorship had in store."

"That is a poor analogy," Gerda said. "I still don't see what makes you predict that communism will be doomed and suffer the same fate."

"Very simple, communism has been already a failure in Russia under Stalin, and that is the truth."

"I cannot believe what you said. Who put all those stupid ideas in your head?"

"We had the best history teachers at the academy, and not all of them were Nazis."

At this point, neither of us said anything. I understood, she was trying to convince me to her way of thinking, but this fifteen-year-old boy had gone and seen enough to finally make his own mind. I broke the silence by saying, "I am a guest in your house. I am sorry, and I apologize if I should have offended you. You have to understand that this is the first time in my life that I speak my own mind. Please don't hate me but forgive me, and I will go."

Gerda had tears in her eyes; she came closer to me, saying, "I have nothing to forgive, nor do I hate you. The truth is I rather love you. Please don't go away."

Before I could say anything, she embraced me, pressing my face to her bosom with affection and kissing me wildly. I was overwhelmed and shocked at the same time by her passion but found it in a way pleasant and began to have feelings of my own toward her, perhaps due to my hormonal activity. I was sure I would have surrendered for whatever Gerda had in mind if at that time the doorbell did not ring. I could see the disappointment on her face; she went to open the door. Two middle-aged men in a street suit, with a bright red badge on the sleeve of their left arm, were entering the apartment. One man carried a big cardboard box with groceries, and the other man came with a briefcase. Gerda introduced me to the men, then asked them to take a chair, explaining to me that she had only contact to the outside world and office by messenger service. Every other day she received new material to work on, and what was completed they would take back to the office. This arrangement was only for the time being and very temporary for Gerda's safety.

In the near future, Mr. Ulbricht, Gerda, and the rest of the staff would occupy the new government building with all the comforts and security. Till then, Berlin would be ruled, together with East Germany, by the Soviet army under Marshal Zhukow, with his military headquarter in Karlshorst. The first German administration in Berlin would be appointed from members of the Communist Party mostly; at a later date, members of the Social Democrats and other parties would be participating in the first free election. Today was the first official day; the men were happily announcing that all of Germany was at peace again, that finally the dreadful war was over. This morning, May 9, 1945, the German military delegation under Field Marshal Keifel, General Stumpf, and Admiral von Friedeburg arrived at Karlshorst to sign the final surrender. The fighting was over, but for rebuilding of our city, the work just started. The soup kitchens were open, but thousands of corpses still needed to be buried. Streets had to be cleaned; utilities must be provided. Factories and repair shops were out of order, and most important, our transportation system had to be restored. To put it all in one sentence, everything must be overhauled, repaired, or completely replaced.

"I noticed that you are wearing red arm badges, am I correct in assuming that you belong to a para police force?"

"That is true, but we carry no weapon. Consider us a liaison between the military police and the public."

"How much longer do you think will the terror in the streets with the Russian soldiers go on?"

"Not much longer," the men said. "Marshal Zhukov told Mr. Ulbricht that all Russian soldiers will be housed in barracks, and any crime committed by them will be severely punished. In conclusion all I can say, in comparison to what we went through, it can only get better." The men ended the conversation and were ready to get up.

"Please wait a few minutes," Gerda said. "We have to celebrate the end of the war and drink for a better future."

"Well," the men said, "why not? We all suffered and waited for this day to come for five miserable years." Gerda took out the bottle of brandy, and we all toasted the new peace.

"Shalom," one of the men said, and I looked at him, not knowing what he was talking about. "That is a Jewish word, it means peace."

"Herbert," Gerda asked me, "is there anything in particular you want to drink to?"

"Yes, may all the people that died in this terrible war rest in peace and never be forgotten. And for all the people on earth, I wish them pax, caritas, et veritas—that is Latin and means peace, love, and truth."

Everybody agreed, and with the last drink, we sealed everybody's testimony before the men parted to go back to work.

After the comrades left, Gerda opened the box to check what kind of groceries she received today as compensation for her secretarial work. The usual things like bread, flour, sugar, rice, tea, milk powder, and canned goods of meat, vegetables, and sunflower oil.

"I am hungry," Gerda said, "for fresh fruits, vegetables, and a glass of real milk. But I should not complain. At least I am not going to bed hungry like many people do these days. What I receive, money could not buy right now. From what I heard, there is already a black market at the Potzdamer Platz, and if you have cigarettes, you can buy anything you want. Look what else I found here in the box, a bottle of genuine Russian vodka. Now let's find out what is in the briefcase today, If I don't work, I don't eat. It is that simple. Here it is, Karlshorst is now trying to get on the good side of the German people. Russian propaganda wants the Berliners to look at Stalin as the liberator and friend of the German people. This will be fun."

Gerda was trying to get my attention. As Marshal Zhukov had given the KPD the authority to thank and praise Generalisimo Stalin for his help, he also was informing the Communist Party to give orders to control the public. The Russians were trying to stop the existing chaos they created in the first place by reversing the attitude that was existing in a form of obstinate opposition toward Soviet authority and occupation. Ulbricht was instructing his staff to accomplish this in a *Zuckerbrot* and *Peitsche* (walk slowly and carry a stick) approach. He received his instruction from the interpreter, passed it on to his writers, and Gerda the editor revised all the material before printing. No newspaper had yet been established, so all information and instruction would be posted in the form of posters on all public buildings for the people to read.

"Here," Gerda said, "if you want to help me, take some of these papers with loose orders and let's put them together in a friendly schematic and organized pattern according to rule without discrimination."

"Maybe we start with the good news first," I said, "by telling them the exact location of all soup kitchens in their city district and how soon the stores will be open again. Now if this is catching their attention, they may go on reading about other orders and regulations given by the Soviet army. For example, to observe the strict order to deliver all arms and any kind of weapons and to observe the exact hours of curfew. All cameras must be given up, bicycles, typewriters, etc. All members of the former Nazi Party must register at the police station, and it goes on and on." Several hours went by before we had composed the different poster designs ready to be picked up by the civil police messengers in two days. While Gerda was preparing some supper for us, she said, "To be honest with you, I don't feel good about the whole thing. I am a tool of the Russians to steal from my own people."

"Don't feel guilty about it," I explained to her. "If you refused to do the dirty work, somebody else would have been forced to do it. This is nothing new. Throughout history, the spoils always go to the victor. We lost the war, remember, and this is 1918 all over again. The Russians and French are eager to steal us blind, they call it reparation. The Russians came here first, and they will take everything to Russia, from a wristwatch to a bread factory. I am afraid they have not learned their lesson yet, and they will squeeze us till they can no longer get blood out of a stone. In the end, they are shocked when the German people, out of deadly desperation, regardless of danger or consequences, follow another crackpot like Hitler all over again."

"You are right," Gerda agreed. "It is obvious that we will see hard times again, but no matter what, we will not survive another war."

"You got that right. Should there ever be another major war, nobody will win or lose, we are all going to be dead. Let us celebrate the peace we just gained, knowing that the fighting, the killing, and the death from the sky is over. For us that is victory, so let them take whatever they want. Our new motto must be 'Let's make love, not war.'"

"I am all for it," Gerda said, and she had already two drinks for us. This time she was serving vodka. "I hope you like my food tonight. It is goulash, gravy and mashed potatoes, bread and butter."

"That is a meal fit for a king, just right for a growing boy." An old candle, left over from the long lonely nights in the air-raid shelter, and some gramophone music made this a lovely evening.

"I would like some hot tea, how about you?"

"Yes, please, I would like it too."

"Make yourself comfortable and give me ten minutes," Gerda said. I was really relaxed as she came in with the tea. "I am so sorry," she said. "I don't have any biscuits in the house."

"I can do without cookies, just let me have some vodka to spike my tea." That was also the way I liked to drink my tea in the evening before I go to bed. The music playing was some vintage recordings, ideal for an evening of relaxation.

"You will be great company tonight, and nobody is going to stop us this time," Gerda said. Catching me by surprise, she threw her arms around me and kissed me. Gerda could now see that it was incredibly exciting for someone like me that had never had sex before, and I succumbed to her desires. She had the experience and led me through a marvelous new world unknown to me until then. This was the night I lost my sexual innocence at the age of fifteen to a woman twice my age. Even later in my life, it never occurred to me until I started writing my memoirs that my introduction to sex in normal times would have been considered outside the law as she was responsible for inducing a minor to drink and having sex with him.

The following day after breakfast, Gerda and I were having a sober conversation about our relationship. There was no need to bring up the question of how we felt for each other. At that particular time, I thought that the passion we demonstrated for each other could be considered as feelings of real love; in any case, time would be the real test. More realistic questions to consider were age, compatibility, education, religion, and profession, just to name a few. Gerda was now giving me her point of view. "We know very little about each other, and we don't have to know everything at once since we are not signing a commitment today or tomorrow. If our mutual attraction will stand the test of time, then we will be closer to making a decision. You are young, and I don't know what your ambition in life will be. Talking about the difference about our age, I can only tell you how I feel about it. If you are comfortable with your partner, I believe age shouldn't be a barrier. This is more than ever true in our times. Because of the war, our society has a severe shortage of men, and a lot of women will end up lonely in their old age. The longer we are single, the harder it is for us women to find a man. As for me, I feel I am still too young to be alone. I want love in my life. Look around the country, all you find are a few old men, a handful of survivors from the Volkssturm. I need someone younger and more exciting. I need a break since I was alone all those years. It is more than obvious that the chances of selection between the two sexes are everything but balanced. That gives you the upper hand in your future, as you are blessed with a wider spectrum of possibilities to choose from. Maybe that is the reason why my view of a relationship as a woman is and has to be more liberal. In my position, to find a man tailor-made is not very realistic, and to wait till the man of my dreams shows up could be a waste of a lifetime. I live in the here and now, and I'd rather take a brief romance than no love at all. If you would decide to go tomorrow with another woman, I would not be less happier over the wonderful time we'll spend together. I am only flexible out of necessity. It goes without saying that I would consider myself the luckiest woman in the world if I could have a man of my own. I am open and honest with my feelings, and you know by now that I want you, and perhaps I love you, but I would never dominate you. I can see it already, if we would stay together, that an early marriage would not be in your best interest. I can give you all the love you want outside of marriage, but you must first study at the university or learn a profession before you consider settling down and have a formal family obligation."

With those words, she really made me feel like I had the freedom of having her or leaving her or having her with no strings attached; I might know a lot about history and war, but I guess she outsmarted me when it came to love and sex. I could only say, "The fact that you put my own development above the advancement of our relationship shows me a great deal about your character. It is indeed a true act of unselfishness regarding my interests as a priority. I can only tell you that I very much appreciate your strong affection and ardent love for me."

As scheduled, the two messengers showed up again, but today for the last time. The good news was that all members of the interim city government would start, day after tomorrow, working in the renovated building next to Haus Vaterland at the Potsdamer Platz. After the two fellows left, Gerda and I saw what was in the box for us to enjoy and check on her last homework. This time they wanted her to prepare a police registration form and a design of an application for employment. Both documents were to contain questions about previous places of employment, residence, and party and military membership. Both of us were sitting down, and each of us prepared a form of our own, lining up questions to put an inquiry together that would make sense, reveal important information, and not give the impression of an interrogation. At the end of the day, we compared our papers and decided what should be added or eliminated for a final draft, which Gerda would type tomorrow in an easy-to-read-and-understand questionnaire. After work, we sat down again for supper without much of a conversation. It seemed like we were both thinking about the same subject. In two days, Gerda would start her full-time employment, and I would continue my journey home. My departure was long overdue; by now everybody was wondering if I was still alive. Over a drink, Gerda and I were beginning to talk about the situation on the outside and how it was beginning to make progress even though we were still far away from a normal proficiency. "When will you be back?" Gerda asked me. "I am already missing you."

"What can I tell you? The only thing I know for sure at this time, as soon as possible."

"That's all I want to know," she said. "That you are coming back to me, period."

"Of course I will. I consider myself very lucky you came my way," I said. It was not easy for me to find the words to explain to her how happy she made me. The same feelings I experienced with Gisela when we expressed our love for each other. But was it really all the same, love and passion? Where was the difference? I guess it was not a true comparison; with my lovely Gisela, it was an innocent first love, but this mature woman had the worldly experience and the mastery of seduction. Gerda knew that she had introduced me into a wonderful new world, that she had made me a real man. Even though in those days I didn't see myself as the fifteen-year-old teen I was, I thought of myself for quite some time as a man.

On the morning of May 15, we both left the house happy at having been able to share a most memorable week. I helped her to put her papers and files together in a large box. Right on time, at 7:00 AM, a car and driver from her office arrived to pick her up. As they were going east, I could catch a ride with them down Hohenzollern Damm to Wilmersdorf first, and they would let me off at Fehrbelliner Platz. Since the end of the war, I could see that in two weeks, the main streets were already free of rubble; and the driver was telling us that in certain places, the U-Bahn was already back in operation. From Gerda's house, I had reached my destination in ten minutes. While the car stopped, Gerda and I had a few minutes left to say good-bye. I was trying to make it short, but Gerda hung on to me, kissing me insistently and asking me again if I would come back soon. I promised her I would, and her last words were "I love you very much."

CHAPTER X

LIFE AFTER THE WAR

Drifting With the Wind

Walking the last two streets toward Inge's house, I was undecided if I should tell her about my encounter with Gerda or better tell her the truth at another more convenient occasion. It might not be appropriate to spoil our meeting with something that may hurt her feelings, and that was the last thing I wanted to do. Inge had suffered enough—first her husband missing in Russia, presumed to be killed in action, and then the tragic death of her only child, Gisela. I would play it by ear and put it for now on the back burner. I rang the doorbell, and Inge opened the door and hugged me. "My prayers are answered," she said. "You are alive, I knew you would survive. Let me look at you." She kissed me with tears in her eyes. This was not an ordinary reunion; this was a celebration of two people who each in their own way escaped alive from the ravages of a bloody war. Over a cup of tea, we were exchanging the experience of adventures, surviving death and adversities. "It is a miracle how you got out of the Flak bunker and how you escaped the Russians at the military medical unit," Inge said. "That is incredible." When I asked Inge how she got through the end of the war, she was rather short on words just telling me, "Nothing spectacular, only happy to be alive."

"Everything happened so fast," Inge said. "I cannot comprehend it yet that there are no more bombs coming down at night or artillery shells busting your eardrums. The damage the Russians have done when they conquered Berlin has not been assessed yet, or at least they don't want to publish it. The radio this morning gave a summary of damages the air raids over Berlin have caused. A total of 310 air raids, 45,517 tons of bombs were dropped over Berlin, more than 150,000 people have been killed, and 30,000 apartments and houses are destroyed."

"Where were you when the Russians came in, at work or at home?" I asked Inge.

"I think two or three days before the end of the war, the SS came and closed our office. They rounded up all of us women, most of us are nurses, and drove us in open trucks to a field hospital in an underground S-Bahn tunnel. One woman doctor and two other surgeons were day and night up to their elbows in blood and broken bones. They were so busy that they had no time to finish a case. Three nurses including myself had to close the skin and stitch them up. One of the trains served as an operating room. We did nothing but emergency open-wound surgery to be treated in a normal hospital at a later date. It was an in-and-out situation. The platform of the train station was full of stretchers, and in one corner of the tunnel, we piled up all the dead soldiers. This went on till the SS stopped fighting in the tunnels and the Russians captured us on May 2. All the men were taken prisoners, and any member of the SS was shot on the spot. Most of the nurses were gang-raped and then dismissed."

After a brief pause, I asked Inge, "Were you among them?"

"No. Like I said, I am only happy to be alive." Inge did not sound too convincing, or it might be that she was still in a state of denial. In either case, I did not want to press the issue, and I changed the conversation.

"Have you heard anything about food distribution for the people left in Berlin?" I asked Inge.

"Yes," she said, "the police district you are registered in as a resident will hand out ration cards on a monthly basis." Inge showed me the food stamps she already picked up. "Take a good look, they are left over from the wartime. The eagle with the swastika are blocked out by hand, and some good news, the stores are already selling potatoes, black bread, and sunflower oil in small quantities. That is what you will eat tonight, courtesy of the Russian military government. Make sure you are also registered with your local employment office, or you will not receive any food ration cards. I already have a new job starting at the Red Cross clinic in Wilmersdorf next Monday as an afternoon supervisor at the outpatient department."

"That is great," I said. "I am happy for you, but you don't have a car anymore."

"I don't need a car for transportation. The hospital is so close I can walk from my house. What are you doing the next few days?" Inge wanted to know.

"Without any further delay, I have to go to Tegel and look for my mother and grandmother. We have not seen or heard from each other since the war was over. My next step will be, if I want to get something to eat, to report at the unemployment office and the local police station in Tegel. When they see my background, without any work experience, they will probably give me the dirtiest job in town that nobody wants to do. But it is all right, it is only temporary anyway. The only thing I am good for is to go back to school. If I could financially afford it, I would like to study medicine. Maybe I'll find a part-time job or get a scholarship. I have never earned a penny in my life, that is why I am eager to get some cash under my belt."

"You are not that poor," Inge said. "The education you have even up to now is like money in the bank. Even if you don't go to college, with an abitur [college entry certificate] in your pocket, you can always get a better—and higher-paying job." The first visit with Inge was short; the following morning I was on my way to Tegel.

It was impossible to travel from point A to point B without interruption. Short and long walks were between the next stations. The time it took me to arrive in Tegel I could have taken a train to Paris. The picture of the city was that of a ghost town; it was hard to believe that Berlin would ever be a clean place to live in again. To see all the rubble around me was heartbreaking, but great happiness came over me when I saw my mother and grandmother being around and unharmed. The feelings were mutual, and all of us were crying for joy. Every day more and more ex-soldiers were coming home, but very few out of Russia, only those that had lost a limb and were useless for keeping over there in labor camps. My mother and grandmother were sharing their meager food from their ration cards with me. I was making it my priority to get a job and some food ration cards, which I would receive after I registered with the local employment office. I did go and register with the necessary public offices, and I noticed that wherever you went these days—train station, post office, police, or any other public office—you would see nothing but huge pictures of Joseph Stalin next to a red flag. I was immediately temporarily assigned to a cleanup crew, and because that was a hard job, I was getting a higher ration card for food. I had to be every day in front of the employment office; a truck would come, pick us up, and take us to work at different locations. I belonged to the Column Friedrich, also known as the gravedigger gang.

Some agency had prepared a map of all the spots in Tegel where Soviet soldiers were temporarily buried till we came and dug them up to be transported to the Soviet Memorial Cemetery in Treptow. These corpses were dirty, half rotten, and stank when exposed to the air. What made it easier for us to carry them was their rigidity; they were as stiff as a board. When you do this for about two weeks and started having nightmares about corpses at night, then they would rotate you for another job. I took a sick leave and went to see Inge for a few days. Together one morning, we visited the black market at Bahnhof Zoo, and I spent the first money I made for some food. The next day I visited the Humboldt University, or what was left of it, to find out how soon they would open again. The only thing I could find was an information office. The university needed a lot of repairs. Prospective students who were willing to participate in the reconstruction would get credit for their work applied as semester fees. I left my name and address to be notified. With 95 percent of the tram system destroyed and a large part of the U-Bahn and S-Bahn system still underwater from the explosions, to visit friends in other parts of the city required time and strength. Just to go to work could be a problem. Practically everybody felt weak from being hungry and had very little ambition to move or go anyplace. Going back to work, I was lucky as they were sending me to work at the *Humboldtmühle*, the grain mill at the lake in Tegel. The place was guarded by Russian soldiers to protect the mill from looters. However, if you worked there, you could chew and swallow all the grain you wanted. If the guards caught you taking the grain or the flour out, that was a different story. It meant the end of your job, and they would put you in the brick, but I had not seen anyone going home with empty pockets at the end of the shift. To hide a pound of grain in the clothes on your body took a lot of ingenuity. But working at the *Humboldmühle* (grain mill) had more than one advantage, besides being able to fill your socks with grain without being detected, at the end of your shift leaving the premises, by the guards.

Needless to say that the Russians needed plenty of soldiers to protect a major food facility like the Humboldmuhle day and night from hungry looters trying to pilfer some food. Those soldiers occupied a packing house and some office buildings behind the mill. A nearby private home was confiscated and served as kitchen and mess hall. Some German women were hired to clean, do the laundry, and prepare their meals. Frequently some of us mill workers were called to work over at the compound to unload heavy supplies or work in the kitchen. When quite often some women didn't show up for work, it was our job to peel potatoes. In no time at all, I learned that the Russian diet called for potatoes in every meal. Kartoschky, kartoschky, and kartoschky—potatoes, potatoes, and potatoes—were prepared in every form three times a day in large quantities. Peeling potatoes was a dumb-but-easy job. Best of all, you were working in the kitchen, and even though your access to the food was restricted, we had access to all the trash cans full of scraps. I was always eagerly volunteering to take the full trash cans out to the backyard. I went through those cans, and I was not ashamed to say that I fought with the vicious watchdogs over the leftovers; but I discovered soon that the dogs would leave me alone as long as I gave them the biggest bone I found. I felt like a caveman scavenging for food to keep me from being hungry.

As the potato peels went, we were making sure to cut the peels extra thick with lots of potato on it; in those days we didn't know the potato peeler, so the potatoes were peeled with a paring knife, and we kept the peels in a separate trash can. At the end of the day, when we were taking all the trash cans to the backyard, the ordinary trash went in the dumpster, and the potato peels can were dumped over the fence. At the end of the workday, we went behind the fence to pick up the potato peels from the ground and share them equally among us to take home. My mother and grandmother were delighted to see me bringing the peels home and whatever grain I could sneak out. We really needed the extra carbohydrates, and I had to admit that it helped very much to enrich our daily menu. My mother and grandmother, among other ways to fix those peels, made the very best potato soup. However, over time I developed a certain aversion to potatoes with peels on them, an aversion that had stayed with me for the rest of my life. This time of the year, the springtime and early summer of 1945, my grandmother's small vegetable garden was producing a good amount of vegetables and tomatoes. The only thing we did not get enough of was protein.

To balance our nutritional needs, I had a remedy of my own for that. Sunday mornings when everybody was still asleep, I would go dynamite fishing at the lake. I knew a spot at the lake far away from civilization behind the bamboo bay where the fishing was good. At the old army rifle range, there was still plenty of ammunition lying around; all I needed was one pineapple (hand grenade) to do the job. When it exploded underwater, most of the noise was muffled, but a few seconds later, all the dead fish came to the surface. No fisherman would ever approve of this method, but I was not doing it as a sport. In one shot, I harvested several kilos of fish. When I returned home we had an all-you-can-eat fish fry. The rest of the fish my grandmother preserved in a big glass jar full of saturated salt solution. We had no refrigerator or freezer in those miserable days.

As soon as trains began to run, thousands of starving Berliners clung on to the roof or the outside of the trains to reach the countryside to find food. Sometimes the rooftops of the trains were overloaded, and people got scraped off and killed at the next low bridge. At the end of June, more S-Bahn and U-Bahn lines were restored. The following weekend, I was living up to my promise and took the S-Bahn to visit Gerda; I only had to switch trains once to go from Tegel to Bahnhof Zoo. Walking over to Gerda's apartment house, I was not sure if she would be home. It was Friday early in the afternoon, and many people were still working. For the weekend, I decided to wear one of my father's suits. When I arrived at her place and Gerda opened the door, she did not recognize me for a split second. My appearance today did not match the image of the dirty escapee that knocked on her door the first time a few weeks ago. A moment later, Gerda was showing me how happy she was to see me. She embraced me and kissed my face as she invited me to come in.

"I have been thinking about you every day, hoping that you come back soon, and here you are. Tell me how things went with you when you did get home." I told Gerda everything, and she felt sorry for me, the way I had to work to make a living.

"Don't worry," I said, "I don't mind. I am a survivor, and things are getting better. I already made up my mind to go back to school. I left my application at the Humboldt University and hope to hear from them soon."

"That is great," Gerda said. "I am all for it, and don't "worry about the money, I will find you a part-time job working for the city, and I hope one of these days you will come and live with me."

"Well," I said, "that may be sooner than you think."

"Right now we have to celebrate your comeback," Gerda said. "Let's have a candlelight dinner." Gerda was a marvelous cook, and like they say in German, "Liebe geht durch den Magen" (love goes through the stomach). Not only did she know how to please me, but for sure, she also knew how to get what she wanted. Then she produced a bottle of genuine Hungarian Slivovitz (plum liquor). Our conversation was now focused on Gerda's new job. She was the number one secretary to Walter Ulbricht; she was sitting in on all the meetings and had her own office. Gerda was taking all the appointments and had two secretaries just to do all the typing.

"Believe me," Gerda said, "our party is working day and night together with the Socialist Party to rebuild and improve conditions in Berlin. Unfortunately, we don't always have the cooperation of the Soviets. What makes it even more complicated is the division of Berlin into four sectors. I have to admit that the Americans are bringing more into West Berlin, while the Russians are still taking things out of East Berlin and East Germany."

"Let's talk about the health condition in Berlin, are the Russians still going around raping and infecting German women?" I asked Gerda.

"Yes! On and off they do, but now they will be severely punished if they catch them."

I said, "According to the Yalta Conference, I am living in a French-occupied sector, but I have not seen any French soldier yet."

"Since the Russians are the only army that captured Berlin, the West is kind of slow at claiming their territory," Gerda explained to me. "Right now Berlin is still under one joint administration, but that will all change in the future, the way the victors have cut up Germany like a pie."

"I doubt it very much that in our lifetime we will ever see Germany reunited, this is my fear and disbelief," I told Gerda.

"Why should we waste our time over things we cannot change? We must live one day at a time and for the moment." And without any more delay, her attention switched to me and she started making love to me. I was still kind of nervous and a little shy but only too eager to learn and experience anything she would teach me. In the ecstasy of the pleasures of the flesh, the time went by at a rapid pace; and before I knew it, it was Sunday morning, and after a hearty breakfast, I was ready to go back to Tegel. This time Gerda had no problem saying good-bye to me; she knew that I was hooked and would come back to her. She really had me under her control, and at that time, I even thought from the two of us I was the fortunate one.

Somehow, instead of changing trains at S-Bahnhof Gesundbrunnen, I found myself at Schonhauser Alle in the middle of the Russian-occupied sector. A major portion of my trip to Tegel was already completed. Since Gerda had fed me well with all the food she was getting from Walter Ulbricht, I hated to go home empty-handed and face my mother and grandmother who were surviving on a meager ration. I still had a few food stamps in my pocket that I was trying to turn in for whatever. My mother gave them to me some days ago, and I had not been able to use them yet. It was difficult to find a store open on a Sunday. On the corner of Schonhauser Alle and Kopenhagener Strasse, I saw a grocery store open. A long line of mostly women waited their turn to get into the store. I hesitated for a moment, but then I decided to get in and place myself at the end of the line.

The line was moving slowly, and I was already waiting for about twenty-five minutes when somebody from behind was pulling me out by my left arm. I was the only male as far as I could see; and when I turned around, I was facing a Russian soldier with an automatic gun hanging loosely over his shoulder. His grip on my arm was firm, and with his head, he motioned me to go with him. I had no idea if he was arresting me or what. A quick look around told me that to run away would be foolish as he might use his weapon on me. In my imagination, I saw myself already as a guest worker, a polite way to call a slave worker, in a Russian gulag. Not understanding most of what he was saying, for the little Russian I knew, this sounded like cussing to me, he was taking me to the curbside, showing me his motorcycle that needed to be repaired. At the same time, he removed a small tool kit from underneath the seat and handed it to me. His gestures toward me were now clear enough in any language; he wanted me to fix his bike, or else. I was looking at the extent of the damage, which apparently was only around the front wheel. He must have driven the bike against something. First I took off the front wheel and patched up the inner rubber tube. To make sure the air was holding, I checked it for leaks in a nearby water hole in the road. More difficult to repair was the two-pronged fork bended apart, unable to hold the axle of the front wheel.

Searching around in the rubble, I found a short piece of iron water pipe to straighten the two ends of the fork. The Russian soldier was apparently very pleased with me and eagerly held the bike for me while I bent the fork till it was aligned. The front wheel was working, and in a few minutes,

I had everything put together again. The bike was in running condition, and it was as good as it could possibly be. I was relieved to get the job done and nervously wiped the sweat off my forehead. To my amazement, the soldier started to jump for joy just like a little boy on Christmas Day. Patting me on the shoulder, he kept saying what sounded like "Karachow, tawarich, karachow tawarich." Very good, my friend, very good, my friend. By now it was about two hours since he'd pulled me out of the line at the grocery store.

He took me again by the arm, and we were walking again back to the store; there was still a long line of people in front of it. Now the Russian soldier pushed me right to the front of the line just to the door of the store, almost one step behind me. Some voices in the background and in the store from people starting to get annoyed, unknown to them that I had been pulled out of the line earlier. The Russian soldier paid no attention to the screams of the angry crowd, and now hanging his semiautomatic weapon in front of him, he took me behind the counter. With his knife, he opened a big bag of potatoes and dumped them on the floor. Holding the empty sack under the store shelves on the wall, he swept with one hand all the various cans of food he could into the empty sack. He threw into the sack any other food items he could grab. Then he made me carry the heavy sack of groceries out of the store while he walked behind me, pointing his gun at the still-angry mob to keep them from attacking me.

Once we were away from the store, he made me sit on the bike behind him and drove me to the S-Bahnhof's station to take my train to Tegel. A quick handshake and he disappeared back into East Berlin.

On my way home, I was truly astonished at how I came across a soldier in a Russian uniform who had a certain sense of fairness and saw to some extent his human side. However, I did not feel too good about taking more than my share of the rationed food, but at the same time, I didn't feel secure enough to contradict my Russian benefactor; I could not tell how he would react if I would turn him down. In these days, I had heard the saying, "He who eats first lives longer"; that was also in the back of my mind.

Sunday evening, I arrived in Tegel just in time for supper. Then my mother gave me a sealed envelope with a note in it. All it said was, "Please come and talk to my father tomorrow." It was signed "Lisa," followed with an address to go. I asked my mother how she received the letter, and she told me that a young woman came to the door, whom she had never seen before, and handed her the letter. My mother did not ask me anything about Lisa, but I knew that the name Lisa was the code word for Werewolf, what my mother wanted to know was what I had in the big burlap sack.

"Probably dirty laundry for you to wash," my grandmother interjected.

"It cannot be, it looks too heavy," my mother said.

"Well, let's stop guessing and take a look in it. I really do not know myself all that it is in it. All I can tell you is that this was given to me by a surprisingly grateful and friendly soldier of the Red Army," I answered.

By now my grandmother was getting up in arms. "Stop trying to fool us, son, and tell us the truth."

As my mother was unpacking the diverse food items, mostly canned goods, I told them the details of the whole story, the way it happened to me this afternoon. "That is amazing. Up to now, I believed that hell would freeze over before a Russian would give you a bite to eat." These were the words my grandmother uttered, still in disbelief.

The Call of the Werewolf

Monday afternoon coming from work at the mill, I was going over to the address that was given to me in the note. It was the high building on the corner of Bolle Strasse and Maxim Gorky Strasse, being the apartment on the fourth floor that belonged to the former *zellen leiter* (group leader) *krüger* of the Nazi Party. I rang the doorbell, and for sure, it was Krüger himself that let me in. I had seen him only once, but I knew that he was in charge of the party business in Neu-Tegel. "I am Wilhelm Krüger," he said. "And you are Herbert Vogt, I presume."

"That is correct, and what is the pleasure I have of being invited by you after the fall of the Third Reich?" I asked him.

"Well," he said, "if you take a seat and give me ten minutes of your time, I will explain why I called on you. As you know, I no longer represent the old government, but I have not given up the idea of helping our people however I can, and I am sure you feel the same way. Right now our people are starving and need our help more than ever before. That is the only reason I am calling on all the Werewolf volunteers in Neu-Tegel. I don't endorse any sabotage against military installations or the killing of any member of the occupation forces. That is stupid and will make our lives even more miserable. The Western powers are slow in supporting us, and the Russians give us nothing; to the contrary, they are taking everything they can put their hands on out of our territory. Just take a traffic count of the daily trains from our two major railroad lines that come from the Russian zone going through the east sector and the French sector loaded with machinery and precious food to be shipped to the Soviet Union."

"According to the Yalta Conference," I objected, "the Russians have no right to do so, and it is the responsibility of the French military police to stop all those trains."

"If you were correct, then I would have no need to talk to you soliciting your help. Your statement is only half true. One clause in the

Yalta agreement states that the Soviet Union reserves the right to control the total railroad system in the east zone of Germany including all Berlin, and the three western sectors within Berlin are no exception. As it stands right now, we have to take the law in our hands. The way I look at it, we are facing an emergency, or more like a disaster. Our misfortune calls for quick action. If the people in our city cannot eat the food our farmers grow on German soil, then we have no choice but to stop those trains. It is not the other material things they are taking out that hurt us the most. No, it is the basic food that we must have to survive as a nation. At this point, I have to call on all former Werewolf volunteers to get a handful of men that are willing to participate in a partisan action."

"Mister Krüger," I said, "I am sure you have a file on my past education, and even so that I am no longer a member of the Hitler Youth, I am still a patriot at heart. Not only will I help my people, but I have plenty of my own personal reasons to fight the Bolsheviks, but I will not go on a suicide mission for a basketful of potatoes. Show me your plan, and then I will make a decision."

"So be it," Mr Krüger said, and that was the end of the conversation for that day.

The weekend that followed, I was over at Inge's house. I was not comfortable the way Inge behaved since the end of the war. She was always nice to me but not as lively as she was before. Inge did not talk very much; many times, when I was telling her something, her mind was somewhere else. I suspected there was something severely bothering her that she was not telling me. Finally I came right out, asking her, "Do you think a drink may cheer you up and make you feel better?"

"I tried it," Inge said. "It is something that does not go away." I was talking to the mother of my deceased girlfriend, who was about twenty years older than me, but we have been through so many things together that we treated each other with familiarity and as peers.

"Perhaps it will make it easy, if you get it off your chest and tell me about it," I said. "I don't recall ever having any secrets between us."

Inge took a deep breath and then started to talk. "I was among the nurses whom the Russians raped that night at the train station. Relax, I am not pregnant. I know how to handle that. It is the VD I contracted that I can't get rid off. It is gonorrhea, which normally is easy to treat, and after two weeks of treatment with the drug sulfonamide, I thought for sure that I recovered. It has been over a month since that happened, but I discovered that I suffered a relapse. I must carry a strain that is immune to sulfa drugs. A woman can easily be fooled of being healed as she always has a little discharge. With a man, that is not the case. One little yellow drop in the morning, and he knows what's going on. What I need is some penicillin, but the Red Cross clinic I am working for has not been supplied with the new antibiotics."

I listened to the whole sad story Inge was telling me, then I slowly put my arm around her and gave her a kiss.

"This is not the end of the world. You could have told me your problem earlier, and we would have taken care of that by now."

"I did not know where to get penicillin," Inge said.

"I don't know either, but let us start to find out right now. We have to make some calls, is your phone in operation again?" I asked Inge.

"I can make some calls, but not all lines are repaired yet," she replied.

"I have an idea," I said. "Please give me Gertrud Rathenow's telephone number. I want to see if I can get her on the phone." I dial her number, and what a luck she answered the phone. "Hi, Gertrud," I said and identified myself. "I see you survived the war, how are you doing? How is your family?"

"All of us are doing fine, thanks to God we have made it so far. Now tell me, how are you and Inge doing? How did you escape the Russians?"

"That is a long story. Inge and I would like to visit you. There is so much we have to tell you, but the phone is not the right place for it."

"I tell you what," Gertrud said, "it is still early, and we have the whole day left. Why don't you and Inge come over and we split a cup of coffee?"

"We would love that very much. Give us some time, and we will see you soon."

"Inge," I said, "today is my lucky day. We will get what you need. Let's go, it is going to be a long walk."

Gertrud was happy about our visit; we had not seen each other for some time, and as always, she had something for us on the table. The center of our conversation was how each of us survived in a different way. Even Gertrud noticed how Inge was suffering from some kind of depression as she was not much into the conversation. Gertrud was trying to open a dialogue with Inge by asking her how she managed to get through the last few days of Hitler's empire. With a cold smile on her face, Inge began to describe the whole brutal and inhumane cruelty of the uncivilized Russian animals. Inge was going to let it all out without holding back any of the bloody details about how the nurses were beaten into submission, screaming and biting as they were gang-raped. While Inge kept on talking, the rest of us can't imagine the infliction of pain and fear those poor and helpless women must have suffered. The more Inge talked about it, the more she felt a relief from within; and then at one point, she became silent. Also, we didn't say anything or ask any questions either. Good old Gertrud, being the mother figure in our group, was beginning to talk softly and kindly, saying that time would help her to overcome the nightmare. "That may be true," Inge said, "but right now, I have an urgent problem that won't go away unless I do something about it immediately. I have a venereal disease, and to be honest about it, this is the main reason we came to visit you."

"Well," Gertrud said, "you have come to the right place. My son is a doctor, remember?"

"Presently I work at the Red Cross clinic in Wilmersdorf, and they treated me with sulfonamide without any lasting results," Inge informed Gertrud. "What I need is some penicillin."

"I heard it is hard to come by, but I know that my son Helmut has some connection with the Americans. Let me call him and see if he is home, then you can talk to him." Gertrud was able to reach her son, who told his mother, after he got the picture, that he had some penicillin, and he would like to see Inge at the Charité Hospital in his office Monday morning from ten to eleven. When we got the good news, we turned into a happy bunch, but nobody was happier than Inge. Over a few drinks, the good mood lasted till it was time for us to break up and go home. Before we left, we thanked Gertrud sincerely for her help.

After the long walk back to Inge's house, both of us were dead tired, so I decided to stay at her place. In the morning, Inge got up and fixed breakfast already before I got out of the sack. It was certainly good to see her being herself again.

Slowly and steadily, the Soviets, in a constant and resolute power-grasping grip, were putting an iron ring around Berlin. In the early days after the war, borderlines only existed between the two superpowers, America and Russia, dividing Germany into a west and east zone. Up to now, the division of Berlin, as agreed in Yalta, only existed on paper. As long as the Russians occupied all of Berlin, there was no political friction. All of that changed the moment the Americans, the British, and the French started to take possession of their designated sectors of Berlin. In reality, the city was now split in two parts, East and West Berlin. Except for some occasional interference by the Western powers, the Russians still kept on plundering Berlin, including West Berlin. As I mentioned before, as far as the railroad system was concerned, the West had no control of it, not even in their own sector. Since Berlin was an island in the east zone, most of the time the Western powers were not even aware of the constant embezzlement of the German goods by the Russian army. From my job at the mill, I could see every day trains going by with all kinds of shipments on a destination to Russia. Yesterday, for instance, I'd seen a whole trainload of potatoes going east through our sector. In my mind I was trying to figure out how many hungry families could get a meal out of one trainload of potatoes.

Today, I received another letter from Lisa, and I was over on my way to see Mr. Krüger. Telling him about my observation from the mill,

I agreed that we had to do something about it. "If times were normal," he said, "I would be the first one to condemn any form of terrorism, but under the circumstances, violence is the only way we can combat hunger and intimidation. I can tell you that the people are beginning to fight back also, that the Werewolf is very much alive, and that alone is very much embarrassing to the Russians in Karlshorst. One major event is the liberation of 466 prisoners by a group of the Werewolf who attacked the NKVD Special Camp number 10. The coup was carried out in the middle of the night as the camp commandant, Major Kyuchkin, attended a banquet at staff headquarters. For the lack of vigilance, Kyuchkin and other senior army officers received strong criticism from the furious commander in chief of the NKVD, Laurenty Beria, himself.

"Our involvement is restricted toward the interruption of Soviet railroad transportation inside the French sector only. The guards of the train, after the intervention, will not attempt a pursuit of the perpetrators after the assault. However, they will shoot with their kalashnikovs from the caboose against anything that moves. The day a food train is scheduled to depart from a certain station and track, one of our men will give us the estimated time of arrival at a specific junction. There are two lines going through our sector, the main line from Magdeburg and the smaller industrial train from Pankow. The second one you see from the mill will be our first target. We are just waiting to get some plastic."

"We don't need any charges to blow the rails," I interrupted Krüger. "All we need is two buckets of used motor oil. On one section by the cemetery is a sharp curve, and when the train reaches the bend, it has to slow down. All we have to do is to cover the rails on both sides, about fifty feet long with motor oil. The reduced speed and the heavy weight of the train will make the wheels of the locomotive go crazy; spinning its wheels on top of the grease, the engine will stop pulling the train. This is the moment of surprise we have to take advantage of. For each wagon, one man with a hammer should jump the railroad car, fast knock the hinges of the sideboards open, and the potatoes will unload themselves. By the time the guards notice the attack, the men should already have disappeared. This assault should best be carried out at nights. All the Russians will do is wipe off the oil from the track or cover them with sand, and without a full load to pull, they will be out and gone in no time. Come daylight, you can be sure the people will come and pick up the potatoes. You can count me in on the attack," I said. "Just let me know the day the train is coming." The same day, when I reached home after supper, my mother gave me a letter from the university. They were giving me a date, I believed it was August 13, to come in for an interview and bring all my academic report cards.

The appointment was on Monday at eight o'clock in the morning, a little early, but it did not matter; on the weekend, I would stay with Gerda since her place was close to the university. My concern right now was to find out how Inge was doing; tomorrow was Friday, and then I would know for sure. Every time I went to town, it took me less time to reach my destination; the transportation system was getting faster, repaired as expected. Inge was surprised too; every time I visited her, I was showing up earlier. Today Inge had excellent news for me. Last Monday Inge visited Dr. Rathenow at the Charité. He was very friendly and gave her the first injection of penicillin G that she badly needed. Penicillin G, the strongest type, was made by an American company. He gave her ten more vials to take to her clinic with the instruction to get one injection every other day, and in three weeks her treatment would be completed.

"Make sure," he said, "to get a lab test after the last dose." Needless to say that Inge was very happy to receive the right treatment. I suggested that we go out of the house tomorrow.

"Maybe we go to Dahlem. I'd like to visit my dead comrades at the Wald Friedhof Cemetery."

"Great," Inge said. "And if we still have time, we could stop by and see if the Eckards are still alive. In the morning, I will make you some hot cereal from the wheat grain you provided. I know you don't like porridge, but that's the best I can do."

"Surprise me," I said, and indeed she did. Inge boiled the cereal slowly in water till it thickened, added some milk powder, and sweetened it with corn syrup. It was delicious; it stuck to your ribs, and I liked it. When you are hungry, even the food you ordinarily like the least tastes wonderful.

The shortest and fastest way to Dahlem was to take the U-Bahn from Ferbelliner Platz to Dahlem Dorf, the end of the line, and we were lucky to make it uninterrupted. Walking through the cemetery gave me a feeling of reverence and sadness. I also saw in Inge's face that she was equally impressed. Perhaps she was thinking right now about her own husband, not knowing for sure if he was among the many dead, or if he was still alive, slaving as a prisoner of war in a Soviet gulag in Siberia or somewhere else in Russia. Passing the old section of the cemetery, we could tell by the landscaping, upkeeping, and care that those graves were already in existence for some years. In the new section, only opened since the beginning of the war, there were hardly any tombstones, mostly rows and rows of fresh-filled graves with a pile of earth and some flowers on top. Long lines of recent military graves were decorated with uniform white wooden crosses, showing a small board placed in the center of the cross, giving the name, rank, and date of birth and death. Looking around, I saw a row with six graves that bore the names of my comrades. We all shared the same barrack, the same duty roster, played poker, and covered up for each other. I saw their faces, heard their voices and screams of pain as they died. These young boys buried here were my buddies from the Schmargendorf Flak Battery. Inge noticed how distressed I was, fighting to hold back my tears. She put her arm gently around me, pulling me away from the graves. "Let it go," Inge said. "You wanted to say good-bye to them, now you must go on with your life."

Dahlem is a prestigious but mostly small residential section of the south. A short walk brought us to the Eckards' place at the end of a cul-de-sac. The passage was flanked with huge villas equal to the size of the Eckard estate. Walking through, we noticed that most buildings were flying the American flag. Suddenly it went through my mind; I had to think of what my grandmother said. She predicted that the Americans, after the war, would make themselves at home in the finest suburban area in Dahlem. From the outside, the Eckards' mansion looked like a large hotel with a circular driveway. In front of the entrance, I saw a big new black Cadillac convertible. Next to it on the sidewalk was a GI in his khaki uniform sitting on a chair. I was not sure if he was a sentry watching the entrance or if he was the chauffeur of the automobile. For a moment, I was hesitating to go any closer till Inge told me to go over and talk to him in English. While he could see me coming over, he stood up to stop me; I gave him a military salute and started talking, "Excuse me, sir, I wonder if you can help me. As it is right now, I am a little confused about a certain family by the name Eckard that used to live in this house. We have not seen them since the end of the war. Frankly, we don't even know if they are still alive."

"Oh yes, very much so," the corporal interrupted me. "The owner of the house is in Russian captivity, and his wife and son are living in the guesthouse in the back. The big house here is now occupied by Colonel Davies and his staff of the American occupation force. Now if you want to see Mrs. Eckard, I can call her and see if she is in and if she wants to come to the gate and see you."

"That would be great, please tell her that Inge and Herbert are here to see her."

The guard took the phone on the wall and called the guesthouse. A male voice answered the phone, and then the soldier handed me the receiver. Immediately, I recognized Peter's voice, and I asked him how he was doing and if it was convenient for him to have us for a visit. "Of course," he said. "I'll be right over at the gate and pick you up." Inge could not figure what it was that took me so long talking to the soldier. I explained to her about the conversation I was having with the corporal, and at that moment, Peter had already come to take us to his house in the back. Halfway over to the guesthouse came Hildegard with a smile to greet us. After all the hugging and embracing, we entered her small cottage, as she called it, and she apologized for not being able to receive us in her big house.

"This house is much bigger than the one I live in," Inge said to make her feel better. As soon as we were seated, we started a lively conversation of asking and answering questions. First Inge and then I. We explained the whole story of how we survived the end of the war and the days after. Finally Inge asked where Otto was. I had to look up to Hildegard and noticed that her face took on a frightful expression.

"On the second of May in the afternoon came a group of Russian officers to our house in the front to arrest Otto for being a high-ranking member of the Nazi Party. Otto ran upstairs to shoot himself with his pistol, but at the last minute Peter was able to stop him from committing suicide. The Russians took Otto into custody, and we have not heard from him since. Peter and I went to see the local commandant to help us. All he could tell us was that Otto is in the hands of the Soviet bureau. We cannot see him, but we will be notified of his trial."

"Even so, that it is bad news," Peter said. "But the fact that my father has not committed any crimes, we hope that he will come out of this alive."

"I will not give up hope," Hildegard said. "But sitting here all day long is driving me crazy, so I decided to go back to work. I went over to the maternity hospital here in Dahlem. They are short on nurses, and they hired me on the spot." Now Inge and I were turning around, looking at Peter, waiting to see what he had to tell us on how he survived and outlived "the thousand-year Reich."

"To give you a complete picture of my last days of WW II," Peter said, "I have to tell you that I never left Spandau from my days as a cadet to the very end. As the Russians came closer to Berlin, we all had to stop our education. According to each individual's age, we either joined the army or we participated in the Hitler Youth home front. During the air raids, I was constantly engaged in firefighting and rescue operations in the city of Spandau. From the beginning of the battle of Berlin, we were put together into panzer fighting units. On the night of April 25, as the Red Army already advanced into Neucölln, it was still unusually quiet in Spandau. My group of twenty Hitler Youths, all from the academy, were sheltering in the cellar of a bombed-out apartment house at the Heer Strasse. Our objective was to defend the bridge over the Havel on the east side. Two more Hitler Youth detachments were placed to defend the Charlottenbrücke leading to the center of Spandau and one group in front of us to protect the Pichelsdorf Bridge. Each of us is equipped with two Panzerfaust, just enough to kill two T-34 Russian tanks. We still had two more days to wait before we would see any action. That alone makes you nervous.

"On April 27, finally the Russian army came in from the northwest to approach Spandau, thereby completely closing the ring around Berlin; but a never-ending stream of refugees were trying to get out of Berlin, and the bridges over the Havel seem to be the only window left to the west. That morning it was raining like crazy, we were freezing and hungry. I was making a fire in the basement to warm up some canned food when all of a sudden hell interrupted our meal. Under heavy artillery fire from the Forty-seventh Army, the Soviets were getting ready to attack Spandau. The massacre at the bridges of civilians and soldiers alike was a horrific slaughter. Many of them were caught in the open by guns of the Russian troops approaching the west side of the riverbank. For the time being, the advancement of the Russians at Spandau was delayed as armored vehicles charged across the bridges, crushing wounded soldiers and civilians pushing westward toward Stacken and safety at the river Elbe. After the bloody attack, we were in a middle of panic-stricken civilians and soldiers looking for a way to escape, to save their own lives if they could. For the severely wounded, there was very little hope; there were too many of them. Besides, if you don't get out of this trap, you are dead for sure. If the barrage of artillery don't kill you, the next wave of Russian infantry will. So here we are, twenty Hitler Youths with two Panzerfaust each. Russian tanks are still in reserve, we are not equiped for a hand-to-hand combat. All of us decided that we must split up and retreat to a better defense line. The majority of the group opted to go back to the center of Berlin. Three of us were trying to escape to the south. I decided to go with them. Our present location is on the east end of the bridge at Heer Strasse. At this point, is the junction of the Stössen see and the north corner of the Grunewald Forest, a large area of woodland and undergrowth. To cross the Grunewald from north to south is about eight kilometers. All three of us are from the same neighborhood—Schmargendorf, Dahlem, and Zehlendorf. At the peak of the Grunewald, we start walking in a direction toward the southwest corner of the forest.

Our first stop is the Teufelsee. Here we are, unloading our Panzerfaust, the lake discreetly swallows our weapons. From now on, we are deserters, and for a moment, we are feeling guilty of forsaking our oath to Adolf Hitler. The next place we are taking a rest is the Jagdschloss Grunewald. We are approaching the schloss, very careful not to be captured if it should be occupied by soldiers, friend or foe. As it turned out, the only person we came across was the caretaker who lived in the basement. He was more afraid of us than we were of him. We asked him for some food, but he told us that he had very little left for him but that he is glad to warm up some leftover potatoes for us. We accepted it, and before we left, he suggested that we get out of our uniforms. He took us over to his nursery and gave each of us a pair of overalls and some tomatoes to eat on the way. In two hours it got dark, just in time for us as we reached the edge of town again. The fellow from Schmargendorf was the first one that left our small group, I am the next one as we reached Dahlem, and the last buddy kept on walking to Zehlendorf. Once I left the Grunewald, I passed Dahlem without any interruption till I reached home."

"That is very impressive," Inge said. "Thank God that you are alive."

"Well," Hildegard interrupted, "we are, but now let me serve you some tea and butter cookies."

While Hildegard was preparing the tray in the kitchen, Peter explained to us, "By choice, we left the big house and are now living in the guesthouse. Surprisingly, the Russians did not give us any more trouble after the arrest of Otto, knowing that the Americans were about to take over Dahlem shortly. It did happen, and now the Americans have taken over possession and are here to stay for a long time. They fell in love with our house and notified us that under U.S. military law, we have two options, either sell it or lease it to them, in either case for a fair market price. We decided to lease it to them completely furnished. The advantage we have living next to the Americans is that nobody will molest us."

After we had tea and cookies, Peter suggested that we left the women alone talking to each other and that the two of us should go to his room and talk for a while. Even though his living quarter had become a lot smaller, he was still very comfortable. His music center was the first thing I recognized as we entered his room. His first question was what I was doing now, and I told him that I was temporarily working at the mill but planning to go back to school in September.

"How about you?" I asked him.

"I have a job, like you, working for the time being as a disc-jockey and part-time bartender at the American club. It is not so much for the money but for the connections I can make with the GIs and officers. From an American GI up to a general, they all know that every item they purchase for pennies in the United States can be sold in Germany for hundreds of marks in our currency. This is particularly true when it comes to food and medicine. Since our money has no value, it has been replaced by cigarettes. Here is how it works. All American soldiers can buy duty—and tax-free in special stores for the military only, one case of cigarettes for one dollar. Any amount he wants, there is no limit. Buyers and sellers are meeting at the black market. There are several of them in the city of Berlin, but they are illegal and frequently raided by the military police. A woman that is desperate for food to feed her starving children goes to the black market and trades her golden wedding band for two cases of cigarettes. Now she can go to the farmer and can buy a pound of butter for two packs of cigarettes, a loaf of bread for one pack, a pound of flour for another pack, or whatever she can purchase. Now let's see how the buyer of the golden ring is making out. He invested two dollars for the two cases of cigarettes he traded for the golden ring. The going rate for an ounce of gold in the U.S. is $30. The net weight of the ring is one-half ounce. If he sells the ring, he made a thirteen-dollar profit on a two-dollar investment. The black market is regulated like any other business, by the law of supply and demand; no shortage no black market. There is no doubt that this unhealthy situation will not go on forever. If you want to go and study at the university, this may be the ticket to pay your tuition and make a living too."

"I don't see where I fit into this game, it sounds good," I said. "But whoever has the cigarettes does not need me as a middleman."

"That's where you are wrong," Peter replied. "You seem not to remember that you are breaking the law when you are going to the black market, and a member of the military arrested by the MP at the black market will be severely punished."

"Well, tell me, why should I stick my neck out, break the law, and go to jail for dealing at the black market?"

"You don't have to go to the black market," Peter is trying to explain to me. "You'll find the same shortage in any outside industry and even on a bigger scale between manufacturer and consumer. It takes two to tango, a U.S citizen to buy low and a German middleman to sell high. As long as you have no competition in Germany, you can name your price. Any legal commodity for some time to come will be highly in demand. Remember, Germany is totally destroyed, and everything we need has to be imported."

"You know," I said, "it makes sense, what you are telling me. I can think of one medication right now that is highly in demand and not available for all the tea in China unless you have some American connection. I would have no problem selling it all day long to clinics and hospitals."

"You are talking about penicillin," Peter told me right away. "The only drug that is able to stop the widespread of VD in Berlin. I have to find out about the manufacturer in the United States and if they have a distributor in West Germany. What is more important is for me to find an American who is interested and trustworthy."

"Peter," I said, "I am serious about it. Do some investigation, and I assure you I will do my part." We sealed our endeavor by shaking hands and left the room to join Hildegard and Inge.

"Time to go home," Inge reminded me, and so we said good-bye, promising to come back soon. Before I left for Tegel, I was asking Inge if she had enough food in the house, if not, I might go to the black market next time I come and trade one of the French brandy bottles. "No," Inge said, "I have enough for now. Let's keep them."

Accident at the Last Mission

Arriving in Tegel, I found everything in order, and again my mother was giving me a letter from Lisa; this time it was saying urgent. Monday after work, I was going over, and my connection told me that sometime tomorrow night, the expected train would pass our sector. "Come over after work, and we will get ready. I am telling everybody," Krüger said, "to meet at the old mausoleum of the Tegel Friedhof at nine o'clock, to bring a hammer, wear tennis shoes and dark clothes. We will be altogether thirty men, fifteen on each side of the train to spread apart one wagon length between each man, hugging the ground till the train stops. Immediately we will jump up, knock the hinges open, and run away from the train. The left-side group of the train will disappear among the nearby huts and cabins of the allotment holders, and the right-side group will run to the cemetery. They will stay under cover behind the tombstones till the train takes off again."

At 9:00 PM, I would go with two other young men to make sure that all the motor oil was applied on the right places. The train was right on schedule, and all the men were in position. The attack proceeded as planned; only one hinge on one side of the last wagon did not open. By the time the Russians realized what happened, our mission was already completed. Afterward, the Russians opened the windows of their caboose and started to shoot with automatic guns aimlessly in all directions. My group was the closest to the train, and we were bombarded with bullets, hiding behind the tombstones, shaking with fright. A strange whistle and shrill sound from the ricochet bullets flying behind our necks scared the living daylight out of us. Luckily, nobody got hurt. In twenty minutes, it was all over; the empty train was leaving for the Russian zone. By the time the French military police arrived to investigate the shooting, all of us were gone. In the morning, the neighbors came and picked up all the potatoes. They had no idea of all the trouble we went through just to provide each of them with an extra ration of potatoes. When I came home with a big sack of potatoes, both women thought Santa Claus was coming early. My grandmother was as happy as could be; she wasted no time preparing a fresh hot potato salad.

The next weekend, I was again at Gerda's house. My time of recovery. She treated me very nice, fed me with food I would not have access to, and she made love to me. Every time I was with her, I was getting more and more relaxed. Gerda and her house had become a sanctuary for me, an escape from the misery of the outside world behind me. My stay with Gerda was always short, but in such time, I regained some of my strength and emotional security.

Very early Monday morning, I was going for my interview at the university. I was introduced to a Professor Dr. Gobel. I gave him my credentials, and after examining them, he told me that the university would not accept my application as it was short on my studies requirements. "Please tell me what I can do to make up for it," I asked him.

"Well," he replied, "you are not the only case, that is why we will conduct extra classes for students like you. In the meantime, you can matriculate for the winter semester."

"I'd like to study medicine," I said. "The war has provided me with the aptitude."

"That is absolutely out of the question," he discouraged me. "This university has already too many previous applications and students that in the middle of their curriculum were called up to serve the military, and they are now the priority for the available registrations. The next best thing I can suggest to you is to become a pharmacist. We have still some openings for that class."

I did not want to go home rejected, and I definitely didn't want to be a blue-collar worker for the rest of my life; I made a real quick decision. "Dr. Gobel," I said, "I have decided to enroll in the pharmacy class, please sign me up."

"Very good," he said and signed a preliminary admission slip, sending me downstairs to the administration office. "And good luck to you," he said at the end of the interview. There was a long line of new students and a lot more of papers to be filled out. Finally, I was admitted, received my ID card, and paid them a deposit. My classes would start on September 10, 1945.

At home I told my mother and grandmother the good news. They were very happy for me, and my mother was handing me another note from Lisa. The same evening, I went over to see Wilhelm Krüger. Before I could say anything, he was congratulating me for the success of last week's mission. "Thank you," I said. "But I cannot continue to participate. I have to make an end to this war business. I am just starting a new life, and I don't want to jeopardize my future."

"Listen to me before you turn me down," he continued. "This time we are not talking potatoes. This is no longer kid stuff. If the Russians should get away with this particular trainload, it would be a loss not only for us but for the whole Western world. At this moment, while I am talking to you, the Russians are assembling a trainload of major art objects they confiscated from all the museums in Berlin, anything of value they could put their hands on. Yesterday, I received a call from the Spree Museum, and they are hauling crates over to the train like crazy. Unfortunately, it is in the east sector of Berlin, and nobody can do anything about it. The train is scheduled to leave the Nord-Bahnhof next Friday night. From there it will take the major route through Tegel, Frankfurt an der Oder, Posen, Warsaw, and Moscow. The only place where that train can be stopped is the French sector. This time we don't have to be around to stop the train. We will blast a hole in front of the train, and that will be the end of its journey to Moscow. The French MP will discover the Russian maneuver, and the French general responsible for his sector will take the cargo in custody. I only need four men to do the job, and the reason I called on you is because you know how to handle explosives. Since we have no ETA [estimated time of arrival] on the train, we will use the British plastic without a timer. We will detonate the charges manually with wire and plunger from a safe distance. A lookout will give us the signal to set off the charges when the train is about three hundred feet from the installation. I leave you now alone to decide with your own conscience if you still want to do something for the greater good of Germany."

Krüger went to the other side of the room and started to light a cigarette. Considering of what was in the scale, I was telling him that I would go, but this would definitely be my last mission. "Now remember," he said, "pilfering food is a minor offense, but blowing up a public transportation is a federal crime. What I am trying to say is you must avoid being arrested."

"I am aware of the risk involved, but I also envision the benefit of a successful operation." "You will accomplish a prosperous intervention of a major crime on the grounds of humanitarian principles. We will see you at my place next Friday at five o'clock." In the afternoon, a group of four was getting together to rehearse the plan one more time, then Krüger was taking us over to his garage; we were selecting some plastic, enough fuse line, and a small detonator. All of us were getting into his VW, and he was taking us to an area he selected between the two train stations Schulzendorf and Heiligensee. He was parking the car at the end of Henningsdorfer Strasse near the border. On the left side of the railroad tracks was the river Havel, and on the right side was a small area of woodland. This was the place where we were hiding out and would set up the detonator. At the end of Schulzendorfer Bahnhof, a railroad bridge crossing the Havel was taking the trains across the border into the Soviet zone.

In a basin-shaped mold covered with brush and close enough to the railroad, we waited for the ambush. Another volunteer and I, as soon as it got dark, were going over to the tracks to set up the charges. Then I wrapped the fuse line several times around a spike and stuck the end of the fuse line deep into the plastic. After I packed both rails, I checked the connections one more time, and now we started running the fuse line back to the hideout, trying to conceal the line under the weeds the best we could. After connecting the fuse line to the detonator, stage one of the attack was completed. My helper and I would stay in the mold at all times. I would push the plunger at the right time when he was getting a signal from a third man when our train was in sight. About three hundred feet from the charges was a tall signal that I could see from our hideout; as soon as the train passed this point, I would set off the charges, enough time for the train to stop.

My partner and the other lookout would stay constantly under communication via two-way radio. After the explosion, there would be plenty of confusion for us, under the cover of tumult and disorder, to escape undetected. We would go back the same route under the railroad tunnel to the west side of Heiligensee where Krüger would be waiting for us at the Henningsdorfer Strasse with the getaway car. That was always the hardest part, to sit, be patient, and wait for the right moment to jump into action. We could hardly keep our eyes open, and it was not till 1:30 AM that the train came into sight. Shortly thereafter, the train passed the signal, and I pushed the plunger down as fast as I could. Instantly a huge explosion ripped the rails apart, and I could hear the sharp squealing sound of the wheels as the engineer applied the brakes. It was time for us to get out of there. Both of us were running toward the street tunnel, my partner first, and I followed him. I could just see him disappear on the other side of the tunnel as two soldiers came around the corner; they spotted me and made a motion to stop me. Before they were able to intercept me, I ran up the stairs on the right side as fast as I could to get to the platform in front of the train. The loud commotion of agitated passengers and turbulent bystanders made it possible for me to shake the MP on my tail and get lost in the crowd. Without being obvious by running, I worked my way up to the front of the train to find another exit, but there was also a guard posted. All I could do was walk and follow the tracks toward the border. In the middle of the railroad bridge over the Havel, I saw two Russian soldiers, each with an assault rifle coming toward me. If I stayed, they would capture me; if I ran back, I would be riddled with bullets like a sieve. Without any hesitation, out of pure instinct, I climbed over the railing and jumped headfirst into the river. The Russians started shooting at me; I could hear it on the way down, but they did not hit me.

That was the good news. Now to the bad news. After I plunged into the water, just underneath the surface, I hit my left shoulder and upper arm on a big object, most likely a sharp piece of iron; as a result, I dislocated my shoulder and suffered a compound fracture on my bone. Surprisingly, I didn't lose my consciousness; apparently, I was so full of adrenaline that I kept swimming underwater away from the bridge till I had to come up for air. With the last energy left in me, I climbed up the riverbank to get to where the car was parked at Henningsdorfer Strasse. Krüger put on the headlights and sent the two guys over to help me. They put me in the car, and Krüger drove me about a mile away from the border. Then in the middle of the Schulzendorfer Forest, they put me down on the grass, cut my shirt off, and stripped me down to my waist. Krüger got the first aid kit out of the car, covered the wound with part of the broken bone sticking out of the skin with some heavy gauze and a tied bandage. With a warm jacket around me, they put me back in the car, and we were now driving back to Tegel. At the corner of Waidmansluster Damm and Berliner Strasse, Krueger stopped the car, and the other two fellows got off. He then asked me what hospital I wanted to go to. I explained to him that first of all, I must go to the American sector; that was the only place where I felt protected and got the right medical care. I gave Krüger Inge's address, and I asked him to drive me over to Wilmersdorf. He did so, and at about 3:00 AM, we arrived at her house. Inge was shocked, but she did not start to ask questions; she helped Krüger to get me to the bedroom. Before Krüger left, I thanked him for his help and asked him to notify my mother to let her know that her son was all right and that I would be home in three to four days. Inge was now taking over using her nursing abilities to make me comfortable and asked Krüger to wait a few more minutes. Then both went to the kitchen, and I knew that Inge did not let Krüger go till he told her the whole bloody story, but she was more interested in how much blood I lost and what kind of treatment and medication I received. The first thing Inge asked me was how severe my pain was, and I told her that right now, I wished somebody would shoot me and get it over with. "I will do something about your pain," Inge was trying to make me feel better. "But first I will have to take your temperature, pulse, blood pressure, and respiration. Your vital signs are OK, except that you have a little temperature, which is expected for your kind of injury. I looked at your dressing, and there is no fresh blood. Tomorrow I will change your bandage and take you to the hospital. For tonight, take the two tablets of codeine, that will lower your pain and let you go to sleep. I will sleep here in the armchair next to you in case you need me."

In the morning, I had only a liquid breakfast; Inge helped me to the bathroom and changed my dressing. By now the pain was coming back, and I also had a little fever. Inge called the hospital where she worked and told them to send over an ambulance to her house. Within the hour, they came to take me to the clinic, and Inge was riding with them. As they put me to bed in a room with three other casualties, Inge took care of all the paperwork in the administration office. Thereafter a resident surgeon was on the way to see me. The doctor examined me and explained that I needed an operation. He also wanted to know who my attending physician was. Inge was doing the talking for me and told him that Dr. Helmut von Rathenow from the Berliner Charité would take care of me.

"Great, then he is in good hands. Please have the doctor call me." And the resident doctor left the room after he ordered some X-rays to be taken and more pain medication for me. Immediately Inge called Dr. Rathenow, and he wanted to know how she was doing.

"I am doing great, but this time I am calling you for my young friend who suffered a compound fracture on his left humerus and needs an open reduction. He specifically asked for you to be his physician."

"I am sorry, I am overloaded with surgeries, but I will send my assistant. He is a qualified orthopedic surgeon."

"Dr. Rathenow," Inge said, "I wish you would reconsider and make it somehow possible to operate on him. The patient we are talking about is the friend of your mother who conducted the undertaking of your father."

"I understand," Dr. Rathenow said. "Of course, I will not let him down, and I will personally take care of him. Unfortunately, I cannot cancel any of my cases, but I will be out of the OR by three o'clock. Please have the X-rays ready and start the IV and the usual pre-op medication at fifteen minutes to five o'clock. I will be there at five o'clock and have your resident surgeon call me. I want him to assist me and get an anesthesiologist."

"It will all be done," Inge said. "And thank you so very much, Doctor." Inge told me the good news, and I was happy that everything would be taken care of. After I came back from the X-ray department, I was exhausted and asked for another painkiller that let me sleep on and off for the rest of the afternoon. Shortly before the operation, Inge came to see me; she had a paper she wanted me to sign.

"Tell me, what is this all about you want me to sign?" I asked her.

"This is a written consent for surgery that everybody has to sign before the operation."

I started to read the paper. At one phrase, I stopped to read and started to smile. "It says here under cause of injury that patient fell down from a ladder and broke his left arm."

"You were painting the outside of his house, Krüger told me, when the accident happened, is that correct?" Inge wanted to know.

"Oh yes," I assured her. "That is exactly what happened, and precisely five minutes later, after he applied the first aid dressing, he drove me, at my request, straight over to Wilmersdorf to see you."

"I believe you," Inge said. "But I never heard of anybody painting the outside of a house in the middle of the night. Another thing that makes no sense to me is the fact that your pants were completely wet when Krüger and I put you to bed."

I just finished signing the paper when the anesthetist came to see me. He asked me some questions about my health. Ten minutes later, they came from the OR to pick me up. Inge gave me a good luck kiss, and off I went. That was all I remembered till I woke up in the recovery room and saw Inge on my bedside taking care of me. After I regained complete consciousness, they were taking me upstairs to a semiprivate room. Inge was holding my good hand, telling me that everything was fine and Dr. Rathenow had no problem fixing the broken bone. As a matter of fact, he would come and see me in the morning. When I started to complain about pain, Inge sedated me so I could make it through the night.

In the morning I felt more relaxed; the pain was not so bad anymore, and I was beginning to be hungry. For the first time, I was really looking at the contraption my arm was cemented in. On top was a window big enough to expose the wound to the air. At 10:00 AM, Dr. Rathenow stopped by to see me. It was the first time we met each other. He had a very pleasant personality and was very friendly to me. I started to ask him questions about the operation, and he took the time to explain things to me.

"You had a nasty fracture close to the shoulder joint and I made a fifteen-centimeter incision right over the spot where the bone penetrated the skin. First I replaced the ball joint back into the shoulder socket, then I lined up the two broken ends of the humerus. The two sharp edges of the bone are like the tip of two spears. Putting them side by side, they were perfectly aligned, but any little muscle reflex could pull them apart before I close the wound. I did not want to take a chance, so I decided for the bone to mend nice and straight to hold it together with a plate and some screws. If it should bother you in the future, it presents no problem to have the hardware removed through a small incision. We will take another X-ray tomorrow, and if everything is OK, you can go home the day after. In two weeks, we will remove the big cast and replace it with a smaller one, and in another few weeks, we take that one off too, and you will be as good as new."

The doctor was looking at his watch, and I told him, "Doctor, I know you are busy, and I will not keep you any longer, but before you go, let me assure you what a pleasure it is for me to know you, and I cannot thank you enough for what you have done for Inge and me."

"Say no more," he said. "Inge and you have been so kind to my mother. I could never repay you. You both come and see us anytime." After the good doctor left, Inge helped me to get out of bed for the first time; she made me sit comfortably in an easy chair, and I learned how to eat with one hand. Patience was not my virtue, but I even learned how to get dressed with one arm. The next day, when I looked at the latest X-ray, I was very pleased as the film showed a picture of the bone back in the right place. I was a fast healer, and I could watch how the scar was beginning to heal together. As scheduled on the second day after the operation, I was getting discharged from the hospital. Inge arranged for somebody from the hospital to drive us home at the end of the day. It felt so good being back in Inge's house, knowing that I survived the accident, and that I was on the road to recovery. Inge took a few days' off and took excellent care of me. She washed the scar every day with hydrogen peroxide, and there was no trace of an infection. I was walking every day to get my strength back, and I felt I was ready to go home; it was now five days after the operation.

"Not so fast," Inge said. "You have to stay at least another three days. It takes a minimum of eight days before I can pull the stitches."

"Yes, but think of my poor mother. She is suffering every day I don't show up." In a couple of days, I was telling Inge that my scar was beginning to itch, and she explained to me that this was a sign that the stitches wanted to come out; the body rejects everything that does not belong to it. After Inge took out the stitches, I could see that the wound was completely closed.

"Today is the day," Inge said. "You got to go home and face your mother."

"I know," I replied. "But I don't know what to tell her."

"Well, you have two choices," Inge put it to me. "You either tell her the truth, or you give her the same fairy tale you are telling me and everybody else."

"Inge, please listen to me. I don't like to keep any secrets from you, but I am between a rock and a hard place. I am in a position where I have to protect the safety of other people. If I would go around telling the truth, I will not only harm myself, but I would also jeopardize the life of others. You will just have to trust me. I am doing what I have to do, but years from now, perhaps even sooner, I will tell you the truth."

Inge was satisfied with my explanation, and that made my departure much easier. Getting in and out of the train with a bulky cast in front of your chest was kind of difficult, especially when the train was loaded with passengers to a maximum capacity. I was glad to arrive in Tegel. The moment I was home and my mother opened the door, I was received with a loud scream. My grandmother had to come, trying to stop her from going on crying.

"May I come in," I said. "I am tired of standing out here." I had not anticipated my mother to be so emotional simply by looking at me. "Don't look at me like I am from out of space. I just broke my arm, that is all. People are breaking their bones all day long. Now the good news is I am alive, and the bad news is I have to run around with this chunk of clay for the next four weeks. Now if you want to know how it happened, let's just say I stepped on a banana peel, fell down, and broke my arm. Or here is another one, make it a piece of soap on the floor of the shower."

"Don't be so sarcastic," my grandmother said. "You are making me mad. If you don't want to tell us the real story, that is your business, but don't make fools out of us."

"I am sorry, Grandma," I said, "I apologize. You have to trust me on this one. In due time, I will no longer hide the truth."

I was planning to stay in Tegel three days. Tomorrow I was going to the mill to pick up my last paycheck, tell them officially that I must terminate my job as I was no longer able to carry heavy sacks. Next day, I had to notify the employment office to remove me from the list of employment seekers and register me as a permanent full-time student. This was important in order to keep on receiving my food ration card. Every day I was beginning to feel stronger, and the pain was also subsiding. In the evening, when the heat cooled off, we sat in the garden watching the sun go down. Friday around noon, I was packing some clean clothes before I took off to see Gerda. In Tegel I received my ration cards and asked them to give them to me in travel tickets as I spent most of my time on the road or in different locations.

Back at Gerda's home was another moment of shock and surprise for her, and I was going through the same routine of a question-and-answer session. The only difference with Gerda was that she was not the mother type, making you feel guilty for not being careful enough or living too much of a dangerous life. Gerda lived in the here and now, as she said it many times, and I knew only too well. She said to me, "What makes me happier than anything else is the fact that you decided to go back to school. I know that you are very disciplined when it comes to education and that you will ultimately settle down. Most boys when they grow up experience a crisis period. A time in their lives where they are driven by wild ideas and behavior and think they can change the world. Later, they undergo a strange metamorphosis process and become mentally more stable and mature. This type of psychological change in young men can often be influenced and shaped by a woman." And Gerda said that she understood very much what I was going through. Gerda was very wise about life to know not to moralize a man; it would only solicit resistance or start a fight.

CHAPTER XI

THE AMERICAN CONNECTION

My Struggle as a Student

Inge—Gisela's mother   Bruno—Inge's husband

September 1 was the day for the removal of the big cast, to be replaced by a not-so-heavy-type smaller support with a sling around my neck. I could not move my arm yet, but it certainly was a big relief to wear something more comfortable, a support, which mitigated pain and stress. It changed my mood and made me happy again. It was a pleasure to walk from the clinic to Inge's house not to have to carry that extra weight with me. I rang the doorbell; no answer. I rang again. Finally the door opened, and I looked at an older skinny man in a shabby worn-out German uniform walking with the support of two crutches. "Hi," I said, "I come to visit Inge, but if she is not here, I will be back some other time." And as I was beginning to turn around, I suddenly stopped, turned around again to take another look at the man. "Wait a minute," I said. "Are you Mr. Behlow?"

"Yes, I am, and I just made it home from Russia."

"Good for you and Inge. She must now be the happiest woman in the world."

"At first she was surprised seeing her dead husband coming home, and may I ask who you are? But first, please come in." He took his crutches and hobbles out of the doorway.

I introduced myself, telling him that I just came back from the clinic where Inge works and had my cast removed and that I didn't see her there, that was why I stopped in their house. I also told him how grateful I was to her for giving me the best care before and after the operation.

"Tell me, what happened to your arm?" he wanted to know.

"Just a freak accident. I was painting my girlfriend's house when I fell down from a high ladder and broke my arm with the bone sticking out. I needed an operation, and the surgeon did a good job putting all the pieces back together with the help of a few screws." I was looking at his left leg, changing the conversation. "I can see that you are not so lucky. You have lost your left foot in the war," I said.

"That is not so. I am one of the few lucky soldiers that survived the war and made it out of Russia. That was the nicest thing that could happen to me when a shrapnel fragment came flying to cut off my foot. That was my ticket home. If I was able to stand on my two feet I would still be in some gulag working every day, twelve hours a day, till I die of starvation or exhaustion."

"Well, if you put it that way, I have to agree with you. As soon as you are equipped with a good fitting prosthesis, you are as good as new. Well, I guess it is time for me to go home. In two weeks I will be back in Wilmersdorf to have my cast permanently removed. I'd like to stop by and say hello to you if you don't mind."

"Oh no, not at all, Inge and I will be happy to see you."

"Thank you very much, sir, and again welcome home."

The first day of the beginning of the winter semester, we got familiar with the facility and university procedures. It was only half a day of orientation. Classes were not scheduled till the following Monday. It took less time to go to school from Gerda's place than it would take to come from Tegel. That was one more reason I stayed with Gerda a lot of the time. It was very convenient in the morning to go to school directly from her place.

The day had come to have my cast removed, and today right after school, I was on my way to the clinic. The moment the cast was off, I was also trying to remove the ugly incident from my mind and go on with my life. I was, as of today, a true 100 percent civilian again, and there would never be for me any more underground Werewolf activities. While I was at the clinic now, it might be the best and also the last time of having a chance to talk to Inge in private. On my way over here, I'd been thinking it over, how I could best handle the situation without giving Inge's husband the wrong impression of my close friendship with her. I was going over to the floor where she was working, and the nurse behind the desk told me that Inge was with a patient. I asked the nurse if she please would be so kind to tell Inge that I would be waiting for her in the visitor's room. Ten minutes after the end of her shift, Inge came to see me. She greeted me with a smile and tears in her eyes. This time they were tears of happiness. "Do you believe in miracles?" Inge asked me.

"Yes, I do, I've seen one the other day when I went to your house and unexpectedly Bruno appeared, answering the door."

"Listen," Inge said, "there is a nice little café around the corner, I'll treat you to a cup of coffee."

"That sounds good, let's go. We have so much to talk about." At the café, we sat down at a table in a private corner. Inge started the conversation by asking me how Bruno and I got acquainted and wanted to know what we talked about. "I only stayed a few minutes, telling him that I stopped by to thank you for the excellent care you gave me before and after the operation. The rest was small talk about my accident and how he was saved in Russia and about his return. I did not say much and didn't mention Gisela." I continued, "The man had just came home. He has been too long away and has a lot of adjusting to do. You cannot tell him everything at once, not that we should hide anything, but just to bring him slowly up-to-date. Can you imagine if I told him that you knew me since the days when Gisela and I went to school together in Tegel? That Gisela was my girlfriend. His next questions would have been all about Gisela, and I think it is not for me to tell him how his only daughter died. I don't know if by now you had the chance to tell him the truth."

"Yes, I did," Inge said. "But not right away. We had to renew our feelings for each other first. After he was comfortable and happy to be home again, I still waited till he started to ask questions about her. When I told him what happened to her, he went out of his mind. He cried like a baby and didn't want to believe it that she is gone. After I told him, I opened a bottle, and we kept drinking till midnight when the bottle was empty. I suffered with him all over again. In the end, we came to the conclusion that Bruno went to hell from one side in Russia, and at his return home, he reentered hell from the other side. I spared him the ugly details of how Gisela died and told him that she was killed instantly. I told him that with the war now over, we have to pick up the pieces and put our lives back together again and put the past behind us."

"You did the right thing," I said. "I agree with you, time is a great healer, and you two are lucky to be back together again. Now that he knows Gisela is dead, tell him the truth about Gisela being my girlfriend and how I suffered when she was taken away. Tell him about our friendship and how when we lost someone we loved so dearly we needed each other for support and survival. I am sure Bruno will respect our friendship. As a matter of fact, he told me that I can come and visit you both. There is one more thing I want to talk to you about, it is my advice not to tell Bruno about the rape and the consequences you suffered. He may be happier if he does not know about it. Some men cannot take it knowing that their wives have been sexually assaulted."

"You may be right," Inge said. "Bruno is not the man that would take it kindly. I may hide it from him for his own good. Weeks ago I have been tested for the last time, and everything turned out negative. I am clean again, and I don't have to fear of being contagious."

"Let us hear from each other. I will be very busy being a full-time student but never too busy to go and visit my friends. One more thing before I forget it, the case of French cognac from Dr. Rathenow is all yours. Turn it into food. It seems to me Bruno could gain a few pounds." And we said good-bye in good spirits.

Back in Tegel, I was telling my mother and grandmother the good news about the homecoming of Inge's husband from Russia. For Inge's sake, they were very happy that she did not have to be alone anymore. After supper, my mother again put a letter on the table in front of me. This time it was not from Lisa; it was a letter from Peter Eckard. I told my mother and grandmother that Peter was a former Napola student from Spandau and lived with his mother in Dahlem. He wrote me that he was still working at the American club in Dahlem. He also gave me the address of the club and wanted me to come and visit him soon one evening. The Americans were always looking for bilingual part-time workers. "Since you are fluent in English, you have no problem being hired, and they are paying good money too."

"I think this might be a good opportunity. Right now I am a little short on cash. I have not even paid the rest of my tuition yet."

"Are you going to stick now with your studies?" my grandmother wanted to know.

"Of course I do. I am registered as a full-time student with the employment office, what else can I do?"

"I'll tell you what," my grandmother said, "if you are serious on getting a better education, I will give you some money. I am an old woman. I have saved money all my life, what for? Inflation takes it away, and what is left to keep it in the bank till I die makes no sense these times. With my retirement pay and Opa's pension, I can live very comfortably. The money is yours, just don't do any more stupid things and risk your life. I know all of your crazy Werewolf activities."

"Grandma," I said, "that is all in the past. I have learned my lesson, and I promise you I will keep my nose clean. You must also know that I am looking for a part-time job to support myself. At the billboard of the university, they are looking for some tutors. You know, chemistry has always been my major, and I don't mean basic chemistry, I am talking about organic chemistry. I will take whatever comes first. What Peter is telling me in his letter sounds pretty interesting. The money you are offering me I consider it as a standby. Primarily, you should spend your money to put more food on the table."

"Oh, we do," she said. "Frequently we are taking the train and visit the farmers in the back country. They still sell their food cheaper as if you had to buy it at the black market. When we visit Senta, she is always taking us to the farmers she knows. Senta is still alone. Her husband took the last Messerschmitt out of Berlin and flew it to West Germany, where he surrendered to the Americans. A fellow flyer from the Bernau squadron visited Senta with a message from Heinz, as they seen each other in the same POW camp, that he is fine and will be home soon. Unlike the Russians, the Americans and the British are beginning to close all camps and send all prisoners home. You can imagine how happy Senta is that they will be reunited soon."

"The only relatives we have not seen yet since the end of the war are Erna and Ingeborg in Kremmen. We hope to check on them also in the near future." Before I left, I told them that I had a strong feeling that we soon would all be together again, and that there was a bright future we could look forward to.

Friday after school, I was going over to see Gerda again. She knew I was coming, so she prepared an out-of-the-ordinary meal. "Can you tell me," I asked her, "what we are celebrating tonight?"

"Don't you remember, four months ago today is when you came into my life."

"Well, happy anniversary. I am sorry I neglected to bring you some flowers."

"That is all right, I will settle for a kiss." I gave her a kiss, and she ended up taking me to her bedroom, and under her spell, I thought, *This is the good life, it can't get any better.*

Later in the evening, I said to Gerda, "All I need is a job to make some money on the side." And I showed her the letter from Peter. "If it is all right with you, tomorrow would be a great day to go and see Peter. During the week time would be too short, and I don't know how long our meeting will be."

"It is OK with me," Gerda said.

Getting a Job at the American Club

The club would open about 11:00 AM to serve lunch and was only for American soldiers and their families. I rang the doorbell and told the porter that I had an appointment with Mr. Eckard; he took me straight over to the bar, and there was my good friend Peter. "Hello, old chum," he said. "I see you got my letter; please sit down and give me a few more minutes while I finish stocking the bar. Saturday is a busy day here. I am glad you came early. So tell me, what is new?"

"Well, a few things happened since I saw you last time. I am back in school studying pharmacy, and I have some really sensational news that will excite great interest especially for your mother."

"Don't keep me in suspense," Peter said. "I am also very emotional."

"About two weeks ago, I was going to visit Inge, and can you imagine who answered the door . . . her husband, Bruno, who all of us thought was dead. He lost a foot in combat. The Germans retreated, but he could not run away and was captured by the Russians. I told him that I was sorry he lost a limb. According to Bruno, this is a small trade-off, for if he was not a cripple, he would still be in Russia, maybe for the rest of his life."

"Unbelievable," Peter remarked. "I am very happy for Inge. To lose a husband and an only child is just too much for any woman."

"Have you heard anything more about your dad? Is he still imprisoned here in Germany?" I am asking Peter.

"We have an attorney, and he is trying to make the Russians deliver him to the authorities in West Germany. For my father, that would be the first step to his freedom." Now he is asking about my father, "Did your father make it to the western zone, or did he get captured by the Russians?"

"We don't know for sure, but since he was stationed in Hungary, close to the Austrian border, we hope that he is in American custody. All we can do right now is pray and wait. My mother would never give up hope. No matter what happens, we all must go on with our lives. What I need at this point is a part-time job, and I believe that is the reason you asked me to come and see you."

"That is correct," Peter agreed. "But first let me tell you, our business adventure as we planned did not materialize. It is virtually impossible to get in on it without a substantial capital investment. The next best thing for us would be a steady part-time employment. I am very satisfied here. The pay is good, and there are many extra benefits. Let's go for lunch, and I will tell you more about the benefits this place has to offer. It is the connections you are making here. That is where the extra money comes in."

Since I was a guest of Peter's, I was allowed, like all of the club members and employees, to order anything up and down the menu for a token of a price in comparison to other restaurants; and on top of it, you didn't have to give up some of your precious food stamps. Needless to say that I was very impressed. No matter what, these days most of us didn't get enough to eat. "Where do you think I would fit in here? Are there any openings at the present time?"

"The club is very unhappy with some of the waiters. The Americans don't want to wait on tables, and most Germans don't speak any English. This presents a problem and leads to a high turnover among the waiters. The American officers and their families are not likely to learn another language. Wherever the Americans go, they expect the whole world to talk to them in English. This is the basic principle of the existence of this club. The Americans don't mingle very well with the German people, and why should they? We were war enemies, and after all, they are the victors. They also want to have a home away from home, and that is what the club is all about.

"There is one thing I have to say about the Americans: they are not stingy whether you are serving behind the bar or serving them food, and if you treat them right, they tip you very generously. Now you think it over, it is up to you. Should you be really interested, I will introduce you to Captain Wilson. He is the manager of the club, and he will be here at three o'clock. I have to go back to the bar and help out. Come with me, and we will talk some more. The bar is not busy, and we have plenty of time to talk in private. Remember the last time we were talking about how cheap Americans can buy cigarettes at the commissary store? Here you can make the right connections once they got to know and trust you. Just tell them that you have connections to some dealers at Bahnhof Zoo and that they will buy any amount of cigarettes you can bring them. The profit for the average GI is very tempting, but they don't want to get involved. They need a middle man, and that is where you come in. Usually, when the merchandise is sold, they will split the profit with you fifty-fifty. I know some guys here who do it all the time. There is a waiter, his wife runs a small clothing store in Kreuzberg full of GI's uniforms and equipment. His American friend is a supply sergeant, for a piece of soap, the Germans are willing to pay a small fortune. Look at the clock," Peter said. "It is three o'clock. I think the captain must be in by now." Peter and I went over to his office, and Peter knocked on the door.

A voice behind the door said, "Come on in." And both of us entered his office; and as he looked up to us, we greeted him, "Good afternoon, sir."

"Captain Wilson," Peter said, "I would like to introduce you to my friend, who is here to apply for a job at the club."

"I don't know if this is the right time," Captain Wilson said. "At the moment, we have only two openings. Unless you are a trumpet player, there is only one job left, that of a busboy."

"Captain, sir, I have done worse than that. I have only held two jobs since the end of the war. I have hauled corpses for the Russians and carried flour sacks at the mill."

"What are you doing now?" the captain wanted to know.

"I am a full-time student at the Humboldt University."

"If you attend a graduate school, then you must have a higher education. Where did you learn to speak such good English?"

"As a former member of the Hitler Youth, I was privileged to get an education in a special government boarding school."

"You mean in an Adolf Hitler school?"

"Yes, sir, that is correct," I replied.

"What do you think about the Nazi Party now?" the captain was asking me.

"That is not for me to say. The jury is still out on it. History will decide and answer your question, but I think it will be in a negative way. But I can tell you that I believe now that not every Nazi is bad and not every Democrat is good."

"You know," the captain said, "I cannot understand you people—Germany, the country of Schiller, Goethe, Einstein, and others, how can you follow a clown like Hitler?"

"I am glad you raised that question," I said. "We were never allowed to do it."

"Well," the captain said, "I like your style. You have two options, you can either start as a busboy now, or wait till one of the evening waiters gives us notice to quit. Since you have no previous experience, I would prefer you get your feet wet as a busboy first."

"That sounds good to me. When do you want me to start?"

"Let's see, how about October first, check in at four o'clock?"

"Thank you for giving me the job, Captain, and I will see you." Peter and I left his office. I was thanking Peter for his effort to get me a job and asked him to give my regards to his mother.

It was a successful day, and I was returning to Gerda with the good news. "Let's celebrate your new job tomorrow," Gerda said. "First we will go out for dinner and then go dancing at a public ballroom near the Potsdamer Platz."

"I have nothing else to do tomorrow. I will go if you don't mind me stepping on your toes."

"We will take it easy and do the slow ones. I am a little rusty myself, don't worry." Gerda is trying to remove my anxiety. Next day, before we leave for the night out in the town, I am under distress, telling her, "You must know that it is very embarrassing, but I am penniless."

"That is no problem," Gerda said. "Also, remember that I am the one that invited you. I never expected you to pay for anything. If it makes you feel better, you must know that I got promoted with a substantial increase of my salary, and that is just for starters. I have not yet climbed to the top of the ladder. Now get this, Ulbricht has promised me a car of my own next month, since my new position in the KPD [German Communist Party] requires more supervision in the different districts. The KPD is now the only party in the German government of the Soviet-controlled parts of Germany. The KPD is strictly interested in the welfare of a common Germany but is not able to minimize the rivalry between east and west. The friction between Russia and America must be stopped or both sides will slip into a state of isolation."

"I am glad to hear that your party has a political comprehension in favor of an all-German state, but my concern is will you be able to stop taking orders from Moscow? Just watch out," I told Gerda, "the moment each side starts printing their own money, then the hostility will turn into an economic war. West Berlin is already surrounded by the Russians. They can take all of Berlin back anytime, who is going to stop them? I certainly would not want to live on an island that is a time bomb for the rest of my life."

"Let us forget about politics. It is such a lovely day. It is time to go and have some fun," Gerda said, and off we went.

In a nice clean Italian restaurant, she ordered dinner and a bottle of Chianti wine. As most of the buildings in Berlin, the dance hall in the city also showed some damage, but repairs and cleaning made it possible to open up the place again. Before the war, there were more than one hundred dance halls and cabarets in Berlin with a swinging nightlife. During the war, dancing and jazz music were absolutely forbidden. Now, if I am correct, there was at least a dozen nightclubs back in business. Some of them were playing ragtime in a boisterous manner. The best—paying customers were members of the occupation armies. All of the soldiers, mostly American and British, were coming with their German girlfriends. The dance hall was very close to the border of the Potsdamer Platz. The plaza was cut up like a pie bordering the Russian, American, and British sectors. As Gerda and I had a good time dancing, shortly before midnight, a handful of animated Russian soldiers, apparently not knowing that they were in the wrong sector, entered the place and started bothering some women that refused to dance with them. As their men came to rescue them, they were beaten up by the Russians. That did not go right with the American and British soldiers; they started to stop the Russian attackers. In a few seconds, the dance hall turned into a battlefield—a few bloody heads and plenty of damage, a state of panic, women were screaming and hiding under the tables. Somebody called the MP, and they did break up the fight and arrested the Russian intruders. For Gerda and me, that was the end of our night out. Luckily, we got out of the place unharmed.

Dancing with Gerda after the war.

At the university, I was able to keep up with my daily classes. In chemistry, I was on top of it; in pharmacology everything was new to me, and I had to learn it. The work at the club was an easy job. I'd been doing it for the last three weeks now, and if there was an opening, I think I would be ready to work as a waiter. My hours were from 4:00 to 9:00 PM—that made it five hours a day. By the time I got home, it was 10:00 to 10:30 PM. At that time I was going straight to bed. I was eating my supper at the club. All I got was six hours of sleep every night; I wished I had a room to sleep between the university and the job. Today was the sixth of October; it was my dear mother's birthday. After I got out of the club, I was going to be free till Monday morning, giving us plenty of time to celebrate her birthday with a big chocolate cake I managed to purchase for the occasion at the club's own bakery. I arrived in Tegel and got off the train at 10:00 PM. Walking fast, I could make it in fifteen minutes. Somehow, I could not explain it. I had a funny feeling that something strange would happen or wait for me at home. Now here it was; I walked into the house and completely unexpected, I saw a man sitting at the table between my mother and my grandmother. For a moment I was stunned, and I almost dropped the cake. The man sitting between them, healthy and alive, was my own father. He got up, and we embraced each other.

"What a wonderful surprise," I said. "When did you get home, Dad?"

"I came home last night." We kept looking at each other, and then he said, "I cannot believe it that the young man in front of me is the boy I left behind some years ago."

I congratulated him for surviving the war and now came a long period of asking questions and giving answers to what each of us experienced. The long session of individual storytelling went on till early in the morning. To get some sleep, we just had to break it up, but next day we started it all over again, and we had so much to talk about that even the weekend would not be long enough to cover it all. Primarily we were trying to get reacquainted for all the years we have been apart and missed each other. During the conversations with my father, he told us how happy he was to be home again, to be reunited with his family, that we were all healthy and have the hope to restore our lives and futures, but he also said that what made him very sad was the fact that Grandfather got killed and that the Lindenhof neighborhood was completely destroyed, and naturally the general destruction of Berlin was very depressing for him too. My mother was apologizing to him (since her mother was living with us) that for the time being we were going to be somewhat crowded in the one-bedroom apartment with only one bathroom.

"Don't complain," my father said. "This is like heaven. You should have seen how we lived in the POW camp, over ten thousand men sleeping on the ground under open sky in rain and sunshine. The latrines were outside of the camp. No way to take a shower, and that lasted for four months."

"Maybe we can find a bigger apartment," my mother suggested.

"You have to face reality," my grandmother said. "In this town, full of homeless people, you could not find a vacant dog house. The only solution

I can come up with is the offer Senta made me to move in with her. She is all alone in the big house and afraid that they could make her share it with some refugees."

"Now," I said, as it was my turn to get in on the subject, "if anybody is moving out, it has to be me. Even if I had the apartment all by myself, I could not stay here any longer. Going to school and having a part-time job at the other end of town, I must have a room somewhere in the south. I am spending over three hours every day riding the train, valuable time I need to sleep and do my homework. I've seen some offers in the university at the bulletin board where they have some furnished rooms for students only. I am willing to take it even if it is just a hole in the wall to sleep."

"Well," my father agrees with me, "that is reasonable. You could not keep it up for three years traveling every day to and from Tegel. You simply must have enough time to study, or you will never graduate. Also, if you cut short on your sleep, you will get sick and have to quit."

Next Friday night, after I got out of the club, I went over to see Gerda. She greeted me tenderly but let me know that I looked tired and stressed. "Well," I said, "I had a very rough week."

"Relax," she said. "Make yourself comfortable and tell me all about it, but first let me know if you want anything to drink or eat."

"No, I am fine. I got something to eat at the club. By the way, I got you some coffee cake, I know you'll like it."

"Thank you for thinking about me. We will have it in the morning."

I was now beginning to tell Gerda about my father. She looked very surprised when I told her that he came home but did not interrupt me and didn't say anything till I told her all the conversations we had about everything. "I am happy for all of you, being together again. You cannot ask for anything more than being reunited with your family. There is one thing I don't agree with you. There is no need for you to look for a room. I encourage you to eliminate the extra travel time, but why live with strangers when you have a home here with me?"

"I would like nothing better than living with you. It would make me very happy, but you forget that I am just a pauper student that could not pay you."

"I don't need your money, I have enough money of my own. What I want is the man I love to be with me every day." Feeling humble and appreciative, I accepted Gerda's offer.

First I went back to Tegel at nights for a few more days till I got the few things, mainly books, that I possessed into my new room. What an advancement this was for me, from sleeping on the sofa in my mother's living room to having a room of my own. At the same time, I was advancing at the club from a busboy to a waiter. My pay had increased, and the tips I was getting were also giving me another financial boost. The weeks went by, and I was getting to know most of my steady customers. Being a waiter in a club was different from being a waiter in a public restaurant; in a club you see the same faces over and over again. Over time you would also get to know each of your customer's likes or dislikes. You try to please them, and they would become more friendly to you. My favored customer was a certain Major Bauermeister from Glendale, California, who came to the club every night to eat his supper. The major was in charge of the American administration office in Dahlem. His grandparents came from Hamburg, but he spoke only a few German words. His favored dish was a Wiener schnitzel, and I told the chef exactly how he liked it done. His family owned a big restaurant in Los Angeles, and he was a part owner. Peter and I had talked to the major many times, and he was giving us some good advice for our future.

One day, coming home from work, I saw a car parked in front that I had never seen before. It was an Opel sedan not older than two or three years. As Gerda opened the door for me, there was a smile all over her face. She must have seen me looking at the car. "That is right, what you are thinking?" Gerda said. "As of today, I am one of the few privileged city employees that has the advantage of driving a government car. I must congratulate you, and I am convinced now that you are a VIP of Ulbricht's inner circle. I have an idea. Let us take an early Christmas vacation and drive to the French Riviera. I understand it is beautiful there this time of the year."

"You dreamer, how far do you think we'll get with those license plates?"

"We can drive around Berlin and the Mark Brandenburg. There are so many places that I have not seen yet we can visit."

"Yes, you are right," I said. "Every weekend we can go someplace else. No more waiting for buses and trains. Best of all, we are not stranded missing the last train. As long as you have this car, I will stay with you."

"Wait a minute," Gerda wanted to know. "Who are you in love with, me or the car?"

"There is no question in my mind, both of you," I responded, smiling.

For openers next Sunday, we were going to visit Gerda's sister (my friend Egon's mother) at Kieler Strasse. It was now seven months ago when I found my first hiding place in a little room over the bakery at Kieler Strasse, thanks to the kindness of Egon's mother. At that time, the corner by the waterfront was a disaster area. This section of town was still surrounded by ruins, but the rubble had been removed, streets were cleaned, and plenty of repairs had been made. We found parking, and Gerda was getting anxious to see if her sister was home. The bakery was closed on Sunday, so we went upstairs to see if anyone was home. Luckily, her sister was in, and what a surprise it was for her to see both of us. She did not understand how we managed to show up at the same time. She remembered that her letter connected me with her sister, but she didn't know the rest of the story. Gerda told her all the details step by step. I didn't remember her saying anything to Gerda, at least not in front of me, for taking such a young lover. Egon's mother always treated me like a son.

"Now to you," Gerda said. "I see you are still alone. What have you heard from your family?"

"This is something I have to tell you. Both my husband and my son are still prisoners. My man wrote me a letter that he is held in an American POW camp and expects to be discharged soon. At least he is very anxious to come home. It took about two months for the letter to reach me and was finally forwarded by the International Red Cross to me. My son Egon is still in England. Officially he is still classified as a prisoner but volunteered to remain in an open labor camp. They work eight hours every day, get paid by the month, and are free to go to town."

"Why is he not coming home?" Gerda interrupted her sister. "Egon was always happy at home. There must be something else that is holding him back."

"Yes, there is." And his mother explained. "Egon was never much of a churchgoer, but one morning he did, and the minister invited him after the service for some coffee and doughnuts in the church hall. The family sitting next to him started a conversation with him as it was obvious that Egon was a stranger in the congregation, and they wanted him to feel as one of them. A beautiful girl sitting next to him was their daughter, and Egon could not stop looking at her. To make a long story short, her folks invited him the following Sunday for a chicken dinner, and now the two youngsters are going steady. They are in love and would not let go of each other."

"Well, that is a sweet real love story," Gerda exclaimed. "What is Egon going to do, is he planning to marry her and stay in England, or are they going to settle down in Germany?"

"Only God knows," her sister complained. "My guess is as good as yours."

"Let us not jump to any conclusion. I am putting my five cents into this conversation: England is not far from here, and if they are getting married, it does not really matter where they live. Once the Europeans get their act together, traveling from London to Hamburg is the same distance as from Hamburg to München and from München to London. In a triangle, all three cities are five hundred miles apart, which equals one hour of traveling time by air from city to city or eight hours by car from Hamburg to München."

"Boy, are you smart." Gerda wanted to know, "Where did you learn all that stuff?"

"That is nothing more than basic geography. I am only trying to make one point. It seems right now, with all our political boundaries, that the two families are worlds apart, when in reality they could visit each other on one weekend. It is a shame that men have developed a massive system of flying squadrons of bombers to destroy all major cities in Europe and at the same time they are unable to produce normal airports and a fleet of friendly airplanes regulated by international aeronautic standards."

"Do you think that could ever happen?" Gerda's sister asked me. "That we could travel with a plane like we are now taking a bus or the train?"

"The question is not if it would happen, it is only a question of when it will happen. In other countries, they have already made the first step in civil aeronautics." The two sisters kept talking till late in the evening and exchanged telephone numbers with the promise to stay in touch.

Next Sunday I was going to visit my parents to see how they were getting along. My father was feeling at home again, and he registered with the employment office but was not in a hurry to take any old job. He was trying to be reinstated to work for the government again. To regain his old status, he must first, like everybody else, undergo the process of denazification. In other words, he had to prove that he was not an NS Party member and demonstrate the accuracy of his statement by several witnesses that he was not guilty of a war crime. My grandmother was reading a letter from her daughter Senta; she was asking her again to come and live with her. Senta was complaining to her mother that she was depressed and did not want to be alone during the coming Christmas holidays. After my grandmother finished reading the letter, there was a moment of silence in the room. Nobody wanted to say anything; it was a decision my grandmother had to make. "I have five children," my grandmother said. "And I love them all equally, but whoever needs me the most, I will stay with them."

"That is a wise decision," my father agreed with her. "Go and take care of Senta. You and Senta are not far from us. We can come and visit you anytime."

A Conflict in Political Ideology

Weihnachten (Christmas) 1945 was the first year we were celebrating the holidays in peace. We didn't have much to give or to celebrate with, but those of us who survived the horrific experiences of World War II had a lot to be thankful for. Not all in our families had been reunited; millions of soldiers were still in prison camps, and millions of people were expelled from their homes and dispersed all over the world. Two members of my family that were the victims of such a crime were Erna and Ingeborg in Kremmen, which was in the Russian side. Some of the neighbors told the Russians that Erna was the widow of a dead Nazi officer. Mother and daughter were abused by the Russians; both women literally had to run away from the Russian soldiers. Their house and small ranch were confiscated by the Soviet government and given to a member of the German Communist Party. According to the editor of the Kremmen newspaper, they were now in a refugee camp in Mecklenburg. I later found out that the informer became the owner of Erna's house. When I discovered what happened to them, for days I was so angry and disturbed I could not hide it from anyone. Gerda noticed that something was bothering me, so I told her about the tragedy in our family.

My anger was directed at the brutality of the Red Army—some of the atrocities that I witnessed and the raping of our women and of my sweet Gisela, who paid with her life. How many German women were raped by Russian soldiers? We will never know; but after the war, it was estimated that two million women had been raped, and in Berlin alone up to 130,000 women of whom about 10,000 committed suicide. Other reports say that 60 to 70 percent of the total female population in East Germany were victims of rape by the Red Army.

I also told her that Hitler was right in one thing, that the danger of communism was the biggest evil known in our times.

"How can you quote a murderer that killed millions of people in his concentration camps?" she asked me in a rage.

"Very simple," I replied. "Stalin killed thirty million people in his own country, mainly in the Ukraine. That makes Hitler a Sunday school teacher compared to Stalin, and I know that two wrongs don't make one right. We are still facing one evil empire that has the ambition to conquer the world as Hitler did. Just look around and see what is going on. Compare how the Russians treat us and what the Americans are doing for us. My friend Peter and his mother had to surrender their villa to the American administration because they needed a certain location in Dahlem. It was well known by the Americans that Peter's father was one of the highest-ranking Nazi officers in Berlin. That did not matter to them at all. They approached the acquisition in a businesslike manner, offering them the option to sell or lease the villa to the American administration for a fair market price. The Eckards elected to lease the villa and are receiving their rent checks quarterly in advance. They are now living in the guesthouse. No American soldier will ever go over and rape Mrs. Eckard or kick them out half naked in the street in the middle of the night. I am very sorry, Gerda, I know where you are coming from. The last thing I want to do is hurt your feelings. I hope one day you'll see the truth. I am in no way defending the Nazi actions. I remember when I really believed the ideas they fed me since I was nine years old, and later, slowly my eyes were opened, and my dreams went up in smoke. Now I really believe in the Americans, and I am not ashamed to say it." After I lectured Gerda, she was really getting furious.

"You know what the trouble is with you?" Gerda told me. "Since you are working at the American club, you are smoking too many of their cigarettes, and that has pickled your brain. Every time an American farts in front of you, you think you smell the fine scent of perfume."

"I apologize for whatever I said that upsets you. All I am trying to outline to you are the extreme opposing different poles of human behavior—barbarism and civility. I am sorry you don't understand and have the sympathy for the pain I suffer for my relatives in the east." To end our first fight, I went to my room and closed the door behind me.

Next day we were making up, and everything between us was normal again. One good thing came out of yesterday's episode: I learned how deeply Gerda loved the Communist Party and how strongly she would defend the system. Ever since the end of the war, refugees in large numbers were migrating to the west in order to escape the Russian/Communist occupation. That was the first mass migration from the east because of the war, but now on a smaller scale eight months later, people from East Germany and East Berlin were beginning to move to West Germany and West Berlin. This created a drain of people, which the Communist Party was desperately trying to stop. Instead of upgrading the standard of living, they reinforced the borders to keep the people behind an iron curtain against their own will. As a direct result, the ring around Berlin was getting tighter and tighter. To move within the City between the different sectors was relatively easy, especially among the British, French, and American sectors, which were called West Berlin, and only the Russian sector was East Berlin. West Berlin was now beginning to be an isolated free island in the middle of a vast Soviet/Russian territory. Despite the political isolation, West Berlin was no longer suffering from a severe food shortage. Food was still rationed and by no means plentiful, but the long lines of people facing the grocery stores were gone. Whatever food stamps you present, you take home your ration for regular prices. Milk, eggs, and other perishable food items were often substituted in powder form or had to be transported in by the U.S. Air Force. The people of West Berlin didn't feel abandoned and were in good spirits; they started making preparations for the upcoming Christmas season. The spirit of hope was with them, and they showed it.

At the university (Humbolt University was located in the Russian sector of the city), the winter semester break would start in a few days and would last till early next year. That would give me the chance to catch up with my studies. This year I was very busy, and I decided not to make any visits over the holidays but just call my friends on the phone or send them a Christmas card. Gerda would be with her sister, my grandmother already left to stay with Senta, and after many years for, the first time my parents and I would be together, just the three of us like it used to be when I was a little boy. It would be a time to relive old memories.

The night before Christmas, Gerda and I had our own private little celebration. I was able to buy at the club two big boxes of chocolate candies already gift-wrapped, one for her and one for my mother. Employees of the club were also allowed to buy some liquor. I purchased two bottles of brandy. I was happy that I had a gift for my father; he liked brandy, and the other bottle Gerda and I started to work on after dinner, before we went to bed. This year we were having a white Christmas, which was a double blessing; it covered all the wounds of a destroyed city and helped you to get into some Christmas spirit. The biggest blessing I had received at this time was that I could eat most of my meals at the club and could save my own food ration coupons and share them with Gerda and my parents.

Christmas Eve, Gerda and I left the apartment at the same time. The nearest train station at her sister's place was the S-Bahnhof Wedding. At this point, I got off the car, and I was not far away from Tegel. My parents were already waiting for me. Whatever my mother was cooking smelled fantastic. In the living room was a cute little Christmas tree all decorated with colorful ornaments and candles. For dinner we were having potato dumplings and Sauerbraten with brown gravy and red cabbage, my father's favored dish. He deserved it as we were also celebrating his homecoming from the war. We felt blessed to have been able to have such meal. For a long time we couldn't have normal meals. There were even those times when we had no meals at all.

After dinner we were having a brandy, and I gave my father a pack of American cigarettes. He really appreciated both; for years he had not enjoyed a shot of brandy and he never tasted before in his life an American cigarette. My mother was very happy with her box of candies; she even had a gift for me. I tore open the wrapper, and there was a beautiful hand-knitted blue vest that I could wear with any jacket. I put it on, and it fit perfectly. I asked my mother if I received any mail, and she gave me a letter from Inge, who wished us all a merry Christmas and let me know that Bruno and she were doing fine but wanted me to call sometimes, and said that we must get together in the New Year. Christmas Day and New Year's Eve, I had to work in the afternoon. I asked Gerda if she wanted to come to the New Year's Eve party at the club; she told me that she was already invited to go with the girls from the office. Peter invited his mother, and I had the chance to talk to Hildegard. She told me that she was not really in the mood to celebrate as her husband was not with her, but Peter insisted that she should go with him and not stay alone at home. "Well," I said, "I certainly agree with him, and it is nice to see you. Inge wrote me a letter telling me that Bruno and she are getting along great, and they asked me to come and visit them."

"That is great." Hildegard encouraged me to go and see them. "I am sure Inge told Bruno that you took good care of her before and after Gisela died, and he is trying to show his appreciation."

"That goes both ways," I replied. "Of course, nobody suffers like a mother does, but Inge also was a great comfort to me. I was very much in love with Gisela." It was getting very busy now at the restaurant, so I had to break up our conversation and go back to work. At seven o'clock, I started taking orders for tonight's special dinner. Even though that I had to work till 2:00 AM, it was a marvelous New Year's party.

CHAPTER XII

FINAL ESCAPE TO FREEDOM

Last Year in Berlin

The year 1946 was a turning point politically for Berlin, as well as for the destination of my own life. The quarrel between SPD and KPD, the two ruling parties in the city government, was boiling to a state of rupture reaching soon a splitting division between East and West Berlin that could not be reversed. I was still attending the Humboldt University in East Berlin and had my job in the American sector. There were some rumors that changes would be made for students living outside of East Berlin. One evening I was serving the major, and I was having a nice conversation with him. He asked me what I knew about a German camera by the name Leica; I told him only what I heard. It was the first 35 mm camera ever developed, famous for its precision optic made by Zeiss Icon. "This must be true," he replied, "because every GI coming to Germany is trying to get a hold of one. One of its desirable features is the compact design, never seen by any other camera on the market. If you could get me one, I will pay you a commission."

"I will try my best to locate one for you," I said. "But I refuse to take one red cent from you."

The two most important black markets were located at the Potsdamer Platz and at the Bahnhof Zoo. At the latter, things were handled with less commotion, and it had not the atmosphere of a flea market. Dealers were whispering to prospective customers and went someplace else to consummate a transaction. Very seldom was the merchandise changing hands at the same place. If you saw a person with a camera hanging around the neck walking up and down the place, you could be sure that it was not a tourist. Ask him or her how much, and they would tell the price they had in mind, but you could always bargain them down. At the Potsdamer Platz, the commodities in trade were usually food items and paid for with cigarettes. At the Bahnhof Zoo, things that were for sale belonged to the more-higher-priced category like gold, jewelry, fur coats, and cameras. These luxury items were almost exclusively acquired with US dollars through a German agent and taken back to America by some member of the military. It was all ruled by the law of supply and demand, and nowhere was it more true than in the city of Berlin. Running the risk of being arrested, hungry people flocked to the black markets every day, searching for some food and willing to give away their golden wedding band if they could bring home some extra food for their family. The first time I went to Bahnhof Zoo, I could not find what I was looking for. Several cameras were for sale, but no Leica was among them. I believed that I might have better luck if I brought Gerda along. Next time we went going on a Saturday. Major Bauermeister gave me two hundred dollars to deal with at my judgment as a barter.

As a University student in 1946

Gerda brought some money of her own; and we were walking around among the crowd, acting like we had some time to spare before we caught our train. So far we had only seen a few people with cameras for sale. One woman pushing a baby carriage up and down caught Gerda's eyes. The woman stopped in front of us, and we were convinced she was not going to show us her baby. She opened the conversation by saying, "I have a terrific bargain for you for the price I am asking." Slowly lifting one corner of the blanket, she kept saying, "Look, this is a complete new dinner set for twelve of rare Meissen porcelain. Today it will be yours for only two hundred dollars."

Gerda answered, "That is a good price, and you should have no problem selling it, but we are on the road looking for a camera."

"You see the man over there by the newsstand with the briefcase, he has some cameras for sale." Now it was my turn, and I casually strolled over to the man to see what he had to offer.

"Hi," I said, "what is new today?"

"What are you looking for?" He came right to the point.

"I might be interested in a camera, if the price is right."

"What kind of a camera?" he wanted to know."

"If it is in good shape, I might go for a Leica."

"It is in excellent condition," he told me. "And for only two hundred dollars, it is a hell of a deal."

"Two hundred dollars is a lot of money these days. Let's go someplace, and I will have to take a good look at it first," I said.

"You should, so you know what I am talking about. Let us go over to Uhland Strasse. There is a little café where we have more privacy."

Gerda and I followed the stranger. At the café, sitting in an out-of-the-way corner, we had all the time to look at the camera he was putting in front of us. It was a very clean Leica with no dents or scratches on the outside; the lens was clear and clean. He was winding up the camera, and every time I pushed the button as the camera was open, I could see the gears of the train for the film moving. All the dials and settings for the speed and focus of the camera were working. After I put the camera back on the table, he guaranteed me that I would be happy with the camera and that it would not lose on value.

"Let me explain to you, the camera is not for me. I am just a middleman like you are, and I am authorized not to pay more than one hundred fifty dollars, and that is the best offer I can make you, take it or leave it."

"If I sell it to you for one hundred fifty," he lamented, "I would not make any profit."

"Trust me," I say, trying to make him feel better, "there is no money in it for me either." He hesitated to accept my offer, and as Gerda and I were ready to get up, he was holding us back and was taking my offer. I put the camera in my pocket and paid him the one-hundred-fifty-dollar cash.

On the way home, Gerda said that I drove a hard bargain. Maybe so, but I was happy to report to the major about what I was able to accomplish for him. The major was delighted with his new camera, and he wanted me to keep the leftover fifty dollars, but I was firm in refusing him. "OK," he said, "I give in, but if I see a chance to make it up to you, I will." The major told me that he was homesick. Right now, in Southern California, the sun was shining; there was no winter. It was summer weather all year round. He showed me pictures of his hometown of Los Angeles—beaches, palm trees, and outdoor swimming pools. At the same time, we were sitting here in Berlin all bundled up surrounded by snow and ice.

On the fifth of February was my father's birthday. I asked him if there was anything I could bring him, and he insisted that he was taken care of and that I should save my money. "Well," he said, "if you bring me some of your American cigarettes, I wouldn't say no to that." From my Hitler Youth days at school, I remembered being taught that smoking was not good for your health, and I knew that my father was a heavy smoker and was addicted to cigarettes, and I should not support his habit. On the other hand, if I told him to stop smoking, he was not going to listen to me anyway, so it was his birthday, let him have the cigarettes. On my father's birthday, my grandmother and Senta were also coming to visit my parents. Senta told us the good news that Heinz had been released from the POW camp and was now in his hometown, Mainz, staying with his parents while he was building a house. He asked Senta and my grandmother to come to West Germany as soon as the house was ready. Senta was very excited, but my grandmother still needed to be persuaded to go and live with them.

On March the 5, 1946, Churchill, at Fulton, Missouri, United States of America, presented in the presence of President Truman the need for Britain and the United States to unite for world peace against the menace of Soviet communism and their ambition for global expansion about Russia's policy. Churchill declared, "Beware . . . time may be short . . . from Stettin in the Baltic to Trieste in the Adriatic, an iron curtain has descended across the continent of Europe."

One day that month of March I asked Gerda if she would come along and drive me over to Wilmersdorf to see Inge and Bruno. Gerda agreed, and I called Inge at work to set it up for the following Sunday. At the club, I purchased a cake, and Gerda managed to get a hold of some flowers. The reception at Inge's house was very cordial; I introduced Gerda to both of them, and they were happy about our visit. Gerda knew the whole story and that they were the parents of my deceased girlfriend, Gisela. Inge greeted us as we arrived and ushered us into the living room. Bruno looked a lot better than when I saw him shortly after he came home from the Russian front. Instead of a ragged, dirty uniform, he was now dressed up in a suit; and I could see that he had put on the extra weight he needed. He also looked younger being shaven and having short hair. As Inge was serving some refreshments, Bruno told us how grateful he was to be home again. "I am still sitting at home not doing very much," he said, "but it will not be long, and one of these days, I will be walking again without crutches. The first thing I am going to do is go back to work and have my wife stay at home the way it should be."

"Don't rush it," Inge said. "I love my job, and if the peaceful situation continues in the future, we have nothing to worry about. Tell me, Gerda, what are you doing for a living?" Inge asked her.

"I have been a secretary all my life long, and I am working for the city of East Berlin. Recently I have been promoted to be the private secretary of Walter Ulbricht."

"Yes," I said, "that is why she is able to drive a car that comes with the job."

"Are you still going to school?" was Inge's next question now directed to me.

"I do, and I am also working part-time at the American club in Dahlem. Peter got me a job as a waiter, he is also still working there as a bartender. He invited his mother on New Year's Eve to the club, and I had a chance to talk to Hildegard. She hopes to be as lucky as you are, for her husband to come home, but they have not heard a word from him yet."

"What about your father?" Bruno got in on the conversation. "Has he returned from the war?"

"Oh yes, we are very lucky. He came home last October, right on my mother's birthday."

"Coming home so early!" Bruno assumed. "He must have had a short and easy stay with the Americans."

"Don't take it for granted that all prisoners captured by the Americans are getting three meals a day and a bed to sleep in," I replied. "Unfortunately, according to my dad, they put him in a camp with 90 percent SS soldiers and officers. The treatment he received was horrible and inhumane. The fact that he was a member of the Luftwaffe saved his life and let him have an early discharge. He is now shuffling coal eight hours a day for the local Gas Co., a low-paying job he had to take to receive his food ration cards. Normally, after working twenty years for the post office, plus his military time, he could retire and receive his government pension, but these are not normal times."

"Sounds familiar," Bruno said. "I was once a captain in a fire station. Now I would be happy if the fire department would give me a desk job."

"Let us not give up hope," Gerda said. "We all went through hell and back. Most of us even lost some loved ones, things can only get better."

"I drink to that," Inge said, and she put a bottle of French brandy in front of Bruno to open it while she was getting out the snifters, arranging them next to us. Bruno filled his glass half full, then he passed the bottle to me, and I poured Gerda's glass. Slowly I turned around and looked at Inge, then I pointed at the label and looked back at her face; she was acknowledging. While I was taking my time pouring her glass, she was looking at me; and without saying anything to each other, our minds were communicating, going back to the days and all the events we lived through together, including the acquisition of the case with the bottles of brandy. We were reliving memories that were bittersweet for us. Inge and I were so close in misery and adventures in the past, outliving even the tragedy of losing our beloved Gisela, but now we were worlds apart. Our lives had taken their normal and hopefully happy course, even though in different directions. I showed her my affection with a subtle smile.

After the second drink, Inge was suggesting that we should now have our coffee and cake, a ritual no German would ever miss on a Sunday afternoon. The two women got up, went over to the kitchen to brew some coffee. Bruno and I were having a chance to talk man to man. "Today, that I know who you really are, I see a little bit of Gisela living in you," Bruno said. "We are sharing the same pain, that brings you closer to Inge and me."

"Those words you just said would make Gisela really happy if she could hear us."

"This house is your home," Bruno assured me. "You come and see us anytime."

A noise was coming in from the kitchen. "Can you guys smell the coffee?" Gerda said. "I really love that smell." We were all sitting down, beginning instantly to enjoy the coffee and cake.

"This is the best cheesecake I ever had in my life. Where did you get it from?" Inge wanted to know.

"What you are eating is a special order, New York cheesecake," I was explaining to them, "coming in frozen to Berlin all the way from America."

"Is that so?" Gerda was telling me in disbelief. "I never heard of such a thing."

"Maybe you have not, but it is a fact, and the American GIs can't get enough of it. They prefer cake from an American bakery as well as other food items."

The conversation went on till the end of the day; and just as we were ready to go home, Inge pulled me over to the side. She opened her purse, trying to give me some money. "What is that for?" I wanted to know. "You don't owe me any money."

"Yes, I do," Inge said. "I sold three bottles of our French brandy at the black market, and I got a good price for it."

"Good for you. I want you to do me a favor and sell the rest of what is left. Take all the money and get Bruno fitted for an artificial limb. It may not be enough money, but at least you can get somebody started to work on it."

"I already made some contacts, and what they tell me is very encouraging. Dr. Sauerbruch, the famous surgeon, has made a revolutionary breakthrough in the development of new artificial limbs. I really appreciate what you are doing for Bruno, and we will be forever thankful," Inge said.

In the back our apartment house in Tegel after a major air raid.

Finally the communist rebels are pushed back into East-Berlin

A close up of a hand to hand struggle between
West-Berlin police and the communist agitators

After the communist invasion is broken up,
the West-Berliners are going home

A ruin with trees growing on top in East-Berlin has never been destroyed by the communist government.

West-Berliner are climbing a wall of reclaimed bricks to watch the street-battle at Bernauer Strasse

West-Berlin police are taking violent demonstrators into custody.

Mass demonstration of communist Youth in West-Berlin

Isolation and Civil Insurrection

At the end of April, I was taking my midterm exam; the twenty-second of this month was also the day the two major political parties in Berlin, the SPD and the KPD, were separating. The Soviets were out to establish in Berlin a one-party system only by fostering the Communist Party. Under pressure, the leaders of the SPD (Otto Grotewohl) and the KPD (Wilhelm Pieck) merged to form a new party called the SED (Socialist Union Party), being nothing but a concealment of the old KPD. The loyal members of the SPD retreated to West Berlin and became the core of a new independent SPD, the ruling party in the west sector. As a result, the gap in the division between east and west was getting bigger, and the first violent confrontations at the borders were taking place. The first of May, normally known as a day of peaceful celebration for the working class, was now being misused by the SED. They sent a huge organized assembly of workers and youth groups in uniform over to West Berlin to forcefully demonstrate to inspire the people in the West to join the revolution of international communism. The few policemen in the west sector were not able to stop the crowd; only the American MP was able to disperse the mass demonstration of East German agitators and push them back across the border to East Berlin. I was very sad that Gerda could not, or would not, see the truth; it did create some friction in our relationship.

Two major events were taking place in June of 1946. As I stayed one weekend with my parents in Tegel, my grandmother and Senta came to visit us. In a way, it was a sad day for all of us, especially for me and my grandmother. They came to say good-bye to us as they were on the way to Mainz to live there permanently in the house that Heinz built for all of them. Somehow, Grandmother and I had the presentiment that we would never see each other again in this life. The second event encouraged me to make the most important decision that changed my life forever. What so far was only an ugly rumor was now becoming a bitter reality. All of us students living in West Berlin received a letter from the administration signed by the dean of the university. We were given two options, either move to East Berlin or we would be expelled from the university at the end of this semester. The ultimatum I received upset me very much. I was always hoping to be with the university till the day I graduated. To move out of West Berlin and into East Berlin was absolutely no option for me; my moral conviction would not let me be intimidated by the ruthless dominion of communism. One night at the club, Major Bauermeister sensed that there was a problem in my mind, and he asked what was upsetting me. I explained to him how my career at the university had ended. The major was like a father to me, and he was always giving good advice. As I served him another cup of coffee, he started telling me, "This is not the end of the world. You have so many options left. In my life, every time something went wrong, there was always something much better coming along. Take a break at your education, you are still young. I know for sure that pretty soon they will open a new university in West Berlin. If you don't want to wait go to West Germany, they have all kinds of universities."

"But I don't know anybody in West Germany. I would be a total stranger," I told him.

"Well, go a step farther west to the land of unlimited opportunities, do like my grandparents did, take a boat and go all the way to America. They had no education, they did not even speak one word of English. You will have a good future better than in Germany. Many emigrants had to pump gas in a filling station, or they washed dishes in a restaurant, but today they are millionaires. I don't want to tell you what to do, but whatever you do, stay cool and don't panic."

"I really appreciate what you are telling me, and I will think about it. Maybe we can talk about it more some other time."

At the end of the semester in July, I put in my resignation and received a certificate of attendance and report card. At the club, they were so busy that they offered me a full-time job, which I accepted gladly. I had made one decision, that I would not go over to the east and join the communists. Maybe my disrespect for communism went back to the days when I was under the influence of Nazi teachings. As much as the NS regime had disappointed us youngsters of the Hitler Youth, they were right in one respect: communism would be the world's biggest danger. I was telling my parents that I was forced to leave the university, and they felt sorry for me. I also let them know that I was contemplating on getting out of Berlin. My mother was not saying anything, but I interpreted her silence as "We don't want you to go away from us again." They both would like me to stay close to them, but my father put his personal feelings behind by saying, "You do whatever you think is best for you. I don't want to be pessimistic, but the way it looks, Berlin is not much of a place for a great future. The biggest fiasco would be if the Russians are annexing West Berlin by force." By repeating what my father said to the major, he assured me that this would never happen.

"How can you be so sure?" I wanted to know. "Berlin is an island encircled by East Germany with no manpower to defend it. For the Russians it would be a cakewalk to come into West Berlin and close that circle since they have control over all the surrounding area."

"Very true," the major said. "But they also know that in two hours, General Patten's Third Panzer Army would be in Berlin to kick ass so fast it will make their heads spin."

"In my opinion," I told him, "that would be the beginning of World War III."

"Precisely, that is my point," the major said. "They cannot afford to mess with us knowing that we will defend Berlin. There is one thing I have to agree with your father: Berlin does not have much of a future to offer for a young man like you. Politically and economically, Berlin will be a testing ground between east and west for a long time to come. If I were you, I would avoid all the struggle and stress by getting out of Germany altogether."

"If I understand you correctly, you are suggesting I immigrate to America."

"All I want you to do is consider my recommendation. The rest is up to you."

"I have spend many nights thinking about it, and I have reached the conclusion that it would be the best for me, but I don't want to set my hopes too high. First of all, I don't know how to go about it. Secondly, they may not even be interested in taking me."

"Well," the major said, "your chances, if I help you, are almost 100 percent. You are young, healthy, honest, educated, single, and speak English. These are the kinds of people America has always taken with open arms. To get a visa, all you need is a sponsor, a letter of employment, and a clean bill of health from your local police office. I will sponsor you and will give you a letter of employment at the same time. A berth on a freighter should be not more than a hundred dollars. First of all, order a passport, then go to the American embassy and apply for a U.S. visa." I did follow the major's instructions, and now I was waiting to be called for an interview with the U.S. consul.

Early in August, ironically, Gerda received a similar notice as I did to move to East Berlin by the end of the year or jeopardize her high-ranking position with the East Berlin city government. Gerda showed me the letter and asked seriously about my feelings at the possibility of her moving to the east side. I had to think hard and carefully put my words together as I answered: "I am very comfortable here with you, but where the future of your life is concerned, it would be very irresponsible on my part to try to influence you as to what is best for you. You have a lot of experience and plenty of time to decide. Think about all the pros and cons before you make a move. At this time, I might tell you what is on my mind and what I am trying to accomplish. As you well know, my career at the university will come to an end the moment I refuse to move to East Berlin. Overnight I can lose my purpose for staying in Berlin, which is my career."

For a few days, I was mentally completely devastated. A good friend helped me to snap out of it and made me an offer too good to decline. He would sponsor and help me to get a visa to immigrate to the United States. If they would not accept my application and turn me down, in that case, I would move to West Germany and go to university there. In either case, I decided to leave Berlin for good at the end of the year or earlier.

Talking to Gerda later on, she told me, "If I understand correctly, our relationship is about coming to an end, and it is all over between us?"

"Let's see how things develop," I explained to her. "If I end up in West Germany and you would come with me, we could probably stay together. It all depends on which way you choose to go. Like I said, sleep on it and find out what will be the most important thing in the future of your life."

A few days later, Gerda told Ulbricht tentatively that she was willing to move to East Berlin provided he could find a house for her to live in. The next few weeks, neither of us heard anything positive in our own endeavors. But in September, the Communist Party offered Gerda a house of her own in a good neighborhood in Treptow, free and clear, and she would get a good title to it. The house still had to be restored, and she would be able to move in the first week in November. Gerda gladly accepted the offer, hoping that I would go with her and go back to school. She was a career woman, could never have children, and she said to me that in her age, she could not find a similar job like the one she had. I was convinced that in her position she made the right choice. In the meanwhile, I received a date to appear at the U.S. Immigration Office to come for an interview. Everything went all right; they sent me for a physical examination and gave me some papers for the major to fill out. I received my passport in the mail, and step-by-step, I was complying with all the requirements to get my visa. My parents were also well informed about my application for a visa to the United States; I even needed their written consent since I was still a minor in the eyes of the law (seventeen). My father signed the papers, and both of them wished me good luck. "If I was younger," my father said, "we would go with you."

The following weekend, Gerda and I were driving over to the east sector to inspect Gerda's new house in Treptow. Treptow is a small town in the southeast part of Berlin. Gerda's house was next to the Treptow Park near the Spree River, a two-story Victorian-style little villa with a nice backyard. The kind of architecture you find in Dahlem and Wannsee. The back door was open, and we were able to see the inside of the house, but they were still painting and fixing the floors. There was a large living room, two bathrooms, a huge kitchen, and four bedrooms. Gerda was so excited; she kept telling me how much she loved the house with the view, the garage, and the fireplace in the living room. "Take two rooms for yourself," Gerda said to me. "Pick the two rooms you like the most."

She took it for granted, after we inspected the house, that I liked the mansion too and would move in with her. She believed the most important thing for me was the chance to go back to university; that part was true, but I could not live under the Communist rule, and I would not live in the east. I could not be easily blinded by the beautiful large house. Deep in my heart, I hoped to get my visa to the United States. On the way home, Gerda was in a very good mood; all she talked about was her new house.

When we got back to her house, she opened a bottle of wine to celebrate the event. She put extra effort that night when she made love to me, like trying to persuade me to go with her to Treptow. In the morning, when I woke up, Gerda kissed me, asking, "Are you still in love with me?"

I answered, "Yes, I am."

"Are you ready to give all of this up for a ticket to America?"

"No, I am not." Somehow I knew that I was fooling myself; I couldn't tell her otherwise as she had the talent to please me and dominate me at the same time. But I felt that she no longer had the complete control over me like she had at the beginning when she introduced me to lovemaking. Even though I was still a teenager, all the dangers and the life experiences packed in my last year somehow helped me to mature, and I knew that I didn't have a future with her. There were a lot of issues between us; among the most important ones the fact that she embraced communism and that I refused to live under that system, and the age difference. I was seventeen; she must have been in her midthirties.

I also knew that was my last summer in Berlin. I loved Lake Tegel, the Wannsee, and the Grunewald—these beautiful places the war did not destroy—and nevertheless, I was willing to give it all up for a better future. Right then I was living in suspense; from day to day, I hoped to find out which route my life would take. Finally, at the end of October, I was notified that my application had been accepted, and that I would receive a permanent immigrant visa to enter the United States of America. For a moment, my heart stopped beating, then I was jumping for joy. A dream that day became a reality for me, and I saw myself already in the new world. This was my lucky day, and the first person I told the good news was my sponsor, Major Bauermeister. He was also very happy about it and would arrange passage for me from Bremerhaven to New York to Los Angeles. He told me that everything would be prepaid and later deducted in payments from my salary. He already informed his brother, who was running the restaurant in Glendale, about my coming to work for him. He drew me a map on a piece of paper and wrote directions as to how to get from the airport in Los Angeles to Glendale. He estimated that my sailing time would be the later part of December.

Next in line for the good news were my parents. Here I had to deal with an emotional factor; they were not ready to accept the fact that I was moving away from them to the other side of the globe. I had to give them time, but they loved me and wanted the best for my future.

Finding the words to tell Gerda about the new direction my life had taken was not easy for me. As I fumbled to put a sentence together, she already knew what I was going to tell her. She made the conversation short and to the point by saying, "We have to follow the road that is good for us, even if each of us has to go a different way." I could see in her eyes the glimpse of a tear, but at the same time, I saw the mature woman that knew exactly what she wanted and how she was going about it; and I had a feeling that she had already accepted what was coming. At that moment, nothing was said anymore as we were both preoccupied with handling our own present inner feelings and our anticipation for our new separate dreams. We hugged and kissed for the last time, like trying to preserve the memory of that moment. In the first week of November, Gerda moved to her beloved house in Treptow.

I spent the last few days with my parents. Saying good-bye was difficult, not knowing when or if we would ever see each other again. First I saw Peter and his mother, and then Inge and Bruno. It was also hard to face Inge and Bruno for the last time. But all of them, they were the most understanding people, and they supported my decision to seek a better life and wished me the best of luck in my new endeavor.

More pleasant and happier was the farewell party I received on my last day of employment at the American club. To me the club was more than just a working place; you could almost call it a second home. All the guys and girls working there respected each other and interacted like a big family; I knew I would miss them all. Much do I owe to Major Bauermeister; he was my benefactor who made it possible for me to have a better chance in life to be successful. Conferring me with such an enormous opportunity made me immensely obligated to him. Shaking hands with him for the last time, I could not find the right words to thank him enough for what he had done for me. "I sincerely hope," I said, "that sometime down the road we will meet again and that I would be able to return the favor."

"You owe me nothing," he replied. "As far as meeting again in the future, that can be arranged. The day my two years are up in Berlin, I will retire from the army and return to California. When you stop being a waiter and move on, leave your forwarding address with my brother at the restaurant, and I will contact you."

"That is a promise," I said. "And if I should ever get married, you will be my best man." One of the American customs was, where there was a party, there was a cake. At the end of my party, they insisted that I should take the rest of the cake home. I did, and it served as a treat for my parents. To make my departure less dramatic, I prepared my parents in advance that I was just out of sight for some time; by no means would this be permanent.

"We are going to stay in communication at all times, either by letter or periodically with a transatlantic telephone call."

"As soon as I have achieved some success, I will send you the money, and you can come and visit me for six months or stay, if you can live without ice and snow, should you like it in sunny California. There is also the possibility that for one reason or another, I may not want to stay in America. In that case, I could be back in Germany very soon. Here is what I want you to remember: by the time you come to visit me, a trip to America will take less than a day's time. You will not go by boat and spend ten days crossing the Atlantic Ocean, like I do. You will fly with a commercial airliner from Frankfurt to New York. In New York you take another airplane and fly from the East Coast across the continent directly to the West Coast and get off the plane in Los Angeles. There I will be waiting for you and drive you home in my new car. I imagine that in the future, they will have travel clubs that will arrange charter flights with round trips at a certain time for much less money."

"You make it all sound," my father said, "like the whole thing going to America is nothing more than a vacation trip to the French Riviera." The moment my parents had overcome the fear of time and distance, it made our parting somewhat easier.

To be all together the last few days, my father took a leave of absence from his job. With whatever food was available, my mother was trying to please me with some dishes that she knew I liked. It was already November, but the weather was still dry and not too cold; we were taking advantage of it by walking every day, either to the Steinberg, Lake Tegel, or to the forest. We also went and did some last-minute shopping. Glancing at all the ruins around every corner, I shook my head, and my father said ironically, "Take a good look at all the rubble, this is the last time. Day after tomorrow there will be nothing that will ever remind you of the war again."

"I don't mind forgetting about the war," I said. "But I would rather take a better image of Berlin with me." The next day I started packing my knapsack, the only piece of luggage I would take with me. As soon as I would get to California, I would not need any more winter clothes. I took only what I needed and things that were light to carry. A good pair of shoes and my trench coat were essential.

Last picture taken in Berlin December 1946
on my way to West Germany

Today was the last day of November, and I was going to depart. My parents wanted to go with me across Berlin to the eastern border where I was going to take a bus at the other side. But I talked them out of it; instead, I suggested that they come with me just to the S-Bahnhof in Tegel and save themselves the trouble of going across town. They agreed, and together we were walking to the train station. I just missed one train and the next one was to arrive in thirty minutes. Sitting in the waiting room, my mother was giving me last-minute advice how to be careful and to take good care of myself. I assured her that I would take care, and I promised them that I would write every week. Finally the train arrived; a short but very emotional good-bye took place, and suddenly we were out of sight, and God only knew when or if we would see each other again. Sitting by the window for the last time, I said good-bye to my hometown and started to daydream about the past. My mind took me back to Kieler Strasse, to Tegel, the lake, and the old schoolhouse; and then I saw Gisela, and a pain went through my heart thinking of her. The sight of Berlin's total destruction reminded me of my firefighting days and the air battle at the Schmargendorf Flak Battery. I realized that this was all history and that I should put all the Berlin memory of previous occurrences back into the faculty of my subconscious mind and start concentrating on the new chapter of my life, which I was about to embark on. Crossing the border from East Germany to West Germany was getting increasingly more difficult. Crossing from West Berlin to East Germany did not present much of a problem. The disadvantage were the larger growing amounts of Volks Polizei (East German Police) stopping everybody trying to get out of the Russian zone into West Germany. Russian sentries were also guarding the border, shooting at anybody making an attempt to escape, regardless if they were trying to get in or out of East Germany. I had researched the situation and decided that I would cross the border up north in the less-populated area, then the main route at Helmstedt. In Gesundbrunnen near downtown, I switched trains and proceeded with another S-Bahn going to Spandau. Two more stations, and the end of the line was Staaken, a small town at the border. Getting off the train, I was walking to the Grenzkontrollstelle (border control check point) at Heer Strasse. At the west side in Staaken, I was already in East Germany. Two policemen were busy checking a truck going to West Berlin and were not paying any attention as I crossed the border.

    At a greasy spoon restaurant, I had some potato soup and black bread for lunch. I talked to the waitress, and she told me how to get to the bus station. Walking a few blocks, I reached the local bus stop. A waiting room next to a parking lot was a dirty place with some wooden benches smelling like a boxcar full of venereal-disease-infected monkeys. I really didn't have much choice but to go into the room full of tobacco smoke so thick that you could hardly see across the room. It was cold outside, and I had to find out at what time I could catch the bus to Wittenberge at the river Elbe. Wittenberge is the bordertown in East Germany about 120 kilometers from here. The bus, if it was on time, was scheduled to leave Staaken at 4:00 PM and should arrive in Wittenberge at 7:00 PM. A prior to WW II vintage bus was pulling in on time, and people traveling to Neustadt or Wittenberge were boarding the bus. The old diesel engine brought it up to speed, but you could feel every pothole in the road; obviously the bus was in need of new shocks. To say something nice, I had to admit that the heater was working. It was getting dark outside, and I was trying to take a nap, a short slumber, and then at about 5:30 PM, the bus arrived at Neustadt for a fifteen-minute bathroom stop and to take on new passengers for the rest of the trip to Wittenberge. At the end of the journey, the bus driver brought his chattering coach to a sudden stop, screaming from the top of his lungs, "End station, *alle aussteigen*" (end of the line, everybody off), loud enough to wake up the dead.

Near the bus station I was happy to find a room in an old but clean hotel for five marks a night, including breakfast. I slept well, but this morning, I got up early to put a plan together on how to cross the border. Maybe I should talk to some local people about the best way to do it, but first my stomach had priority, and I was going downstairs to the dining room for some food. There were already many people seated for breakfast. At a buffet, everybody got the same thing—toast, *Bratkartoffeln* (cottage fries), one boiled egg, and tea. With a tray in my hands, I looked for an empty table, but I could not locate one. There was one young lady sitting alone on her table, noticing how helpless I was. She came to my rescue by inviting me to share a table with her. I introduced myself, and her name was Anna Peters. During our conversation, it turned out that she was a local girl on business in Wittenberge. Anna had spotted me immediately for somebody that was trying to get out of East Germany.

Lüneburger Heide

She made it clear by asking me for what reason I was abandoning the glorious communist state. "I am not escaping at all," I told her. "I am a pharmacy student at the Humboldt University in Berlin on the way to the Lüneburger Heide."

Anna wanted to know, "What on earth is a pill pusher looking for in a godforsaken heath moorland?"

"As a prerequisite to graduate, each student has to produce a herbarium," I explained to her.

Again, she asked me impatiently, "What the hell is a herbarium?"

"Don't be intolerant, I am trying to give you a description. A herbarium is a press-dried collection of medicinal plants arranged in a book form. One of the best places in West Germany to find a good variety of species listed in the DAB 6 Deutsches Arznei Buch (German Pharmacopoea) is the Lüneburger Heide." I could see that my story was not very convincing; that was why I showed Anna my student pass from the university. "Somehow I have the feeling that you are going to discourage me from passing the border to the west. If that is the case, I am about to forget the whole thing and will make a U-turn to go back."

"You will go home and start blaming yourself for not giving it your best shot," Anna said. "I don't think you should give it up that easy since you are now already close to your project. The border is only twenty kilometers from here."

"It may be easy for you living in these parts around the river Elbe, you propably know every corner in this section. My chances are, not knowing the borderland, I will walk right into a nest of border guards."

"You have a point there," Anna said. "It would be better if you had some help to cross the border."

"Do you know somebody that would take on the job?" I asked her. "I will pay with a carton of American cigarettes."

"You must be really desperate to get your silly weeds from the Lüneburger Heide. I might be able to help you. As I told you, I am here on business in Wittenberge. My contact will come at noon to the hotel, check the merchandise in my room, and pay me COD. After we close the transaction, I am going back tonight across the border to West Germany. If you don't ask me what I am smuggling, I will take you across the river with me."

"It is a deal," I said. "I do trust you and will not ask any questions."

"Be ready and wait for me in the lobby at noon; it may be that I am a few minutes late." After she said that, we parted to go to our individual rooms.

Ten minutes after twelve, Anna showed up carrying a big handbag over her shoulder; she was wearing pants, an overcoat, and hiking boots. Both of us were now going back to the bus station. Buses to or from Wittenberge were connected with all major cities in East Germany. There were only two local bus lines serving the little communities around the Elbland. We were taking the bus that was going north along the river Elbe toward Dömitz but got off at Olenzen twenty kilometers outside of Wittenberge. It was only a half-hour drive, but the bus was packed with people. All seats were taken, and we must ride standing. The dirt road was uneven, and the bus driver had a talent for finding every pothole. The Opel bus was on its last leg, a 1936 model; it had balding tires, a leaky radiator, a clutch that slipped, and a loud knock in the engine. I was holding myself to the handrail overhead and spread my feet on the floor, but each lurch took me by surprise, and the metal back of the seat behind me hit my back with a sickening thud that jarred every nerve in my spine. Some twenty minutes after the bus turned off the dirt road and followed into the paved main street, we were enjoying an instant relief. Finally the bus came to a stop at the station in Olenzen; the doors opened quietly, then Anna and I were stepping down softly from the bus. Sitting down for a few minutes, we both tried to relax.

Our next stop, after we were back on our feet, was what they called the Uferwald, a medium-sized forest between the Overland Road and the east shore of the Elbe. It was only a short walk, not more than two kilometers north of Olenzen till we reached the forest. I broke the silence, "May I ask why we are going at this particular spot across the border?"

"Very simple," Anna said. "The river Elbe crosses East Germany all the way from Torgau, Magdeburg, Wittenberge, to Hamburg. At Olenzen the Elbe and the border joined for the first time, and the river became the borderline. Olenzen is on the river shore at East Germany, and across on the other side of the Elbe was a little town called Schnackenburg, which was already in West Germany. Almost 100 percent of the people tried to cross the frontier at the dry borderline south of Olenzen; this was also the main concentration point of the Russian and East German border patrol. Crossing the Elbe north of Olenzen is almost impossible unless you had a motorboat. The shore forest is an ideal place to hide, giving us enough cover should we encounter some armed guards. Now I am sure you want to know how we are going to cross the river without a canoe."

"You don't have to read my mind," I replied. "Unless we have a transportation, I don't see any other solution to make it to the other side."

"You are absolutely right, and I am going to tell you who is going to take us across the Elbe. You guessed it by now that going back and forth is part of my business. This is the only route I ever take. At the waterfront surrounded by the forest, there is a fishery with a big smokehouse and a marine chandlery owned by a long-time friend of mine. He is doing business with both sides of the border, and every time I come to see him, he is always taking me to Schnackenburg without being stopped crossing the river. Everybody around the Elbe knows his blue and white *Fischdampfer* [trawler]."

"I am very impressed with what you are telling me, Anna. It gives me much confidence in your leadership and what you are doing."

"Let's go," Anna said. "We are running out of daylight, but a full moon shining over us will help definitely a great deal getting through to our destination. Our border crossing will start here." Anna explained to me. "The moment we enter the forest our heading is straight west toward the Elbe. We must stay on the little trail, which takes us directly to the fishery."

A trail through the woods was exactly where she said it would be; we followed the narrow footpath bordered by tall pine trees. The going was easy enough, but looking out for the presence of standing Russian patrols in the area made us move cautiously, stopping every thirty yards or less to listen. No sounds at all, except for a faint noise of a distant truck grinding away in low gear. A hare was suddenly taking fright and bolting across our path; we didn't encounter the presence of any other living beings. Up to now we had not noticed any sight or sound of the Russian patrols who were supposed to be manning the river outpost line. The fisherman's place was only half a mile away from where we started the journey through the forest, and we were already close to an hour on the footpath. The moment Anna was satisfied that we were out of the danger zone, she went faster on the move. In a catlike reaction, Anna led me straight forward to the entrance of her friend's house without losing any observation of the last section of the trail. The front door was open, and we entered the hallway. A man in his early thirties appeared to greet us. Anna introduced me to him, and his name was Andreas Ruben.

"My friends call me Andy," he said. "I am glad to meet you and welcome to my house. You are just in time for supper. We don't have much fancy food but plenty of fish to eat. Let me call my wife and tell her that we have company." His wife must have heard us; she came in, asking us to follow her to the dining room.

"These are my two boys, Gerhard, thirteen years old, and Richard, ten years old; and my name is Irma, but I am not telling you my age," she said half-jokingly, and everybody was laughing. Andy and Irma were down-to-earth folks and made me feel at home even though I was a total stranger to them. "How do you like our food?" Irma wanted to know. "What you are eating tonight is eel in aspic, a real delicatessen. We don't catch water snakes very often."

"I like it," I said. "But where I come from in Berlin, seafood is rare and very expensive. Most of what we eat is pork."

Andy and Anna were starting to talk about the good old days when they went to school at St. Thomas in Wittenberge. "I was at my first year in high school," Anna said. "And Andy graduated the same year when we got to know each other."

"Tomorrow morning I will take you both across the river," Andy said. "You have to stay here tonight."

"How much will I owe you, Andy?"

"Nothing, I have to go to the other side anyway."

"OK, in that case, let me pay for the board and room." And I was handing him a carton of American cigarettes. First he did not want to accept my gift, but I insisted, and he said, "Thank you very much." Next morning we got up and had a hearty breakfast; then we said good-bye to Irma while Andy got the boat started. In less than five minutes, he ferried us across the river Elbe.

My First Steps to Freedom

The first glance at Schnackenburg was nothing more than a boardwalk and a filling station with two floating slips for a tie-down. As I disembarked from the trawler and put my feet on the ground, I could not believe that I was in West Germany. We said good-bye to the skipper and started walking inland. Passing the ridge over the shoreline, the whole view of the town was now in front of us. This was the moment I had been long waiting for. I was overjoyed and overcame by my feelings in my moment of happiness. I grabbed Anna and kissed her. To my total surprise, she responded to my kiss in the same enthusiastic fashion.

We were starting to walk again. I didn't have to worry where I was going; Anna knew these parts of the country, and all I had to do was follow her. We arrived at the bus station in Schnackenburg. It felt good to enter the heated waiting room. "If you want to go to the Lüneburger Heide," Anna said, "then we can go together. I live in Lüneburg and will stay there for two days, then I must take the train to Hamburg to pick up some more merchandise."

"I will be happy to continue my traveling with you. Tell me please about our bus schedule for today."

"At eleven o'clock, the first bus will take us from here to Dannenberg, that is only a thirty-kilometer ride. In Dannenberg, we have to wait till three o'clock to catch the second bus that will arrive in Lüneburg about five o'clock. In Dannenberg we have almost three hours to kill. It is a nice little town, and I know a restaurant in a *Gasthof* [pension] where we can go for lunch."

What a difference, right on time we were boarding a newer bus, all painted and in good repair. In less than an hour, we arrived in Dannenberg. Walking through town, we window-shopped. I noticed immediately that contrast to East Germany; here in the west, you could buy a lot more things than in the east. Anna took me to a typical German Gasthof with a cozy restaurant; we ordered some homemade German dishes and a bottle of wine. Listening to an old record player for background music, we had a nice conversation about several subjects, including the hospitality of Andy and Irma. "By the way," Anna said, "I think it was very nice of you to give Andy a whole carton of your American cigarettes. Every time Andy takes me to the other side to West Germany, and that is at least twice a month, he would never take any money from me. On my way back from Hamburg, I always go by train across the border to Wittenberge. Sometime ago Irma developed diabetes and requires insulin injections to treat her condition. She is now taking a kind of insulin mixture not available in East Germany. I keep her supplied by buying the insulin in Hamburg without charging her for it. That way I feel good to make it up to them."

Soon it was time for us to go back to the bus station. "Are you ready for the last sixty kilometers to go?" Anna wanted to know. "We will be on the road for another two hours."

Looking at the almost-new bus, I told Anna, "With a streamlined conveyance like this bus, it must feel like flying to Lüneburg." We were the first two people embarking on the bus and had the choice to pick any seat in the house. I left it up to Anna, and she took me all the way to the end of the coach to occupy the last two seats in the corner. Anna turned off the overhead lights, and both of us lay back in a comfortable position. After we were resting for a while and most of the passengers were occupying their seats, Anna leaned to one side, getting closer to me. I remained silent and motionless. I had to think of Gerda, what was I doing here again with an older woman? Anna must be in her thirties.

Lüneburg, the quiet little city of hospitality and serene setting in a countrylike atmosphere. Wherever we were going from the bus station to Anna's apartment, I saw charming and friendly stores where people could look around or enjoy the local cafés. Nobody seemed to be in a hurry. There was hardly any traffic on the streets or highways intersecting the city. I was surprised when we reached Anna's place to find a roomy bungalow surrounded by a nicely landscaped garden. "I don't have to ask you why you have selected Lüneburg as your hometown."

"You like my place?" Anna asked.

"What I have seen tonight shows me that you have good taste and a distinct preference for the better things in life."

"I have lived in Hamburg, a big international harbor of commerce, but I find it more relaxing to live in Lüneburg." Anna asked me to open a bottle of wine while she put something to munch on the table. "Would you like me to make you a sandwich?"

"Thank you," I said. "I am not hungry, I had enough for the rest of the day with the big meal we had for lunch. I really have to thank you again for such an outstanding treat."

"Let's drink to our friendship," Anna said and tipped her glass against mine. Looking out of the window while she was standing next to me with one arm around me, both of us noticed how it started to snow.

Kind of sarcastic, Anna whispered in my ear, "Good luck with your herbarium. If it keeps on snowing, all you will collect are frozen vegetables." There was no longer any reason not to tell Anna the truth about my real purpose coming to West Germany. Somehow I had the feeling Anna never did believe my story in the first place. Now that I was safely in West Germany, I could tell anybody what I was about to do. "Here we are, looking at the outside getting covered with snow, and in Santa Monica people are going swimming at the beach."

"What are you talking about, where is Santa Monica?"

"Santa Monica is a famous beach in Los Angeles, where I will be in about three weeks, just in time for Christmas."

"Are you telling me that you are going to America, or is that just another line of lies you are feeding me?"

"No, this time I am telling you the truth, and I will prove it to you."

"There was no need for you to lie to me. You could have told me where you intend to go in Wittenberge," she replied.

"I could not. I did not know you, and you did not tell me that you live in West Germany. I was instructed to keep my mouth shut as long as I am in East Germany. You have no idea how difficult it is to get an immigration visa to enter the United States, and I was not going to jeopardize it by being arrested by the Stasi and turned over to the Russians. Here, this should ascertain my argument and establish the evidence by you looking at a genuine immigration visa signed and stamped into my West German passport by the American consulate."

Without saying anything, Anna handed the passport back to me, but by the expression in her face I could tell that she was not very happy with the news she received. She reopened the conversation by saying, "Please pour me another glass of wine."

I did, and then I asked her if she was mad at me. "I am happy for you that you have a chance to get out of this country that has very little to offer for your future, but I am also at the same time disappointed that I will never see you again. It may sound selfish to you, but I want you to understand that I am beginning to care for you."

"Let's drink to our friendship," I said, "and let it go at that. At the age of seventeen and having witnessed enough death and violence, I am fascinated with the prospect of a new world of freedom, and I appreciate and will remember the nice people like you who helped me to reach that freedom. A better future is waiting for me in America, a once-in-a-lifetime opportunity I can't let go. From the very beginning, we are sharing these experiences with the awareness of being two strangers traveling in different directions. You have voluntarily befriended me, and I hope I have not given you the idea of a future mutual relationship."

Regardless, it would be a lie if I would say that there was no emotional background. Some kind of bonding evolved when one did spend all those days together crossing illegally the dangerous Russian-occupied East Germany, sharing perils and uncertainty. Available men in Germany in those days were in short supply, and fortunately or unfortunately for me, perhaps she saw me as the accessible man for her. I was having a lump in my throat at the final moment of departure. Anna was giving me her last-minute statement that I could always come back to her if I didn't like it in America. Anna was walking with me to take the bus to Bremerhaven, then she would catch the next train from Lüneburg to Hamburg.

Driving through the Lüneburger Heide reminded me of pictures I had seen from the regions of the Arctic hemisphere or the Russian tundra, a flat stretch of undulated snow-covered plains. The moorlands, covered with endless waves of heather, a small evergreen flowering shrub with rose-colored flowers, were known to be in the summertime the best-liked landscape in Northern Germany. Artist, painters, and nature lovers came here to seek inspiration and enjoy the tranquility and multitude of protected animals. I was in a depressed mood, but my attitude changed when I arrived in Bremerhaven. The city of Bremerhaven, on the North Sea, was Germany's second biggest port. The old town of Bremen has many historic buildings including the gothic Romanesque cathedral and town hall. I was having some late lunch at a small counter in a merchant store. I was going over my instructions, and the local people were telling me that the quarantine encampments for emigrants were located outside of town in the harbor district. One of the local buses was taking me to my last destination in Germany. The camp was a renovated old *Luftstalag* for the prisoners of the American and British air force during WW II. At the gate, I produced my passport and immigration papers to be registered and admitted to a room in a certain block. I was assigned to G-block, room 19. The clerk told me, "All of you will be here for about a week before you are shipping out. I suggest for the time that you are our guest, make yourselves at home, and take the opportunity to write a last few letter to your friends and family. Nobody is allowed to leave the compound. For your comfort and entertainment, we have a large mess hall serving you three meals a day, a general store, and a bar for your enjoyment."

Walking down the one and only street, I could see a big black letter *G* painted on the corner of one of the blocks ahead of me.

Room 19 was a large dormitory holding several bunk beds. The first thing I did was claim one of the empty beds, drop my belongings in the footlocker, and stretch out on top of the bed. Looking at the white-painted plywood ceiling, the whole setup reminded me very much of the Flak battery barracks in Schmargendorf. The only difference was that here I would not be kicked out of bed by an air raid in the middle of the night and run to the shelter to be alive in the morning. A few of my roommates were asking me to go with them to the mess hall to eat some supper. The meals were simple, but there was plenty of food to eat. Next morning after breakfast, I looked at the bulletin board for official camp reports and announcements of interest for all emigrants. One list that was published by the camp clinic showed all names, days, and time for each individual to show up for a secondary health appraisal by the camp doctor.

Each maritime quarantine station had a senior medical officer in command giving a true statement to a port inspection officer about the health status of crew and passengers. The ship was allowed to leave dock if all its members were free from infectious disease. The screening took place in the quarantine station. Any person diagnosed with an infectious disease was put in a strict isolation unit and kept from boarding the ship. International quarantine laws had proved effective in reducing death rates and in checking the spread of epidemics. Most of us, or I should say practically everybody, were coming out from the physical examination with a clean bill of health. Only one guy in our room on the day of his doctor visits did not show up the night to go to sleep; his bunk remained empty for the rest of the days. We later found out that he suffered from tuberculosis and was remaining in isolation. The last two days in the quarantine station, I witnessed an outbreak of carnival season rejoicing in singing and dancing before our departure. Everybody went to the bar and started drinking till he had spent the last deutsche mark, useless for us once we were in America. The loudest noise came from the crew of the ship; they were singing, or rather screaming, old English popular songs and tunes from both world wars like "It is a long way to Tipperary" and "Lilly, from Picadilly, she is the ugliest girl in town." One cheerful party went on till early next morning, but most of the fellows went to bed by midnight. I think all of us by now were suffering from cabin fever; we had been locked up for too long. Finally, the day had come on December 17 when they handed out the boarding cards, a four-by-six-inch green cardboard name tag attached to a string, to hang around the neck. This was the ticket to America; without it there was no way to get aboard the ship. In a single file, we were walking up the plank; and the moment you put one foot on the ship, the green card would be checked against the manifest and taken away from you.

Looking back to Bremerhaven—a last farewell to Germany

By the time the last passenger had checked in, we were all assembling at the railing, watching the pedestrian below us at the pier. Some of them were relatives or friends waving, with white handkerchiefs, a final good-bye to their loved ones above. It was a long-standing custom with the town of Bremerhaven to send their emigrants away with farewell songs played by a brass band. At the same time, the ship's anchor went up, and the captain at the bridge gave the signal to start the engines. Slowly the ship moved away from the pier. The sound of the music and the sight of the city was fading away by the minute. The English Channel was taking us to the Atlantic Ocean, and the last seagulls were flying back to the coast. In a week or so, we shall reach New York Harbor, and the Statue of Liberty would be the first one to welcome us to America.

However, as destiny dictated it, we never reached the safe haven of New York.

Storm Over the Atlantic

The ship we were sailing was an old freighter ready to retire, but somehow, instead of being dismantled it ended up as a ship to transport emigrants across the Atlantic Ocean. One of the officers told us that this was her second voyage to New York under the Swedish flag. The ship left the English Channel in complete darkness, and there was no more land in sight anywhere.

A converted freighter like this took me across the Atlantic to America

Most of us had taken by now our small bags with our meager belongings and went below deck. Long ladders leading to the interior were going up and down with every wave in a steady rhythm. The steward was telling everybody to hang on with both hands firmly to the sides of the ladder. We still had our land legs and didn't know how to balance our steps. A little practice, and soon I would get the hang of it as to how to stay on my two feet. Some of us were already beginning to get seasick. What could one do about it? The steward's best advice was to put some food in our stomach. According to him, he had crossed the Atlantic many times, and he was always getting sick for the first two days or so.

The dining room was in the middle of the ship for a good reason, since the center of the vessel was almost motionless. The aroma of the good food directed us to the entrance of the galley. It was a large room with long tables and benches which were permanently attached to the dinning room floor. The ship's kitchen or caboose was next to the galley. Both rooms were only divided by a wall of glass windows which would be open at mealtimes to serve all immigrants a hot meal three times a day. Unbelievable to us, it was an all-you-can-eat affair. I had never seen in my entire life so many people gulping down food in such quantities, especially during the first few days aboard. We could not shake off our war-leftover syndrome. "Eat all you can. Tomorrow you might not be able to get any food."

Another curiosity that I noticed was the fact that nobody would take the black bread, but everybody would eat the white bread—something we had not seen in years. "Too bad," the head cook explained. "This is your last chance to eat wholesome Westphalian high-fiber pumpernickel rye bread. Once you get off this boat, you will find it very difficult to find dark bread anywhere in America."

In between meals, we didn't have anything to do other than staying belowdecks or walking along the railing from stern to bow. The most interesting viewpoints were the front and the rear of the ship. The second day after dinner, when I was standing by the railing at the rear, watching the waves turning into ocean spray, I noticed two kitchen helpers carrying several huge buckets of food, which they dumped overboard. I could not believe my eyes; big shanks of food among what it looked to me like half a side of beef, some other kind of still frozen meat, whole loaves of bread, and butter were discarded as if it was garbage. I failed to comprehend what I was witnessing. After all the hunger I saw around me and personally experienced, having good food had become to mean a special blessing and wasting it a mortal sin. There were still people in Europe and all over the world dying of starvation, and many young children were still going to bed hungry every night. Next morning, after breakfast, I could not resist to tell the chef my experience. He just smiled at me and said to all of us, "Well, I agree with you, but there is nothing I can do about it. It is maritime law to prevent infestation by rodents and other pests and the spread of disease. Once the food is taken out from refrigeration, it cannot be taken back and is considered kitchen refuse and must be discarded. That is also the reason we observe a strict rule that no food is to be taken out of the dining room. I hope that this will make sense to all of you people."

The third day at sea, we must be already somewhere in the middle of the Atlantic. Between midnight and daybreak, the ship would start rolling up and down, fighting its way through a stormy weather. Specifically the Atlantic Ocean was known for its mighty hurricanes. All of us were scared and clutching with both hands the sides of the bunk beds, trying not to fall out. I was assigned to a lower bunk bed in a forty-bed sleeping room. The steady hammering beat of the laboring engines did not allow us to get much sleep, but like everything else, we got used to it. However, tonight was different; it felt like riding a roller coaster as the ship was going up and down. Nobody wanted to get out of the berth, hoping that the hurricane would soon slow down. The lower deck had four bathrooms overcrowded with seasick men in a hurry to find a spot to empty their stomachs. Some men who made it to the upper deck were hanging over the railing, feeding the fish. Late in the afternoon, the strong gale was almost over, making us feel better again; but I was dead tired and had to catch up on my sleep.

The more pleasant side of my ocean trip was the spiritual part that came over me. My favorite place to spend some time alone was the bow, the most forward place on the ship, where both sides of the railing are coming together. I squeezed my body into that narrow most tiny spot and pretend that there was nothing behind me. It gave me the feeling of being all alone in the middle of the ocean. At nights this experience was even more dramatic. The ocean and the sky were melting together into one big endless body of the cosmos. Looking at the moon and observing all the stars with only my feet remaining in contact with the ship, a certain trance in which my soul appeared to be absent from my body was taking over. Temporary suspension of sensation and volition, while my heart and lungs continued to act, put my mind into a state of catalepsy being transposed to the firmament my bodiless soul was trying to find a permanent connection with the divine spirit of the universe. This sacred conjecture remained in my mind even after the reuniting of my body and soul.

This breathtaking experience of being transposed to the infinite of the universe was giving me a special peace of mind. Somehow my mind was getting very calm, and my soul was going through a certain metamorphosis. I felt suddenly connected to the endless substance of the universe. It was so overwhelming and convincing to me that from this day on, I was a believer in metaphysics. Any church or cathedral had become small to me in comparison to the new discovery of the universe. Seeking a solution to all the problems here on this planet and asking myself the question why men could not live in peace was no longer my main concern. After I had been exposed to the true meaning of peace and tranquility in the universe, my connection to God had been renewed in a more spiritual and independent way.

The days were going by, and on Christmas Eve, as our voyage was much closer to the shoreline of the American continent, an emergency in the engine room occurred. Whatever holiday spirit any of us would have had was overshadowed by the fear of being stranded in the Atlantic Ocean and the uncertainty as to when help would arrive. The ship was no longer operating under full speed, and the captain decided to shut off the power completely in order for the engineers to find out where and what the problem of the power failure was. The ship was now drifting helplessly in the ocean, and on the second day without power, they sent down a diver to take a look at the ship's two huge propellers. As it turned out, the diver detected a broken propeller shaft. Even though the ocean was calm, the accident could not be taken care of at high sea for two reasons. Number one, the ship did not carry any big spare parts, and second, such a major repair job could only be done in a dry dock. As a result, the captain had no other choice but to get to the nearest harbor; in our case, it would be Quebec, Canada.

Operating a ship with one propeller only took a lot of skill. It had to be done with low speed only to avoid unnecessary torque to one side. Under high speed, the ship would go in circles. To keep the ship going forward in a straight line, the officer in charge of the bridge must slightly compensate with the rudder. Not being able to sail under full speed, our trip across the Atlantic was delayed by three extra days. Finally on the tenth day, land came in sight, and what a beautiful view that was. Everyone of us emigrants was taking part in an assemblage at the upper deck. Our eyes were set on the far-distant-appearing coast. The margin of the land next to the sea at first was nothing more than a long dark line under the clouds. As we got closer to the shore, the land split into two halves, exposing in the middle a big body of water; what we were detecting was the Gulf of Saint Lawrence, the great estuary that blends with the Saint Lawrence River.

The Saint Lawrence Seaway is the world's largest inland waterway open to deep-sea navigation. It permits large ocean-going ships to sail from the Atlantic Ocean to the ports of Quebec and Montreal. The mouth of the river at the gulf is about a hundred miles wide and narrows down on the way to the city of Quebec to two miles or less. Between Quebec and the city of Montreal, the river of Saint Lawrence is only less than a mile wide. Considering the slow speed of the oceanliner and the narrowness of the river, it gave us a perfect twenty-four hours' sightseeing trip of both sides of the shorelines. The beautiful view of the Canadian coast was our first impression of the American continent. It was magnificent to see long rows of clean houses, tall trees, and a highway with cars and trucks passing us on both sides of the ship. On the north side of the river, we were passing the city of Quebec. It was already dark, and the thousands of shining lights from the town were visible. Our journey came to an end as we arrived late on a Friday night, the twenty-seventh of December, at Montreal.

That we were all eager to go on land was an understatement; the bad news was that we couldn't disembark till Monday. Over the weekend the Canadian Immigration Office was closed, and unfortunately, nobody could leave the ship till we got official clearance. Most of the population in Montreal were French-speaking citizens. They had hardly ever seen a German but knew so many bad things about all German people instilled by their own propaganda. Right after the war, for obvious reasons, the immigration quota for Germans to the United States and Canada was at an all-time low. Perhaps the emergency situation of our ship to enter the harbor of Montreal was the first opportunity for some Canadians to meet a ship full of real German immigrants in their own country.

The word must have gotten around, and before we knew it, people crowded the pier to come and see us, like monkeys in the zoo. We could not get off the ship, and they were not allowed to come aboard. We were hanging out at the railing, and those of us who were able to speak English engaged in conversation and answered their questions. It was curiosity more than anything else that drove them to come and see us. At first they were reluctant to talk to us, giving me the impression that they were afraid to come close to us. The only spectators that came right out in the beginning were a few German descendant Canadians who started a friendly conversation in German language with us. In their greetings, they seemed to be genuinely happy to meet some countrymen from the old country. Some of them still had relatives in Germany and asked us all kinds of questions.

A few French Canadians, as they looked us over and convinced themselves that we looked and behaved like any other normal human beings, started to ask us questions in English. This interaction between German immigrants and Canadians went on for some time. I remembered in particular a young Canadian woman with a young infant in her arms. In her French accent, she spoke to the young fellow next to me and wanted to know if it was true that some German soldiers would eat newborn babies. Being perplexed at first, he would not dignify her question with an answer but instead leaned all the way over the railing, spread his arms wide open with a mischievous smile, and asked her if he could hold her baby for a moment. The young mother started to scream from the top of her lungs, took a step backward from the pier, and ran away as fast as she could. Some readers might think this was funny, but for us young folks, this was very sad to see what ignorance and hate could spread.

Monday morning, finally the waiting was over, and by an ordinance of the Canadian Immigration, officers were coming aboard the ship. Once more we were standing in line, and our papers were checked. A few questions were asked about our destination, and since we were all going to the United States, our passports were stamped with a transit visa. After we disembarked from the large freighter, some buses from the immigration office took us to the Montreal International Airport. At 3:00 PM the same day, I was able to catch a flight to Los Angeles. I spent two nights at the Glendale Salvation Army, and as soon as I could, I made contact with my new boss. He was already expecting me, and he had arranged for me to rent a furnished room. I liked my job, and at my first day off, I spent the whole day at the beach of Santa Monica, enjoying the sunshine and listening to the waves of the Pacific Ocean.

The will of a former Hitler Youth to survive succeeded. The story ended in Germany and found a new beginning in the United States of America, a land of freedom and many opportunities that only an immigrant appreciates in a very special way.

Russian soldiers are raising the communist flag over the Reichstag (Parliament) in May 1945 as a symbol of their victory over Germany

The trees along the wall are in West-Berlin.
The empty church is in the middle of the death trap.

The old Parliament building in West-Berlin under restoration

The wall at Bernauer Strasse

Another section of the Berlin Wall

A monument for Ida Seikmann, one of the seven people shot at this section of the wall trying to escape to freedom.

A minefield between two walls preventing the people to escape from East to West Berlin

Visiting Berlin 1989 in front of the border at the Brandenburg Gate

CPSIA information can be obtained at www.ICGtesting.com
Printed in the USA
BVOW071330060113

309544BV00003B/3/P